EDEXCEL A LEVEL

ECONOMICS A

2

PETER SMITH

DYNAMIC LEARNING

HODDER EDUCATION
AN HACHETTE UK COMPANY

Orders

Please contact Bookpoint Ltd, 130 Milton Park, Abingdon, Oxon OX14 4SB. Telephone: (44) 01235 827720. Fax: (44) 01235 400454. Email education@bookpoint.co.uk Lines are open from 9 a.m. to 5 p.m., Monday to Saturday, with a 24-hour message answering service. You can also order through our website: www.hoddereducation.co.uk

ISBN: 978 1 4718 3005 1

© Peter Smith 2015

First published in 2015 by
Hodder Education,
An Hachette UK Company
Carmelite House
50 Victoria Embankment
London EC4Y 0DZ

www.hoddereducation.co.uk

Impression number   10 9 8 7 6 5 4 3 2
Year   2019 2018 2017 2016

Typeset by Integra Software Services Pvt., Pondicherry, India.
Printed in Dubai.

A catalogue record for this title is available from the British Library.

The Publishers would like to thank the following for permission to reproduce copyright material.

Photo credits

Cover Stripped Pixel; **p4** Julio Etchart/Alamy; **p9** Dragon Images/Fotolia; **p13** qaphotos.com/Alamy; **p23** Bloomberg/Getty Images; **p24** Dinodia Photos/Alamy; **p29** Stephen Brashear/Getty Images; **p41** txakel/Fotolia; **p45** Ana Malin/Fotolia; **p49** Mark Richardson/Alamy; **p57** TopFoto; **p61** Tristar Photos/Alamy; **p68** Keith Morris/Alamy; **p73** somkanokwan/Fotolia; **p75** easyJet; **p77** HappyAlex/Fotolia; **p83** wellphoto/Fotolia; **p89** Gregory Wrona/Alamy; **p96** Jeffrey Blackler/Alamy; **p100** Allstar Picture Library/Alamy; **p108** Kumar Sriskandan/Alamy; **p111** martin33/Fotolia; **p115** Lev/Fotolia; **p133** Mariusz Prusaczyk/Fotolia; **p137** Sonny Tumbelaka/AFP/Getty Images; **p143** Kadmy/Fotolia; **p145** Clynt Garnham Business/Alamy; **p153** VanderWolf Images/Fotolia; **p156** Robert Hoetink/Fotolia; **p163** SC Photos/Alamy; **p166** Universal Images Group Limited/Alamy; **p174** Hulton Archive/Stringer; **p179** Xinhua/Alamy; **p193** DB images/Alamy; **p205** Tyler Olson/Fotolia; **p210** Thakala/Fotolia; **p220** asab974/Fotolia; **p225** JB Dodane/Alamy; **p229** leeyiutung/Fotolia; **p236** Andrew Aitchison/Alamy; **p240** Alan Gignoux/Alamy; **p244** Dinodia Photos/Alamy; **p250** Georg Kristiansen/Alamy; **p256** Morane/Fotolia; **p263** F Geoffroy/Fotolia; **p268** Tidchun/Fotolia; **p275** Greg Balfour Evans/Alamy; **p281** Alistair Cotton/Fotolia; **p282** Lloyds of London; **p285** Chris Dorney/Fotolia; **p294** Stephen Jaffe/IMF via Getty Images; **p296** Kostas Pikoulas/Alamy; **p300** David Levenson/Alamy; **p309** poco_bw/Fotolia; **p312** Margit Power/Fotolia

Get the most from this book

In combination with Book 1, this textbook provides an introduction to economics. It has been tailored explicitly to cover the content of the Edexcel specification for A level in Economics A. The specification is divided into four themes: Book 2 covers Themes 3 and 4.

The text provides the foundation for studying Edexcel Economics A, but you will no doubt wish to keep up to date by referring to additional topical sources of information about economic events. This can be done by reading the serious newspapers, visiting key sites on the internet, and reading such magazines as *Economic Review*.

Special features

Learning objectives
A statement of the intended learning objectives for each chapter.

Prior knowledge needed
The knowledge required for the course that you have already met in your first year of studies.

Study tips
Short pieces of advice to help you present your ideas effectively and avoid potential pitfalls.

Extension material
Extension points to stretch your understanding.

Synoptic links
Synoptic links showing the connections between the themes.

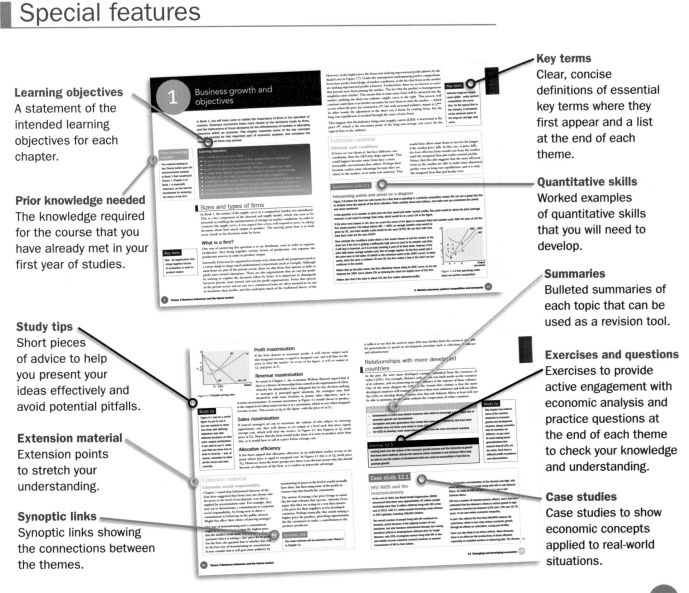

Key terms
Clear, concise definitions of essential key terms where they first appear and a list at the end of each theme.

Quantitative skills
Worked examples of quantitative skills that you will need to develop.

Summaries
Bulleted summaries of each topic that can be used as a revision tool.

Exercises and questions
Exercises to provide active engagement with economic analysis and practice questions at the end of each theme to check your knowledge and understanding.

Case studies
Case studies to show economic concepts applied to real-world situations.

Contents

Theme 4 A global perspective

Introduction

Prior learning, knowledge and progression

This book builds upon the material that was covered in Book 1. At key points during the text you will find references to particular chapters in Book 1 that will support your understanding.

Find out more about the Edexcel Economics A offering, or other related qualifications, at **http://qualifications.pearson.com/en/home.html**.

Assessment objectives

In common with other economics specifications, Edexcel Economics A entails four assessment objectives. Candidates will thus be expected to:

- demonstrate knowledge of terms/concepts and theories/models to show an understanding of the behaviour of economic agents and how they are affected by and respond to economic issues
- apply knowledge and understanding to various economic contexts to show how economic agents are affected by and respond to economic issues
- analyse issues within economics, showing an understanding of their impact on economic agents
- evaluate economic arguments and use qualitative and quantitative evidence to support informed judgements relating to economic issues.

The structure of assessment

The A level in Economics A will be assessed by three examinations. The first two deal respectively with 'markets and business behaviour' and the 'national and global economy'. The third is a synoptic paper covering topics from both microeconomics and macroeconomics. Each will be a written paper lasting 2 hours. Further details are provided on the Edexcel website.

Economics in this book

The study of economics requires a familiarity with recent economic events in the UK and elsewhere, and candidates will be expected to show familiarity with 'recent historical data' — broadly defined as covering the last 25 years. The following websites will help you to keep up to date with recent trends and events:

- Recent and historical data about the UK economy can be found at the website of the Office for National Statistics (ONS) at: **www.ons.gov.uk**

- Also helpful is the site of HM Treasury at: **www.gov.uk/government/ organisations/hm-treasury**. Especially useful is the Treasury's *Pocket Databank*, which is updated weekly, providing major economic indicators and series for both domestic and international economies: **www.gov.uk/government/statistics/ weekly-economic-indicators**
- The Bank of England site is well worth a visit, especially the *Inflation Report* and the Minutes of the Monetary Policy Committee: **www.bankofengland.co.uk**
- The Institute for Fiscal Studies offers an independent view of a range of economic topics: **www.ifs.org.uk**

It is also important to be able to put the UK experience into an international context. There are many helpful websites that enable this. The World Bank offers an extensive array of indicators about almost every country at **http://data.worldbank.org/** or you can use their data visualiser at **http://devdata.worldbank.org/DataVisualizer/** which allows you to construct all sorts of interesting graphs to trace how countries have changed through time. You can also visit the UNDP at **http://hdr.undp.org/ en/data-explorer**. Other data are available via OCED at www.oecd.org or via the European Commission at **http://ec.europa.eu/eurostat**.

Finally, for answers to case studies, exercises etc. featured in this book, please visit **https://www.hoddereducation.co.uk/Product?Product=9781471830051** and click 'Download answers'.

How to study economics

There are two crucial aspects of studying economics. The first stage is to study the theory, which helps us to explain economic behaviour. However, in studying A level Economics A it is equally important to be able to apply the theories and concepts that you meet, and to see just how these relate to the real world.

If you are to become competent at this, it is vital that you get plenty of practice. In part, this means carrying out the exercises that you will find in this text. However, it also means thinking about how economics helps us to explain news items and data that appear in the newspapers and on the television. Make sure that you practise as much as you can.

In economics, it is also important to be able to produce examples of economic phenomena. In reading this text, you will find some examples that help to illustrate ideas and concepts. Do not rely solely on the examples provided here, but look around the world to find your own examples, and keep a note of these ready for use in essays and exams. This will help to convince the examiners that you have understood economics. It will also help you to understand the theories.

Enjoy economics

Most important of all, I hope you will enjoy your study of economics. I have always been fascinated by the subject, and hope that you will capture something of the excitement and challenge of learning about how markets and the economy operate. I also wish you every success with your studies.

Acknowledgements

I would like to express my deep gratitude to Russell Dudley-Smith, whose thorough reading of the book's precursor and insightful and helpful comments were invaluable in improving the scope and focus of this book. I am also grateful to the reviewer who commented on this edition, whose remarks and suggestions have enabled improvements in the content and style of this new edition. I would also like to thank the team at Hodder Education, especially Naomi Holdstock, Rachel Furse and Chris Bessant, for their efficiency in production of this book, and for their support and encouragement.

Many of the data series shown in figures in this book were drawn from the data obtained from the National Statistics website **www.ons.gov.uk** and contain public sector information licensed under the Open Government Licence v3.0.

Other data were from various sources, including OECD, World Bank, United Nations Development Programme and other sources as specified.

While every effort has been made to trace the owners of copyright material, I would like to apologise to any copyright holders whose rights may have unwittingly been infringed.

Peter Smith

THEME 3

BUSINESS BEHAVIOUR AND THE LABOUR MARKET

1 Business growth and objectives

In Book 1, you will have come to realise the importance of firms in the operation of markets. Business economics looks more closely at the decisions made by firms, and the implications of those decisions for the effectiveness of markets in allocating resources within an economy. This chapter examines some of the key concepts that are needed for this important part of economic analysis, and considers the objectives that firms may pursue.

Prior knowledge needed

The material relating to this Theme builds upon the microeconomic analysis in Book 1 that constituted Theme 1. Chapter 3 of Book 1 is especially important, as this laid the foundations for analysing the theory of the firm.

Learning objectives

After studying this chapter, you should:
→ be aware of the reason for the birth of firms, and the desire for their growth
→ be familiar with alternative ways in which firms grow
→ be able to distinguish between horizontal, vertical and conglomerate mergers
→ be aware of the need for firms to grow if they wish to compete in global markets
→ be familiar with short- and long-run cost curves and their characteristics
→ understand the significance of economies of scale in the context of the growth of firms
→ understand the profit maximisation motive and its implications for firms' behaviour
→ be aware of the principal-agent issue, and its influence on the motivations of firms
→ be familiar with alternative motivations for firms and how these affect decision making

Sizes and types of firms

In Book 1, the notion of the supply curve in a competitive market was introduced. This is a key component of the demand and supply model, which was seen to be powerful in enabling the interpretation of changes in market conditions. In order to construct the supply curve, it was argued that a firm will respond to price in taking decisions about how much output to produce. The starting point here is to look more closely at the decisions made by firms.

What is a firm?

Key term

firm an organisation that brings together factors of production in order to produce output

One way of answering this question is to say that **firms** exist in order to organise production: they bring together various factors of production, and organise the production process in order to produce output.

Internally, firms may be organised in various ways, from small sole proprietors (such as a corner shop) to mega-sized multinational corporations (such as Google). Although most firms are part of the private sector, there are also firms that operate as fully or partly state-owned enterprises. There are also organisations that are not-for-profit. In seeking to explain the decisions taken by firms, it is important to distinguish between private, state-owned and not-for-profit organisations. Firms that operate in the private sector and are run on a commercial basis are often assumed to set out to maximise their profits, and this underpins much of the traditional theory of the firm in economic analysis. In other words, they are assumed to take decisions that make as much surplus of revenue over costs as possible. It will be seen later that this may not always be the case, but it is a helpful working assumption.

It is important to recognise that not all private firms may operate in this way. Charities and other enterprises may work on a not-for-profit basis, aiming to cover their costs but not make a surplus above that level. Firms that are state-owned may also have other objectives. For example, they may be established in order to provide services rather than to earn a profit, perhaps aiming for efficiency in provision and customer coverage rather than monetary profit. Their decisions will therefore be taken with these alternative objectives in mind.

A key decision that all firms face concerns the scale of their operations. This decision turns partly on the nature of the market that they are serving, but it also depends upon the technology of the sector in which they operate and the structure of costs that they face.

Some firms may need to grow in order to compete with other large-scale competitors in global markets. There may be many reasons why firms wish to expand their operations. This chapter will begin to explain why this is so, and show how the decision about how much output to produce depends upon what it is that a firm is trying to achieve, and on the market environment in which it is operating.

In some sectors, there are examples of both large and small firms. For example, your local gymnasium may be a relatively small enterprise, but there are also some big players in the market, such as Chelsea FC and Sky. There may be small local taxi firms that are part of the transport sector, but there are also large firms such as British Airways.

The nature of the activity being undertaken by the firm and its scale of operation will help to determine its most efficient form of organisation. For firms to operate successfully, they must minimise the transaction costs of undertaking business.

> ### Exercise 1.1
>
> Identify firms that are operating in your town or city. Which of them would you classify as being relatively small-scale enterprises, and which operate on a more national or international basis?

The growth of firms

A feature of the economic environment in recent years has been the increasing size of firms. Some, such as Microsoft, Walmart and Google, have become giants. Why is this happening?

Firms may wish to increase their size in order to gain market power within the industry in which they are operating. A firm that can gain market share, and perhaps become dominant in the market, may be able to exercise some control over the price of its product, and thereby influence the market. However, firms may wish to grow for other reasons, which will be explained later in the chapter.

Organic growth

Some firms grow simply by being successful. For example, a successful marketing campaign may increase a firm's market share, and provide it with a flow of profits that can be reinvested to expand the firm even more. Some firms may choose to borrow in order to finance their growth, perhaps by issuing shares (equity).

Such *organic growth* may encounter limits. A firm may find that its product market is saturated, so that it can grow further only at the expense of other firms in the market. If its competitors are able to maintain their own market shares, the firm may need to diversify its production activities by finding new markets for its existing product, or perhaps offering new products.

There are many examples of such activity. Tesco, the leading UK supermarket, has launched itself into new markets by opening branches overseas, and has also introduced a range of new products, including financial services, to its existing customers. Microsoft has famously used this strategy in the past, by selling first its internet browser and later its media player as part of its Windows operating system, in an attempt to persuade existing customers to buy its new products.

Diversification may be a dangerous strategy: moving into a market in which the firm is inexperienced and existing rival firms already know the business may pose quite a challenge. In such circumstances, much may depend on the quality of the management team.

A Tesco store in China — diversifying into new markets is one way to maintain growth

Mergers and acquisitions

Instead of growing organically — that is, based on the firm's own resources — many firms choose to grow by merging with, or acquiring, other firms. The distinction here is that an *acquisition* (or takeover) may be hostile, whereas a *merger* may be the coming together of equals, with each firm committed to forming a single entity.

Growth in this way has a number of advantages: for example, it may allow some rationalisation to take place within the organisation. On the other hand, firms tend to develop their own culture, or way of doing things, and some mergers have foundered because of an incompatibility of corporate cultures.

Mergers (or acquisitions) can be of three different types. A **horizontal merger** is a merger between firms operating in the same industry and at the same stage of the production process: for example, the merger of two car assembly firms. The car industry has been characterised by such mergers in the past, including the takeover of Rover by BMW in 1994 and the merger of Daimler-Benz with Chrysler in 1998. A more recent example was the acquisition of Kerry Foods by Pork Farms: both firms produce chilled savoury pastry products (pork pies, sausage rolls, pasties and slices, quiches and scotch eggs). The result of such a merger is known as **horizontal integration**.

A horizontal merger can affect the degree of market concentration, because after the merger takes place there are fewer independent firms operating in the market. This may increase the market power held by the new firm.

A car assembly plant merging with a tyre producer, on the other hand, is an example of the second type of merger: a **vertical merger**. Vertical mergers may be either upstream or downstream. If a car company merges with a component supplier, that is known as backward integration, as it involves merging with a firm that is involved in an earlier part of the production process. **Forward integration** entails merging in the other direction, as for example if the car assembly plant decided to merge with a large distributor.

Vertical integration may allow rationalisation of the process of production. Car producers often work on a just-in-time basis, ordering components for the production line only as they are required. This creates a potential vulnerability, because if the supply of components fails then production has to stop. If a firm's component supplier is part of the firm rather than an independent operator, this may improve the reliability of, and confidence in, the just-in-time process, and in consequence may make life more difficult for rival firms. However, vertical mergers have different implications for concentration and market power.

The third type of merger — **conglomerate merger** — involves the merging of two firms that are operating in quite different markets or industries. For example, companies like Unilever and Nestlé operate in a wide range of different markets, partly as a result of acquisitions.

One argument in favour of conglomerates is that they reduce the risks faced by firms. Many markets follow fluctuations that are in line with the business cycle but are not always fully synchronised. By operating in a number of markets that are on different cycles, the firm can even out its activity overall. However, this is not necessarily an efficient way of doing business, as the different activities undertaken may require different skills and specialisms. In recent years, conglomerate mergers seem to have become less popular.

Exercise 1.2

Categorise each of the following as a horizontal, vertical or conglomerate merger:

a the merger of a firm operating an instant coffee factory with a coffee plantation

b the merger of a brewer and a bakery

c the merger of a brewer and a crisp manufacturer

d the merger of a soft drinks manufacturer with a chain of fast-food outlets

e the merger of an internet service provider with a film studio

f a merger between two firms producing tyres for cars

Globalisation

Since the 1980s, advances in the technology of transport and communications and deregulation of international markets have led to a process known as *globalisation*. This has had a significant effect on the growth of firms. The whole process of marketing goods and services has been revolutionised with the spread of the internet and e-commerce.

Multinational corporations will make a number of appearances in the following chapters of the book, and their increasing role in the global economy will be evaluated. One motive for mergers and acquisitions has been defensive — that is, to try to compete with other large firms in the global market. However, there are many firms that aspire to operate as multinationals in order to have access to larger international markets, to obtain competitively priced resources or to become more efficient by outsourcing parts of their production chain.

Key terms

vertical merger a merger between two firms in the same industry, but at different stages of the production process

backward integration a process under which a firm merges with a firm that is involved in an earlier part of the production chain

forward integration a process under which a firm merges with a firm that is involved in a later part of the production chain

conglomerate merger a merger between two firms operating in different markets

multinational corporation a firm that conducts its operations in a number of countries

Study tip

Make sure that you are familiar with the three types of merger (horizontal, vertical and conglomerate) and be ready with examples of each to illustrate your answers.

Evaluation

Mergers and acquisitions seem at first glance to be an attractive option for a firm wishing to expand. Organic growth may offer a more controlled environment for growth, as it builds on the known existing strengths of the growing firm. However, it may be a slower process, as the rate of growth may be constrained by the availability of finance, whereas a merger offers an instant expansion of market share and of the expertise available within the merged firm. It also seems to offer the potential for cost savings through rationalisation of key functions within the internal organisation of a firm.

In the case of a horizontal merger, the advantages may be seen as providing instant access to increased economies of scale, and an increase in market share, perhaps leading to increased market power. In practice, this may also be a disadvantage, because such gains in market share may attract the attention of the regulator, as will be discussed in Chapter 6.

A vertical merger, whether forward or backward, offers greater control over the supply chain. If the firm after the merger now has its own suppliers of components, or its own distribution chain, it is clearly less subject to interruptions in supply, and has more control over the margins at each stage of the production process.

A conglomerate merger may also offer advantages because a diversified portfolio of production activities may leave the firm less vulnerable to recession, if different activities are affected to different degrees by fluctuations in the general level of economic activity. There may also be possibilities for cost savings, if the merged firms can find synergies in core business functions such as financial accounting and marketing. On the other hand, there may be managerial diseconomies if the management team do not understand all aspects of the new diversified business.

In practice, not all mergers turn out to be successful. In some cases it may be that the costs of integrating the managements of two different firms are underestimated before the event. Computer or production systems may not be compatible, and it may not be as easy as expected to make staff cuts. Corporate cultures may collide, especially where the merger takes place across national borders. This may mean that the expected gains in market share or profits do not materialise. Once two firms have merged, reversing the process by separating can turn out to be costly and acrimonious.

Constraints on the growth of firms

In practice, there may be constraints on the growth of firms. The size of the market may be an important factor here. If a firm is operating in a niche market, then there may be clear limits on the size to which the firm can grow. It may also be that the market for a good or service is localised, so that there may be limited scope for expansion. An example might be hairdressing salons, which tend to have a local and loyal clientele. The technology of the production process may also limit the extent to which a firm is able to grow — this will be discussed later in this chapter.

Some firms may choose to remain small-scale, perhaps because the owner does not feel the need to expand. A sole proprietor of a small business may prefer to stay in charge, rather than handing over to a management team. Small businesses may also find it more difficult to raise finance for expansion, and be limited by their own resources. Having reached a certain size, firms may not wish to grow further for fear of attracting the attention of the regulator.

The principal–agent problem

One issue for many larger firms — especially public limited companies — is that the owners may not be directly involved in running the business. This gives rise to the **principal–agent** (or **agency**) **problem**. In a public limited company, the shareholders delegate the day-to-day decisions concerning the operation of the firm to managers who act on their behalf. In this case the shareholders are the *principals*, and the managers are the *agents* who run things for them.

If the agents are fully in sympathy with the objectives of the owners, there is no problem and the managers will take exactly the decisions that the owners would like. Problems arise when there is conflict between the aims of the owners and those of the managers.

One simple explanation of why this problem arises is that the managers like a quiet life, and therefore do not push to make as much profit as possible, but do just enough to keep the shareholders off their backs. Herbert Simon referred to this as 'satisficing' behaviour, where managers aim to produce satisfactory profits rather than maximum profits.

Another possibility is that managers become negligent because they are not fully accountable. One manifestation of this may be *organisational slack* in the organisation: costs will not be minimised, as the firm is not operating as efficiently as it could. The principal–agent problem arises primarily from an information asymmetry. This arises because the agents have better information about the effects of their decisions than the owners (the principals), who are not involved in the day-to-day running of the business. In order to overcome this, the owners need to overcome the information problem by improving their monitoring of the managers' actions, or to provide the managers with an incentive to take decisions that would align with the owners' objectives. For example, by offering bonuses related to profit, the managers would be more likely to try to maximise profits.

Exercise 1.3

The principal-agent distinction is applicable in many different contexts. In each of the following cases, identify which is the principal and which is the agent:

a the owners of a firm and the managers hired to run it

b a department store and its employees

c a department store and its customers

d an electricity supplier and consumers of electricity

e a dentist and his or her patients

Demergers

Mergers do not always turn out to be as successful as had been anticipated. Indeed, in many cases the expected cost savings do not seem to be reaped, and shareholder value does not seem to be enhanced as a result of the merger or acquisition. In extreme cases, it could be that the firm has to admit failure and seek to reverse the process by demerging. This may simply be a case of the firm realising that the merger was a mistake, or it may be that the regulator steps in and insists that the firms demerge. For example, the British Airports Authority was forced by the regulator to sell some of the airports that had come under its control, including Gatwick.

A merged firm will inevitably look to reap the benefits of operating on a large scale, perhaps by looking for efficiencies in core functions. A merged firm may not need two accounting divisions, or multiple marketing sections. It is thus likely to consolidate these functions, shedding staff and perhaps relocating some functions. Reversing this process during a demerger is equally disruptive for the firm and for the workers who have been displaced or discharged. It may also be confusing for the consumers. Where the merger was effectively an acquisition, in which a large firm took over a smaller firm and tried to assimilate it, there may be little possibility of the smaller firm recovering the position it held before the merger.

Summary

- A firm is an organisation that exists to bring together factors of production in order to produce goods or services.
- Firms range, in the complexity of their organisation, from sole proprietors to public limited companies.
- Firms may undergo organic growth, building upon their own resources and past profits.
- If limited by the size of their markets, firms may diversify into new markets or products.
- Firms may also grow through horizontal, vertical or conglomerate mergers and acquisitions.
- Globalisation has enabled the growth of giant firms operating on a global scale.
- There may be constraints on the growth of firms in some market situations.
- For many larger firms, where day-to-day control is delegated to managers, a principal–agent problem may arise if there is conflict between the objectives of the owners (principals) and those of the managers (agents).
- The process of demerging can be costly for businesses, workers and consumers.

Costs facing firms

Firms have to make key decisions about the quantity of output that they wish to produce. This also involves taking decisions about the inputs of factors of production needed to produce this output, and the ways in which those factors are combined. An important element in taking these decisions concerns the way in which the costs of production vary with the level of output to be produced, which depends upon the prices of the factors of production and the way in which they are combined.

This section focuses on the relationship between costs and the level of output produced by a firm. For simplicity, assume that the firm produces a single product using two factors of production — labour and capital.

In exploring the firm's decisions, it is important to distinguish between the **short run** and the **long run**. In the short run, the firm faces limited flexibility. Varying the quantity of labour input that the firm uses may be relatively straightforward — it can increase the use of overtime, or hire more workers, fairly quickly. However, varying the amount of capital that the firm has at its disposal may take longer. For example, it takes time to commission a new piece of machinery, or to build a new factory — or a Channel Tunnel! Hence labour is regarded as a flexible factor and capital as a fixed factor. The short run is defined as the period over which the firm is free to vary the input of variable factors, but not of the fixed factors. In the long run, the firm is able to vary inputs of both variable and fixed factors.

The nature of technology in an industry will determine the way in which output varies with the quantity of inputs. However, one thing is certain. If the firm increases

Key terms

short run the period over which a firm is free to vary the input of one of its factors of production (labour), but faces a fixed input of the other (capital)

long run the period over which the firm is able to vary the inputs of all its factors of production

Additional computer programmers increase production provided they have machines to use

the amount of inputs of the variable factor (labour) while holding constant the input of the other factor (capital), it will gradually derive less additional output per unit of labour for each further increase. This is known as the **law of diminishing returns**, and is one of the few 'laws' in economics. It is a *short-run* concept, as it relies on the assumption that capital is fixed.

It can readily be seen why this should be the case. Suppose a firm has 10 computer programmers working in an office, using 10 computers. The 11th worker may add some extra output, as the workers may be able to 'hot-desk' and take their coffee breaks at different times. The 12th worker may also add some extra output, perhaps by keeping the printers stocked with paper. However, if the firm keeps adding programmers without increasing the number of computers, each extra worker will be adding less additional output to the office. Indeed, the 20th worker may add nothing at all, being unable to get access to a computer.

Total costs in the short run

Because the firm cannot vary some of its inputs in the short run, some costs may be regarded as fixed, and some as variable. For example, a firm may have contracted to lease a piece of machinery or rent a factory for a period of time, so cannot vary this. In this short run, some **fixed costs** are **sunk costs**: that is, costs that the firm cannot avoid paying even if it chooses to produce no output. **Variable costs** are those such as operating costs, or wages paid to short-term contract staff. Total costs are the sum of fixed and variable costs:

total costs = total fixed costs + total variable costs

Total costs will increase as the firm increases the volume of production, because more of the variable input is needed to increase output. A common assumption made by economists is that in the short run, at very low levels of output, total costs will rise more slowly than output, but that as diminishing returns set in, total costs will accelerate, as shown in Figure 1.1.

Key terms

law of diminishing returns a law stating that if a firm increases its inputs of one factor of production while holding inputs of the other factor fixed, it will eventually derive diminishing marginal returns from the variable factor

fixed costs costs that do not vary with the level of output

sunk costs short-run costs that cannot be recovered if the firm closes down

variable costs costs that vary with the level of output

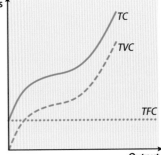

Figure 1.1 Costs in the short run

Average and marginal costs

Average cost (total cost divided by the amount of output produced) varies with the level of output, importantly because of diminishing marginal returns. Firms may often take decisions at the margin: for example, by checking whether or not producing an additional (marginal) unit of output will add to profit. **Marginal cost** is the cost of producing an additional unit of output. These terms are closely related.

Quantitative skills 1.1

The relationship between output and costs

Table 1.1 provides an arithmetic example to illustrate the relationship between these different aspects of costs. The firm represented here faces fixed costs of £225 per week (column 2). The table shows the costs of production for up to 6,000 units of the firm's product per week. Column 3 shows total variable costs of production: you can see that these rise quite steeply as the volume of production increases. Adding fixed and variable costs gives the total costs (*TC*) at each output level. This is shown in column 4, which is the sum of columns 2 and 3.

Table 1.1 The short-run relationship between output and costs (in £s)

(1) Output (000 units per week)	(2) Fixed costs (*TFC*)	(3) Total variable costs (*TVC*)	(4) Total costs (2) +(3) (*TC*)	(5) Average total cost (4)/(1) (*SRAC*)	(6) Marginal cost Δ(4)/Δ(1) (*MC*)	(7) Average variable cost (3)/(1) (*AVC*)	(8) Average fixed cost (2)/(1) (*AFC*)
1	225	85	310	310		85	225
2	225	150	375	187.5	65	75	112.5
3	225	210	435	145	60	70	75
4	225	300	525	131.25	90	75	56.25
5	225	475	700	140	175	95	45
6	225	870	1,095	182.5	395	145	37.5

Short-run average cost (*SRAC* – column 5) is calculated as total cost divided by output. To calculate marginal cost, you need to work out the additional cost of producing an extra unit of output at each output level. This is calculated as the change in costs divided by the change in output (Δ column 4 divided by Δ column 1, where Δ means 'change in').

Finally, average variable costs (*AVC*, i.e. column 3/column 1) and average fixed costs (AFC, i.e. column 2/column 1) can be calculated.

Notice that *SRAC* falls as output increases, but after 4,000 units of output it begins to increase. Notice that *SRAC* is composed of average variable and average fixed costs (*AVC* and *AFC*). *AFC* falls continuously as output increases, because the fixed costs are being spread out across more units of output. This helps to explain why *SRAC* initially falls. However, as diminishing marginal returns set in, average variable costs begin to increase, and this helps to explain the way that *SRAC* varies with output.

Graphing short-run costs

Quantitative skills 1.1 showed the arithmetic relationship between the components of short-run costs. The short-run average and marginal curves based on these data are plotted in Figure 1.2. First, notice that the short-run average total cost curve (SRAC) takes on a U-shape. This form is often assumed in economic analysis. SRAC is the sum of average fixed and variable costs (SAFC and SAVC, respectively). The average fixed cost curve slope downwards throughout – this is because fixed costs do not vary with the level of output, so as output increases, SAFC must always get smaller, as the fixed costs are spread over more and more units of output. However, SAVC also shows a U-shape, and it is this that gives the U-shape to SRAC.

A very important aspect of Figure 1.2 is that the short-run marginal cost curve (SMC) cuts both SAVC and SRAC at their minimum points. This is always the case. If you think about this for a moment, you will realise that it makes good sense. If you are adding on something that is greater than the average, the average must always increase. For a firm, when the marginal cost of producing an additional unit of a good is higher than the average cost of doing so, the average cost must rise. If the marginal cost is the same as the average cost, then average cost will not change.

An example can show how general this rule is. Suppose that a team newly promoted to football's premier league brings in a new striker, whose wage far exceeds that of existing players. What happens to the average wage? Of course it must increase, as the marginal wage of the new player is higher than the previous average wage. This is quite simply an arithmetic property of the average and the marginal, and always holds true.

Another feature of the figure is that the SAVC curve gets closer to SRAC at higher levels of output. This is because the difference between them is AFC, which gets smaller as output increases.

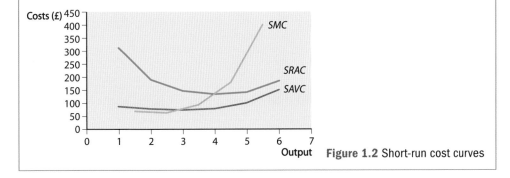

Figure 1.2 Short-run cost curves

Costs in the long run

In the long run, a firm is able to vary both capital and labour. It is thus likely to choose the level of capital that is appropriate for the level of output that it expects to produce. Figure 1.3 shows a number of short–run average cost curves corresponding to different expected output levels, and thus different levels of capital. With the set of *SRAC* curves in Figure 1.3, the long-run average cost curve (*LAC*) can be seen to take on a U–shape.

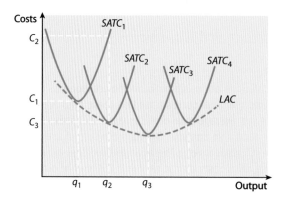

Figure 1.3 Short-run cost curves with different levels of capital input

Economies of scale

> **Key term**
>
> **economies of scale**
> occur for a firm when an increase in a firm's scale of production leads to production at lower long-run average cost

One of the reasons why firms find it beneficial to be large is the existence of **economies of scale**. These occur when a firm finds that it is more efficient in cost terms to produce on a larger scale.

It is not difficult to imagine industries in which economies of scale are likely to arise. For example, recall the notion of the division of labour, which you encountered in Chapter 1 of Book 1. When a firm expands, it reaches a certain scale of production at which it becomes worthwhile to take advantage of division of labour. Workers begin to specialise in certain stages of the production process, and their productivity increases. Because this is only possible for relatively large-scale production, this is an example of economies of scale. It is the size of the firm (in terms of its output level) that enables it to produce more efficiently — that is, at lower average cost.

Although the division of labour is one source of economies of scale, it is by no means the only source, and there are several explanations of cost benefits from producing on a large scale. Some of these are industry-specific, and thus some sectors of the economy exhibit more significant economies of scale than others — it is in these activities that the larger firms tend to be found. There are no hairdressing salons that come into the top ten largest firms, but there are plenty of oil companies.

Technology

One source of economies of scale is in the technology of production. There are many activities in which the technology is such that large-scale production is more efficient.

One source of technical economies of scale arises from the physical properties of the universe. There is a physical relationship between the volume and surface area of an object, whereby the storage capacity of an object increases proportionately more than its surface area. Consider the volume of a cube. If the cube is 2 metres each way, its surface area is $6 \times 2 \times 2 = 24$ square metres, while its volume is $2 \times 2 \times 2 = 8$ cubic metres. If the dimension of the cube is 3 metres, the surface area is 54 square metres (more than double the surface area of the smaller cube) but the volume is 27 cubic metres (more than three times the volume of the smaller cube). Thus the larger the cube, the lower the average cost of storage. A similar relationship applies to other shapes of storage containers, whether they be barrels or ships.

What this means in practice is that a large ship can transport proportionally more than a small ship, or that large barrels hold more wine relative to the surface area of the barrel than small barrels. Hence there may be benefits in operating on a large scale.

Furthermore, some capital equipment is designed for large-scale production, and would only be viable for a firm operating at a high volume of production. Combine harvesters cannot be used in small fields; a production line for car production would not be viable for small levels of output. In other words, there may be *indivisibilities* in the production process.

The Channel Tunnel — the construction costs were enormous compared to the costs of running trains through the tunnel

In addition to indivisibilities, there are many economic activities in which there are high *overhead* expenditures. Such components of a firm's costs do not vary directly with the scale of production. For example, having built a factory, the cost of that factory is the same regardless of the amount of output that is produced in it. Expenditure on research and development could be seen as such an overhead, which may be viable only when a firm reaches a certain size.

Notice that there are some economic activities in which these overhead costs are highly significant. For example, think about the Channel Tunnel. The construction (overhead) costs were enormous compared to the costs of running trains through the tunnel. Thus the overhead cost element is substantial — and the economies of scale will also be significant for such an industry.

There are other examples of this sort of cost structure, such as railway networks and electricity supply. The largest firm in such a market will always be able to produce at a lower average cost than smaller firms. This could prove such a competitive advantage that no other firms will be able to become established in that market, which may therefore constitute what is known as a **natural monopoly**. Intuitively, this makes sense. Imagine having several underground railway systems operating in a single city, all competing against each other on the same routes!

Management and marketing

A second source of economies of scale pertains to the management of firms. One of the key factors of production is managerial input. A certain number of managers are required to oversee the production process. As the firm expands, there is a range of volumes of output over which the management team does not need to grow as rapidly as the overall volume of the firm, as a large firm can be managed more efficiently. Notice that there are likely to be limits to this process. At some point, the organisation begins to get so large and complex that management finds it more difficult to manage. At this point **diseconomies of scale** are likely to cut in — in other words, average costs may begin to rise with an increase in output at some volume of production.

Similarly, the cost of marketing a product may not rise as rapidly as the volume of production, leading to further scale economies. One interpretation of this is that we might see marketing expenses as a component of fixed costs — or at least as having a substantial fixed cost element.

Finance and procurement

Large firms may have advantages in a number of other areas. For example, a large firm with a strong reputation may be able to raise finance for further expansion on more favourable terms than a small firm. This, of course, reinforces the market position of the largest firms in a sector and makes it more difficult for relative newcomers to become established.

Once a firm has grown to the point where it is operating on a relatively large scale, it will also be purchasing its inputs in relatively large volumes. In particular, this relates to raw materials, energy and transport services. When buying in bulk in this way, firms may be able to negotiate good deals with their suppliers, and thus again reduce average cost as output increases.

It may even be the case that some of the firm's suppliers will find it beneficial to locate in proximity to the firm's factory, which would reduce costs even more.

External economies of scale

The factors listed so far that may lead to economies of scale arise from the internal expansion of a firm. If the firm is in an industry that is itself expanding, there may also be **external economies of scale**.

In Figure 1.4, if the firm expands its output up to $q^\star$, long-run average cost falls. Up to $q^\star$ of output is the range over which there are economies of scale. To the right of $q^\star$, however, long-run average cost rises as output continues to be increased, and the firm experiences diseconomies of scale. The output $q^\star$ itself is at the intermediate state of **constant returns to scale**.

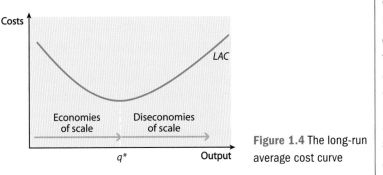

Figure 1.4 The long-run average cost curve

Some of the most successful firms of recent years have been involved in activities that require high levels of technology and skills. The computer industry is one example of an economic activity that has expanded rapidly. As the sector expands, a pool of skilled labour is built up that all the firms can draw upon. The very success of the sector encourages people to acquire the skills needed to enter it, colleges may begin to find it viable to provide courses and so on. Each individual firm benefits in this way from the overall expansion of the sector. The greater availability of skilled workers reduces the amount that individual firms need to spend on training.

Computer engineering is by no means the only example of this. Formula 1 development teams, pharmaceutical companies and others similarly enjoy external economies of scale.

Economies of scope

There are various ways in which firms expand their scale of operations. Some do so within a relatively focused market, but others are multi-product firms that produce a range of different products, sometimes in quite different markets.

For example, look at Nestlé. You may immediately think of instant coffee, and indeed Nestlé produces 200 different brands of instant coffee worldwide. However, Nestlé also produces baby milk powder, mineral water, ice cream and pet food, and has diversified into hotels and restaurants.

Such conglomerate companies can benefit from **economies of scope**, whereby there may be benefits of size across a range of different products. These economies may arise because there are activities that can be shared across the product range. For example, a company may not need a finance or accounting section for each different product, nor human resource or marketing departments.

If the firm is operating at the lowest possible level of long-run average costs, it is said to be in a position of **productive efficiency** because at this point the firm has chosen the appropriate combination of the factors of production and is producing the maximum output possible from those inputs. The level of output at which long-run average cost stops falling as output rises is known as the **minimum efficient scale**.

The long-run average cost curve (LAC) in Figure 1.4 is drawn as a U-shape because of the assumptions that were made about the technology of production. The underlying assumption here is that the firm faces economies of scale at relatively low levels of output, so that LAC slopes downwards. However, at some point decreasing returns to scale set in, and LAC then begins to slope upwards.

This turns out to be a convenient representation, but in practice the LAC curve can take on a variety of shapes. Figure 1.5 shows some of these. LAC_1 is the typical U-shape, which has already been discussed. LAC_2 shows an example of a situation in which there are economies of scale up to a point, after which long-run average cost levels out and there is a long flat range over which the firm faces constant returns to scale. LAC_3 is a bit similar, except that the constant returns to scale (flat) segment eventually runs out and diseconomies of scale set in. In LAC_4 the economies of scale continue over the whole range of output shown. This could occur in a market where the fixed costs are substantial, dominating the influence of variable costs.

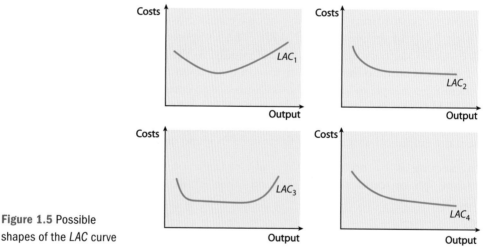

Figure 1.5 Possible shapes of the LAC curve

Exercise 1.4

Which of the following reflects a movement *along* a long-run average cost curve, and which would cause a shift *of* a long-run average cost curve?

a A firm becomes established in a market, learning the best ways of utilising its factors of production.

b A firm observes that average cost falls as it expands its scale of production.

c The larger a firm becomes, the more difficult it becomes to manage, causing average cost to rise.

d A firm operating in the financial sector installs new, faster computers, enabling its average cost to fall for any given level of service that it provides.

Summary

- A firm may face inflexibility in the short run, with some factors being fixed in quantity and only some being variable.
- The short run is defined in this context as the period over which a firm is free to vary some factors but not others.
- The long run is defined as the period over which the firm is able to vary the input of all of its factors of production.
- The law of diminishing returns states that, if a firm increases the input of a variable factor while holding input of the fixed factor constant, eventually the firm will get diminishing marginal returns from the variable factor.
- Short-run costs can be separated into fixed, sunk and variable costs.
- There is a clear and immutable relationship between total, average and marginal costs.
- For a U-shaped average cost curve, marginal cost always cuts the minimum point of average cost.
- The minimum efficient scale is the point at which the long-run average cost curve stops sloping downwards.
- In practice, long-run average cost curves may take on a variety of shapes, according to the technology of the industry concerned.

Exercise 1.5

A firm faces long-run total cost conditions as in Table 1.2.

a Calculate long-run average cost and long-run marginal cost for each level of output.

b Plot long-run average cost and long-run marginal cost curves on a graph. (Hint: don't forget to plot *LMC* at points that are halfway between the corresponding output levels.)

c Identify the output level at which long-run average cost is at a minimum.

d Identify the output level at which *LAC* = *LMC*.

e Within what range of output does this firm enjoy economies of scale?

f Within what range of output does the firm experience diseconomies of scale?

g If you could measure the nature of returns to scale, what would characterise the point where *LAC* is at a minimum?

Table 1.2 Output and long-run costs

Output (000 units per week)	Total cost (£000)
0	0
1	32
2	48
3	82
4	140
5	228
6	352

A firm's revenues

Chapter 2 of Book 1 introduced the notion of the demand curve and its relationship with the revenues received by a firm from selling different levels of output. Indeed, ignoring indirect taxes, the price of a good is the average revenue received by the firm, and the total revenue is the price multiplied by the quantity sold. You saw earlier that there is a fixed mathematical relationship between total, average and marginal costs. The same applies to total, average and marginal revenue. Marginal revenue is the additional revenue received by the firm when it sells an additional unit of output.

Prior knowledge needed

You are advised to remind yourself of the discussion in Book 1, Chapter 2, which explored the relationship between average and total revenue and the price elasticity of demand.

The relationship between sales and revenue

Table 1.3 provides an arithmetic example to illustrate the relationship between these different aspects of revenue.

Table 1.3 The relationship between sales and revenue

(1) Quantity sold	(2) Average revenue (Price, £)	(3) Total revenue (TR)	(4) Marginal revenue (MR)
0	12	0	
			10
20	10	200	
			6
40	8	320	
			2
60	6	360	
			–2
80	4	320	
			–6
100	2	200	
			–10
120	0	0	

Columns 1 and 2 plot out the demand curve for this product, showing the quantities sold at each price. Column 3 calculates total revenue (TR) as column 1 multiplied by column 2. Marginal revenue is shown in column 4. This is calculated by taking the change in revenue between the points on the demand curve, expressed per unit. For example, if price goes from £10 to £8, the quantity sold increases from 20 to 40, and total revenue goes from £200 to £320, so revenue increases by £(320 – 200) = £120, which is £6 per unit sold. In the table the values for marginal revenue are shown halfway between the values in the other columns, as we are looking at the change between the successive points.

Figure 1.6 plots these values (I have not plotted all of the negative values of MR). This shows the relationship between AR and MR. The two lines (curves) share the same intercept with the y-axis, and the MR curve is exactly twice as steep as the AR line (curve). This relationship always holds.

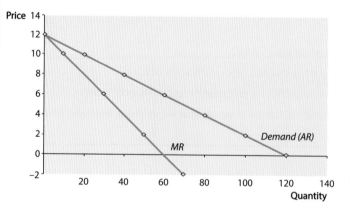

Figure 1.6 Average and marginal revenue

Notice that the MR line cuts the x-axis at the quantity 60, which is the point at which TR is at a maximum. This is also a mathematical feature of the relationship.

Business objectives

The opening section of this chapter stated that firms exist to organise production, by bringing together the factors of production in order to produce output. This begs the question of what motivates them to produce particular *levels* of output, and at what price. In the remainder of this chapter, consideration will be given to alternative objectives that firms may set out to achieve.

Profit maximisation

Traditional economic analysis has tended to start from the premise that firms set out with the objective of maximising profits. It is important to be clear about what is meant by 'profits' in this context.

All firms need to make enough profit to cover the cost of being in business. If a firm does not cover the opportunity cost of operating in a market, it has no incentive to remain in the market. This normal rate of return is known as **normal profit**. It can be seen as the opportunity cost of capital: the rate of return that is sufficient to prevent the firm from exiting from the market. Normal profit is viewed by economists as being part of the total cost faced by the firm. Profits made by a firm above that level are known as **supernormal profits**, or **abnormal profits**.

Notice that in the short run, a firm may choose to remain in a market even if it is not covering its opportunity costs, provided its revenues are covering its variable costs. Since the firm has already incurred fixed costs, if it can cover its variable costs in the short run, it will be better off remaining in business and paying off part of the fixed costs than exiting the market and losing all of its fixed costs. Thus, the level of average variable costs represents the shut-down price, below which the firm will exit from the market in the short run.

How does a firm choose its output level if it wishes to maximise profits? Suppose a firm is a relatively small player in a big market, and thus has no influence over the price of its product. Its total revenue is then proportional to the amount of output it sells. If it faces a total cost curve like the one that was introduced earlier in the chapter, its output decision can be analysed by reference to Figure 1.7. To maximise profits, the firm needs to choose the output level at which total revenue is as far above the total cost curve as possible. This happens at $q^\star$.

Key terms

normal profit profit that covers the opportunity cost of capital and is just sufficient to keep the firm in the market

supernormal profits/ abnormal profits/ economic profit terms referring to profits that exceed normal profit

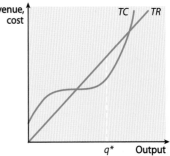

Figure 1.7 Profit maximisation

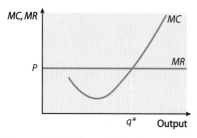

Figure 1.8 Profit maximisation again

Key term

marginal revenue the additional revenue gained by a firm from selling an additional unit of output

Study tip

The $MR = MC$ rule for profit maximisation is an important one, as it applies in any market situation where a firm sets out to maximise profits, so make sure you understand and remember it.

An alternative way of looking at the profit-maximising decision is to draw the marginal cost and marginal revenue curves. In this case, the firm has no influence over the price of the product, as it was assumed that the firm is a small player in the market. This means that the firm receives the same revenue from the sale of each unit of the good. In other words, the **marginal revenue** that it receives from selling each unit of output is the same. Consider Figure 1.8. Marginal revenue (MR) is shown as a horizontal straight line, and marginal cost is given by MC, having a U-shape as before.

It turns out that the level of output that maximises profit will be found where $MC = MR$. If the firm is producing less output than this, it will find that the marginal revenue from selling an additional unit of output is higher than the marginal cost of producing it, so the firm can add to its profits by increasing output. In contrast, if the firm is producing more than $q^{\star}$, it will find that the marginal revenue from selling an extra unit fails to cover the cost of producing the unit, so it will not pay the firm to produce beyond $q^{\star}$. Therefore, $q^{\star}$ can be seen as the level of output that maximises the firm's profits.

The $MC = MR$ rule is a general rule for firms that want to maximise profits, and it holds in all market situations. For example, suppose the firm faces a downward-sloping demand curve for its product, such that it can sell more by reducing the price. You may recall from Book 1 that a linear demand curve is associated with a total revenue curve like that shown in Figure 1.9. Assume that the firm faces the usual shape of short-run total cost curve TC. Profits are again maximised where the distance of TR above TC is as large as possible. This occurs at q_π.

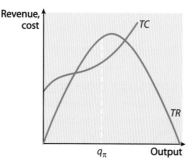

Figure 1.9 Profit maximisation with a downward-sloping demand curve

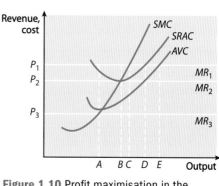

Figure 1.10 Profit maximisation in the short run

Exercise 1.6

Figure 1.10 shows a firm in short-run equilibrium. The firm is operating in a market in which it has no influence over price, so it gains the same marginal revenue from the sale of each unit of output. Marginal revenue and average revenue are thus the same. P_1, P_2 and P_3 represent three possible prices that could prevail in the market.

a For each price level, identify the output level that the firm would choose in order to maximise profits.

b For each of these output levels, compare the level of average revenue with that of average cost, and consider what this means for the firm's profits.

Will a firm always operate as efficiently as it can? Earlier in the chapter, the principal–agent phenomenon was introduced, and it was noted that this could lead to some managerial slack, if management are not fully accountable to the owners of the firm. This is an example of what is called **X-inefficiency**. For example, in Figure 1.11 $LAC\star$ represents the long-run average cost curve showing the most efficient cost positions for the firm at any output level. With X-inefficiency, a firm could end up producing on a long-run average cost curve such as LAC_1 that is above the most efficient that could be achieved. For example, at output q_1, the firm would produce at an average cost of AC_1, although it could have produced at $AC\star$ if it were not for the X-inefficiency. Thus, in the presence of X-inefficiency the firm will be operating *above* its lowest-possible long-run average cost curve.

Key term

X-inefficiency a situation arising when a firm is not operating at minimum cost, perhaps because of organisational slack

Some writers have argued that the managers may be pursuing other objectives. For example, some managers may enjoy being involved in the running of a *large* business, and may prefer to see the firm gaining market share — perhaps beyond the profit-maximising level. Others may like to see their status rewarded and so will want to divert part of the profits into managerial perks — large offices, company cars and so on. Or they may feel that having a large staff working for them increases their prestige inside the company. These sorts of activity tend to reduce the profitability of firms.

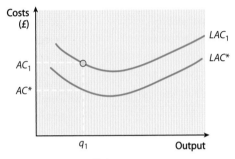

Figure 1.11 X-inefficiency

Revenue maximisation

William Baumol argued that managers may set out with the objective of maximising revenue. The effects of such action can be seen in Figure 1.12. As before, q_π represents the profit-maximising level of output. However, you can see that total revenue is maximised at the peak of the TR curve at q_r. Thus, a revenue-maximising firm will produce more output than a profit-maximising one, and will need to charge a lower price in order to sell the extra output. Notice that the revenue maximisation point occurs at the level of output at which marginal revenue is equal to zero ($MR = 0$).

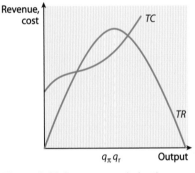

Figure 1.12 Revenue maximisation

Baumol pointed out that the shareholders might not be too pleased about this. The way the firm behaves then depends upon the degree of accountability that the agents (managers) have to the principals (shareholders). For example, the shareholders may have sufficient power over their agents to be able to insist on some minimum level of profits. The result may then be a compromise solution between the principals and the agents, with output being set somewhere between q_π and q_r.

Sales maximisation

In some cases, managers may focus more on the volume of sales than on the resulting revenues. This could lead to output being set even higher, as shown in Figure 1.13. The firm would now push for higher sales up to the point where it just breaks even at q_s. This is the point at which total revenue only just covers total cost and where average cost equals average revenue. Remember that total cost includes normal profit — the opportunity cost of the resources tied up in the firm. The firm would have to close down if it did not cover this opportunity cost.

Again, the extent to which the managers will be able to pursue this objective without endangering their positions with the shareholders

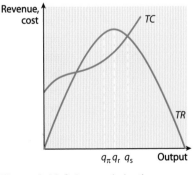

Figure 1.13 Sales maximisation

depends on how accountable the managers are to the shareholders. Remember that the managers are likely to have much better information about the market conditions and the internal functioning of the firm than the shareholders, who view the firm only remotely. This may be to the managers' advantage.

Behavioural theories

Businesses may not set out to maximise anything, either consciously because they have other motivations, or as a result of the principal–agent issue. For example, it might be that managers simply prefer a quiet life, and therefore do not push for the absolute profit-maximising position, but do just enough to keep the shareholders off their backs. Herbert Simon referred to this as '**satisficing**' behaviour, where managers aim to produce satisfactory profits rather than maximum profits.

Firms may wish to develop a favourable reputation by demonstrating a commitment to acting in ways that benefit society at large, or that improve the welfare of their employees and the community in which they are located. This notion of **corporate social responsibility** (CSR) has become widespread, with firms devoting resources to promoting community programmes of various kinds and encouraging their employees to engage in volunteering activities.

Exercise 1.7

Google 'corporate social responsibility' with the name of some large firms with which you are familiar, and check out the range of activities in which firms engage under this banner.

Has this now become a prerequisite for firms' survival? If it is perceived that failure to engage with CSR has a major impact on firms' sales, then it becomes crucial for a firm to be able to demonstrate its commitment in order to compete with its rivals. Devoting resources to CSR then becomes part of a firm's strategy to safeguard its market position.

Why assume profit maximisation?

The discussion has revealed a range of reasons explaining why firms may depart from profit maximisation. Does this mean that it should be abandoned as an assumption?

It could be argued that some of the strategies adopted by firms seem to diverge from profit maximisation in the short run, but may result in the maximisation of profits in the long run. For example, if all firms in a market are engaging in CSR in order to improve their credibility for their customers, then it could be argued that this expenditure becomes part of operating costs, and a necessary part of maintaining the market share needed to maximise profits in the long term.

From an economic modelling perspective, being able to assume that firms maximise profits allows the economist to come to an understanding of firms' behaviour under a simple and clear assumption. This offers much more straightforward insights into firms' behaviour than trying to implement some of the more complex assumptions that could be made about what motivates firms' decisions. Profit maximisation then provides a benchmark for other more complex models that enables an evaluation of how differently firms may behave under alternative assumptions. So even if it is not the case that firms always act to maximise profits, it is a useful starting point to ask how they would behave if they did maximise profits, and then explore alternative theories using profit maximisation as the benchmark against which to compare other models of behaviour.

Summary

- Traditional economic analysis assumes that firms set out to maximise profits.
- The opportunity cost of a firm's resources is viewed as a part of fixed costs. This is known as normal profit.
- Profits above this level are known as supernormal profits.
- A firm maximises profits by choosing output such that marginal revenue is equal to marginal cost.
- This may lead to satisficing behaviour and to X-inefficiency.
- William Baumol suggested that managers may set out to maximise revenue rather than profits; others have suggested that sales or the growth of the firm may be the managers' objectives.
- For an individual firm, productive efficiency can be regarded as having been achieved when the firm is operating at minimum long-run average cost.

Case study 1.1

A failed merger

This case study examines an episode in which a merger did not turn out the way that the firms involved anticipated.

In 2001 negotiations began between two firms in the telecoms-equipment business — the French firm Alcatel and Lucent Technologies of America — and 5 years later, in April 2006, an agreement was reached that the two firms would merge.

There seemed to be good commercial reasons for coming together. Alcatel, the bigger of the two firms, would gain entry into the lucrative American market, and the merger would make the combined firm one of the world's largest in the market. The combined revenue of the two firms from sales of network equipment would be slightly larger than that of Cisco Systems, the market leader at the time.

It was expected that the merger would not only give the firm a higher profile in the two key markets of America and Europe, but also enable the exploitation of economies of scale. By combining the companies, it was expected that about 10% of the existing workforce could be cut, saving $1.7 billion. This would be achieved by eliminating overlapping administrative, procurement and marketing costs, as well as reducing the workforce.

However, things did not work out as expected, and the merged company ran into problems. The firm found cost savings difficult to realise, in spite of 16,500 job losses from a workforce of 88,000 — and found that prices in the market were falling, squeezing profitability. The firm faced competition from new entrants, particularly from Chinese firms, and found difficulty in keeping up with the pace of technological change. It was also reported that the firm was suffering from a clash of cultures between the French and American parts of the business.

The result of all this was that in July 2008 it was announced that the French chairman (who was formerly the boss of Alcatel) and the American chief executive (formerly the boss of Lucent) were leaving the company and being replaced by a new executive team charged with the task of taking the company forward. The new chairman was neither French nor American.

Even the most carefully planned mergers can end up as failures

Follow-up question

From the passage, identify the factors that led to the failure of the merger.

Coke vs Pepsi in India

In the mid-2000s it was reported that Coca-Cola and PepsiCo were fighting to increase their sales in India. A pesticide scare in the previous year had caused sales to plummet, and the two firms were anxious to recover the situation.

The tactics they adopted were to reduce the size of the bottles for sale in order to appeal to consumers with low incomes, to cut prices, to increase the availability of the products in rural areas, and to encourage more at-home consumption in the urban areas.

It was seen that there was plenty of scope for growth in the market, as India showed one of the lowest average levels of consumption of fizzy drinks in the world, and was substantially below the Asian average. This may partly reflect the way that children have been discouraged from drinking colas by their teachers at school.

The prices being charged were rated as being the world's lowest prices for cola as the two firms battled to increase their market shares. However, in consequence the firms faced reductions in their profit margins, and continued to face competition from local producers. The logistics of supplying such a geographically large and diverse region, given the need to ensure refrigeration, added significantly to costs. Attempts were made to counter this by reducing the weight of the bottles and by making use of cheap transport in the form of bullock carts and cycle rickshaws in the rural areas.

Market analysts said that soft-drink companies should be able to improve profits, but executives remained bent on boosting volumes. The vice-president of Coca-Cola marketing in India was quoted as saying that 'any affordability strategy will put pressure on margins, but it is critical to build the market'.

The pesticide issue proved to be a long-lasting controversy, and the Kerala government filed a criminal complaint against PepsiCo over its environmental impact, although this was rejected by the Supreme Court of India in 2010. Indeed, the US Department of State named PepsiCo as one of the 12 multinationals that displayed 'the most impressive corporate social responsibility credentials in emerging markets'.

Coke and Pepsi compete for market share in India

Follow-up questions

a Given the statements in the passage, do you think that Coca-Cola and PepsiCo were trying to maximise short-run profits?

b Explain your answer to (a) and comment on what the firms were trying to achieve by their strategies.

c Identify ways in which the firms were seeking to influence their costs.

d How do you think PepsiCo's record on CSR will have affected its position in the market?

e Discuss what you think the firms would want to achieve in the long run.

2 Market structure: perfect competition and monopoly

Book 1 introduced the notion of market failure — describing situations in which free markets may not produce the best outcome for society in terms of efficiency. One of the reasons given for this concerned what is termed 'imperfect competition'. It was argued that, if firms can achieve a position of market dominance, they may distort the pattern of resource allocation. It is now time to look at market structure more closely in order to evaluate the way that markets work, and the significance of this for resource allocation. The fact that firms try to maximise profits is not in itself bad for society. However, the structure of a market has a strong influence on how well the market performs. 'Structure' here is seen in relation to a number of dimensions, but in particular to the number of firms operating in a market and the way in which they interact. This chapter considers two extreme forms of market structure: perfect competition and monopoly. It begins with a discussion of efficiency.

Learning objectives

After studying this chapter, you should:
→ be familiar with the economist's notions of efficiency
→ understand what is meant by market structure, and why it is important for firms
→ appreciate the significance of barriers to entry in influencing the market structure
→ be familiar with the assumptions of the model of perfect competition
→ understand how a firm chooses profit-maximising output under perfect competition
→ appreciate how a perfectly competitive market reaches long-run equilibrium
→ understand how the characteristics of long-run equilibrium under perfect competition affect the performance of the market in terms of productive and allocative efficiency
→ be familiar with the assumptions of the model of monopoly
→ understand how a monopoly firm chooses output and sets price
→ understand why a monopoly can arise in a market
→ understand how the characteristics of equilibrium under monopoly affect the performance of the market in terms of productive and allocative efficiency
→ be aware of the relative merits of perfect competition and monopoly in terms of market performance
→ be aware of the conditions under which price discrimination may be possible

Efficiency

Book 1 introduced the ideas of productive and allocative efficiency. The extent to which markets will deliver efficiency will be explored in the following chapters, but it is also important to refine these notions further. Indeed, it has already been noted that the principal–agent problem can lead to X-inefficiency, which is one reason why the ideal combination of productive and allocative efficiency will not be achieved.

productive efficiency
occurs when firms have
chosen appropriate
combinations of factors of
production and produce
the maximum output
possible from those
inputs, thus producing at
minimum long-run average
cost

static efficiency
efficiency at a particular
point in time

allocative efficiency
achieved when society is
producing the appropriate
bundle of goods and
services relative to
consumer preferences

dynamic efficiency a view
of efficiency that takes
into account the effect of
innovation and technical
progress on productive
and allocative efficiency in
the long run

Study tip

These notions of efficiency
are important, and will be
central to the discussion
of market structures,
so make sure that you
understand them before
moving on.

Productive efficiency

The notion of **productive efficiency** is closely tied to the costs faced by firms, particularly in relation to the average total cost of production. Productive efficiency can be seen in terms of the minimum average cost at which output can be produced, recognising that average cost is likely to vary at different scales of output. For example, in Figure 1.4 the point $q^\star$ may be regarded as the optimum level of output, in the sense that it minimises average cost per unit of output.

From the firm's perspective, the decision process can be viewed as a three-stage procedure. First, the firm needs to decide how much output it wants to produce. Second, it chooses an appropriate combination of factors of production, given that intended scale of production. Third, it attempts to produce as much output as possible, given those inputs. Another way of expressing this is that, having chosen the intended scale of output, the firm tries to minimise its costs of production.

Notice that when the firm starts this decision process, it is likely to choose its desired output level on the basis of current or expected market conditions. However, remember the distinction between the short and the long run. Once the firm has chosen its desired scale of production, and installed the necessary capital, it is tied into that level of capital stock in the short run. If it needs to change its decision in the future, it will take time to implement the changes. In the short run, a firm may thus be in a situation of **static efficiency**, choosing the minimum average cost, given the market conditions at that time.

Allocative efficiency

The notion of **allocative efficiency** relates to the issue of whether an economy allocates its resources in such a way as to produce a balance of goods and services that matches consumer preferences. In an individual market, this would mean that firms were producing the ideal amount of a good that consumers wish to buy. This is related to the notion of equilibrium in the demand and supply model, in which prices act as signals to consumers and producers to bring demand and supply into equilibrium. However, Book 1 demonstrated that there are situations in which market failure can occur, thus preventing the best allocation of resources from society's point of view.

Dynamic efficiency

The discussion of efficiency so far has been conducted in terms of how to make the best use of existing resources, producing an appropriate mix of goods and services and using factor inputs as efficiently as possible, given existing knowledge and technology. This is good as far as it goes, but it does represent a relatively static view of efficiency.

Dynamic efficiency goes one step further, recognising that the state of knowledge and technology changes over time. For example, investment in research and development today means that production can be carried out more efficiently at some future date. Furthermore, the development of new products may also mean that a different mix of goods and services may serve consumers better in the long term.

The notion of dynamic efficiency stemmed from the work of Joseph Schumpeter, who argued that a preoccupation with static efficiency may sacrifice opportunities for greater efficiency in the long run. In other words, there may be a trade-off between achieving efficiency today and improving efficiency tomorrow.

Summary

- A society needs to find a way of using its limited resources as efficiently as possible.
- Productive efficiency occurs when firms have chosen appropriate combinations of factors of production and produce the maximum output possible from those inputs.
- Allocative efficiency occurs when firms produce an appropriate bundle of goods and services, given consumer preferences.
- An individual market exhibits aspects of allocative efficiency when the marginal benefit received by society from consuming a good or service matches the marginal cost of producing it — that is, when price is equal to marginal cost.
- Dynamic efficiency recognises that there may be a trade-off between efficiency in the short run and in the long run.

Market structure

Firms cannot take decisions without having some awareness of the market in which they are operating. In some markets, firms find themselves to be such small players that they cannot influence the price at which they sell. In others, a firm may find itself to be the only firm, which clearly gives it much more discretion in devising a price and output strategy. There may also be many intermediate situations where the firm has some control over price, but needs to be aware of rival firms in the market.

Economists have devised a range of models that allow such different **market structures** to be analysed. Before looking carefully at the most important types of market structure, the key characteristics of alternative market structures will be introduced. The main models are summarised in Table 2.1. In many ways, we can regard these as a spectrum of markets with different characteristics.

Key term

market structure the market environment within which firms operate

Table 2.1 A spectrum of market structures

	Perfect competition	Monopolistic competition	Oligopoly	Monopoly
Number of firms	Many	Many	Few	One
Freedom of entry	Not restricted	Not restricted	Some barriers to entry	High barriers to entry
Firm's influence over price	None	Some	Some	Price maker, subject to the demand curve
Nature of product	Homogeneous	Differentiated	Varied	No close substitutes
Examples	Cauliflowers	Fast-food outlets	Cars	PC operating systems
	Carrots	Travel agents	Mobile phones	Local water supply

Perfect competition

At one extreme is *perfect competition*. This is a market in which each individual firm is a *price taker*. This means that no individual firm is large enough to be able to influence the price, which is set by the market as a whole. This situation arises where there are many firms operating in a market, producing a product that is much the same whichever firm produces it. You might think of a market for a particular sort of vegetable, for example. One cauliflower is very much like another, and it would not be possible for a particular cauliflower-grower to set a premium price for its product.

Such markets are also typified by freedom of entry and exit. In other words, it is relatively easy for new firms to enter the market, or for existing firms to leave it to produce something else. The market price in such a market will be driven down to that at which the typical firm in the market just makes enough profit to stay in business. If firms make more than this, other firms will be attracted in, and thus abnormal profits will be competed away. If some firms in the market do not make sufficient profit to want to remain in the market, they will exit, allowing price to drift up until again the typical firm just makes enough to stay in business.

Monopoly

At the other extreme of the spectrum of market structures is *monopoly*. This is a market where there is only one firm in operation. Such a firm has some influence over price, and can choose a combination of price and output in order to maximise its profits. The monopolist is not entirely free to set any price that it wants, as it must remain aware of the demand curve for its product. Nonetheless, it has the freedom to choose a point along its demand curve.

The nature of a monopolist's product is that it has no close substitutes — either actual or potential — so it faces no competition. An example might be Microsoft, which for a long time held a global monopoly for operating systems for PC computers. At the time of the famous trial in 1998, Microsoft was said to supply operating systems for about 95% of the world's PCs.

Another condition of a monopoly market is that there are barriers to the entry of new firms. This means that the firm is able to set its price such as to make profits that are above the minimum needed to keep the firm in business, without attracting new rivals into the market.

Monopolistic competition

Between the two extreme forms of market structure are many intermediate situations in which firms may have some influence over their selling price, but still have to take account of the fact that there are other firms in the market. One such market is known as *monopolistic competition*. This is a market in which there are many firms operating, each producing similar but not identical products, so that there is some scope for influencing price, perhaps because of brand loyalty. However, firms in such a market are likely to be relatively small. Such firms may find it profitable to make sure that their own product is differentiated from other goods, and may advertise in order to convince potential customers that this is the case. For example, small-scale local restaurants may offer different styles of cooking.

On trial in 1998, Microsoft was found to have a global monopoly on PC operating systems

Oligopoly

Another intermediate form of market structure is *oligopoly*, which literally means 'few sellers'. This is a market in which there are just a few firms that supply the market. Each firm will take decisions in close awareness of how other firms in the market may react to their actions. In some cases, the firms may try to *collude* — to work together in order to behave as if they were a monopolist — thus making higher profits. In other cases, they may be intense rivals, which will tend to result in abnormal profits being competed away. The question of whether firms in an oligopoly collude or compete has a substantial impact on how the overall market performs in terms of resource allocation, and whether consumers will be disadvantaged as a result of the actions of the firms in the market.

Barriers to entry

It has been argued that if firms in a market are able to make abnormal profits, this will act as an inducement for new firms to try to gain entry into that market in order to share in those profits. A *barrier to entry* is a characteristic of a market that prevents new firms from joining the market. The existence of such barriers is thus of great importance in influencing the market structure that will evolve.

For example, if a firm holds a patent on a particular good, this means that no other firm is permitted by law to produce the product, and the patent-holding firm thus has a monopoly. The firm may then be able to set price such as to make abnormal profits without fear of rival firms competing away those profits. On the other hand, if there are no barriers to entry in a market, and if the existing firms set price to make abnormal profits, new firms will join the market, and the increase in market supply will push price down until no abnormal profits are being made.

Summary

- The decisions made by firms must be taken in the context of the market environment in which they operate.
- Under conditions of perfect competition, each firm must accept the market price as given, but can choose how much output to produce in order to maximise profits.
- In a monopoly market, where there is only one producer, the firm can choose output and price (subject to the demand curve).
- Monopolistic competition combines some features of perfect competition, and some characteristics of monopoly. Firms have some influence over price, and will produce a differentiated product in order to maintain this influence.
- Oligopoly exists where a market is occupied by just a few firms. In some cases, these few firms may work together to maximise their joint profits; in other cases, they may seek to outmanoeuvre each other.

Exercise 2.1

For each of the market situations listed below, select the form of market structure that is most likely to apply. In each case, comment on the way in which the firm's actions may be influenced by the market structure.

Forms of market structure:

A perfect competition

B monopoly

C monopolistic competition

D oligopoly

a A fairly large number of fast-food outlets in a city centre, offering various different styles of cooking (Indian, Chinese, fish and chips, burgers, etc.) at broadly similar prices.

b An island's only airport.

c A large number of farmers selling parsnips at the same price.

d A small number of large firms that between them supply most of the market for commercial vans.

The model of perfect competition

Key term

perfect competition a form of market structure that produces allocative and productive efficiency in long-run equilibrium

At one end of the spectrum of market structures is **perfect competition**. This model has a special place in economic analysis, because if all its assumptions were fulfilled, and if all markets operated according to its precepts, the best allocation of resources would be ensured for society as a whole. Although it may be argued that this ideal is not often achieved, perfect competition nonetheless provides a yardstick by which all other forms of market structure can be evaluated.

Assumptions

The assumptions of the model of perfect competition are as follows:

1 Firms aim to maximise profits.

2 There are many participants (both buyers and sellers).

3 The product is homogeneous.

4 There are no barriers to entry to or exit from the market.

5 There is perfect knowledge of market conditions.

6 There are no externalities.

Profit maximisation

The first assumption is that firms act to maximise their profits. You might think that this means that firms, acting in their own self-interest, are unlikely to do consumers any favours. However, it transpires that this does not interfere with the operation of the market. Indeed, it is the pursuit of self-interest by firms and consumers which ensures that the market works effectively.

Many participants

This is an important assumption of the model: that there are so many buyers and so many sellers that no individual trader is able to influence the market price. The market price is thus determined by the operation of the market.

On the sellers' side of the market, this assumption is tantamount to saying that there are limited economies of scale in the industry. If the minimum efficient scale is small relative to market demand, then no firm is likely to become so large that it will gain influence in the market.

A homogeneous product

This assumption means that buyers of the good see all products in the market as being identical, and will not favour one firm's product over another. If there were brand loyalty, such that one firm was more popular than others, then that firm would be able to charge a premium on its price. By ruling out this possibility the previous assumption is reinforced, and no individual seller is able to influence the selling price of the product.

No barriers to entry or exit

By this assumption, firms are able to join the market if they perceive it to be a profitable step, and they can exit from the market without hindrance. This assumption is important when it comes to considering the long-run equilibrium towards which the market will tend.

Perfect knowledge

It is assumed that all participants in the market have perfect information about trading conditions in the market. In particular, buyers always know the prices that firms are charging, and thus can buy the good at the cheapest possible price. Firms that try to charge a price above the market price will get no takers. At the same time, traders are aware of the product quality.

No externalities

Book 1 described externalities as a form of market failure that prevents the attainment of allocative efficiency. Here externalities are ruled out in order to explore the characteristics of the perfect competition model.

The firm under perfect competition

With the above assumptions, it is possible to analyse how a firm will operate in the market. An important implication of these assumptions is that no individual trader can influence the price of the product. In particular, this means that the firm is a **price taker**, and has to accept whatever price is set in the market as a whole.

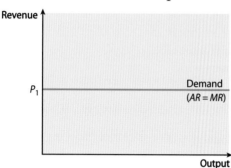

Figure 2.1 The firm's demand curve

As the firm is a price taker, it faces a perfectly elastic demand curve for its product, as is shown in Figure 2.1. In this figure, P_1 is the price set in the market, and the firm cannot sell at any other price. If it tries to set a price above P_1 it will sell nothing, as buyers are fully aware of the market price and will not buy at a higher price, especially as they know that there is no quality difference between the products offered by different firms in the market. What this also implies is that the firm can sell as much output as it likes at that going price — which means there is no incentive for any firm to set a price below P_1. Thus, all firms charge the same price, P_1.

Extension material

Competition and the internet

The assumption of perfect knowledge of market conditions can seem to be unrealistic in some situations, but it is necessary for the model of perfect competition to work. This is because if some traders have better information than others, they may be able to exploit the situation, and firms may not all face the same price. Book 1, Chapter 7 explored some of the implications of asymmetric information for a market.

If you think about it, the internet has had an enormous impact on the information available to buyers — and to sellers in relation to their competitors. The proliferation of price comparison sites makes it easy to look for good deals when buying goods and services. In this context, the assumption of perfect knowledge begins to appear rather less unrealistic. So we might argue that the arrival of the internet has made it more likely that firms in some markets will indeed be price takers, less able to charge high prices because consumers are better informed.

Study tip

Remember from the previous chapter that *SMC* cuts the minimum points of *AVC* and *SRAC*. In Figure 2.2, as the demand curve is horizontal, the firm faces constant average and marginal revenue and will choose output at q_1, where *MR* = *MC*.

The firm's short-run supply decision

If the firm can sell as much as it likes at the market price, how does it decide how much to produce?

Chapter 1 explained that to maximise profits a firm needs to set output at such a level that marginal revenue is equal to marginal cost. Figure 2.2 illustrates this rule by adding the short-run cost curves to the demand curve.

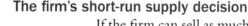

Figure 2.2 The firm's short-run supply decision

If the market price were to change, the firm would react by changing output, but always choosing to supply output at the level at which $MR = MC$. This suggests that the short-run marginal cost curve represents the firm's short-run supply curve: in other words, it shows the quantity of output that the firm would supply at any given price.

However, there is one important proviso to this statement. If the price falls below short-run average variable cost, the firm's best decision will be to exit from the market, as it will be better off just incurring its fixed costs. So the firm's **short-run supply curve** is the *SMC* curve above the point where it cuts *SAVC* (at its minimum point).

Industry equilibrium in the short run

One crucial question not yet examined is how the market price comes to be determined. To answer this, it is necessary to consider the industry as a whole. In this case there is a conventional downward-sloping demand curve, of the sort met in Book 1. This is formed according to preferences of consumers in the market and is shown in Figure 2.3.

On the supply side, it has been shown that the individual firm's supply curve is its marginal cost curve above *SAVC*. If you add up the supply curves of each firm operating in the market, the result is the industry supply curve, also shown in Figure 2.3. The price will then adjust to P_1 at the intersection of demand and supply. The firms in the industry will between them supply Q_1 output, and the market will be in equilibrium.

The firm in short-run equilibrium revisited

As this seems to be a well-balanced situation, with price adjusting to equate market demand and supply, the only question is why it is described as just a *short-run equilibrium*. The clue to this is to be found back with the individual firm.

Figure 2.4 returns to the position facing an individual firm in the market. As before, the firm maximises profits by accepting the price P_1 as set in the market and producing up to the point where $MR = MC$, which is at q_1. However, now the firm's average revenue (which is equal to price) is greater than its average cost (which is given by AC_1 at this level of output). The firm is thus making supernormal profits at this price. (Remember that 'normal profits' are included in average cost.) Indeed, the amount of total profits being made is shown as the shaded area on the graph. Notice that average revenue minus average costs equals profit per unit, so multiplying this by the quantity sold determines total profit.

This is where the assumption about freedom of entry becomes important. If firms in this market are making profits above opportunity cost, the market is generating more profits than other markets in the economy. This will prove attractive to other firms, which will seek to enter the market — and the assumption is that there are no barriers to prevent them from doing so.

This process of entry will continue for as long as firms are making supernormal profits. However, as more firms join the market, the *position* of the industry supply curve, which is the sum of the supply curves of an ever-larger number of individual firms, will be affected. As the industry supply curve shifts to the right, the market price will fall. At some point the price will have fallen to such an extent that firms are no longer making supernormal profits, and the market will then stabilise.

If the price were to fall even further, some firms would choose to exit from the market, and the process would go into reverse. Therefore price can be expected to stabilise such that the typical firm in the industry is just making normal profits.

Key term

short-run supply curve
for a firm operating under perfect competition, the curve given by its short-run marginal cost curve above the price at which $MC = SAVC$; for the industry, the horizontal sum of the supply curves of the individual firms

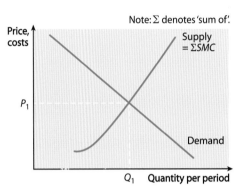

Note: Σ denotes 'sum of'.

Figure 2.3 A perfectly competitive industry in short-run equilibrium

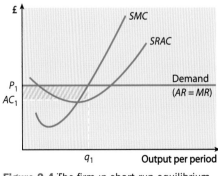

Figure 2.4 The firm in short-run equilibrium

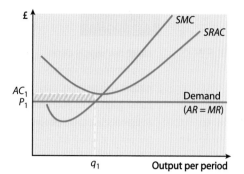

Figure 2.5 The firm in short-run equilibrium again

Figure 2.5 shows a different situation. This firm also tries to maximise profits by setting $MC = MR$, but finds that its average cost exceeds the price. It makes losses shown by the shaded area, and in the long run will choose to leave the market. As this and other firms exit from the market, the market supply curve shifts to the left, and the equilibrium price will drift upwards until firms are again making normal profits.

Perfect competition in long-run equilibrium

Figure 2.6 shows the situation for a typical firm and for the industry as a whole once long-run equilibrium has been reached and firms no longer have any incentive to enter or to exit the market. The market is in equilibrium, with demand equal to supply at the going price. The typical firm sets marginal revenue equal to marginal cost to maximise profits, and just makes normal profits.

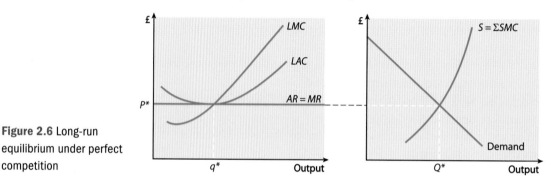

Figure 2.6 Long-run equilibrium under perfect competition

The long-run supply curve

Suppose there is an increase in the demand for this product. Perhaps, for some reason, everyone becomes convinced that the product is really health promoting, so demand increases at any given price. This disturbs the market equilibrium, and the question then is whether (and how) equilibrium can be restored.

Figure 2.7 reproduces the long-run equilibrium that was shown in Figure 2.6. Thus, in the initial position market price is at $P\star$, the typical firm is in long-run equilibrium producing $q\star$, and the industry is producing $Q\star$. Demand was initially at D_0, but with the increased popularity of the product it has shifted to D_1. In the short run this pushes the market price up to P_1 for the industry because, as market price increases, existing firms have the incentive to supply more output: that is, they move along their short-run supply curves. So in the short run a typical firm starts to produce q_1 output. The combined supply of the firms then increases to Q_1.

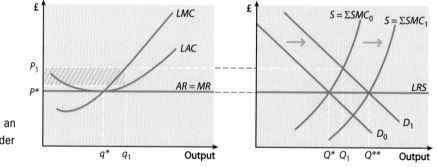

Figure 2.7 Adjusting to an increase in demand under perfect competition

However, at the higher price the firms start making supernormal profits (shown by the shaded area in Figure 2.7). Under the assumptions underpinning perfect competition, firms have perfect knowledge of market conditions, so the fact that firms in the market are making supernormal profits is known. Furthermore, there are no barriers to entry that prevent new firms joining the market. The fact that the product is homogeneous simplifies entry further. This means that in time more firms will be attracted into the market, pushing the short-run industry supply curve to the right. This process will continue until there is no further incentive for new firms to enter the market — which occurs when the price has returned to $P\star$, but with increased industry output at $Q\star\star$. In other words, the adjustment in the short run is borne by existing firms, but the long-run equilibrium is reached through the entry of new firms.

This suggests that the **industry long-run supply curve (LRS)** is horizontal at the price $P\star$, which is the minimum point of the long-run average cost curve for the typical firm in the industry.

Extension material

Different cost conditions

If firms are not identical, but face different cost conditions, then the *LRS* may slope upwards. This could happen because some firms face a more favourable environment than others. Perhaps their location confers some advantage because they are closer to the market, or to some raw material. This would then allow some firms to survive for longer if the market price falls. In this case, as price falls, the least efficient firms would exit from the market until the marginal firm just makes normal profits. Notice that this also suggests that the most efficient firms in the market are able to make some abnormal profits even in long-run equilibrium, and it is only the marginal firm that just breaks even.

Quantitative skills 2.1

Interpreting points and areas on a diagram

Figure 2.8 shows the short-run cost curves for a firm that is operating in a perfectly competitive market. We can use a graph like this to analyse some key aspects of the firm's situation. Think carefully about what follows, and make sure you understand the points and areas mentioned.

A first question is to consider at what price the firm would just make 'normal' profits. This point would be where the price (average revenue) is just equal to average total costs, which would be at a price *OA* in the figure.

If the price were indeed at *OA*, then we could find areas of the figure to represent fixed and variable costs. With the price at *OA* the firm would produce *OQ* output (where *MC = MR*), so average variable costs would be given by *OE*, and total variable costs would be the area *OEHQ*. We can then infer that total fixed costs are the area *EADH*.

Now consider the conditions under which a firm would choose to exit the market. In the short run, if the firm is getting a sufficiently high price to cover to its variable cost then it will stay in business, as it is at least covering a part of its fixed costs. However, if the price falls below average variable cost, this no longer applies. So the firm would exit if the price were to fall below *OI* (which is the minimum point of the *SAVC* curve). In other words, when the price is between *OI* and *OE* the firm makes a loss in the short run but continues in the market.

Notice that as the price varies, the firm effectively moves along its *SMC* curve, so we can interpret the *SMC* curve (above *OI*) as showing the short-run supply curve of the firm.

Notice also that if the price is above *OA*, the firm makes abnormal profits.

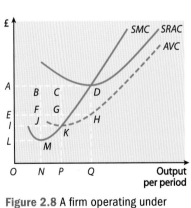

Figure 2.8 A firm operating under short-run perfect competition

Study tip

These diagrams can be quite confusing until you get used to them, and you would be well advised to practise both interpreting and drawing them, so you can be confident in using them when you need to do so.

Exercise 2.2

Starting from a diagram like Figure 2.6, track the response of a perfectly competitive market to a decrease in market demand for a good — in other words, explain how the market adjusts to a leftward shift of the demand curve.

Efficiency under perfect competition

Having reviewed the characteristics of the long-run equilibrium of a perfectly competitive market, you may wonder what is so good about such a market in terms of productive and allocative efficiency.

Productive efficiency

For an individual market, productive efficiency is reached when a firm operates at the minimum point of its long-run average cost curve. Under perfect competition, this is indeed a feature of the long-run equilibrium position. So productive efficiency is achieved in the long run — but not in the short run, when a firm need not be operating at minimum average cost.

Allocative efficiency

For an individual market, allocative efficiency is achieved when price is set equal to marginal cost. This was explained in Chapter 4 of Book 1 Again, the process by which supernormal profits are competed away through the entry of new firms into the market ensures that price is equal to marginal cost within a perfectly competitive market in long-run equilibrium. So allocative efficiency is also achieved. Indeed, firms set price equal to marginal cost even in the short run, so allocative efficiency is a feature of perfect competition in both the short run and the long run.

Evaluation of perfect competition

A criticism sometimes levelled at the model of perfect competition is that it is merely a theoretical ideal, based on a sequence of assumptions that rarely holds in the real world. Perhaps you have some sympathy with that view.

It could be argued that the model does hold for some agricultural markets. One study in the USA estimated that the elasticity of demand for an individual farmer producing sweetcorn was −31,353, which is pretty close to perfect elasticity.

However, to argue that the model is useless because it is unrealistic is to miss a very important point. By allowing a glimpse of what the ideal market would look like, at least in terms of resource allocation, the model provides a measure against which alternative market structures can be compared. Furthermore, economic analysis can be used to investigate the effects of relaxing the assumptions of the model, which can be another valuable exercise. For example, it is possible to examine how the market is affected if firms can differentiate their products, or if traders in the market are acting with incomplete information.

So, although there may be relatively few markets that display all the characteristics of perfect competition, that does not destroy the usefulness of the model in economic theory. It will continue to be a reference point when examining alternative models of market structure.

Summary

- The model of perfect competition describes an extreme form of market structure. It rests on a sequence of assumptions.
- Its key characteristics include the assumption that no individual trader can influence the market price of the good or service being traded, and that there is freedom of entry and exit.
- In such circumstances, each firm faces a perfectly elastic demand curve for its product, and can sell as much as it likes at the going market price.
- A profit-maximising firm chooses to produce the level of output at which marginal revenue (*MR*) equals marginal cost (*MC*).
- The firm's short-run marginal cost curve, above its short-run average variable cost curve, represents its short-run supply curve.
- The industry's short-run supply curve is the horizontal summation of the supply curves of all firms in the market.
- Firms may make supernormal profits in the short run, but because there is freedom of entry these profits will be competed away in the long run by new firms joining the market.
- The long-run industry supply curve is horizontal, with price adjusting to the minimum level of the typical firm's long-run average cost curve.
- Under perfect competition in long-run equilibrium, both productive efficiency and allocative efficiency are achieved.

The model of monopoly

At the opposite end of the spectrum of market structures is **monopoly**, which is a market with a single seller of a good.

There is a bit more to it than that, and economic analysis of monopoly rests on some important assumptions. In the real world, the Competition and Markets Authority (CMA), the official body in the UK with responsibility for monitoring monopoly markets, is empowered to investigate a merger if it results in the combined firm having more than 25% of a market. The operations of the CMA will be discussed in Chapter 6.

Key term

monopoly a form of market structure in which there is only one seller of a good or service

Assumptions

The assumptions of the monopoly model are as follows:

1 There is a single seller of a good.

2 There are no substitutes for the good, either actual or potential.

3 There are barriers to entry into the market.

It is also assumed that the firm aims to maximise profits. You can see that these assumptions all have their counterparts in the assumptions of perfect competition, and that in one sense this model can be described as being at the opposite end of the market structure spectrum.

If there is a single seller of a good, and if there are no substitutes for the good, the monopoly firm is thereby insulated from competition. Furthermore, any barriers to entry into the market will ensure that the firm can sustain its market position into the future. The assumption that there are no potential substitutes for the good reinforces the situation. (Chapter 4 will explore what happens if this assumption does not hold.)

A monopoly in equilibrium

The first point to note is that a monopoly firm faces the market demand curve directly. Thus, unlike in perfect competition, the demand curve slopes downwards. For the monopolist, the demand curve may be regarded as showing average revenue. Unlike a firm under perfect competition, therefore, the monopolist has some influence over price, and can make decisions regarding price as well as output. This is not to say that the monopolist has complete freedom to set the price, as the firm is still constrained by market demand. However, the firm is a *price maker* and can choose a location *along* the demand curve.

As a preliminary piece of analysis, recall from Book 1 that there is a relationship between the own-price elasticity of demand along a straight-line demand curve and total revenue. The key graphs are reproduced here as Figure 2.9. The price elasticity of demand is elastic above the mid-point of the demand curve and inelastic in the lower half, with total revenue increasing with a price fall when demand is elastic and falling when demand is inelastic.

The marginal revenue curve (*MR*) has been added to the figure. This has a fixed relationship with the average revenue curve (*AR*). This is for similar mathematical reasons as those that explained the relationship between marginal and average costs in the previous chapter. *MR* shares the intercept point on the vertical axis (point *A* in Figure 2.9) and has exactly twice the slope of *AR*.

As with the firm under perfect competition, a monopolist aiming to maximise profits will choose to produce at the level of output at which marginal revenue equals marginal cost. This is at Q_m in Figure 2.10. Having selected output, the monopolist then identifies the price that will clear the market for that level of output — in Figure 2.10 this is P_m. Notice that a monopoly will always produce in the segment of the demand curve where *MR* is positive, which implies that demand is price elastic.

This choice allows the monopolist to make supernormal profits, which can be identified as the shaded area in the figure. As before, this area is average revenue minus average cost, which gives profit per unit, multiplied by the quantity.

It is at this point that barriers to entry become important. Other firms may see that the monopoly firm is making healthy supernormal profits, but the existence of barriers to entry will prevent those profits from being competed away, as would happen in a perfectly competitive market.

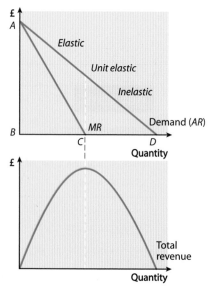

Figure 2.9 Elasticity and total revenue

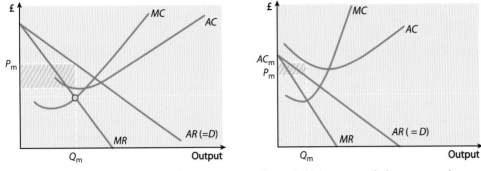

Figure 2.10 Profit maximisation and monopoly

Figure 2.11 Losses made by a monopoly

It is important to notice that the monopolist cannot be guaranteed always to make such substantial profits as are shown in Figure 2.10. The size of the profits depends upon the relative position of the market demand curve and the position of the cost curves. For example, if the cost curves in the diagram were higher, as in Figure 2.11, the monopoly would actually incur losses, as if the monopoly tries to maximise profits by choosing the output at which $MR = MC$, it will charge a price (P_m) that is below average cost (AC_m).

Exercise 2.3

Table 2.2 shows the demand curve faced by a monopolist.

a Calculate total revenue and marginal revenue for each level of demand.

b Plot the demand curve (AR) and marginal revenue on a graph.

c Plot total revenue on a separate graph.

d Identify the level of demand at which total revenue is at a maximum.

e At what level of demand is marginal revenue equal to zero?

f At what level of demand is there unit own-price elasticity of demand?

g If the monopolist maximises profits, will the chosen level of output be higher or lower than the revenue-maximising level?

h What does this imply for the price elasticity of demand when the monopolist maximises profits?

Table 2.2 Demand curve for a monopolist

Demand (000 per week)	Price (£)
0	80
1	70
2	60
3	50
4	40
5	30
6	20
7	10

A monopoly and an increase in demand

If a monopoly experiences (or can induce) an increase in the demand for its product, it will benefit. In Figure 2.12, suppose that initially the monopoly faces the demand curve D_0. It maximises profits by setting $MR = MC$, producing Q_0 output and charging a price P_0. If the demand curve shifts to the right, notice that the MR curve will also shift, as this has a fixed relationship with the demand curve. After the increase in demand, the monopoly chooses to produce Q_1 output, where $MR = MC$, and now sets a higher price at P_1, making higher profits.

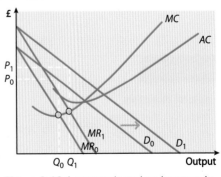

Figure 2.12 A monopoly and an increase in demand

How do monopolies arise?

Monopolies may arise in a market for a number of reasons. In a few instances, a monopoly is created by the authorities. For example, for 150 years the UK Post Office held a licence giving it a monopoly on delivering letters. This service was opened to some competition in the 2000s, although any company wanting to deliver packages weighing less than 350 grams and charging less than £1 could do so only by applying for a licence. The Post Office monopoly formerly covered a much wider range of services, but its coverage was eroded over the years, and competition in delivering larger packages has been permitted for some time. It was fully privatised (transferred into private ownership) in 2013. Nonetheless, it remains an example of one way in which a monopoly can be created.

The patent system offers a rather different form of protection for a firm. The patent system was designed to provide an incentive for firms to innovate through the development of new techniques and products. By prohibiting other firms from copying the product for a period of time, a firm is given a temporary monopoly.

A natural monopoly

In some cases the technology of the industry may create a monopoly situation. In a market characterised by substantial economies of scale, there may not be room for more than one firm in the market. This could happen where there are substantial fixed costs of production but low marginal costs. For example, building a high-speed rail link entails substantial expenditure in the form of fixed costs to create new track, upgraded stations and new rolling stock. However, once it is in operation, the marginal cost of carrying an additional passenger is very low.

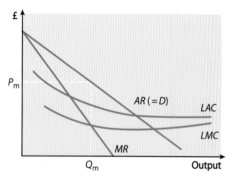

Figure 2.13 illustrates this point. The firm in this market enjoys economies of scale right up to the limit of market demand. Any new entrant into the market will be operating at a lower scale, so will inevitably face higher average costs. The existing firm will always be able to price such firms out of the market. Here the economies of scale act as an effective barrier to the entry of new firms and the market is a **natural monopoly**. A profit-maximising monopoly would thus set $MR = MC$, produce at quantity Q_m and charge a price P_m.

Figure 2.13 A natural monopoly

Such a market poses particular problems regarding allocative efficiency. Notice in the figure that marginal cost is below average cost over the entire range of output. If the firm were to charge a price equal to marginal cost, it would inevitably make a loss, so such a pricing rule would not be viable. This problem is analysed in Chapter 6.

The sort of market where a natural monopoly may emerge is one in which there may be substantial fixed costs of operation but relatively low marginal cost. An example might be an underground railway system in a city or a Channel Tunnel. The setup costs of building a rail network under a city or a tunnel under the Channel are enormous compared with the marginal cost of carrying an additional passenger. Some cities (e.g. Kuala Lumpur) do have more than one underground railway system, but they do not compete on the same routes. It would not make economic sense to have parallel rail systems competing for the same passengers on a particular route, any more than it would be sensible to have two Channel Tunnels close to each other. Notice that although the Channel

Tunnel may seem an obvious natural monopoly, this does not mean that the firm operating it faces no competition. The tunnel has to compete with ferry companies and airlines.

The London Underground is an example of a natural monopoly

Another example of a natural monopoly might seem to be the manufacture of passenger aircraft. Building a plane capable of carrying large numbers of passengers on long-haul routes has large economies of scale. There are indivisibilities in the production process, and any firm producing such aircraft has to make substantial investment in research and development upfront. Thus there are large economies of scale in the production process. Furthermore, the market is relatively small, in the sense that the number of aircraft sold in a year is modest. However, looking at the market, it is clear that it is not a monopoly as there are two firms operating in the market — Boeing and Airbus. These are the only effective global competitors.

Does this negate the natural monopoly theory? The answer is no. In fact, this market has aroused much transatlantic debate and contention. Boeing, the US producer, has accused European governments of unfairly subsidising Airbus's R&D programme. In return, Airbus has responded by pointing to the benefits that Boeing has received from the US military research programme. Without being drawn into this debate at this stage, the net effect of the interventions has been to create a duopoly situation (a market with just two firms) in which Boeing and Airbus compete for market share. Later discussion will examine why such competition is regarded as being more favourable for consumers than allowing an unregulated natural monopoly to develop.

There are markets in which firms have risen to become monopolies by their actions in the market. Such a market structure is sometimes known as a *competitive monopoly*. Firms may get into a monopoly position through effective marketing, through a process of merger and acquisition, or by establishing a new product as a widely accepted standard.

In the first Microsoft trial in 1998, it was argued that Microsoft had gained 95% of the world market for operating systems for PC computers. The firm claimed that this was because it is simply very good at what it does. However, part of the reason why Microsoft was on trial was that not everyone agreed with this claim, and they alleged unfair market tactics.

Monopoly and efficiency

The characteristics of the monopoly market can be evaluated in relation to productive and allocative efficiency (see Figure 2.10).

Productive efficiency

A firm is said to be productively efficient if it produces at the minimum point of its long-run average cost curve. It is clear from the figure that this is extremely unlikely for a monopoly. The firm will produce at its minimum long-run average cost only if it so happens that the marginal *revenue* curve passes through this exact point — and this would happen only by coincidence. Furthermore, if a monopoly is protected by barriers to entry, the incentive to become and remain productively efficient may be lacking. In this case, complacency could lead to X-inefficiency, which was discussed in Chapter 1.

Allocative efficiency

For an individual firm, allocative efficiency is achieved when price is set equal to marginal cost. It is clear from Figure 2.10 that this will not be the case for a profit-maximising monopoly firm. The firm chooses output where MR equals MC; however, given that MR is below AR (i.e. price), price will always be set above marginal cost.

Perfect competition and monopoly compared

It is possible to identify the extent to which a monopoly by its behaviour distorts resource allocation, by comparing the monopoly market with the perfectly competitive market. To do this, the situation can be simplified by setting aside the possibility of economies of scale. This is perhaps an artificial assumption to make, but it can be relaxed later.

Suppose that there is an industry with no economies of scale, which can be operated either as a perfectly competitive market with many small firms, or as a monopoly firm running a large number of small plants.

Figure 2.14 shows the market demand curve ($D = AR$), and the long-run supply curve under perfect competition (LRS). If the market is operating under perfect competition, the long-run equilibrium will produce a price of P_{pc}, and the firms in the industry will together supply Q_{pc} output. Consumer surplus is given by the area $AP_{pc}E$, which represents the surplus that consumers gain from consuming this product. In other words, it is a measure of the welfare that society receives from consuming the good, as was explained in Book 1.

Now suppose that the industry is taken over by a profit-maximising monopolist. The firm can close down some of the plants to vary its output over the long run, and the *LRS* can be regarded as the monopolist's long-run marginal cost curve. As the monopoly firm faces the market demand curve directly, it will also face the *MR* curve shown, so will maximise profits at quantity Q_m and charge a price P_m.

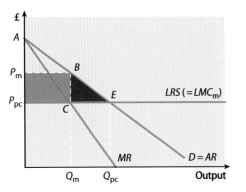

Figure 2.14 Comparing perfect competition and monopoly

Thus, the effect of this change in market structure is that the profit-maximising monopolist produces less output than a perfectly competitive industry and charges a higher price.

It is also apparent that consumer surplus is now very different, as in the new situation it is limited to the area AP_mB. Looking more carefully at Figure 2.14, you can see that the loss of consumer surplus has occurred for two reasons. First, the monopoly firm is now making profits shown by the shaded area P_mBCP_{pc}. This is a redistribution of welfare from consumers to the firm, but, as the monopolist is also a member of society, this does not affect overall welfare. However, there is also a deadweight loss, which represents a loss to society resulting from the monopolisation of the industry. This is measured by the area of the triangle *BCE*. Chapter 6 examines whether the authorities need to worry about this situation and explores the sort of policy that could be adopted to tackle the issue.

Summary

- A monopoly market is one in which there is a single seller of a good.
- The model of monopoly used in economic analysis also assumes that there are no substitutes for the goods or services produced by the monopolist, and that there are barriers to the entry of new firms.
- The monopoly firm faces the market demand curve, and is able to choose a point along that demand curve in order to maximise profits.
- Such a firm may be able to make supernormal profits, and sustain them in the long run because of barriers to entry and the lack of substitutes.
- A monopoly may arise because of patent protection or from the nature of economies of scale in the industry (a 'natural monopoly').
- A profit-maximising monopolist does not achieve allocative efficiency, and is unlikely to achieve productive efficiency in the sense of producing at the minimum point of the long-run average cost curve.
- A comparison of perfect competition with monopoly reveals that a profit-maximising monopoly firm operating under the same cost conditions as a perfectly competitive industry will produce less output, charge a higher price and impose a deadweight loss on society.

Study tip

Remember that there are some key concepts (such as consumer surplus, mentioned in this section) that you will have learned in Book 1 which are important here as well.

Price discrimination

Are there any conditions in which a monopoly firm would produce the level of output that is consistent with allocative efficiency?

Consider Figure 2.15. Suppose this market is operated by a monopolist who faces constant marginal cost *LMC*. (This is to simplify the analysis.) Under perfect competition the market outcome would be at price $P\star$ and quantity $Q\star$. What would induce the monopolist to produce at $Q\star$?

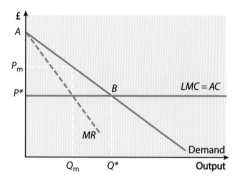

Figure 2.15 Perfect price discrimination

One of the assumptions made throughout the analysis so far is that all consumers in a market get to pay the same price for the product. In Figure 2.15, if the market were operating under perfect competition and all consumers were paying the same price, consumer surplus would be given by the area $AP^\star B$. If the market were operated by a monopolist, also charging the same price to all buyers, then profits would be maximised where $MC = MR$: that is, at quantity Q_m and price P_m.

But suppose this assumption is now relaxed; suppose that the monopolist is able to charge a different price to each individual consumer. A monopolist is then able to charge each consumer a price that is equal to his or her willingness to pay for the good. In other words, the demand curve effectively becomes the marginal revenue curve, as it represents the amount that the monopolist will receive for each unit of the good. It will then maximise profits at point B in Figure 2.15, where MR (i.e. AR) is equal to LMC. The difference between this situation and that under perfect competition is that the area $AP^\star B$ is no longer consumer surplus, but producer surplus: that is, the monopolist's profits. The monopolist has hijacked the whole of the original consumer surplus as its profits.

From society's point of view, total welfare is the same as it is under perfect competition (but more than under monopoly without discrimination). However, now there has been a redistribution, from consumers to the monopoly — and presumably to the shareholders of the firm. This situation is known as **perfect price discrimination**, or **first-degree price discrimination**.

Perfect price discrimination is fairly rare in the real world, although it might be said to exist in the world of art or fashion, where customers may commission a painting, sculpture or item of designer jewellery and the price is a matter of negotiation between the buyer and supplier.

However, there are situations in which partial price discrimination is possible. For example, students or old-age pensioners may get discounted bus fares, the young and/ or old may get cheaper access to sporting events or theatres etc. In these instances, individual consumers are paying different prices for what is in fact the same product. This is known as **third-degree price discrimination**.

There are three conditions under which a firm may be able to price discriminate:

1 The firm must have market power.

2 The firm must have information about consumers and their willingness to pay — and there must be identifiable differences between consumers (or groups of consumers).

3 The consumers must have limited ability to resell the product.

Market power

Clearly, price discrimination is not possible in a perfectly competitive market, where no seller has the power to charge other than the going market price. So price discrimination can take place only where firms have some ability to vary the price.

Information

From the firm's point of view, it needs to be able to identify different groups of consumers with different willingness to pay. What makes price discrimination

Key terms

perfect/first-degree price discrimination a situation arising in a market whereby a monopoly firm is able to charge each consumer a different price

third-degree price discrimination a situation in which a firm is able to charge groups of consumers a different price for the same product

Perfect price discrimination exists in the art world

profitable for firms is that different consumers display different sensitivities to price: that is, they have different price elasticities of demand.

Ability to resell

If consumers could resell the product easily, then price discrimination would not be possible, as consumers would engage in **arbitrage**. In other words, the group of consumers who qualified for the low price could buy up the product and then turn a profit by reselling to consumers in the other segment(s) of the market. This would mean that the firm would no longer be able to sell at the high price, and would no longer try to discriminate in pricing.

In the case of student discounts and OAP concessions, the firm can identify particular groups of consumers; and such 'products' as bus journeys and dental treatment cannot be resold. But why should a firm undertake this practice?

The simple answer is that, by undertaking price discrimination, the firm is able to increase its profits. This is shown in Figure 2.16, which separates two distinct groups of consumers with differing demand curves. Thus, panel (a) shows market A and panel (b) shows market B, with the combined demand curve being shown in panel (c), which also shows the firm's marginal cost curve.

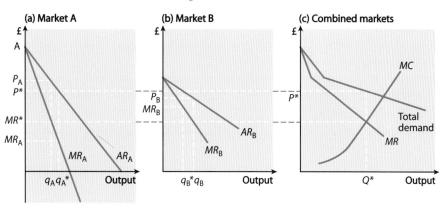

Figure 2.16 A price-discriminating monopolist

If a firm has to charge the same price to all consumers, it sets marginal revenue in the combined market equal to marginal cost, and produces Q^* output, to be sold at a price of P^*. This maximises profits when all consumers pay the same price. The firm sells q_A^* in market A, and q_B^* in market B.

However, if you look at panels (a) and (b), you will see that marginal revenue in market A is much lower (at MR_A) than that in market B (at MR_B). It is this difference in marginal revenue that opens up a profit-increasing opportunity for the firm. By taking sales away from market A and selling more in market B, the firm gains more extra revenue in B than it loses in A. This increases its profit. The optimal position for the firm is where marginal revenue is equalised in the two markets. In Figure 2.16 the firm sells q_A in market A at the higher price of P_A. In market B sales increase to q_B with price falling to P_B. Notice that in both situations the amounts sold in the two sub-markets sum to Q^*.

The consumers in market B seem to do quite well by this practice, as they can now consume more of the good. Indeed, it is possible that with no discrimination the price would be so high that they would not be able to consume the good at all.

An extreme form of price discrimination was used by NAPP Pharmaceutical Holdings, as a result of which the firm was fined £3.2 million by the Office of Fair Trading (OFT). NAPP sold sustained-release morphine tablets and capsules in the UK. These are drugs administered to patients with incurable cancer.

NAPP realised that the market was segmented. The drugs were sold partly to the NHS for use in hospitals, but were also prescribed by GPs. As these patients were terminally ill, they tended to spend a relatively short time in hospital before being sent home. NAPP realised that GPs tended to prescribe the same drugs as the patients had received in hospital. It therefore reduced its price to hospitals by 90%, thereby forcing all competitors out of the market and gaining a monopoly in that market segment. It was then able to increase the price of these drugs prescribed through GPs, and so maximise profits. The OFT investigated the firm, fined it and instructed it to stop its actions, thus saving the NHS £2 million per year.

Study tip

Be ready with the three conditions necessary if a firm is to be able to use price discrimination:

- The firm must have market power.
- The firm must be able to identify different consumers (or groups of consumers) and differences in their elasticities of demand.
- There must be limited ability for consumers to resell the product.

Exercise 2.5

In which of the following products might price discrimination be possible? Explain your answers.

a hairdressing

b peak and off-peak rail travel

c apples

d air tickets

e newspapers

f plastic surgery

g beer

Summary

- In some markets a monopolist may be able to engage in price discrimination by selling its product at different prices to different consumers or groups of consumers.
- This enables the firm to increase its profits by absorbing some or all of the consumer surplus.
- Under first-degree price discrimination, the firm is able to charge a different price to each customer and absorb all consumer surplus.
- The firm can practise price discrimination only where it has market power, where consumers have differing elasticities of demand for the product, and where consumers have limited ability to resell the product.

Of cabbages and rings

Ted Greens has a farm on which he grows a variety of crops, including cabbages that grow well on his south field, which seems especially suited to the crop. When Ted takes his cabbage crop to market, hoping to make as much profit as possible, he finds that the price he can charge for cabbages depends on market conditions — after all, one cabbage is very much like any other. He thus has to accept the price that he can get, which is the same as that charged by his many rival producers. If he tries to set a higher price, he sells nothing as all traders in the market have good awareness of market conditions, but as he can sell as much as he likes at the going price, there is no need to drop price below that prevailing in the market. Price tends to fluctuate from one harvest season to the next, and in some years when cabbages are plentiful, Ted finds that he barely covers his costs.

Edward de Vere owns a diamond mine — the only such mine in the country. His company cuts the stones and uses them to produce diamond rings. In selling the rings, Edward takes into account the strength of demand, choosing a price that will clear the market. He finds that by restricting the number of rings that he produces, he is able to charge a higher price. By doing so he is able to increase the profits that he makes. As he controls the only source of diamonds, Edward does not have to worry about other producers entering the market, and there are no acceptable substitutes for diamonds that people are prepared to accept.

Follow-up questions

a Which of the two producers appears to operate under conditions of perfect competition, and which is a monopoly?

b Explain your answer to part (a), referring to the assumptions that underlie the two theories of market structure.

c Under what conditions would Ted Greens decide to give up growing cabbages?

d Can you think of steps that Ted Greens might take in order to improve his profits on cabbages?

e Draw a diagram to explain how Edward de Vere would react to an increase in the demand for diamond rings.

f Suppose that a foreign firm starts to import diamond rings into the country in competition with Edward de Vere. How would you expect him to react?

Market structure: monopolistic competition and oligopoly

The previous chapter introduced the models of perfect competition and monopoly, and described them as being at the extreme ends of a spectrum of forms of market structure. In between those two extremes are other forms of market structure, which have some but not all of the characteristics of either perfect competition or monopoly. It is in this sense that there is a spectrum of structures. Attention in this chapter is focused on some of these intermediate forms of market structure.

Learning objectives

After studying this chapter, you should:

→ be familiar with the range of market situations that exists between the extremes of perfect competition and monopoly
→ understand the meaning of product differentiation and its role in the model of monopolistic competition
→ understand the significance of concentration in a market and how to measure it
→ understand the notion of oligopoly and be familiar with approaches to modelling firm behaviour in an oligopoly market
→ understand the benefits that firms may gain from forming a cartel — and the tensions that may result
→ be familiar with the characteristics of a monopsony market

Monopolistic competition

If you consider the characteristics of the markets that you frequent on a regular basis, you will find that few of them display all of the characteristics associated with perfect competition. However, there may be some that show a few of these features. In particular, you will find some markets in which there appears to be intense competition among many buyers, but in which the products for sale are not identical. For example, think about restaurants. In many cities, you will find a wide range of restaurants, cafés and pubs that compete with each other for business, but do so by offering slightly different products.

The theory of **monopolistic competition** was devised by Edward Chamberlin, writing in the USA in the 1930s, and his name is often attached to the model, although Joan Robinson published her book on imperfect competition in the UK at the same time. The motivation for the analysis was to explain how markets worked when they were operating neither as monopolies nor under perfect competition.

The model describes a market in which there are many firms producing similar, but not identical, products, such as travel agents, hairdressers or fast-food outlets. In the case of fast-food outlets, the high streets of many cities are characterised by large numbers of different types of takeaway — burgers, fish and chips, Indian, Chinese, fried chicken and so on.

Key term

monopolistic competition a market that shares some characteristics of monopoly and some of perfect competition

The monopolistic competition model describes the fast-food market in many cities

Model characteristics

Three important characteristics of the model of monopolistic competition distinguish this sort of market from others.

Product differentiation

First, firms produce differentiated products, and face downward-sloping demand curves. In other words, each firm competes with the others by making its product slightly different. This allows the firms to build up brand loyalty among their regular customers, which gives them some influence over price. It is likely that firms will engage in advertising in order to maintain such brand loyalty, and heavy advertising is a common characteristic of a market operating under monopolistic competition.

Because other firms are producing similar goods, there are substitutes for each firm's product, which means that demand will be relatively price elastic. However, it is not perfectly price elastic, as was the case with perfect competition. These features — that the product is not homogeneous and demand is not perfectly price elastic — represent significant differences from the model of perfect competition.

Freedom of entry

Second, there are no barriers to entry into the market. Firms are able to join the market if they observe that existing firms are making supernormal profits. New entrants to the market will be looking for some way to differentiate their product slightly from the others — perhaps the next fast-food restaurant will be Nepalese, or Peruvian.

This characteristic distinguishes the market from the monopoly model, as does the existence of fairly close substitutes.

Low concentration

Third, the concentration ratio in the industry tends to be relatively low, as there are many firms operating in the market. For this reason, a price change by one of the firms will have negligible effects on the demand for its rivals' products.

> **Key term**
>
> **product differentiation** a strategy adopted by firms that marks their product as being different from their competitors'

This characteristic means that the market is also different from an oligopoly market, where there are a few firms that interact strategically with each other.

Overview

Taking these three characteristics together, it can be seen that a market of monopolistic competition has some of the characteristics of perfect competition and some features of monopoly; hence its name.

Short-run equilibrium

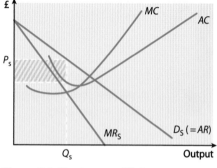

Figure 3.1 represents short-run equilibrium under monopolistic competition. D_s is the demand curve, and MR_s is the corresponding marginal revenue curve. AC and MC are the average and marginal cost curves for a representative firm in the industry. If the firm is aiming to maximise profits, it will choose the level of output such that $MR_s = MC$. This occurs at output Q_s, and the firm will then choose the price that clears the market at P_s.

This closely resembles the standard monopoly diagram that was introduced in Chapter 2. As with monopoly, a firm under monopolistic competition faces a downward-sloping demand curve, as already noted. The difference is that under monopolistic competition it is assumed that there is free entry into the market, so that Figure 3.1 represents equilibrium only in the short run. This is because the firm shown in the figure is making supernormal profits, shown by the shaded area (which is $AR - AC$ multiplied by output).

Figure 3.1 Short-run equilibrium under monopolistic competition

The importance of free entry

This is where the assumption of free entry into the market becomes important. In Figure 3.1 the profits being made by the representative firm will attract new firms into the market. The new firms will produce differentiated products, and this will have two important effects on demand for the representative firm's product. First, the new firms will attract some customers away from this firm, so that its demand curve will tend to shift to the left. Second, as there are now more substitutes for the original product, the demand curve will become more elastic — remember that the availability of substitutes is an important influence on the own-price elasticity of demand.

Long-run equilibrium

This process will continue as long as firms in the market continue to make profits that attract new firms into the activity. It may be accelerated if firms are persuaded to spend money on advertising in an attempt to defend their market shares. The advertising may help to keep the demand curve downward sloping, but it will also affect the position of the average cost curve, by pushing up average cost at all levels of output.

Figure 3.2 shows the final position for the market. The typical firm is now operating in such a way that it maximises profits (by setting output such that $MR = MC$); at the same time, the average cost curve (AC) at this level of output is at a tangent to the demand curve. This means that $AC = AR$, and the firm is just making normal profit (i.e. is just covering opportunity cost). There is thus no incentive for more firms to join the market. In Figure 3.2 this occurs when output is at Q_1 and price is set at P_1.

Efficiency

One way of evaluating the market outcome under this model is to examine the consequences for productive and allocative efficiency. It is clear from Figure 3.2 that neither of these conditions will be met. The representative firm does not reach the minimum point on the long-run average cost curve, and so does not attain productive efficiency; furthermore, the price charged is above marginal cost, so allocative efficiency is not achieved.

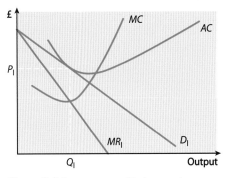

Figure 3.2 Long-run equilibrium under monopolistic competition

Evaluation

If the typical firm in the market is not fully exploiting the possible economies of scale that exist, it could be argued that product differentiation is damaging society's total welfare, in the sense that it is the product differentiation that allows firms to keep their demand curves downward sloping. In other words, too many different products are being produced. However, this argument could be countered by pointing out that consumers may enjoy having more freedom of choice. The very fact that they are prepared to pay a premium price for their chosen brand indicates that they have some preference for it.

Another crucial difference between monopolistic competition and perfect competition is that under monopolistic competition firms would like to sell more of their product at the going price, whereas under perfect competition they can sell as much as they like at the going price. This is because price under monopolistic competition is set above marginal cost.

The use of advertising to attract more customers and to maintain consumer perception of product differences may be considered a problem with this market. It could be argued that excessive use of advertising to maintain product differentiation is wasteful, as it leads to higher average cost curves than needed. On the other hand, the need to compete in this way may result in less X-inefficiency than could arise under a complacent monopolist.

Examples of monopolistic competition

The theory of monopolistic competition describes a market with some features of monopoly and some features of perfect competition. Entry barriers are low, so the market has many firms. However, firms in the market use product differentiation to influence consumers, and thus face downward-sloping demand curves. What sorts of market in the real world might typify this structure?

When you journey along a motorway or trunk road in the UK, observe the heavy goods vehicles (HGVs) and smaller vans that you pass. You will see HGVs and vans in a wide variety of liveries, from a wide range of countries and carrying a wide diversity of loads.

This is a market characterised by many competing firms, many of which operate in niche markets. Firms try to differentiate their offering by carrying particular categories of products — building materials, perhaps, or electronic goods. Some may trade between certain destinations. They advertise by broadcasting these specialisms on their vehicles, in the *Yellow Pages* or on the internet.

Another part of the road transport market that may typify monopolistic competition is local taxi markets. Count the local taxi companies in your local *Yellow Pages*.

Again, firms may seek to differentiate their products through having a fleet livery, by advertising pre-booking only or by offering a limousine service. There may also be firms that specialise in longer-distance trips, say to airports.

Another example is food outlets. The number of restaurants and fast-food outlets has mushroomed in recent decades, and on many high streets in UK towns there is a proliferation of eating places and takeaways. One of the characteristics of a market operating under monopolistic competition is the product differentiation that takes place. Each individual seller sets out to be different from its competitors. This is certainly a characteristic of the fast-food sector, where outlets offer different styles of cuisine — burgers, Indian, Chinese, Thai, Mexican and so on. Before condemning such a market as being damaging to consumers because of the effect on productive and allocative efficiency, it is worth being aware that this market offers consumers a wide range of choice for fast food. If they value this choice, then this should be seen as a benefit that arises because of the market structure.

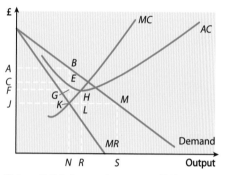

Figure 3.3 A firm under monopolistic competition

Exercise 3.1

Figure 3.3 shows a firm under monopolistic competition.

a Identify the profit-maximising level of output.

b At what price would the firm sell its product?

c What supernormal profits (if any) would be made by the firm?

d Is this a short-run or a long-run equilibrium? Explain your answer.

e Describe any subsequent adjustment that might take place in the market (if any).

f At what level of output would productive efficiency be achieved? (Assume that AC represents long-run average cost for this part of the question.)

Summary

- The theory of monopolistic competition has its origins in the 1930s, when economists such as Edward Chamberlin and Joan Robinson were writing about markets that did not conform to the models of perfect competition and monopoly.
- The model describes a market where there are many firms producing similar, but not identical, products.
- By differentiating their product from those of other firms, it is possible for firms to maintain some influence over price.
- To do this, firms engage in advertising to build brand loyalty.
- There are no barriers to entry into the market, and concentration ratios are low.
- Firms in the short run may make supernormal profits.
- In response, new entrants join the market, shifting the demand curves of existing firms and affecting their shape.
- The process continues until supernormal profits have been competed away, and the typical firm has its average cost curve at a tangent to its demand curve.
- Neither productive nor allocative efficiency is achieved in long-run equilibrium.
- Consumers may benefit from the increased range of choice on offer in the market.

Market concentration

Chapter 2 pointed out that the models of perfect competition and monopoly produce very different outcomes for productive and allocative efficiency. Perfect competition produces a 'good' allocation of resources, but monopoly results in a deadweight loss. In the real-world economy it is not quite so simple. In particular, not every market is readily classified as following either of these extreme models. Indeed, you might think that the majority of markets do not correspond to either of the models, but instead display a mixture of characteristics.

An important question is whether such markets behave more like a competitive market or more like a monopoly. There are many different ways in which markets with just a few firms operating can be modelled, because there are many ways in which the firms may interact. Some of these models will be explored later in the chapter.

It is helpful to have some way of gauging how close a particular market is to being a monopoly. One way of doing this is to examine the degree of concentration in the market. Later it will be seen that this is not all that is required to determine how efficiently a market will operate; but it is a start.

Concentration is normally measured by reference to the **concentration ratio**, which measures the market share of the largest firms in an industry. For example, the three-firm concentration ratio measures the market share of the largest three firms in the market; the five-firm concentration ratio calculates the share of the top five firms, and so on. Concentration can also be viewed in terms of employment, reflected in the proportion of workers in any industry that are employed in the largest firms.

Key term

n-firm concentration ratio a measure of the market share of the largest n firms in an industry

Quantitative skills 3.1

Calculating a concentration ratio

Consider the following example. Table 3.1 gives average circulation figures for the firms that publish national newspapers in the UK (with a circulation of more than 100,000 per day). In the final column these are converted into market shares. Where one firm produces more than one newspaper, their circulations have been combined (e.g. News Corporation publishes both the *Sun* and *The Times*).

Table 3.1 Concentration in the UK newspaper industry, April 2013

Firm	Average circulation	Market share (%)
News Corporation	2,661,364	32.4
Associated Newspapers	1,803,327	22.0
Trinity Mirror	1,298,943	15.8
Express Newspapers	1,057,443	12.9
Telegraph Group	549,037	6.7
Independent Newspapers	379,890	4.6
Financial Times	266,169	3.2
Guardian Newspapers	196,004	2.4
Total	8,212,177	100.0

The market shares are calculated by expressing the average circulation for a firm as a percentage of the total. For example, the market share of the *Financial Times* is 100 × 266,169/8,212,177 = 3.2%.

The three-firm concentration ratio is calculated as the sum of the market shares of the biggest three firms: that is, 32.4 + 22.0 + 15.8 = 70.2%.

Source: www.abc.org.uk

Concentration ratios may be calculated on the basis of either shares in output or shares in employment. In the above example, the calculation was on the basis of output (daily circulation). The two measures may give different results because the largest firms in an industry may be more capital-intensive in their production methods, which means that their share of employment in an industry will be smaller than their share of output. For purposes of examining market structure, however, it is more helpful to base the analysis of market share on output.

This might seem an intuitively simple measure, but it is too simple to enable an evaluation of a market. For a start, it is important to define the market appropriately: for instance, in the above example are the *Financial Times* and the *Sun* really part of the same market?

There may be other difficulties too. Table 3.2 gives some hypothetical market shares for two markets. The five-firm concentration ratio is calculated as the sum of the market shares of the largest five firms. For market A this is 68 + 3 + 2 + 1 + 1 = 75; for market B it is 15 + 15 + 15 + 15 + 15 = 75. In each case the market is perceived to be highly concentrated, at 75%. However, the nature of likely interactions between the firms in these two markets is very different because the large relative size of firm 1 in market A is likely to give it substantially more market power than any of the largest five firms in market B. Nonetheless, the concentration ratio is useful for giving a first impression of how the market is likely to function.

Table 3.2 Market shares (% of output)

Largest firms in rank order	Market A	Market B
Firm 1	68	15
Firm 2	3	15
Firm 3	2	15
Firm 4	1	15
Firm 5	1	15

Figure 3.4 shows the five-firm concentration ratio for a number of industrial sectors in the UK. Concentration varies from 5% in construction and 12% in printing and publishing to 71% in cement and 99% in tobacco products. In part, the difference between sectors might be expected to reflect the extent of economies of scale, and this makes sense for many of the industries shown.

Summary

- It is important to be able to evaluate the degree of concentration in a market.
- While not a perfect measure, the concentration ratio is one way of doing this, by calculating the market share of the largest firms.

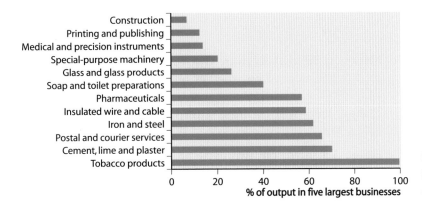

Figure 3.4 Concentration in UK industry, 2004

Source: ONS

Oligopoly

A number of markets seem to be dominated by relatively few firms — think of motor vehicle manufacturing or commercial banking in the UK, or the newspaper industry. A market with just a few sellers is known as an **oligopoly** market. An important characteristic of such markets is that when making economic decisions each firm must take account of its rivals' behaviour and reactions. The firms are therefore interdependent.

An important characteristic of oligopoly is that each firm has to act strategically, both in reacting to rival firms' decisions and in trying to anticipate their future actions.

There are many different ways in which a firm may take such strategic decisions, and this means that there are many ways in which an oligopoly market can be modelled, depending on how the firms are behaving. This chapter reviews just a few such models.

Oligopolies may come about for many reasons, but perhaps the most convincing concerns economies of scale. An oligopoly is likely to develop in a market where there are modest economies of scale — economies that are not substantial enough to require a natural monopoly, but are large enough to make it difficult for too many firms to operate at minimum efficient scale.

Within an oligopoly market, firms may adopt rivalrous behaviour or they may choose to cooperate with each other. The two attitudes have implications for how markets operate. Cooperation will tend to take the market towards the monopoly end of the spectrum, whereas non-cooperation will take it towards the competitive end. In either scenario, it is likely that the market outcome will be somewhere between the two extremes.

The kinked demand curve model

One such model revolves around how a firm *perceives* its demand curve. This is called the kinked demand curve model, and was developed by Paul Sweezy in the USA in the 1930s.

The model relates to an oligopoly in which firms try to anticipate the reactions of rivals to their actions. One problem that arises is that a firm cannot readily observe its demand curve with any degree of certainty, so it must form expectations about how consumers will react to a price change.

Figure 3.5 shows how this works. Suppose the price is currently set at $P\star$; the firm is selling $Q\star$, and is trying to decide whether to alter price. The problem is that it

> **Key term**
>
> **oligopoly** a market with a few sellers, in which each firm must take account of the behaviour and likely behaviour of rival firms in the industry

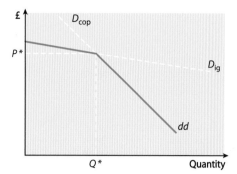

Figure 3.5 The kinked demand curve

knows for sure about only one point on the demand curve: that is, when price is $P\star$, the firm sells $Q\star$.

However, the firm is aware that the degree of sensitivity to its price change will depend on whether or not the other firms in the market will follow its lead. In other words, if its rivals ignore the firm's price change, there will be more sensitivity to this change than if they all follow suit.

Figure 3.5 shows the two extreme possibilities for the demand curve which the firm perceives that it faces. If other firms ignore its action, D_{ig} will be the relevant demand curve, which is relatively elastic. On the other hand, if the other firms copy the firm's moves, D_{cop} will be the relevant demand curve.

The question then is under what conditions will the other firms copy the price change, and when will they not? The firm may imagine that if it raises price there is little likelihood that its rivals will copy. After all, this is a non-threatening move that gives market share to the other firms. So for a price *increase*, it is D_{ig} that is the relevant section.

On the other hand, a price reduction is likely to be seen by the rivals as a threatening move, and they are likely to copy in order to preserve their market positions. For a price *decrease*, then, it is D_{cop} that is relevant.

Putting these together, the firm perceives that it faces a kinked demand curve (*dd*). The firm then faces a difficult choice. If it increases price, it will lose customers because rivals are not expected to react, and will continue to sell at the old price. On the other hand, if the firm reduces price, it will face intense competition from rivals, and will be unlikely to gain many customers. Its best strategy may thus be to do nothing.

Game theory

A more recent development in the economic theory of the firm has been in the application of **game theory**. This began as a branch of mathematics, but it became apparent that it had wide applications in explaining the behaviour of firms in an oligopoly.

Game theory itself has a long history, with some writers tracing it back to correspondence between Pascal and Fermat in the mid-seventeenth century. Early applications in economics were by Antoine Augustin Cournot in 1838, Francis Edgeworth in 1881 and J. Bertrand in 1883, but the key publication was the book by John von Neumann and Oskar Morgenstern, *Theory of Games and Economic Behaviour*, published in 1944. Other famous names in game theory include John Nash (played by Russell Crowe in the film *A Beautiful Mind*), John Harsanyi and Reinhard Selton, who shared the 1994 Nobel prize for their work in this area.

Almost certainly, the most famous game is the **prisoners' dilemma**, introduced in a lecture by Albert Tucker (who taught John Nash at Princeton) in 1950. This simple example of game theory turns out to have a multitude of helpful applications in economics.

Study tip

Although this is a popular model, remember that it is just one attempt to model strategic behaviour between firms. There are many ways in which firms may interact, so there are many different ways of trying to model the interactions.

Key terms

game theory a method of modelling the strategic interaction between firms in an oligopoly

prisoners' dilemma an example of game theory with a range of applications in oligopoly theory

Russell Crowe playing the part of mathematician and game theorist John Nash in *A Beautiful Mind*

Two prisoners, Al Fresco and Des Jardins, are being interrogated about a major crime, and the police know that at least one of the prisoners is guilty. The two are kept in separate cells and cannot communicate with each other. The police have enough evidence to convict them of a minor offence, but not enough to convict them of the major one.

Each prisoner is offered a deal. If he turns state's evidence and provides evidence to convict the other prisoner, he will get off — *unless* the other prisoner also confesses. If both refuse to deal, they will just be charged with the minor offence. Table 3.3 summarises the sentences that each will receive in the various circumstances.

Table 3.3 The prisoners' dilemma: possible outcomes (years in jail)

		Des			
		Confess		**Refuse**	
Al	Confess	10	10	0	15
	Refuse	15	0	5	5

If both Al and Des refuse to deal, they will be convicted of the minor offence, and each will go down for 5 years. However, if Al confesses and Des refuses to deal, Al will get off completely free, and Des will take the full rap of 15 years. If Des confesses and Al refuses, the reverse happens. However, if both confess, they will each get 10 years.

Think about this situation from Al's point of view, remembering that the prisoners cannot communicate, so Al does not know what Des will choose to do and vice versa. You can see from Table 3.3 that, whatever Des chooses to do, Al will be better off confessing. John Nash referred to such a situation as a **dominant strategy**.

The dilemma is, of course, symmetric, so for Des too the dominant strategy is to confess. The inevitable result is that if both prisoners are selfish they will both confess — and both will then get 10 years in jail. If they had both refused to deal, they would *both* have been better off; but this is too risky a strategy for either of them to adopt. A refusal to deal might have led to 15 years in jail.

What has this to do with economics? Suppose there are two firms (Diamond Tools and Better Spades) operating in a duopoly market (i.e. a market with only two firms). Each firm has a choice of producing 'high' output or 'low' output. The profit made by one firm depends on two things: its own output, and the output of the other firm.

Table 3.4 shows the range of possible outcomes for a particular time period. Consider Diamond Tools: if it chooses 'low' when Better Spades also chooses 'low', it will make £2 million profit (and so will Better Spades); but if Diamond Tools chooses 'low' when Better Spades chooses 'high', Diamond Tools will make zero profits and Better Spades will make £3 million.

The situation that maximises joint profits is for both firms to produce low; but suppose you were taking decisions for Diamond Tools — what would you choose?

Key terms

dominant strategy a situation in game theory where a player's best strategy is independent of those chosen by others

Nash equilibrium a situation occurring within a game when each player's chosen strategy maximises payoffs given the other player's choice, so that no player has an incentive to alter behaviour

Table 3.4 Diamond Tools and Better Spades: possible outcomes (profits in £m)

		Better Spades			
		High		**Low**	
Diamond Tools	High	1	1	3	0
	Low	0	3	2	2

If Better Spades produces 'low', you will maximise profits by producing 'high', whereas if Better Spades produces 'high', you will still maximise profits by producing high! So Diamond Tools has a dominant strategy to produce high — it is the profit-maximising action whatever Better Spades does, even though it means that joint profits will be lower.

Given that the table is symmetric, Better Spades faces the same decision process, and also has a dominant strategy to choose high, so they always end up in the northwest corner of the table, even though southeast would be better for both of them. Furthermore, after they have made their choices and seen what the other has chosen, each firm feels justified by its actions, and thinks that it took the right decision, given the rival's move. This is known as a **Nash equilibrium**, which has the characteristic that neither firm needs to amend its behaviour in any future period. This model can be used to investigate a wide range of decisions that firms need to take strategically.

Exercise 3.2

Suppose there are two cinemas in a market, X and Y; you are taking decisions for firm X. You cannot communicate with the other firm; both firms are considering only the next period. Each firm is choosing whether to set price 'high' or 'low'. Your expectation is that the payoffs (in terms of profits) to the two firms are as shown in Table 3.5 (firm X in orange, firm Y in blue):

Table 3.5 Cinemas X and Y: possible outcomes

		Firm Y chooses:			
		High price		Low price	
Firm X chooses:	High price	0	10	1	15
	Low price	15	1	4	4

a If firm Y sets price high, what strategy maximises profits for firm X?

b If firm Y sets price low, what strategy maximises profits for firm X?

c So what strategy will firm X adopt?

d What is the market outcome?

e What outcome would maximise the firms' joint profit?

f How might this outcome be achieved?

g Would the outcome be different if the game were played over repeated periods?

Cooperative games and cartels

Look back at the prisoners' dilemma game in Table 3.4. It is clear that the requirement that the firms be unable to communicate with each other is a serious impediment from the firms' point of view. If both firms could agree to produce 'low', they would maximise their joint profits, but they will not risk this strategy if they cannot communicate.

If they could join together in a **cartel**, the two firms could come to an agreement to adopt the low–low strategy. However, if they were to agree to this, each firm would have a strong incentive to cheat because if each now knew that the other firm was going to produce low, they would also know that they could produce high and dominate the market — at least, given the payoffs in the table.

This is a common feature of cartels. Collusion can bring high joint profits, but there is always the temptation for each of the member firms to cheat and try to sneak some additional market share at the expense of the other firm/s in the cartel.

Extension material

You can see how a cartel might operate in Figure 3.6, which shows the situation facing a two-firm cartel (a duopoly). Panels (a) and (b) show the cost conditions for each of the firms, and panel (c) shows the whole market.

If the firms aim to maximise their joint profits, then they set $MR = MC$ at the level of the market

(shown in panel (c)). This occurs at the joint level of output $Q_1 + Q_2$, with the price set at $P\star$. Notice that the joint marginal cost curve is the sum of the two firms' marginal cost curves.

The critical decision is how to divide the market up between the two firms. In the figure, the two firms have different cost conditions, with firm 1 operating at lower short-run average cost than firm 2. If the firms agree to set price at $P\star$, and each produces up to the point where marginal cost equals the level of (market) marginal revenue at $MR\star$, then the market should work well. Firm 1 produces Q_1 and firm 2 produces Q_2. Joint profits are maximised, and there is a clear rule enabling the division of the market between the firms.

However, notice that firm 2 is very much the junior partner in this alliance, as it gets a much smaller

market share. The temptation to cheat is obvious. If firm 2 accepts price $P\star$, it sees that its profits will be maximised at $Q_2\star$, so there is a temptation to try to steal an extra bit of market share.

Of course, the temptation is also there for firm 1, but as soon as either one of the firms begins to increase output the market price will have to fall to maintain equilibrium, and the cartel will be broken: the market will move away from the joint profit-maximising position.

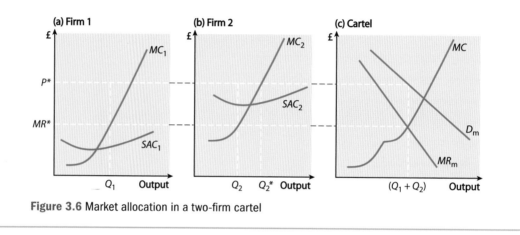

Figure 3.6 Market allocation in a two-firm cartel

There is another downside to the formation of a cartel. In most countries around the world (with one or two exceptions, such as Hong Kong) they are illegal. For example, in the UK the operation of a cartel is illegal under the UK Competition Act, under which the Competition and Markets Authority is empowered to fine firms up to 10% of their turnover for each year the cartel is found to have been in operation.

This means that **overt collusion** is rare. The most famous example is not between firms but between nations, in the form of the Organisation of the Petroleum Exporting Countries (OPEC), which over a long period of time has operated a cartel to control the price of oil.

Conditions favouring collusion

Some conditions may favour the formation of cartels — or at least, some form of collusion between firms. The most important of these is the ability of each of the firms involved to monitor the actions of the other firms, and so ensure that they are keeping to the agreement.

In this context, it helps if there are a relatively small number of firms; otherwise it will be difficult to monitor the market. It also helps if they are producing similar goods; otherwise one firm could try to steal an advantage by varying the quality of the product. When the economy is booming it may be more difficult to monitor market shares, because all firms are likely to be expanding. If firms have excess capacity, this may increase the temptation to cheat by increasing output and stealing market share; on the other hand, it also makes it possible for the other firms to retaliate quickly. The degree of secrecy about market shares and market conditions is also important.

> ### Key term
>
> **overt collusion** a situation in which firms openly work together to agree on prices or market shares

Collusion in practice

Although cartels are illegal, the potential gains from collusion may tempt firms to find ways of working together. In some cases, firms have joined together in rather loose strategic alliances, in which they may work together on part of their business, perhaps undertaking joint research and development or technology swaps.

For example, in 2000 General Motors (GM) and Fiat took an equity stake in each other's companies, with GM wanting to expand in Europe and needing to find out more about the technology of making smaller cars. Such alliances have not always been a success, and in the GM–Fiat case GM and Fiat separated in 2005.

The airline market is another sector where strategic alliances have been important, with the Star Alliance and the One World Alliance carving up the long-haul routes between them. Such alliances offer benefits to passengers, who can get access to a wider range of destinations, business-class lounges and frequent-flier rewards, and to the airlines, which can economise on airport facilities by pooling their resources. However, the net effect is to reduce competition, and the regulators have interfered with some suggested alliances, such as that between British Airways and American Airlines in 2001, which was investigated by regulators on both sides of the Atlantic. The conditions under which the alliance would have been permitted were such that British Airways withdrew the proposal.

Alternatively, firms may look for **tacit collusion**, in which the firms in a market observe each other's behaviour very closely and refrain from competing on price, even if they do not actually communicate with each other. Such collusion may emerge gradually over time in a market, as the firms become accustomed to market conditions and to each other's behaviour.

One way in which this may happen is through some form of *price leadership*. If one firm is a dominant producer in a market, then it may take the lead in setting the price, with the other firms following its example. It has been suggested that the OPEC cartel operated according to this model in some periods, with Saudi Arabia acting as the dominant firm.

> ### Key term
>
> **tacit collusion** a situation occurring when firms refrain from competing on price, but without communication or formal agreement between them

The alliance between British Airways and American Airlines attracted the attention of the regulators in 2001

An alternative is *barometric price leadership*, in which one firm tries out a price increase and then waits to see whether other firms follow. If they do, a new higher price has been reached without the need for overt discussions between the firms. On the other hand, if the other firms do not feel the time is right for the change, they will keep their prices steady and the first firm will drop back into line or else lose market share. The initiating firm need not be the same one in each round. It has been argued that the domestic air travel market in the USA has operated in this way on some internal routes. The practice is facilitated by the ease with which prices can be checked via the computerised ticketing systems, so that each firm knows what the other firms are doing.

The frequency of anti-cartel cases brought by regulators in recent years suggests that firms continue to be tempted by the gains from collusion. The operation of a cartel is now a criminal act in the UK, as it has been in the USA for some time. This will be discussed in Chapter 6.

Monopsony

The discussion of market structure so far has focused on the number of sellers in a market, and the interrelationships between them. However, it is also important to consider the number of traders who are potential buyers in a market. An extreme situation would be where there is a single buyer of a good or service. Such a market structure is known as a **monopsony**.

A single buyer may be able to exert substantial influence over the suppliers of the good when drawing up contracts on the price and quality of goods. Suppose that a firm is producing computer chips in competition with other similar firms, but enters into a contract to sell all of its output to a particular computer manufacturer. This may have advantages for the firm, which is assured of a secure market for its output. However, in return for this it may have to agree a competitive price and production schedule with the buyer, which is effectively acting as a monopsonist. The monopsonist gains by keeping its costs down and by being assured of regular supply of components. The consumer gains indirectly because of the monopsonist's low cost base.

Another example might occur in some labour markets. There may be towns in which there is a single large employer that employs a significant proportion of the local labour force. Again, such an employer might be seen to have market power within that local labour market. This could constitute another form of market failure, in which the buyer can exert influence in the market. The effects of this will be explored in Chapter 5.

Think about the supermarkets in the UK. It is possible that the sheer buying power of the large chains would leave the relatively fragmented suppliers in a weak bargaining position. The supermarkets would then be able to keep their costs down by using their bargaining strength. This has been a matter of concern for the competition authorities in the past. In this case, it might seem that there is not a single buyer, as this market is dominated by a few large supermarkets. This might therefore be considered to be an **oligopsony**, rather than a monopsony. However, once a supplier enters into an exclusive contract to supply a particular firm, the relationship becomes more like a monopsony.

As in the example above, the supermarkets gain from establishing regular low-cost suppliers, the consumers gain from lower prices, and the suppliers gain from knowing they have a regular buyer for their products. However, this supposes that the buyers do not exploit their market power to reach unreasonable deals with their suppliers. There may also be knock-on effects for other parts of the grocery sector, as small retailers may find it difficult to obtain produce at a price that allows them to remain profitable. The end result of this may be a lessening of consumer choice.

Exercise 3.3

Discuss the extent to which consumers gain or lose as a result of supermarkets' buying power with their suppliers.

Exercise 3.4

For each of the following markets, identify the model that would most closely describe it (i.e. perfect competition, monopoly, monopolistic competition or oligopoly):

a a large number of firms selling branded varieties of toothpaste

b a sole supplier of postal services

c a large number of farmers producing cauliflowers, sold at a common price

d a situation in which a few large banks supply most of the market for retail banking services

e a sole supplier of rail transport

f a single employer of unskilled labour in a town

Study tip

It is often helpful to be able to include examples. In the context of this chapter, it is helpful to be ready with some examples of markets that conform to the various types of market structure. You need to think about this before the exam period, so that you are ready to use them.

Summary

- An oligopoly is a market with a few sellers, each of which takes strategic decisions based on likely rival actions and reactions.
- Because there are many ways in which firms may interact, there is no single way of modelling an oligopoly market.
- One model is the kinked demand curve model, which argues that firms' perceptions of the demand curve for their products are based on their views about whether or not rival firms will react to their own actions.
- This suggests that price is likely to remain stable over a wide range of market conditions.
- Game theory is a more recent and more flexible way of modelling interactions between firms.
- The prisoners' dilemma can demonstrate the potential benefits of collusion, but also shows that in some market situations each firm may have a dominant strategy to move the market away from the joint profit-maximising position.
- If firms could join together in a cartel, they could indeed maximise their joint profits — but there would still be a temptation for firms to cheat, and try to steal market share. Such action would break up the cartel, and move the market away from the joint profit-maximising position.
- However, cartels are illegal in most societies.
- Firms may thus look for covert ways of colluding in a market: for example, through some form of price leadership.
- A monopsony is a market in which there is a single buyer of a good or service.

Competition in oligopolistic markets

An oligopolistic market is one in which firms engage in strategic competition. Strategic competition exists when the actions of one firm have an appreciable effect on its rival or rivals. Common textbook examples of oligopoly include the oil industry, motor manufacturing, soft drinks and airlines operating between particular city pairs. But oligopolists are not necessarily large firms. Close to the university campus in Southampton there is a road containing several small restaurants and takeaways. They are engaged in strategic competition because if one firm were to change its prices this would have an appreciable effect on the sales and thus profits of the others. So you can see that many firms will find themselves competing in oligopolistic markets and thus it is important that, as economists, we try to understand how such markets operate.

Modelling oligopoly

The defining characteristic of oligopoly is that the actions of one firm have an appreciable effect on its rival(s) and thus when modelling such a market it is natural to begin by assuming that each firm recognises this interdependence and takes it into account when formulating its strategy. To keep things simple, let's suppose there are just two firms in the market and each of them is thinking about what price to charge for its product. Again, just for simplicity, we will focus on two possibilities.

What is the highest price that they might conceivably choose? To answer this, consider the maximum aggregate profit that the two firms could theoretically generate. Figure 3.7 depicts the case of two firms producing identical products with identical horizontal marginal cost (average cost) curves.

The market demand curve is D and MR shows the (joint) marginal revenue accruing to the firms if they set the same price. This is the same marginal revenue curve that would have existed had the market been a monopoly.

If the firms were producing different products (as is usually the case) then the analysis would be more complex but again we could take the monopoly price or prices to be the upper limit on possible choices.

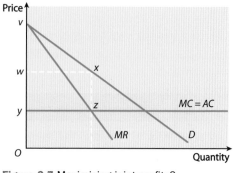

Figure 3.7 Maximising joint profits?

An alternative option for each of our two firms would be to set a price below the monopoly level. If one firm were to choose the monopoly price and the other a lower price, then the latter would gain a larger market share and, provided the price was not too low, a larger profit. But if both chose the low price, each would earn less profit than if they had both chosen the monopoly price. The situation facing the firms is illustrated in Table 3.6.

Table 3.6 Profits of two firms

		Firm B chooses:			
		High price		**Low price**	
Firm A chooses:	High price	2	2	0	3
	Low price	3	0	1	1

The two firms, A and B, must choose either a high price or a low price and the decisions are assumed to be made simultaneously, in the sense that each firm makes its decision without knowledge of the other firm's choice. The figures represent the profits of the two firms, with the first number in each cell denoting the profit of firm A and the second the profit of firm B. Thus, for example, if both opt for high (the monopoly price) then each will earn a profit of 2 (half the monopoly profit), but if, say, A chooses high and B chooses low, A will make a profit of 0 and B will make 3.

Follow-up questions

a What is the maximum joint profit that the firms could theoretically generate? Explain how this could be achieved.

b What prices will the two firms choose?

c The passage described the situation close to the campus at the University of Southampton, in which there are several restaurants operating in close proximity. Discuss whether they would be able to maximise their joint profits.

Pricing strategies and contestable markets

Having examined a range of models of market structure, it is time to investigate the sorts of pricing strategy that firms may adopt, and how they decide which to go for. This chapter also discusses ways in which firms may try to prevent new firms from joining a market, in terms of both pricing and non-price strategies. The theory of contestable markets is investigated as well.

Learning objectives

After studying this chapter, you should:

→ be aware of the possible pricing rules that can be adopted by firms
→ understand the notion of cost-plus pricing, and how this may relate to profit maximisation
→ be familiar with the idea of predatory pricing
→ be aware of the concept of limit pricing
→ understand the notion of contestable markets and its implication for firms' behaviour
→ be familiar with other entry deterrence strategies
→ understand the conditions under which price discrimination is possible and how this affects consumers and producers

Pricing rules

In the analysis of market structure, it was assumed that firms set out to maximise profits. However, Chapter 1 pointed out that sometimes they may set out to achieve other objectives. The price of a firm's product is a key strategic variable that must be manipulated in order to attain whatever objective the firm wishes to achieve.

Figure 4.1 illustrates the variety of pricing rules that are possible. The figure shows a firm operating under a form of market structure that is not perfect competition — because the firm faces a downward-sloping demand curve for its product shown by $AR (= D)$. Remember that under perfect competition the firm is a price-taker, so the only possible pricing rule is to accept the price prevailing in the market. However, in other forms of market structure, firms may have some power to influence the price of their product.

An important influence on the pricing strategies adopted by firms is the extent to which they face competition in their product markets. One of the key assumptions of the perfect competition model is that there is freedom of entry into and exit from the market. This chapter highlights the importance of **barriers to entry** in determining the pricing strategy adopted by firms. A barrier to entry is an obstacle that makes it difficult for new firms to join a market. Such barriers may exist for several reasons, including the technology of production (as in the case of the natural monopoly discussed earlier), legal protection in the form of patent regulations, and other reasons that will emerge during the discussion.

Key term

barrier to entry
a characteristic of a market that prevents new firms from readily joining the market

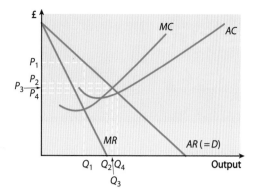

Figure 4.1 Possible pricing rules

Profit maximisation

If the firm chooses to maximise profits, it will choose output such that marginal revenue is equal to marginal cost, and will then set the price to clear the market. In terms of the figure, it will set output at Q_1 and price at P_1.

Revenue maximisation

As noted in Chapter 1, the economist William Baumol argued that if there is a divorce of ownership from control in the organisation of a firm, whereby the shareholders have delegated day-to-day decision making to managers (a principal–agent situation), the managers may find themselves with some freedom to pursue other objectives, such as revenue maximisation. A revenue maximiser in Figure 4.1 would choose to produce at the output level where total revenue is at a maximum, which occurs when marginal revenue is zero. This occurs at Q_2 in the figure, with the price set at P_2.

Sales maximisation

If instead managers set out to maximise the volume of sales subject to covering opportunity cost, they will choose to set output at a level such that price equals average cost, which will clear the market. In Figure 4.1 this happens at Q_4 (with price at P_4). Notice that the firm would make losses if it were to produce more than this, as it would have to sell at a price below average cost.

Allocative efficiency

It has been argued that allocative efficiency in an individual market occurs at the point where price is equal to marginal cost. In Figure 4.1 this is at Q_3 (with price P_3). However, from the firm's perspective there is no obvious reason why this should become an objective of the firm, as it confers no particular advantage.

Study tip

Figure 4.1 may be a useful figure for you to use if you are required to show how firms with differing objectives may take different decisions on their price–output combination. If you wish to use it, make sure that you know how to draw it correctly — and, of course, remember to label all the curves and axes correctly.

Extension material

Corporate social responsibility

Chapter 1 noted that behavioural theories of the firm have suggested that firms may not always take decisions in the kind of mechanistic way that is implied by maximisation rules. For example, they may try to demonstrate a commitment to corporate social responsibility, by being seen to show a commitment to behaving in the public interest. Might this affect their choice of pricing strategy?

One way of demonstrating such a commitment might be to refrain from setting the highest price that the market could stand. For example, a firm may announce that it is setting a 'fair' price for its products. For the firm, the question here is whether this will be the best way of demonstrating its commitment. It may consider that it will gain more publicity by

maintaining its prices at the level it would normally have done, but then using some of the profits in various ways that benefit the community.

The notion of setting a fair price brings to mind the *fair trade* schemes that operate, whereby firms argue that they are acting in a way that ensures a fair price for their suppliers in less developed countries. Perhaps ironically, this entails setting a higher price for produce, providing opportunities for the consumers to make a contribution to the primary producers.

Synoptic link

Fair trade schemes will be examined under Theme 4 in Chapter 12.

Pricing in practice

It seems clear that in practice most firms do not know the shape of their revenue and cost curves with any great precision. It might thus be argued that they cannot actually adopt any of these rules, and need to find alternative ways of devising a pricing strategy.

One such approach would be to make a series of small (marginal) changes, and observe the effects each time, thereby moving gradually towards whatever objective the firm wishes to attain. However, if you were to ask managers how they decide on price, many of them would probably say that they use **cost-plus pricing** (sometimes known as mark-up pricing). In other words, they calculate average cost at their chosen output level, and then add on a mark-up to bring them some profit per unit. Indeed, when the Bank of England conducted a survey of British companies to see how they set their prices, 37% said that they set prices using a mark-up pricing rule.

Does this nullify the profit-maximising hypothesis? Not necessarily. Saying that a firm sets price as a mark-up on average cost leaves a very important question unanswered: namely, what determines the size of the mark-up that the firm can add to average cost?

The Bank of England survey also discovered that firms in markets in which there were few competitors set higher mark-ups than those in markets in which there were more firms. Mark-ups were also higher in markets where there were differentiated products than in markets producing homogeneous ones.

This pattern of behaviour is entirely compatible with the profit-maximisation hypothesis, where mark-ups are expected to be lower in the presence of a high degree of competition. In other words, mark-up pricing may be a strategy used by firms to find the profit-maximising level of price and output, albeit through a process of trial-and-error. In other words, a firm may experiment with different prices in order to iterate towards the profit-maximising level.

> **Key term**
>
> **cost-plus pricing** a pricing policy whereby firms set their price by adding a mark-up to average cost

Summary

- There are many pricing rules that a firm may choose to adopt, depending on the objectives it wishes to achieve.
- In practice, firms may not know their cost and revenue curves with any accuracy.
- By making marginal changes and observing the effects, they may be able to move towards the price that would achieve their chosen objective.
- Many firms use mark-up pricing, adding a profit margin to average cost.
- The size of the mark-up may depend upon the degree of competition in the market and the extent to which the product is differentiated.
- Mark-up pricing is not inconsistent with profit maximisation.

Price wars

Another finding of the Bank of England's survey was that firms were very strong in saying that they wished to avoid price wars. This could be expected from the kinked demand curve model, where firms in an oligopoly realise that a price reduction is likely to be matched by rivals, leaving all firms with lower profits but having relatively little effect on market shares.

And yet, price wars do break out from time to time. For example, in May 2002 a price war broke out in the UK tabloid newspaper market. It was initiated by the *Express*, but the main protagonists were the *Mirror* and the *Sun*, which joined in after a couple of weeks. The *Mirror* cut its price from 32p to 20p, and the *Sun* from 30p to 20p.

After a week at these lower prices, the editor of the *Sun* was serving champagne in the newsroom in celebration. Their reading of the situation was that the *Mirror* had not expected the *Sun* to follow the price cut. Three weeks after the *Mirror*'s price cut, it put its price back up again — followed by the *Sun*. Analysts and observers commented that the only gainers had been the readers, who had enjoyed three weeks of lower prices.

Why should firms act in this way? The *Mirror* argued that it was trying to re-brand itself, and capture new readers who would continue to read the paper even after the price returned to its normal level. This may hint at the reason for a price war — to affect the long-run equilibrium of the market. The *Sun*'s retaliation was a natural defensive response to an aggressive move.

In some cases a price war may be initiated as a strategy to drive a weaker competitor out of the market altogether. The motivation then is clear, especially if the initiator of the price war ends up with a monopoly or near-monopoly position in the market. It could be argued that this represents an attempt to maximise profits in the long run by establishing a monopoly position.

A price war broke out in the UK tabloid market in 2002

Predatory pricing

Perhaps the most common context in which price wars have broken out is where an existing firm or firms have reacted to defend the market against the entry of new firms.

One such example occurred in 1996, in the early years of easyJet, the low-cost air carrier, which was then trying to become established. When easyJet started flying the London–Amsterdam route, charging its now well-known low prices, the incumbent firm (KLM) reacted very aggressively, driving its price down to a level just below that of easyJet. The response from easyJet was to launch legal action against KLM, claiming it was using unfair market tactics.

So-called **predatory pricing** is illegal under English, Dutch and EU law. It should be noted that, in order to declare an action illegal, it is necessary to define that action very carefully — otherwise it will not be possible to prove the case in the courts. In the case of predatory pricing, the legal definition is based on economic analysis.

Chapter 1 defined the shut-down price for the firm, pointing out that if a firm was failing to cover average variable costs, its strategy should be to close down immediately, as it would be better off doing so. The courts have backed this theory, and state that a pricing strategy should be interpreted as being predatory if the price is set below average variable costs, as the only motive for remaining in business while making such losses must be to drive competitors out of business and achieve market dominance. This is known as the *Areeda–Turner principle* (after the case in which it was first argued in the USA).

On the face of it, it would seem that consumers have much to gain from such strategies through the resulting lower prices. However, a predator that is successful in driving out the opposition is likely to recoup its losses by putting prices back up to profit-maximising levels thereafter, so the benefit to consumers is short lived.

Having said that, the low-cost airlines survived the attempts of the established airlines to hold on to their market shares. Indeed, in the post-9/11 period, which was a tough one for the airlines for obvious reasons, the low-cost airlines flourished while the more conventional established airlines went through a very difficult period indeed.

In some cases, the very threat of predatory pricing may be sufficient to deter entry by new firms, if the threat is a credible one. In other words, the existing firms need to convince potential entrants that they, the existing firms, will find it in their best interests to fight a price war, otherwise the entrants will not believe the threat. The existing firms could do this by making it known that they had surplus capacity, so that they would be able to increase output very quickly in order to drive down the price.

Whether entry will be deterred by such means may depend in part on the characteristics of the potential entrant. After all, a new firm may reckon that, if the existing firm finds it worth sacrificing profits in the short run, the rewards of dominating the market must be worth fighting for. It may therefore decide to sacrifice short-term profit in order to enter the market — especially if it is diversifying from other markets and has resources at its disposal. The winner will then be the firm that can last the longest; but, clearly, this is potentially very damaging for all concerned.

Key term

predatory pricing an anti-competitive strategy in which a firm sets price below average variable cost in an attempt to force a rival or rivals out of the market and achieve market dominance

Study tip

Notice the importance of firms' perceptions in this analysis. Firms take decisions based on their perceptions of their own position in the market, and on their expectations of how rival firms will react. This is a key feature of oligopoly markets — and of economists' models that attempt to explain firms' behaviour.

Exercise 4.2

Discuss the extent to which consumers benefit from a price war.

Limit pricing

An associated but less extreme strategy is **limit pricing**. This assumes that the incumbent firm has some sort of cost advantage over potential entrants: for example, economies of scale.

Figure 4.2 shows a firm facing a downward-sloping demand curve, and thus having some influence over the price of its product. If the firm is maximising profits, it is setting output at Q_0 and price at P_0. As average revenue is comfortably above average cost at this price, the firm is making healthy supernormal profits.

Suppose that the natural barriers to entry in this industry are weak. The supernormal profits will be attractive to potential entrants. Given the cost conditions, the incumbent firm is enjoying the benefit of economies of scale, although producing below the minimum efficient scale.

If a new firm joins the market, producing on a relatively small scale, say at Q_1, the impact on the market can be analysed as follows. The immediate effect is on price, as now the amount $Q_0 + Q_1$ is being produced, pushing price down to P_2. The new firm (producing Q_1) is just covering average cost, so is making normal profits and feeling justified in having joined the market. The original firm is still making supernormal profits, but at a lower level than before. The entry of the new firm has competed away part of the original firm's supernormal profits.

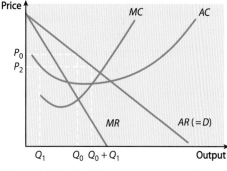

Figure 4.2 Limit pricing

One way in which the firm could have guarded against entry is by charging a lower price than P_0 to begin with. For example, if it set output at $Q_0 + Q_1$ and price at P_2, then a new entrant joining the market would push the price down to a level below P_2, and without the benefit of economies of scale would make losses and exit the market. In any case, if the existing firm has been in the market for some time, it will have gone through a process of learning by doing, and therefore will have a lower average cost curve than the potential entrant. This makes it more likely that limit pricing can be used.

Thus, by setting a price below the profit-maximising level, the original firm is able to maintain its market position in the longer run. This could be a reason for avoiding making too high a level of supernormal profits in the short run, in order to make profits in the longer term.

Notice that such a strategy need not be carried out by a monopolist, but could also occur in an oligopoly, where existing firms may jointly seek to protect their market against potential entry.

Contestable markets

It has been argued that in some markets, in order to prevent the entry of new firms, the existing firm would have to charge such a low price that it would be unable to reap any supernormal profits at all.

This theory was developed by industrial economist William Baumol, and is known as the theory of **contestable markets**. It was in recognition of this theory that the monopoly model in Chapter 2 included the assumption that there must be no substitutes for the good, *either actual or potential*.

For a market to be contestable, it must have no barriers to entry or exit and no sunk costs. *Sunk costs* refer to costs that a firm incurs in setting up a business and which cannot be recovered if the firm exits the market. Furthermore, new firms in the market must have no competitive disadvantage compared with the incumbent firm(s): in other words, they must have access to the same technology, and there must be no significant learning-by-doing effects. Entry and exit must be rapid.

Under these conditions, the incumbent firm cannot set a price that is higher than average cost, because as soon as it does it will open up the possibility of *hit-and-run entry* by new firms, which can enter the market and compete away the supernormal profits.

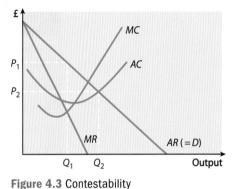

Figure 4.3 Contestability

Consider Figure 4.3, which shows a monopoly firm in a market. The argument is that, if the monopolist charges the profit-maximising price, then if the market is contestable the firm will be vulnerable to hit-and-run entry — a firm could come into the market, take some of the supernormal profits, then exit again. The only way the monopolist can avoid this happening is to set price equal to average cost, so that there are no supernormal profits to act as an incentive for entry.

On the face of it, the conditions for contestability sound pretty stringent. In particular, the firm in Figure 4.3 enjoys some economies of scale, so you would think that some sunk costs had been incurred.

However, suppose a firm has a monopoly on a domestic air route between two destinations. An airline with surplus capacity — that is, a spare aircraft sitting in a hangar — could enter this route and exit again without incurring sunk costs in response to profits being made by the incumbent firm. This is an example of how contestability may limit the ability of the incumbent firm to use its market power.

Notice in this example that, although the firm only makes normal profits, neither productive nor allocative efficiency is achieved.

A moot point is whether the threat of entry will in fact persuade firms that they cannot set a price above average cost. If entry and exit are so rapid, perhaps the firms can risk making some profit above normal profits and then respond to entry very aggressively if and when it happens. After all, it is difficult to think of an example in which there are absolutely no sunk costs. Almost any business is going to have to advertise in order to find customers, and such advertising expenditure cannot be recovered.

This will be re-examined in the next chapter when discussing competition policy, as it is an important issue in that context, and the degree of contestability may affect the perception of how much market power is in the hands of existing firms.

Contestability and the internet

The growth of the internet has had a significant impact on the contestability of markets and hence on competitiveness. By making information more freely available, the internet has given consumers improved knowledge of market conditions and enabled them to make more informed choices. Furthermore, the growth of online sales has made it much easier for new firms to enter markets.

One good example of this is the travel industry. In 2012 UK residents made more than 56 million trips abroad, so this is a significant sector. In the past, many overseas trips, especially holidays, were arranged by the high street travel agents. Although there were many retail outlets, the largest chains of travel agents were responsible for a significant market share. The internet has revolutionised this sector, with online firms competing effectively with the established firms, and individual consumers able to make their own travel arrangements much more effectively. This is an example of where increased contestability of a market has resulted in an increase in competitiveness.

Exercise 4.3

Discuss the extent to which the following markets may be considered to be contestable — or to have become more so in recent years:

a opticians

b travel agents

c financial services

d the postal service

e aircraft manufacture

Other entry deterrence strategies

Pricing is not the only strategy that firms adopt in order to deter entry by new firms. Another approach that has been used over a wide range of economic activities is to raise the fixed costs of being in the industry.

Advertising and publicity

Advertising can be regarded as a component of fixed costs because expenditure on it does not vary directly with the volume of output. If the firms in an industry typically spend heavily on advertising, it will be more difficult for new firms to become established, as they too will need to advertise widely in order to attract customers.

Similarly, firms may spend heavily on achieving a well-known brand image that will ensure customer loyalty. Hence they may invest a lot in the design and packaging of their merchandise. One example was the high-profile TV campaign run by Sunny Delight when trying to gain entry into the soft drinks market in the early part of the twenty-first century.

Notice that such costs are also sunk costs, and cannot be recovered if the new firm fails to gain a foothold. It has sometimes been suggested that the cost of excessive advertising should be included in calculations of the social cost of monopoly.

Research and development

A characteristic of some industries is the heavy expenditure undertaken on research and development (R&D). A prominent example is the pharmaceutical industry, which spends large amounts on researching new drugs — and new cosmetics.

This is another component of fixed costs, as it does not vary with the volume of production. Again, new firms wanting to break into the market know that they will need to invest heavily in R&D if they are going to keep up with the new and better drugs and cosmetics always coming on to the market.

The high costs of R&D in the pharmaceutical industry can deter new firms entering the market

Exercise 4.4

For each of the following, explain under what circumstances the action of the firm constitutes a barrier to entry and discuss whether there is a strategic element to it, or whether it might be regarded as a 'natural' or 'innocent' barrier.

a A firm takes advantage of economies of scale to reduce its average costs of production.

b A firm holds a patent on the sale of a product.

c A firm engages in widespread advertising of its product.

d A firm installs surplus capacity relative to normal production levels.

e A firm produces a range of very similar products under different brand names.

f A firm chooses not to set price at the profit-maximising level.

g A firm spends extensively on research and development in order to produce a better product.

Market structure and competitiveness

A good way of gaining insight into the way in which market structure can affect the intensity of competitiveness in a market is to look at examples of markets that have experienced a change in market conditions that has induced a change in market structure. The process of deregulation affords such an opportunity, and there have been several examples of this in recent years. The low-cost airlines have transformed the face of air travel. They show some of the effects of changing market structure, and how firms are able to become profitable by understanding some economic analysis.

The low-cost airlines appeared on the scene as long ago as 1971, with the advent of Southwestern in the USA, followed by Ryanair in 1985 and easyJet in 1995. The model has now been copied by Air Asia and other airlines operating in South East Asia.

This market provides an illustration of how intensified competition can affect the operation of markets. Before the advent of the low-cost airlines, the market for air travel was dominated by large national carriers, in many cases either state-run or heavily subsidised by governments. As time went by, these large airlines began to join together in strategic alliances that enabled them to work together yet maintain their individual characters. The market seemed to be consolidating and was effectively becoming more concentrated.

Deregulation provided an opening for changes in the market structure, by reducing the barriers to entry of new firms. However, in order to exploit that opening, the budget airlines needed a good understanding of economic analysis. Their success has been built on a thorough understanding of cost structures and a recognition of the contestability of airlines, together with the judicious use of price discrimination.

Focus on costs

Profits depend upon costs as well as revenue. EasyJet (not to mention other budget airlines, such as Ryanair and Flybe) took a close look at the structure of costs. By focusing on each individual item of costs and looking for ways of cutting costs to a minimum, the budget airlines were able to achieve profitability.

In part, this has been connected with the understanding of demand. As the budget airlines developed, they offered a 'no frills' approach, doing away with pre-assigned seats and pre-issued tickets, free in-flight catering, a separate business class and so on. They also used more remote airports, where charges were relatively low. But the savings went way beyond these conspicuous items.

In particular, the budget airlines followed a pattern established by the Texas-based airline Southwestern, which set out four key rules.

First, only fly one type of plane. This reduces maintenance costs and avoids the need to hold a wide range of spare parts. This is one source of potential economies of scale.

Second, drive down costs every year. This may be achieved while the airline is still expanding if there are economies of scale to be reaped. For example, it may be achieved by negotiating improved deals from suppliers — of fuel, insurance, etc.

Third, minimise the time that aircraft spend parked on the tarmac. The no frills and no tickets approach enables a much quicker turn-round of aircraft — which, after all, only earn money for the company when they are in the air. For example, an easyJet plane flying between Luton and Nice can make four round-trips per day, by spending only about half-an-hour on the tarmac at each end.

Fourth, do not try to sell anything except seats. Schemes that offer loyalty bonuses or air miles cost money to administer, and are more complicated than they are worth.

Following these rules, and paying careful attention to the various forms of costs, the budget airlines were able to expand, to make profits and to transform air travel.

Pricing strategy

The focus on costs was only part of the strategy. As far as its pricing strategy was concerned, easyJet claimed on its website that it 'operates a very simple fare structure... based on supply and demand'. The nature of the price structure is that passengers who book early pay the lowest prices, whereas those who book close to their travel time pay the highest prices. This is an illustration of how a firm can use price discrimination.

The arrival of low-cost airlines transformed the market structure for air travel

You might expect that in a competitive market, the price structure would be the opposite. If prices follow costs, the marginal cost to easyJet of carrying an extra passenger is likely to be pretty low, so the flight could be filled up by offering last-minute deals, with the price being driven close to marginal cost. But this is clearly not happening at easyJet, as the later a passenger books, the higher the price that they face.

This suggests that easyJet took a different view, taking into account the nature of demand, and using price discrimination on its flights. People who book at the last minute are likely to be business travellers who need to fly urgently, perhaps for a business meeting or to clinch a deal. Such customers are likely to have low elasticity of demand, and thus be prepared to pay a higher price for their ticket. This is in contrast to those who can book well in advance, who are more likely to be people travelling for pleasure — visiting relatives or going on holiday. For these travellers, the choice of when to fly is more flexible. This means there are more possible flights from which they can choose. And we know that when there are substitutes for a commodity, the price elasticity of demand is high. It is for these customers that easyJet can offer the low prices that we see being advertised. After all, at the prices that easyJet advertises, it probably costs some customers more to get to the airport than it costs for the flight! EasyJet can make use of this difference in demand elasticity to charge different prices to different customers, even if the product (such as the flight from London to Nice) is the same for all of them.

The entry of the budget airlines caused the existing firms to reconsider the way in which they operate. Some reacted by setting up their own budget subsidiaries, with varying degrees of success. Others had to accept that they needed to focus on longer-haul flights.

The budget airlines case therefore provides another example of how competition can transform a market, and how contestability can affect firms' behaviour. Why can the airline business be regarded as contestable? After all, it might be argued that the set-up costs of establishing an airline are likely to be high, so it is difficult to claim that there are no sunk costs faced by firms. However, the key issue is that market conditions on particular routes may well encourage contestability. Once the airline is established, the costs of flying a new route are relatively low. There are bound to be some advertising costs, but otherwise an airline can switch aircraft to new routes quite quickly. It could then switch to other routes if profits were disappointing. In other words, hit-and-run entry is possible on particular routes. This may mean that existing airlines will not set prices at such levels that entry is attracted.

It is also worth noting that the low-cost airlines flourished not only by taking customers away from the existing airlines, but also by tapping a new customer base. By offering low fares and easy accessibility, they have attracted passengers who would not otherwise have dreamed of flying. As these airlines became more established, and as competition amongst them intensified, they began to bring back some premium facilities, such as choice of seat, so non-price competition began to come into play.

It is interesting to note, however, that not all firms have adopted the approach of low-cost airlines. Many theatres have approached price discrimination in a different way, by selling last-minute tickets at knock-down prices, realising that the marginal cost of admitting extra people when seats have not all been sold is very low. This can then appeal to consumers who are happy to be flexible in their plans rather than booking well in advance. Theatregoers who are anxious not to miss the latest hit production will be prepared to book early and pay a higher price as they have inelastic demand. People who are happy to queue for returned tickets and run the risk of missing out in order to get a cheaper seat have elastic demand.

Summary

- Although price wars are expected to be damaging for the firms involved, they do break out from time to time.
- They may occur when firms wish to increase their market shares, or when existing firms wish to deter the entry of new firms into the market.
- Predatory pricing is an extreme strategy that forces all firms to endure losses. It is normally invoked in an attempt to eliminate a competitor, and is illegal in many countries.
- Limit pricing occurs when a firm or firms choose to set price below the profit-maximising level in order to prevent entry. The limit price is the highest price that an existing firm can set without allowing entry.
- In some cases, the limit price may enable the incumbent firm or firms to make only normal profit. Such a market is said to be contestable.
- Contestability requires that there are no barriers to entry or exit and no sunk costs – and that the incumbent firm(s) have no cost advantage over hit-and-run entrants.
- Firms have adopted other strategies designed to deter entry, such as using advertising or R&D spending to raise the cost of entry by adding to required fixed costs.

Case study 4.1

Airline contestability

At the time of US deregulation a number of influential economists argued that an absence of actual competitors in airline markets did not indicate a lack of competition. Airline markets, they argued, are *contestable*, and therefore the mere threat of entry is sufficient to keep prices at or near competitive levels. To what extent is this a correct interpretation of these markets?

Aircraft are, by nature, highly mobile ('capital with wings'). This is the basis of the argument that airline markets are contestable — if an aircraft can easily be moved between markets then there are no sunk costs associated with its use in any particular market. There have been many empirical studies of US airline markets in the almost 30 years since deregulation, and the particular question of whether the markets are contestable has been investigated in a number of ways.

One approach is to see whether prices depend upon the number of actual competitors on a route. If the market is contestable, then there should be no relationship between the two. Many studies have found, however, that actual competition does matter. For example, some research by Weiher, Sickles and Perloff found that the average ratio of price to marginal cost was 3.3 on routes operated by a monopolist but 2.2 for routes with two airlines.

A second approach is to seek to compare the effect of actual and potential competitors. This, of course, raises the question of how to identify potential competitors. One method is to define a potential entrant to a city-pair as an airline that serves one or both of the endpoints but not the route itself. Studies of this type find that the impact of a potential entrant on prices is between one-tenth and one-third of the impact of an actual competitor.

Finally, there has been some analysis of the impact of actual entry onto or exit from a route. The evidence here suggests that both entry and exit have an impact on price, the former reducing price by about 9% on average and the latter causing price to rise by about 10%.

Taken together, the research provides strong evidence that airline markets are not contestable and that, whilst potential entrants do have some impact on prices, their effect is small in relation to that of actual competitors.

There are a number of reasons why airline markets are not contestable. First, in practice passengers do not respond instantaneously to price differentials, and so incumbents can react before an entrant is able to capture the entire market. Furthermore, entry typically does involve set-up costs that cannot be recovered if the firm subsequently exits the market. Thus hit-and-run entry is unlikely to be a profitable strategy. Second, experience has shown that incumbent airlines have a variety of means of deterring entry, in addition to price retaliation. For example, frequent flyer programmes increase the relative attractiveness of airlines with extensive networks over small entrants.

To what extent are airline markets contestable?

Follow-up questions

a Explain the key characteristics of a contestable market, and why economists initially thought that airline markets would be a good example.

b Explain and evaluate the evidence presented in the passage which suggests that contestability might not be as strong as had been thought.

5 The labour market

An important market in any economy is the market for labour, and no doubt you will one day be part of that market, if you are not already. Labour is a crucial factor of production for firms, so the demand for labour comes from firms wanting to hire workers. People need to work in order to earn income, which is done through the medium of supplying labour. In this chapter, you will see the way in which the demand for labour from firms and the supply of labour by workers come together in the labour market. The chapter also discusses the nature of equilibrium in the labour market, and some reasons why it might not always be possible to reach equilibrium.

Prior knowledge needed

This chapter builds upon material that was contained in Book 1, especially the early chapters that developed the demand and supply model. This chapter applies this analysis to the labour market. The concepts of elasticity, producer surplus and externalities will also be drawn into the discussion.

Learning objectives

After studying this chapter, you should:
→ understand the factors which influence the demand for and supply of labour
→ appreciate that the demand for labour is a derived demand
→ understand the factors that influence the supply of labour to a particular occupation
→ be aware of how market failure can affect labour markets
→ be able to demonstrate labour market equilibrium
→ be able to use demand and supply analysis to examine the effects of government policies that affect the labour market
→ appreciate the significance of the elasticity of demand for and supply of labour

Key term

derived demand
demand for a good or service not for its own sake, but for what it produces, e.g. labour is demanded for the output that it produces

Study tip

There are two key things to remember here: that the wage rate is seen as the price of labour and that the demand for labour is a derived demand. Be clear in your mind about this notion of a derived demand, as it underpins much of the discussion of labour markets.

The demand for labour

What do firms do and why do they demand labour? In Chapter 1, a firm was defined as 'an organisation that brings together factors of production in order to produce output'. The aim of a firm, therefore, is to produce output to sell in order to generate revenue and make profits. Labour is one of the key factors of production used by firms as part of this process.

This means that firms do not demand labour for its own sake, but for the sake of the revenue that is obtained from selling the output that labour produces. The demand for labour is thus an example of a **derived demand**, and understanding this is crucial for an analysis of the labour market.

To illustrate this, consider a firm that manufactures cricket bats. The firm hires labourers to operate the machinery that is used in production. However, the firm does not hire a labourer because he or she is a nice person. The firm aims to make profit by selling the cricket bats produced, and the labourer is needed because of the labour services that he or she provides. This notion of derived demand underpins the analysis of labour markets.

It is important to be aware that although there is a tendency to talk about 'the' labour market, or about 'unemployment' in the aggregate, in reality there is not a single market in the economy, but a multitude of sub-markets. This partly reflects the fact that individual workers differ from each other in terms of their characteristics and skills. There are different markets for different types of labour, such as lawyers, accountants, cleaners and bricklayers. There may also be geographic sub-markets, given that labour may be relatively immobile. An employer may perceive that it operates in a particular industry, so there may be a labour market for an industry, or for particular skills within an industry. Indeed, a firm may find itself operating in several different sub-markets.

This interlocking pattern of labour markets is likely to evolve over time, as technology changes, bringing with it the need for different skills, and a different balance of skills.

The demand curve for labour

Consider the demand for a particular type of labour — in other words, a particular labour market. Given that the demand for labour is a derived demand, the first factor that will determine the demand for labour is the output that labour produces. Given the law of diminishing returns, which was introduced in Chapter 1, the additional output produced by labour as more labour is deployed is expected to diminish, other things remaining equal. This is because capital becomes relatively scarcer as the amount of labour increases without a corresponding increase in capital.

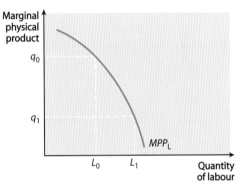

Important for the firm, then, is the **marginal physical product of labour**, which is the amount of additional output produced if the firm increases its labour input by 1 unit (e.g. adding 1 more person-hour), holding capital constant. An example is shown in Figure 5.1. When labour input is relatively low, such as at L_0, the additional output produced by an extra unit of labour is relatively high, at q_0, since the extra unit of labour has plenty of capital with which to work. However, as more labour is added, the marginal physical product falls, so at L_1 labour the marginal physical product is only q_1.

Figure 5.1 The marginal physical product of labour

Although the marginal physical product is important, what really matters to the firm is the *revenue* that it will receive from selling the additional output produced. In considering the profit-maximising amount of labour to employ, therefore, the firm needs to consider the marginal physical product multiplied by the marginal revenue received from selling the extra output, which is known as the **marginal revenue product of labour (MRP_L)**.

If the firm is operating under perfect competition, then marginal revenue and price are the same and MRP_L is MPP_L multiplied by the price. However, if the firm faces a downward-sloping demand curve for its product, it has to reduce the selling price in order to sell the additional output. Marginal revenue is then lower than price, as the firm must lower the price on *all* of the output that it sells, not just on the last unit sold.

Consider a firm operating under perfect competition, and setting out to maximise profits. Figure 5.2 shows the marginal revenue product curve. The question to consider is how the firm chooses how much labour input to use. This decision is based partly on the knowledge of the MRP_L, but it also depends on the cost of labour.

Key terms

marginal physical product of labour (MPP_L) the additional quantity of output produced by an additional unit of labour input

marginal revenue product of labour (MRP_L) the additional revenue received by a firm as it increases output by using an additional unit of labour input, i.e. the marginal physical product of labour multiplied by the marginal revenue received by the firm

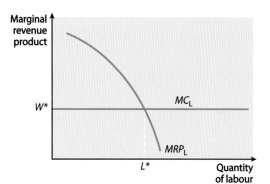

Figure 5.2 The labour input decision of a profit-maximising firm under perfect competition

The main cost of using labour is the wages paid to the workers. There may be other costs — hiring costs and so on — but these can be set aside for the moment. Assuming that the labour market is perfectly competitive, so that the firm cannot influence the market wage and can obtain as much labour as it wants at the going wage rate, the wage can be regarded as the *marginal cost of labour* (MC_L).

If the marginal revenue received by the firm from selling the extra output produced by extra labour (i.e. the MRP_L) is higher than the wage, then hiring more labour will add to profits. On the other hand, if the MRP_L is lower than the wage, then the firm is already hiring too much labour. Thus, it pays the firm to hire labour up to the point where the MRP_L is just equal to the wage. On Figure 5.2, if the wage is $W\star$, the firm is maximising profits at $L\star$. The MRP_L curve thus represents the firm's demand for labour curve. This approach is known as **marginal productivity theory**.

Extension material

Marginal productivity theory and profit maximisation

This profit-maximising condition can be written as:

wage = marginal revenue × marginal physical product of labour

which is the same as:

marginal revenue = wage/MPP_L

Remember that capital input is fixed for the firm in the short run, so the wage divided by the MPP_L is the firm's cost per unit of output at the margin. This shows that the profit-maximising condition is the same as that derived for a profit-maximising firm in Chapter 2: in other words, profit is maximised where marginal revenue equals marginal cost. This is just another way of looking at the firm's decision.

Key term

marginal productivity theory a theory which argues that the demand for labour depends upon balancing the revenue that a firm gains from employing an additional unit of labour against the marginal cost of that unit of labour

Quantitative skills 5.1

Marginal physical product and marginal revenue product

Table 5.1 shows how the total output produced by labour varies with labour input for a firm operating under perfect competition in the product market. The price of the product is £5.

Table 5.1 Output and labour input

Labour input per period	Output (goods per period)
0	0
1	7
2	15
3	22
4	27
5	29

→

Chapter 1 showed how marginal cost could be calculated from total cost. The same principle applies in calculating the MPP_L from the total output produced by different amounts of labour input. For example, suppose labour input is increased from 2 units to 3. The output produced by labour increases from 15 to 22, so the MPP_L is $22 - 15 = 7$.

The MRP_L is then the MPP_L multiplied by the selling price of the output, which is $7 \times 5 = 35$. This is the additional revenue that the firm receives from selling the additional output produced by the third unit of labour employed.

Test your understanding of this as part of the following exercise.

Exercise 5.1

This exercise builds on Quantitative skills 5.1.

a Calculate the marginal physical product of labour (MPP_L) at each level of labour input.

b Calculate the marginal revenue product of labour (MRP_L) at each level of labour input.

Suppose that the firm is also operating in perfect competition in the labour market, where the wage is £30.

c Plot the MRP_L on a graph and identify the profit-maximising level of labour input.

d Suppose that the firm faces fixed costs of £10. Calculate total revenue and total costs at each level of labour input, and check the profit-maximising level.

Factors affecting the position of the demand for labour curve

There are a number of factors that determine the *position* of a firm's labour demand curve. Remember that the demand for labour is a derived demand, so firms demand labour for the sake of the output that labour produces. This suggests that the amount of output that labour is able to produce will be an important factor. If labour becomes more productive for some reason, then this will lead to an increase in the demand for labour. For example, if a new technological advance raises the productivity of labour, it will also affect the position of the labour demand curve.

In Figure 5.3, you can see how the demand for labour would shift if there were an increase in the productivity of labour as a result of new technology. Initially, demand is at D_{L0}, but the increased technology pushes the curve to D_{L1}. If the wage remains at $W^\star$, the quantity of labour hired by the firm increases from L_0 to L_1. Similarly, in the long run, if a firm expands the size of its capital stock, this will also affect the demand for labour.

It can also be seen that because the demand for labour is a derived demand, a change in the revenue that the firm receives from selling the output that labour produces will affect the demand for labour. For example, suppose that in a competitive market, the equilibrium price of a good falls — perhaps as a result of a shift in the demand curve for the good. This will have a knock-on effect on the firm's demand for labour, as illustrated in Figure 5.4. Initially, the firm was

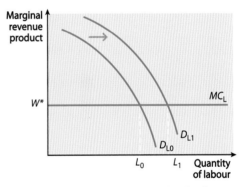

Figure 5.3 The effect of improved technology

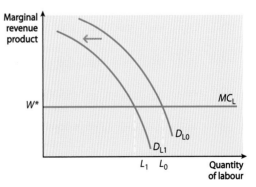

Figure 5.4 The effect of a fall in the demand for a firm's product on the demand for labour

demanding L_0 labour at the wage rate $W^\star$, but the fall in demand for the product leads to a fall in the revenue that the firm receives from selling the good (even though the physical productivity of labour has not changed), so the labour demand curve shifts from D_{L0} to D_{L1}. Only L_1 labour is now demanded at the wage rate $W^\star$. It is important to understand that this arises because the demand for labour is a derived demand that is intimately bound up with the demand for the firm's product.

Summary

- The demand for labour is a derived demand, as the firm wants labour not for its own sake, but for the output that it produces.
- In the short run, a firm faces diminishing returns to increases in labour input if capital is held constant.
- The marginal physical product of labour is the amount of output produced if the firm employs an additional unit of labour, keeping capital input fixed.
- The marginal revenue product of labour is the marginal physical product multiplied by marginal revenue.
- With perfect competition in the product market, marginal revenue and price are the same, but if the firm needs to reduce its price in order to sell additional units of output, then marginal revenue is smaller than price.
- A profit-maximising firm chooses labour input such that the marginal cost of labour is equal to the marginal revenue product of labour. This is equivalent to setting marginal revenue equal to marginal cost.
- The firm has a downward-sloping demand curve for labour, given by the marginal revenue product curve.
- The position of the firm's labour demand curve depends on those factors that influence the marginal physical product, such as technology and efficiency, but also on the price of the firm's product.

Wage elasticity of the demand for labour

In addition to the factors affecting the *position* of the demand for labour curve, it is also important to examine its *shape*. In particular, what factors affect the firm's elasticity of demand for labour with respect to changes in the wage rate? In other words, how sensitive is a firm's demand for labour to a change in the wage rate (the cost of labour)?

Book 1, Chapter 2 examined the influences on the price elasticity of demand, and identified the most important as being the availability of substitutes, the relative size of expenditure on a good in the overall budget, and the time period over which the elasticity is measured. In looking at the elasticity of demand for labour, similar influences can be seen to be at work.

One significant effect on the elasticity of demand for labour is the extent to which other factors of production, such as capital, can be substituted for labour in the production process. If capital or some other factor can be readily substituted for labour, then an increase in the wage rate (ceteris paribus) will induce the firm to reduce its demand for labour by relatively more than if there were no substitute for labour. The extent to which labour and capital are substitutable varies between economic activities, depending on the technology of production, as there may be some sectors in which it is relatively easy for labour and capital to be substituted, and others in which it is quite difficult.

Whether capital can be substituted for labour varies, depending on the technology of production

Second, the share of labour costs in the firm's total costs is important in determining the elasticity of demand for labour. In many service activities, labour is a highly significant share of total costs, so firms tend to be sensitive to changes in the cost of labour. However, in some capital-intensive manufacturing activities, labour may comprise a much smaller share of total production costs.

Third, capital will tend to be inflexible in the short run. Therefore, if a firm faces an increase in wages, it may have little flexibility in substituting towards capital in the short run, so the demand for labour may be relatively inelastic. However, in the longer term the firm will be able to adjust the factors of production towards a different overall balance. Therefore, the elasticity of demand for labour is likely to be higher in the long run than in the short run.

These three influences closely parallel the analysis of what affects the price elasticity of demand. However, as the demand for labour is a derived demand, there is an additional influence that must be taken into account: the price elasticity of demand for the product. The more price elastic is demand for the product, the more sensitive will the firm be to a change in the wage rate, as high elasticity of demand for the product limits the extent to which an increase in wage costs can be passed on to consumers in the form of higher prices.

In order to derive an industry demand curve for labour, it is necessary to add up the quantities of labour that firms in that industry would want to demand at any given wage rate, given the price of the product. As individual firms' demand curves are downward sloping, the industry demand curve will also slope downwards. In other words, more labour will be demanded at a lower wage rate, as shown in Figure 5.5.

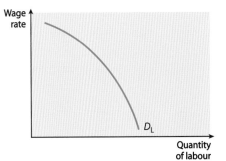

Figure 5.5 An industry demand for labour curve

Summary

- The elasticity of demand for labour depends on the degree to which capital may be substituted for labour in the production process.
- The share of labour in a firm's total costs will also affect the elasticity of demand for labour.
- Labour demand will tend to be more elastic in the long run than in the short run, as the firm needs time to adjust its production process following a change in market conditions.
- As the demand for labour is a derived demand, the elasticity of labour demand will also depend on the price elasticity of demand for the firm's product.

Exercise 5.2

Using diagrams, explain how each of the following will affect a firm's demand for labour:

a a fall in the selling price of the firm's product

b adoption of working practices that improve labour productivity

c an increase in the wage (in a situation where the firm must accept the wage as market determined)

d an increase in the demand for the firm's product

Labour supply

On the supply side of the labour market, it is important to consider the factors that will influence the quantity of labour that workers wish to supply. Again, it may be supposed that this will depend partly on the wage rate.

So far, labour supply has been considered only as it is perceived by a firm, and the assumption has been that the firm is in a perfectly competitive market for labour, and therefore cannot influence the 'price' of labour. Hence the firm sees the labour supply curve as being perfectly elastic, as drawn in Figure 5.2, where labour supply was described as MC_L.

However, for the industry as a whole, labour supply is unlikely to be flat. Intuitively, you might expect to see an upward-sloping labour supply curve. The reason for this is that more people will tend to offer themselves for work when the wage is relatively high. However, this is only part of the background to the industry labour supply curve.

An increase in the wage rate paid to workers in an industry will have two effects. On the one hand, it will tend to attract more workers into that industry, thereby increasing labour supply. However, the change may also affect the supply decisions of workers already in that industry, and for existing workers an increase in the wage rate may have ambiguous effects.

Individual labour supply

Consider an individual worker who is deciding how many hours of labour to supply. Every choice comes with an *opportunity cost*, so if a worker chooses to take more leisure time, he or she is choosing to forgo income-earning opportunities. In other words, the wage rate can be seen as the opportunity cost of leisure. It is the income that the worker has to sacrifice in order to enjoy leisure time.

Now think about the likely effects of an increase in the wage rate. Such an increase raises the opportunity cost of leisure. This in turn has two effects. First, as leisure time is now more costly, there will be a substitution effect against leisure. In other words, workers will be motivated to work longer hours.

However, as the higher wage brings the worker a higher level of real income, a second effect comes into play, encouraging the consumption of more goods and services — including leisure, if it is assumed that leisure is a *normal good*.

Notice that these two effects work against each other. The substitution effect encourages workers to offer more labour at a higher wage because of the effect of the change in the opportunity cost of leisure. However, the real income effect encourages the worker to demand more leisure as a result of the increase in income. The net effect could go either way.

It might be argued that at relatively low wages the substitution effect will tend to be the stronger. However, as the wage continues to rise, the income effect may gradually become stronger, so that at some wage level the worker will choose to supply less labour and will demand more leisure. The individual labour supply curve will then be backward bending, as shown in Figure 5.6, where an increase in the wage rate above W^* induces the individual to supply fewer hours of work in order to enjoy more leisure time.

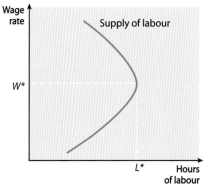

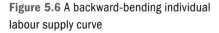
Figure 5.6 A backward-bending individual labour supply curve

It is important to realise that decisions about labour supply may also be influenced by job satisfaction. A worker who finds his or her work to be satisfying may be prepared to accept a lower wage than a worker who really hates every minute spent at work. Indeed, firms may provide other **non-pecuniary benefits** — in other words, firms may provide benefits that are not fully reflected in wages. These are sometimes known as *fringe benefits*. They might include a subsidised canteen or other social facilities. They could also include in-work training, pension schemes or job security. If this is the case, then in choosing one job over another, workers may consider not only the wage rate, but the overall package offered by employers. In other words, by providing non-pecuniary benefits, firms may effectively shift the position of their labour supply curves, as workers will be prepared to supply more labour at any given wage rate. It may also be seen as a way in which firms can encourage loyalty, and thus hold on to workers when the job market is tight.

> **Key term**
>
> **non-pecuniary benefits**
> benefits offered to workers by firms that are not financial in nature

Industry labour supply

The labour supply curve for a market can be expected to be upward sloping, as in Figure 5.7. The reason for this is that more people will tend to offer themselves for work when the wage is relatively high. People will join the market at a higher wage rate, either from outside of the workforce altogether or from other industries where wages have not risen. In this way, wages act as a signal to workers about which industries are offering the best returns to work. This is another example of the way in which the price mechanism operates to allocate resources within a society.

A number of factors may influence the position of the labour supply curve. An increase in the rate of unemployment benefits payable could mean that for some industries the number of people prepared to offer themselves for work may fall, resulting in a leftward shift of the labour supply curve. An increase in the rate of immigration to a country could shift the supply curve of labour to the right.

Figure 5.7 A labour supply curve

An important issue here concerns the decision of individuals about whether to participate in the workforce. The **participation rate** measures the proportion of the population of working age who are employed or looking for work. This excludes people such as students, those who have taken early retirement, and those who for other reasons are not looking for work. Those not looking for work may include parents undertaking childcare, but also *discouraged workers*: those who have failed to gain employment and are no longer seeking work.

The wage elasticity of supply

There are several factors that may influence the elasticity of labour supply: in other words, to what extent an increase in the wage rate in a labour market will encourage an increase in the supply of labour. First, this may depend upon whether there is unemployment, so that there are workers ready to take up jobs. However, there are also likely to be obstacles to flexibility in labour supply. For example, the unemployed workers available for work may not have the skills needed for the vacancies available, so that training may be needed. It could be that the workers who are available are located in areas remote from where the vacancies are appearing. If the available workers are living in Newcastle, but the vacancies are in London, then they may not respond to the higher wages on offer, given the costs of transport, moving house, finding new schools for their children — or even the difficulty of finding out that the jobs are available. Labour supply may thus be relatively inelastic in the short run.

In the long run if wage differentials persist, labour supply may be more elastic. More people may be attracted into high-paid occupations, industries or regions. Alternatively, firms may shift their locations to where labour is more plentiful.

Summary

- For an individual worker, a choice needs to be made between income earned from working and leisure.
- The wage rate can be seen as the opportunity cost of leisure.
- An increase in the wage rate will encourage workers to substitute work for leisure through the substitution effect.
- However, there is also an income effect, which may mean that workers will demand more leisure at higher income levels.
- If the income effect dominates the substitution effect, then the individual labour supply curve may become backward bending.
- However, when aggregated to the industry level, higher wages will encourage more people into the industry, such that the industry supply curve is not expected to be backward bending.
- Labour supply is likely to be more elastic in the long run than in the short run.

Labour market equilibrium

Bringing demand and supply curves together for an industry shows how the equilibrium wage is determined. Figure 5.8 shows a downward-sloping demand curve (D_L) and an upward-sloping labour supply curve (S_L). Equilibrium is found at the intersection of demand and supply. If the wage is lower than $W^\star$ employers will not be able to fill all their vacancies, and will have to offer a higher wage to attract more workers. If the wage is higher than $W^\star$ there will be an excess supply of labour, and the wage will drift down until $W^\star$ is reached and equilibrium obtains.

Synoptic link

Notice that in this chapter, labour market equilibrium is being discussed from a microeconomic perspective. Macroeconomic analysis sees unemployment in an overall context as it views the economy in aggregate. However, macroeconomics also takes into account 'the' labour market, and views unemployment as a total for the economy. It is important to make these links between microeconomic analysis of individual markets and macroeconomic analysis of the aggregates.

Comparative static analysis can be used to examine the effects of changes in market conditions. For instance, a change in the factors that determine the position of the labour demand curve will induce a shift of labour demand and an adjustment in the equilibrium wage. Suppose there is an increase in the demand for the firm's product. This will lead to a rightward shift in the demand for labour, say from D_{L0} to D_{L1} in Figure 5.9. This in turn will lead to a new market equilibrium, with the wage rising from W_0 to W_1.

This may not be the final equilibrium position, however. If the higher wages in this market now encourage workers to switch from other industries in which wages have not risen, this will lead to a longer-term shift to the right of the labour supply curve. In a free market, the shift will continue until wage differentials are no longer sufficient to encourage workers to transfer.

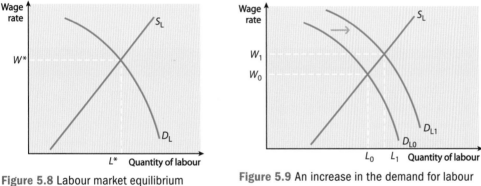

Figure 5.8 Labour market equilibrium

Figure 5.9 An increase in the demand for labour

Exercise 5.3

Using diagrams, explain how the market equilibrium will change for an industry if:

a there is an increase in the rate of immigration into a country

b new health and safety legislation raises the cost of labour

c there is an increase in the selling price of a firm's product

Extension material

Explaining wage differentials

A common topic of debate concerns why there should be such large differences in pay between people in different occupations. For example, why should footballers in the top teams get paid so much? Demand and supply in the labour market can provide part of the answer.

Consider an example of differential earnings — say, surgeons and butchers. First think about the surgeons. Surgeons are in relatively inelastic supply, at least in the short run. The education required to become a surgeon is long and demanding, and is certainly essential for entry into the occupation. Furthermore, not everyone is cut out to become a surgeon, as this is a field that requires certain innate abilities and talents. This implies that the supply of surgeons is limited, and does not vary a great deal with the wage rate.

The situation may be reinforced by the fact that, once an individual has trained as a surgeon, there may be few alternative occupations to which, if disgruntled, he or she could transfer. There is a natural limit to how many surgeons there are *and* to their willingness to exit from the market.

What about butchers? The training programme for butchers is less arduous than for surgeons, and a wider range of people is suitable for employment in this occupation. Labour supply is thus likely to be more elastic than for surgeons. If butchers were to receive high enough wages, more people would be attracted to the trade and wage rates would eventually fall.

In addition, there are other occupations into which butchers can transfer when they have had enough of cutting up all that meat; they might look to other sections of the catering sector, for example. This reinforces the relatively high elasticity of supply.

Is this the whole of the story? The discussion so far has centred entirely on the supply side of the market. But demand is also important. Indeed, it is the position of the demand curve when interacting with supply that determines the equilibrium wage rate in a labour market. It may well be that the supply of workers skilled in underwater basket weaving is strictly limited; but if there is no demand for underwater basket weavers then there is no scope for that skill to earn high wages. In the above example, it is the relatively strong demand for surgeons relative to their limited supply that leads to a relatively high equilibrium wage in the market.

Summary

- Labour market equilibrium is found at the intersection of labour demand and labour supply.
- This determines the equilibrium wage rate for an industry.
- Comparative static analysis can be used to analyse the effects of changes in market conditions.
- Changes in relative wages between sectors may induce movement of workers between industries.

Labour mobility

In some situations, labour markets in practice can be seen to be inflexible. One reason for this is that workers are not perfectly mobile. Mobility here can be seen in two important dimensions. First, there may be geographic immobility, where workers may be reluctant to move to a new region in search of appropriate employment. Second, there may be immobility between occupations. Both sorts of immobility can hinder the free operation of labour markets.

Geographic mobility

There are a number of reasons that help to explain why workers may not be freely mobile between different parts of the country. This will cause problems for the labour market if the available jobs and the available workers are not located in the same area. A key issue involves the costs that are entailed in moving to a new job in a new region. These could be considerable in social terms — people do not like to move away from their friends and relatives, or to leave the area that they know or where their favourite football team plays. Parents may not wish to disrupt their children's education. However, there are also strong economic considerations.

The relatively high rate of owner-occupied housing in the UK means that workers who are owner-occupiers may need a strong inducement to move to another part of the country in search of jobs. For council house tenants, too, it may be quite difficult to relocate to a different area for employment purposes because they will have to return to the bottom of the waiting list for housing. Differences in house prices in different parts of the country add further to the problem of matching workers to jobs.

There may also be information problems, in that it may be more difficult to find out about job availability in other areas. The internet may have reduced the costs of job search to some extent, but it is still easier to find jobs in the local area, where the reputation of firms is better known to locals. Where both partners in a relationship are working, this may also make it more difficult to find jobs further afield, and there is some evidence that females tend to be less mobile geographically than males.

International mobility of labour has increased in recent years, especially since the expansion of the EU in 2004, with the addition of ten new member countries. One of the features of the Single Market measures of 1992 was to allow free movement of people, goods, services and capital within the EU. Not all of the existing EU members allowed free movement of labour from the new members, but the UK did. As a result, it experienced large waves of migration from eastern Europe, especially from Poland. This was partly a response to the wage differential between the countries. As the marginal product of labour was higher in the UK than in Poland and other countries, wages in the UK were relatively high. This wage differential acted as an incentive for workers to move to the UK.

Exercise 5.4

Draw two labour market diagrams to represent the demand and supply of labour in the UK and Poland before the EU expansion. Show on the diagrams how the two markets would adjust to a flow of workers from Poland to the UK.

A Polish shop in London — higher wages attract Polish workers to the UK

Occupational mobility

The difficulty that people face in moving between occupations is an important source of labour market inflexibility, and may result in structural unemployment. Over time, it is to be expected that the pattern of consumer demand will change, and if the pattern of economic activity is to change in response, it is important that some sectors of the economy decline to enable others to expand. As the UK economy has moved away from manufacturing towards service sector activities, people have needed to be occupationally mobile to find work.

There are costs involved for workers switching between occupations. A displaced farm worker may not be able to find work as a ballet dancer without some degree of retraining! Firms may be expected to underprovide training to their workers because of the free-rider problem. There may therefore be a need for some government intervention to ensure that training is provided in order to combat the problem of structural unemployment and to facilitate occupational mobility.

As with geographic mobility, another factor that may impede occupational mobility is the question of information. Workers may not have enough information to enable them to judge the benefits from occupational mobility. For example, they may not be aware of their aptitude for different occupations, or the extent to which they may gain job satisfaction from a job that they have not tried. These arguments do not apply only to workers displaced by structural change in the economy. They are equally valid for workers who are in jobs that may not necessarily be the best ones for them.

Summary

- Geographic immobility may impede the operations of the labour market, if workers are not readily able to move between different parts of the country.
- Occupational immobility may also contribute to the inflexibility of the labour market.

Monopsony in a labour market

Key term

monopsony a market in which there is a single buyer of a good, service or factor of production

One type of market failure in a product market occurs when there is a single *seller* of a good: that is, a monopoly market. As you may recall, a firm with this sort of market dominance is able to restrict output, and maximise profits by setting a higher price. A similar form of market power can occur on the other side of the market if there is a single *buyer* of a good, service or factor of production. Such a market is known as a **monopsony**. This was introduced in Chapter 3.

So far, it has been assumed that firms in the labour market face perfect competition, and therefore must accept the market wage. However, suppose that one firm is the sole user of a particular type of labour, or is the dominant firm in a city or region, and thus is in a monopsony situation.

Such a monopsonist faces the market supply curve of labour directly, rather than simply accepting the equilibrium market wage. It views this supply curve as its average cost of labour because it shows the average wage rate that it would need to offer to obtain any given quantity of labour input.

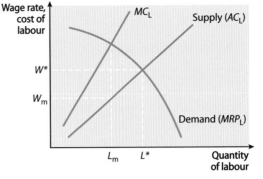

Figure 5.10 shows a monopsonist's demand curve for labour, which is the marginal revenue product curve (MRP_L), and its supply curve of labour, seen by the firm as its average cost curve of labour (AC_L). If the market were perfectly competitive, equilibrium would be where supply equals demand, which would be with the firm using $L^\star$ labour at a wage rate $W^\star$.

Figure 5.10 A monopsony buyer of labour

From the perspective of the monopsonist firm facing the supply curve directly, if at any point it wants to hire more labour, it has to offer a higher wage to encourage more workers to join the market — after all, that is what the AC_L curve tells it. However, the firm would then have to pay that higher wage to all its workers, so the *marginal cost* of hiring the extra worker is not just the wage paid to that worker, but the increased wage paid to all the other workers as well. So the marginal cost of labour curve (MC_L) can be added to the diagram.

If the monopsonist firm wants to maximise profit, it will hire labour up to the point where the marginal cost of labour is equal to the marginal revenue product of labour. Therefore it will use labour up to the level L_m, which is where $MC_L = MRP_L$. In order to entice workers to supply this amount of labour, the firm need pay only the wage W_m. (Remember that AC_L is the supply curve of labour.) You can see, therefore, that a profit-maximising monopsonist will use less labour, and pay a lower wage, than a firm operating under perfect competition. From society's perspective, this entails a cost, just as was seen in the comparison of monopoly and perfect competition in Chapter 2.

Exercise 5.5

Figure 5.11 shows a firm in a monopsonistic labour market.

a What would the wage rate be if this market were perfectly competitive, and how much labour would be employed?

b As a monopsony, what wage would the firm offer to its workers, and how much labour would it employ?

c Which area represents the employer's wage bill?

d What surplus does this generate for the firm?

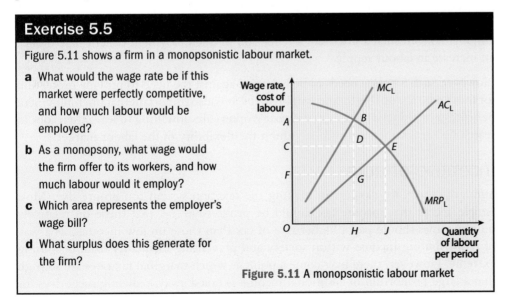

Figure 5.11 A monopsonistic labour market

Bilateral monopoly

It is important to notice that much of this analysis has treated the firm as being very passive in the negotiations. Suppose, however, that there is a *bilateral monopoly*, in which the monopoly trade union seller of labour faces a firm that is a monopsony buyer of labour. The resulting situation is illustrated in Figure 5.12. If unhindered by the trade union, the firm would offer a wage W_m and use L_m labour. However, if the union now negotiates a higher wage rate, what happens is that, as the wage moves upwards from W_m, the firm will take on *more* labour. The market will then move back towards the perfectly competitive level (at wage $W^\star$ and quantity $L^\star$).

In this situation, the market power of the two protagonists works against both of them to produce an outcome that is closer to perfect competition. It is not possible to predict where the final resting place for the market will be, but it will lie somewhere between L_m and $L^\star$, depending upon the relative strengths and negotiating skills of the firm and the union.

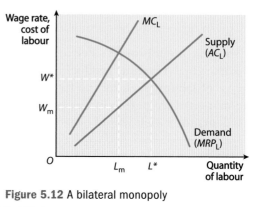

Figure 5.12 A bilateral monopoly

Effects of government intervention in the labour market

There are various ways in which governments intervene in labour markets, either in an attempt to protect vulnerable workers, or to improve the flexibility and effectiveness with which labour markets operate.

Unemployment benefits

An important influence on labour supply, particularly for low-income workers, is the level of unemployment benefit. If unemployment benefit is provided at too high a level, it may inhibit labour force participation, in that some workers may opt to live on unemployment benefit rather than take up low-skilled (and low-paid) employment. In such a situation, a reduction in unemployment benefit may induce an increase in labour supply.

However, such a policy needs to be balanced against the need to provide protection for those who are unable to find employment. It is also important that unemployment benefit is not reduced to such a level that workers are unwilling to leave their jobs to search for better ones, as this may inhibit the flexibility of the labour market.

Incentive effects

Similarly, there are dangers in making the taxation system too progressive. Most people accept that income tax should be progressive (i.e. that those on relatively high incomes should pay a higher rate of tax than those on low incomes) as a way of redistributing income within society and preventing inequality from becoming extreme. However, there may come a point at which marginal tax rates are so high that a large proportion of additional income is taxed away, reducing incentives for individuals to supply additional effort or labour. Again, however, it is important to balance these incentive effects against the distortion caused by having too much inequality in society.

Minimum wage

In its manifesto published before the 1997 election, the Labour Party committed itself to the establishment of the National Minimum Wage (NMW). This was the first time that such a measure had been used in the UK on a nationwide basis, although **minimum wages** had sometimes been set in particular industries.

A Low Pay Commission was set up to oversee the implementation of the policy, which came into force in April 1999. The level of the NMW depends upon age. Initially, the NMW was set at £3.60 per hour for those aged 22 and over, and £3 for those aged 18–21. The rates are revised each year: in 2014 the NMW was set at £6.50 per hour for those aged 21 or over; the rate was £5.13 for those aged between 18 and 20, and £3.79 for those under 18. Apprentices were guaranteed £2.73 per hour.

The objectives of the minimum wage policy are threefold. First, it is intended to protect workers against exploitation by the small minority of bad employers. Second, it aims to improve incentives to work by ensuring that 'work pays', thereby tackling the problem of voluntary unemployment. Third, it aims to alleviate poverty by raising the living standards of the poorest groups in society.

The policy has been a contentious one, with critics claiming that it meets none of these objectives. It has been argued that the minority of bad employers can still find ways of exploiting their workers: for example, by paying them on a piecework rate so that there is no set wage per hour. Another criticism is that the policy is too indiscriminate to tackle poverty, and that a more sharply focused policy is needed for this purpose: for example, many of the workers receiving the NMW may not in fact belong to poor households, but may be women working part time whose partners are also in employment. But perhaps most contentious of all is the argument that, far from providing a supply-side solution to some unemployment, a national minimum wage is causing an increase in unemployment because of its effects on the demand for labour.

First, consider a firm operating in a perfectly competitive market, so that it has to accept the wage that is set in the overall market of which it is a part. In Figure 5.13 the firm's demand curve is represented by its marginal revenue product curve (MRP_L), and in a free market it must accept the equilibrium wage $W^\star$. It thus uses labour up to $l^\star$.

If the government now steps in and imposes a minimum wage, so that the firm cannot set a wage below W_{min}, it will reduce its labour usage to d_{min}, since it will not be profitable to employ labour beyond this point.

This effect will be similar for all the other firms in the market, and the results of this can be seen in Figure 5.14. Now the demand curve is the combined demand of all the firms in the market, and the supply curve of labour is shown as upward sloping, as it is the market supply curve. In free market equilibrium the combined demand of firms in the market is $L^\star$, and $W^\star$ emerges as the equilibrium wage rate.

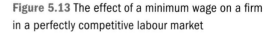

Figure 5.13 The effect of a minimum wage on a firm in a perfectly competitive labour market

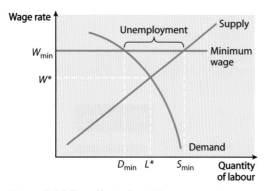

Figure 5.14 The effect of a minimum wage in a perfectly competitive labour market

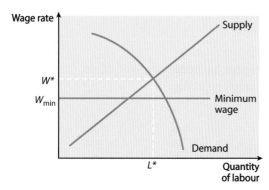

Figure 5.15 A non-binding minimum wage in a perfectly competitive labour market

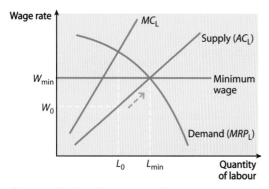
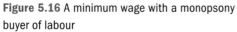

Figure 5.16 A minimum wage with a monopsony buyer of labour

When the government sets the minimum wage at W_{min}, all firms react by reducing their demand for labour at the higher wage. Their combined demand is now D_{min}, but the supply of labour is S_{min}. The difference between these ($S_{min} - D_{min}$) is unemployment. Furthermore, it is involuntary unemployment — these workers would like to work at the going wage rate, but cannot find a job.

Notice that there are two effects at work. Some workers who were formerly employed have lost their jobs — there are $L^{\star} - D_{min}$ of these. In addition, however, the incentive to work is now improved (this was part of the policy objective, remember?), so there are now an additional $S_{min} - L^{\star}$ workers wanting to take employment at the going wage rate. Thus, unemployment has increased for two reasons.

It is not always the case that the introduction of a minimum wage leads to an increase in unemployment. For example, in the market depicted in Figure 5.15 the minimum wage has been set below the equilibrium level, so will have no effect on firms in the market, which will continue to pay $W^{\star}$ and employ $L^{\star}$ workers. At the time of the introduction of the NMW, McDonald's argued that it was in fact already paying a wage above the minimum rate set.

This is not the only situation in which a minimum wage would *not* lead to unemployment. Suppose that the labour market in question has a monopsony buyer of labour. The firm's situation is shown in Figure 5.16. In the absence of a minimum wage, the firm sets its marginal cost of labour equal to its marginal revenue product, hiring L_0 labour at a wage W_0. A minimum wage introduced at the level W_{min} means that the firm now hires labour up to the point where the wage is equal to the marginal revenue product and, as drawn in Figure 5.16, this takes the market back to the perfectly competitive outcome.

Notice that the authorities would have to be very knowledgeable to set the minimum wage at exactly the right level to produce this outcome. However, any wage between W_0 and W_{min} will encourage the firm to increase its employment to some extent as the policy reduces its market power. Of course, setting the minimum wage above the competitive equilibrium level will again lead to some unemployment. Thus, it is critical to set the wage at the right level if the policy is to succeed in its objectives.

It is also important to remember that there is not just a single labour market in the UK. In fact, it could be questioned whether a single minimum wage set across the whole country could be effective, as it would 'bite' in different ways in different markets. For example, wage levels vary across the regions of the UK, and it must be questioned whether the same minimum wage could be as effective in, say, London as in Northern Ireland or the north of England.

Extension material

The living wage

A twenty-first-century development has been the concept of the living wage. The UK Living Wage Campaign was launched by a community alliance in 2001 and has since grown into a national movement. The campaign began because it was seen that the NMW was not providing people with enough funds to live on. The living wage is thus based on a calculation of the basic cost of living in the UK. It is an estimate of how much income households need to afford an acceptable standard of living, calculated by the Centre for Research in Social Policy at Loughborough University.

In 2014, the living wage was set at £9.15 per hour in London and £7.85 in other parts of the country, compared with the NMW at £6.50. The difference between the living wage and the NMW has been growing over time (especially in London).

Unlike the NMW, the living wage has no legal status. However, the campaign for the living wage has been influential in affecting pay levels, particularly by appealing to firms' commitment to corporate social responsibility.

A maximum wage?

The controversy over the bonuses paid to bankers and other top executives has led some commentators to recommend that, in addition to setting a minimum wage, the authorities should set a maximum wage, or a wage ceiling. It is argued that this would stem the excesses that characterise executive pay. An argument often put forward in this context is that high salaries and bonuses are needed to provide incentives for effort, but supporters of the maximum wage counter this by saying that the incentive effects are not strong at those levels of pay. This could reflect the diminishing marginal utility of income — the idea that additional increments of income provide less additional utility as incomes rise. It is also likely that attempts to introduce such a measure would be fraught with difficulties. For example, how would the level of the maximum wage be set? And, of course, the political pressures against such a policy would be enormous.

Public sector wages

One sector in which the government can intervene more easily is the public sector. After all, it determines and negotiates the wages that it pays to its employees. This can distort the overall labour market, if the private sector sets wages according to labour market conditions, but the public sector offers wages that are significantly different.

If the public sector sets wages that are lower than equilibrium in the overall market, then it will have difficulty in recruiting, and may end up hiring the least well-qualified workers. In many less developed countries, the opposite problem has been encountered, where public sector pay (and job security) is high, so all of the best workers gravitate into the public sector, leaving the private sector struggling to find employees.

Exercise 5.6

Sketch some diagrams to explore how the elasticity of demand for and the supply of labour influence the impact on market equilibrium of the imposition of a minimum wage.

Anger at bankers' bonuses — should the authorities set a maximum wage?

Policies to improve the flexibility of the labour market

What steps could the government take to promote flexibility? A number of obstacles to flexibility have been identified. To what extent are these amenable to policy intervention?

Training, skills and information

The process of structural change in an economy may be impeded if the people looking for work, perhaps because they have been released from a declining sector, do not have the skills needed for the sectors that are expanding. It is also important for unemployed workers to have good information about the jobs available.

The 1997 Labour government launched a package of policy measures known as the New Deal, which was aimed at reducing long-term unemployment. These measures were aimed at three age groups, responding to the fact that youth unemployment was perceived as a particular problem. Young people aged 18–24 years old who had been unemployed for a period of more than 6 months were to be assigned a personal adviser to provide them with information about available jobs and contacts with potential employers. If they were still without a job after a further 4 months, they would either enter a year of full-time education or training; or take up a job with the voluntary sector or the environmental task force for 6 months; or go into subsidised employment which would include on-the-job training. Similar targeted programmes were provided for the older age groups.

Such measures are designed to improve the flexibility of the labour market, by providing unemployed workers with information and skills training. Furthermore, employers receive a subsidy to take on workers, who can then be observed in the workplace, which provides a better insight into their potential than any interview or other screening process.

Trade union reform

A further question concerns the extent to which the trade unions have affected the operation of labour markets. By negotiating for a wage that is above the equilibrium level, trade unions may trade off higher wages for lower levels of employment. The potential disruption caused by strike action can also impede the workings of a labour market.

Some indication of this disruption can be seen in Figure 5.17. Clearly, compared with the 1970s and 1980s, the amount of disruption through strikes in recent years has been very low, although even the 1979 figure pales into insignificance besides the 162 million working days lost in the General Strike of 1926. In fact, however, the 1970s and 1980s were a tempestuous period, in which trade union action severely disrupted UK industry. So why has life become so much quieter?

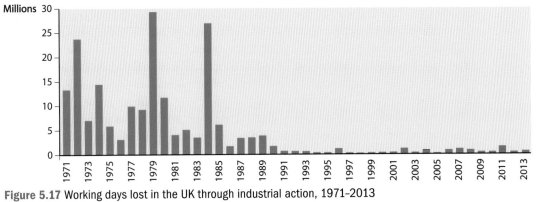

Figure 5.17 Working days lost in the UK through industrial action, 1971–2013
Source: ONS

It was perhaps no surprise that unions should have worked hard to protect their members during the 1980s, when unemployment was soaring and the Thatcher government was determined to control inflation — including inflation of wages. Legislation was introduced in the early 1980s to begin to reform the trade unions, and after the highly disruptive miners' strike ended in 1985, the government introduced a number of further reforms designed to curb the power of the trade unions, making it more difficult for them to call rapid strike action. For example, secret ballots were to be required before strike action could be taken. This may help to explain why trade union membership has been in decline since the 1980s. By weakening the power of trade unions in this way, some labour market inflexibility has been removed.

Another factor may have been changes in the structure of economic activity during this period. Manufacturing employment was falling, whereas the service sectors were expanding. Traditionally, union membership has been higher among workers in the manufacturing sector than in services.

Regional policy

There have always been differences in average incomes and in unemployment rates between the various regions of the UK. In broad terms, there are two possible responses to this — either persuade workers to move to regions where there are more jobs, or persuade the firms to move to areas where labour is plentiful. Each of these solutions poses problems. Housing markets limit the mobility of workers, and it is costly for firms to relocate their activities.

The regions most affected in the past have been those that specialised in industries that subsequently went into decline: for example, coal mining areas or towns and regions dominated by cotton mills. In a broad context, it is desirable for the economy to undergo structural change as the pattern of international comparative advantage changes, but it is painful during the transition period. Thus, successive governments have implemented regional policies to try to cope with the problems experienced in areas of high unemployment.

At the same time, the booming regions can be affected by the opposite problem — a shortage of labour. Thus, measures have been taken to encourage firms to consider relocating to regions where labour is available. These have included leading by example, with some civil service functions being moved out of London.

EU funding has helped in this regard, with Scotland, Wales and Northern Ireland all qualifying for grants. Between 1999 and 2012, Regional Development Agencies (RDAs) set up by the Labour government had responsibility for promoting economic development in their regions. There were nine of these agencies covering the country. Although differentials have narrowed, it is difficult to know how much of this narrowing can be attributed to the success of regional policy. It has also been pointed out that there are some areas that have been receiving regional aid for more than 70 years, but are still disadvantaged, so it is difficult to argue that regional policy has had outstanding success. The RDAs were abolished as part of government efforts to reduce the budget deficit, and ceased operating in March 2012.

Technology and unemployment

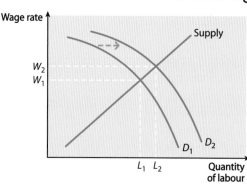

Figure 5.18 An increase in capital

One of the greatest fallacies perpetuated by non-economists is that technology destroys jobs. Bands of labourers known as Luddites rioted between 1811 and 1816, destroying textile machines, which they blamed for high unemployment and low wages. In the twenty-first century there is a strong lobbying group in the USA arguing that outsourcing and cheap labour in China are destroying US jobs.

In fact, new technology and an expansion in the capital stock should have beneficial effects — so long as labour markets are sufficiently flexible. Consider a market in which new technology is introduced. If firms in an industry invest in technology and expand the capital stock, this affects the marginal revenue product of labour and hence the demand for labour, as shown in Figure 5.18, where demand shifts from D_1 to D_2. In this market, the effect is to raise the wage rate from W_1 to W_2 and the employment level from L_1 to L_2.

However, it is important to look beyond what happens in a single market, as the argument is that it is all very well expanding employment in the technology sector — but what about the old industries that are in decline? Suppose the new industries absorb less labour than is discarded by the old declining industries? After all, if the effect of technology is to allow call centres to create jobs in India at the expense of the USA or the UK, does this not harm employment in those countries?

The counter-argument to this lies in the notion of the gains from specialisation introduced in Book 1, Chapter 1. This argues that countries can gain from international trade through specialising in certain activities. Setting up call centres in India frees UK workers to work in sectors in which the UK has a comparative advantage, with the result that the UK can import (and thus consume) more labour-intensive goods than before.

There is one proviso, of course. It is important that the workers released from the declining sectors have (or can obtain) the skills that are needed for them to be absorbed into the expanding sectors. This recalls the question of whether the labour market is sufficiently flexible to allow the structure of economic activity to adapt to changes in the pattern of comparative advantage. However, it also serves as a reminder that policy should be aimed at enabling that flexibility, and not at introducing protectionist measures to reduce trade, which would be damaging overall for the economy.

Summary

- Governments have intervened in labour markets in various ways.
- This includes providing unemployment benefits and setting the National Minimum Wage.
- An important factor influencing the rate of unemployment is the degree of flexibility in labour markets.
- The New Deal was a package of measures introduced with the objective of reducing long-term unemployment, through providing information to jobseekers and training.
- Trade union reforms were introduced during the 1980s and have contributed to flexibility in labour markets.
- Regional policy has attempted to reduce the differentials in unemployment rates between the regions of the UK.
- Adjustment in labour markets is needed in order to cope with the changing international pattern of specialisation.

Case study 5.1

Valuing professional footballers

The football transfer market was buoyant in the summer of 2014. Among the most prominent traders were the top English Premiership clubs such as Manchester United, Liverpool and Chelsea. The FA Premier League has the highest revenues of any domestic football league in the world, grossing more than £3 billion in revenues in the 2013/14 season according to Deloitte. The top Premiership clubs also compete in the highly lucrative UEFA Champions League. The battle between TV firms for broadcasting rights is a key factor in generating these revenues.

So not surprisingly, the top English Premiership clubs are able to outbid most of their rivals to attract the best players in the world. A survey published in November 2014 revealed that the average salary of a footballer playing in the English Premier League in the 2013/14 season had reached £2.3 million per year (£43,717 per week), comfortably more than

footballers playing in the top leagues in Germany, Italy and Spain. These figures suggest that a high proportion of the TV revenues goes into players' salaries — rather than into lower ticket prices.

But is there any economic justification for Barcelona paying a transfer fee of £75 million to Liverpool for Luis Suárez or Manchester United paying £59.7 million to Real Madrid to obtain the services of Ángel di María?

From an economic and financial perspective, professional footballers are complex productive assets who are expected to provide a flow of services both on and off the field over the period of their employment contract. One way of valuing a professional footballer is to calculate the value of the expected flow of net benefits accruing to the holder of the asset — that is, the club. In other words, the value of a professional footballer should be related to the marginal revenue product (*MRP*) of the player.

$\rightarrow$

Calculating the *MRP* of a professional footballer requires estimating the expected additional cash flows accruing to the club as a consequence of signing that player. Broadly speaking, there are two types of revenue stream that a player can generate. Firstly, there are the revenue streams associated with the player's on-the-field contribution to team performance. Team revenues tend to be 'win-elastic'. Winning teams tend to attract more spectators, generating higher match-day revenues. Media revenues can also be win-elastic with bigger viewing audiences for the more successful teams.

Sponsorship and merchandising revenues also tend to be higher for more successful teams. But a player's value will also depend on his expected image value off-the-field. Star players can generate greater revenues by virtue of being star players irrespective of their actual impact on team performance. Glamour as well as glory makes money in professional team sports, which when all is said and done are part of the entertainment industry. So from the economic perspective the fundamental value of a professional footballer can be stated as:

$$MRP = (MPC \times MWR) + PIV$$

where *MPC* is the (expected) marginal playing contribution, *MWR* is the marginal win revenue and *PIV* is the player image value. Calculating a player's value requires an estimate of the incremental impact of the player on the team performance, an estimate of the sensitivity of the team's revenues to team performance and an estimate of the off-the-field marketing value of the player.

Luis Suárez — is he worth the transfer fee?

Follow-up questions

a Explain what is meant by the 'marginal revenue product' of a footballer.

b What is meant by the statement that team revenues tend to be 'win-elastic'?

c Explain why 'glamour as well as glory makes money'.

d To what extent does the discussion of a footballer's *MRP* help to explain why professional footballers command such high wages?

Government intervention to promote competition

If resources are going to be allocated efficiently within a society, it is crucial that business organisations make the appropriate economic decisions. Previous chapters have shown that firms may sometimes be able to gain market dominance, giving them sufficient market power to take decisions that cause a distortion in resource allocation. This chapter explores the major policy areas in which authorities attempt to influence firms' economic decision making. It looks first at competition policy, through which the authorities attempt to encourage competition in markets and protect the interests of consumers. It then examines measures introduced to regulate privatised industries, most of which are natural monopolies posing particular problems for resource allocation. There is also discussion of ways in which the private sector has become involved in public sector organisations.

Learning objectives

After studying this chapter, you should:
→ understand the economic underpinnings of competition policy
→ appreciate that there may be situations in which unremitting competition may not be in the best interests of society
→ be familiar with the role of the Competition and Markets Authority
→ be aware of the issues that may affect the judgements of a market under investigation
→ be familiar with the general institutional background of competition policy in the UK and the EU
→ be familiar with the process for investigating mergers
→ appreciate the arguments for and against privatisation
→ understand the need to regulate natural monopolies and some of the problems that may arise in attempting to do so
→ be familiar with ways in which private sector involvement in public sector organisations has been encouraged

Competition and the government

An awareness of the market failure that can arise from imperfect competition has led governments to introduce measures designed to promote competition and protect consumers. Such measures are known as **competition policy**.

A key focus of such legislation in the past has been monopoly, as economic analysis highlighted the allocative inefficiency that can arise in a monopoly market if the firm sets out to maximise profit. In particular, policy has tended to focus on situations in which the merger of previously separate firms could potentially lead to market dominance. More recently, the scope of legislation has widened, and since 1997 competition policy has been toughened significantly.

> **Key term**
>
> **competition policy** a set of measures designed to promote competition in markets and protect consumers in order to enhance the efficiency of markets

Underlying this aspect of government policy has been the growing belief that competition induces firms to eliminate X-inefficiency as well as encouraging better resource allocation. However, this must always be balanced against the possible sacrifice of economies of scale if competition can only be enabled by fragmentation of the production process. The question of contestability is also important, as it is possible that the very threat of competition may be sufficient to affect firms' behaviour.

X-inefficiency does not occur only in the private sector, and a further set of measures has tried to address the question of efficiency in the provision of public sector services by encouraging the private sector to be involved in partnership with the public sector in its economic activities.

Economic analysis and competition policy

The final section of Chapter 2 undertook a comparison of perfect competition and monopoly, and it is this analysis that lies at the heart of competition policy. Figure 6.1 should remind you of the discussion.

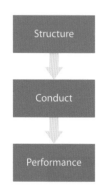

Figure 6.1 Perfect competition and monopoly compared

Here it is assumed there is an industry that can operate either under perfect competition, with a large number of small firms, or as a multi-plant monopolist. For simplicity, it is also assumed that there is no cost difference between the two forms of market structure, so that the long-run supply schedule (*LRS*) under perfect competition is perceived by the monopolist as its long-run marginal cost curve. In other words, in long-run equilibrium the monopoly varies output by varying the number of plants it is operating.

Under perfect competition, output would be set at Q_{pc} and market price would be P_{pc}. However, a monopolist will choose to restrict output to Q_m and raise price to P_m. Consumer surplus will be reduced by this process, partly by a transfer of the blue rectangle to the monopoly as profits, and partly by the red triangle of deadweight loss. Competition policy is intended to alleviate this deadweight loss, which imposes a cost on society.

Indeed, this analysis led to a belief in what became known in the economics literature as the *structure–conduct–performance paradigm*. At the core of this belief, illustrated in Figure 6.2, is the simple idea that the structure of a market, in terms of the number of firms, determines how firms in the market conduct themselves, which in turn determines how well the market performs in achieving productive and allocative efficiency.

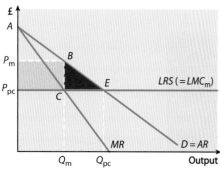

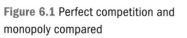

Figure 6.2 The structure-conduct-performance paradigm

> ## Study tip
>
> Be sure that you understand why it is argued that structure, conduct and performance are linked in this way. If necessary look back at Chapters 2 and 3, which discuss alternative market structures and how the structure of the market influences decision making by firms.

Thus, under perfect competition firms cannot influence price, and all firms act competitively to maximise profits, thereby producing good overall performance of the market in allocating resources. On the other hand, under monopoly the single firm finds that it can extract consumer surplus by using its market power, and as a result the market performs less well.

This point of view leads to a distrust of monopoly — or, indeed, of any market structure in which firms might be seen to be conducting themselves in an anti-competitive manner. Moreover, it is the structure of the market itself that leads to this anti-competitive behaviour.

If this line of reasoning is accepted, then monopoly is always bad, and mergers that lead to higher concentration in a market will always lead to allocative inefficiency in the market's performance. Thus, legislation in the USA tends to presume that a monopoly will work against the interests of society. However, there are some important issues to consider before pinning too much faith on this assumption.

Cost conditions

The first issue concerns the assumption that cost conditions will be the same under perfect competition as under monopoly. This simplifies the analysis, but there are many reasons to expect economies of scale in a number of economic activities. If this assumption is correct, then a monopoly firm will face lower cost conditions than would apply under perfect competition.

In Figure 6.3, *LRS* represents the long-run supply schedule if an industry is operating under perfect competition. The perfectly competitive equilibrium would be at output level Q_{pc} with the price at P_{pc}. However, suppose that a monopolist had a strong cost advantage, and was able to produce at constant long-run marginal cost LMC_m. It would then maximise profit by choosing the output Q_m, where MR_m is equal to LMC_m, and would sell at a price P_m. In this situation the monopolist could actually produce more output at a lower price than a firm operating under perfect competition.

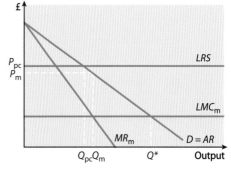

Figure 6.3 Suppose that monopoly offers much better cost conditions

Notice that in the monopoly situation the market does not achieve allocative efficiency, because with these cost conditions, setting price equal to marginal cost would require the firm to produce Q^* output. However, this loss of allocative efficiency is offset by the improvements in productive efficiency that are achieved by the monopoly firm. This is sometimes known as dynamic efficiency, whereas allocative efficiency is a more static concept that considers the best use of existing resources with existing technologies.

It could be argued that the monopolist should be regulated, and forced to produce at Q^*. However, what incentives would this establish for the firm? If a monopolist knows that whenever it makes supernormal profits the regulator will step in and take them away, it will have no incentive to operate efficiently. Indeed, Joseph Schumpeter argued that monopoly profits were an incentive for innovation, and would benefit society, because only with monopoly profits would firms be able to engage in research and development (R&D). In other words, it is only when firms are relatively large, and when they are able to make supernormal profits, that they are able to devote resources to R&D. Small firms operating in a perfectly competitive market do not have the resources or the incentive to be innovative.

Figure 6.4 illustrates a less extreme case. As before, equilibrium under perfect competition produces output at Q_{pc} and price at P_{pc}. The monopoly alternative faces lower long-run marginal cost, although with a less marked difference than before: here the firm produces Q_m output in order to maximise profits, and sets price at P_m.

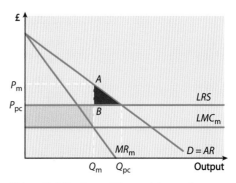

Figure 6.4 Cost conditions again — a less extreme example

Analysis of this situation reveals that there is a deadweight loss given by the red triangle; this reflects the allocative inefficiency of monopoly. However, there is also a gain in productive efficiency represented by the blue rectangle. This is part of monopoly profits, but under perfect competition it was part of production costs. In other words, production under the monopoly is less wasteful in its use of resources in the production process.

Is society better off under monopoly or under perfect competition? In order to evaluate the effect on total welfare, it is necessary to balance the loss of allocative efficiency (the red triangle) against the gain in productive efficiency (the blue rectangle). In Figure 6.4 it would seem that the rectangle is larger than the triangle, so society overall is better off with the monopoly. Of course, there is also the distribution of income to take into account — the area $P_{m}ABP_{pc}$ would be part of consumer surplus under perfect competition, but under monopoly becomes part of the firm's profits.

Contestability

A second important issue concerns contestability, which was introduced in Chapter 4. If barriers to entry into the market are weak, and if the sunk costs of entry and exit are low, the monopoly firm will need to temper its actions to avoid potential entry.

Thus, in judging a market situation, the degree of contestability is important. If the market is perfectly contestable, then the monopoly firm cannot set a price that is above average cost without allowing hit-and-run entry. In this case, the regulator does not need to intervene. Even without perfect contestability, the firm may need to set a price that is not so high as to induce entry. In other words, it may choose not to produce at the profit-maximising level of output, and to set a price below that level.

Concentration and collusion

The structure–conduct–performance argument suggests that it is not only monopolies that should be the subject of competition policy, but any market in which firms have some influence over price. In other words, oligopolies also need careful attention because of the danger that they will collude, and act *as if* they were a joint monopoly. After all, it was argued that where a market has just a small number of sellers there may be a temptation to collude, either in a cartel or tacitly. Government authorities may therefore be wary of markets in which concentration ratios are simply high, even if not 100%.

For this reason, it is important to examine whether a concentrated market is *always* and *necessarily* an anti-competitive market. This is tantamount to asking whether structure necessarily determines conduct. A high concentration ratio may mean that there is a small number of firms of more or less equal size, or it could mean that there is one large firm and a number of smaller competitors. In the latter case you might expect the dominant firm to have sufficient market power to control price.

With a small number of equally sized firms, it is by no means certain that they will agree to collude. They may be very conscious of their respective market shares, and so act in an aggressively competitive way in order to defend them. This may be especially true where the market is not expanding, so that a firm can grow only at the expense of the other firms. Such a market could well display intense competition, causing it to drift towards the competitive end of the scale. This would suggest that the authorities should not presume guilt in a merger investigation, since the pattern of market shares may prove significant in determining the firms' conduct, and hence the performance of the market.

Globalisation

Another significant issue is that a firm that comes to dominate a domestic market may still face competition in the broader global market. This may be especially significant within the Single European Market.

In this regard, there has been a longstanding debate about how a domestic government should behave towards its large firms. Some economists believe that the government should allow such firms to dominate the domestic market in order that they can become 'national champions' in the global market. This has been especially apparent in the airline industry, where some national airlines are heavily subsidised by their national governments in order to allow them to compete internationally. Others have argued that if a large firm faces competition within the domestic market, this should help to encourage its productive efficiency, enabling it to become more capable of coping with international competition.

> ### Exercise 6.1
>
> Discuss the extent to which a firm's performance in terms of efficiency is dictated by the market environment in which it operates.

Summary

- Competition policy refers to a range of measures designed to promote competition in markets and to protect consumers in order to enhance the efficiency of markets in resource allocation.
- One view is that market structure determines the conduct of firms within a market, and this conduct then determines the performance of the market in terms of allocative efficiency.
- A profit-maximising monopolist will produce less output at a higher price than a perfectly competitive market, causing allocative inefficiency.
- However, there may be situations in which the monopolist can enjoy economies of scale, and thereby gain in productive efficiency.
- In the presence of contestability, a monopolist may not be able to charge a price above average cost without encouraging hit-and-run entry.
- In a concentrated market, the pattern of market shares may influence the intensity of competition between firms.
- A firm that is a monopoly in its own country may be exposed to competition in the international markets in which it operates.

Competition policy in the UK

In the UK, competition policy has tended to be less rigid than in the USA, where there has been a natural distrust of monopoly. Policy has therefore been conducted in such a way as to take account of the issues discussed above. This has meant that cases of monopoly or concentrated markets have been judged on their individual merits on a case-by-case basis.

This pragmatic approach was embedded in UK legislation from the start — which was the 1948 Monopolies and Restrictive Practices (Inquiry and Control) Act. This Act set up the Monopolies and Restrictive Practices Commission to investigate markets in which a single firm (or a group of firms in collusion) supplied more than one-third of a market. The commission was asked to decide whether such a market was operating in the public interest, although at that stage the legislation was not very precisely defined.

Since then the legislation has been steadily tightened through a sequence of Acts, the most recent of which are the Competition Act of 1998 and the Enterprise Act of 2002. The Competition Act is in two sections ('chapters'), one dealing with anti-competitive agreements between parties (e.g. firms) and the other dealing with anti-competitive practices by one or more parties — that is, the abuse of a dominant position in a market.

Cartels are covered by Chapter 1 of the 1998 Act, but less formal agreements between firms are also within the scope of the Act: for example, price fixing, agreements to restrict output and agreements to share a market. The Enterprise Act elevated the operation of a cartel to a criminal offence (as opposed to a civil offence).

From April 2014, the conduct of the policy has been entrusted to the Competition and Markets Authority (CMA) (previously it was implemented by two agencies: the Office of Fair Trading (OFT) and the Competition Commission). The CMA investigates mergers and anti-competitive practices in markets. The expectation was that merging the OFT and the Competition Commission into a single body would simplify the implementation of competition policy in the UK, thus avoiding duplication and saving costs. The CMA will also be able to operate with shorter time frames for investigations, reducing the uncertainty faced by firms that find themselves under investigation.

The main functions of the CMA are:

- investigating mergers which could potentially give rise to a substantial lessening of competition (SLC)
- investigating markets to assess particular markets in which there are suspected competition problems
- antitrust enforcement by investigating possible breaches of UK or EU prohibitions against anti-competitive agreements and abuse of a dominant position
- criminal cartels: the CMA is able to bring criminal proceedings against individuals who commit the cartel offence
- consumer protection

A merger is subject to investigation by the CMA if the firms involved in the proposed merger or acquisition have a combined market share in the UK of more than 25% and if the combined assets of the firms exceed £70 million worldwide.

The CMA has a wide range of powers that it can invoke should it find that a merger is likely to result in an SLC. However, there is no presumption that the CMA will find anything wrong with a market, and the result of an investigation may be that a proposed merger raises no concerns about there being an SLC. Indeed, on a number of occasions the CMA's predecessor, the OFT, launched a consumer awareness campaign, having found that the problem with a market lay in the way consumers understood its workings, and not with the market itself.

Probably the best way of understanding how competition policy operates is by exploring an example of how it has worked in practice. First, however, there is a very important issue to be examined.

The relevant market

The first step in any investigation is to identify the **relevant market**. Until the scope of the market has been defined, it is not possible to calculate market shares or concentration ratios.

> ### Key term
>
> **relevant market** a market to be investigated under competition law, defined in such a way that no major substitutes are omitted but no non-substitutes are included

How should the market be defined in this context? In other words, which products should be included? Or over which region should the market be defined? Take the market for sugar — is this defined as the market for all sugar, or just for granulated sugar? Is organic sugar a separate product? Or, regarding the market for rail travel in Scotland, do bus services need to be considered as part of the Scottish market for travel?

One way of addressing this question is to apply the *hypothetical monopoly test*. Under this approach, the product market is defined as the smallest set of products and producers in which a hypothetical monopolist controlling all such products could raise profits by a small increase in price above the competitive level.

Extension material

The hypothetical monopoly test is effectively a question about substitution. If in a hypothetical market an increase in price will induce consumers to switch to a substitute product, then the market has not been defined sufficiently widely for it to be regarded as a monopoly. This is demand-side substitutability. One way of evaluating it would be to consult the cross-price elasticity of demand — if it could be measured. This would determine which products were perceived as substitutes for each other by consumers.

For example, in 2003 a number of supermarkets put in bids to take over the Safeway chain. The first step in the investigation was to define the relevant market. One issue that was raised was whether discount stores such as Lidl and Aldi, which sell a limited range of groceries, should be considered part of the same market as supermarkets selling a wide range of grocery products. In the south of the country, the cross-price elasticity of Sainsbury's demand was 0.05 with respect to Lidl's price, but 1.48 with respect to Tesco's price. This suggested that Sainsbury and Tesco were in the same market, but Lidl was not.

It is also important to consider the question of substitutes on the supply side: in other words, whether an increase in price may induce suppliers to join the market. Supply-side substitutability is related to the notion of contestability, in the sense that one way a market can be seen to be contestable is if other firms can switch readily into it — that is, if there are potential substitutes.

An example of an investigation: airports

BAA plc

In 1987 the British Airports Authority was privatised, and BAA plc was established. The new company was responsible for the airports that had previously been under the aegis of the British Airports Authority — namely, the three London airports (Heathrow, Gatwick and Stansted), plus airports in Scotland (Aberdeen, Edinburgh, Glasgow and Prestwick). Prestwick was sold in 1991, and Southampton was acquired in 1990. This meant that BAA plc had an effective monopoly on flights in and out of London and a stranglehold on flights in and out of Scotland.

One of the objectives in setting up BAA plc was to have a single enterprise that would be able to take strategic decisions to plan ahead, and to provide the airport capacity needed to meet the expected growth in demand. In addition, it was hoped that the provision of the infrastructure needed for air travel would help to encourage competition amongst the airlines providing the transport services.

In the event, things did not work out well, and after 20 years of operation, BAA plc was seen to have failed to provide sufficient capacity to meet demand in the South East region. There was also mounting criticism of the way that BAA was managing its airports — especially Heathrow. In March 2007, the OFT referred the case to the Competition Commission for investigation under the Enterprise Act 2002. The brief for the investigation was 'to investigate whether any feature, or combination of features, of the market or markets for airport services in the UK as exist in connection with the supply of airport services by BAA Limited prevents, restricts or distorts competition in connection with the supply or acquisition of any goods or services in the UK or a part of the UK. If so there is an "adverse effect on competition"' (Competition Commission, 2008).

In terms of market share, it was clear that BAA was in a very strong position. The Competition Commission noted that its seven airports accounted for more than 60% of all passengers using UK airports. In the South East, Heathrow, Gatwick, Stansted and Southampton between them accounted for 90% of air passengers; in Scotland, 84% of air passengers were accounted for by Edinburgh, Glasgow and Aberdeen. The key issue is whether this market position was damaging competition, and hence working against consumer interests.

BAA's dominant market position was found to be having an adverse effect on competition

Competition between airports

An important aspect of this is whether there is scope for competition between airports, and what effect such competition would have on the nature and quality of service that would be offered. In order to approach this question, the Competition Commission looked at evidence relating to non-BAA airports that could be regarded as being in potential competition with each other — for example, Birmingham International Airport and East Midlands Airport, Cardiff International Airport and Bristol International Airport, and other combinations. Some evidence was found which suggested that there could be competition between airports, particularly in relation to the low-cost airlines. However, competition is most likely where there is spare capacity — which is not the case for Heathrow and Gatwick.

Competition also requires there to be the potential for substitution in demand. In other words, there needs to be some overlap in the potential catchment area for competing airports. In relation to BAA's airports in Scotland, it was found that there was some overlap in catchment between Glasgow and Edinburgh — but not with Aberdeen. In the South East, there was little evidence of competition between BAA's London airports and non-BAA airports (apart from some competition between Southampton and Bournemouth). However, there was significant overlap in the catchment areas of these airports, suggesting the possibility of some competition (subject to capacity constraints).

The Competition Commission came to the view that the shortage of capacity in the South East had partly arisen from the common ownership of the three BAA London airports, and that had these airports been under separate ownership, the incentives to expand capacity and improve the quality of service being offered would have been higher.

Having concluded that there was evidence that the market structure was having an adverse effect on competition, the Competition Commission in its provisional findings recommended that BAA should sell two of its three airports in the South East, and should not be allowed to continue to own airports in both Glasgow and Edinburgh.

Since that time, BAA has become Heathrow Airport Holdings Ltd, owning four airports: Heathrow, Southampton, Glasgow and Aberdeen. It sold Gatwick in 2009, Edinburgh and Prestwick in 2012, and Stansted in 2013. Southampton Airport was acquired by AGS Airports in 2014.

Study tip

Although it is helpful to be aware of case studies like this, do not spend lots of time studying the details. What is important is that you understand the underlying economic analysis that underpins the work of the CMA.

Competition policy in the European Union

With increasing integration within the European Union (EU), it has become important to be able to investigate possible monopoly situations that arise at an EU level. Accordingly, the EU has a competition policy that enables it to investigate potential abuse of market power when such abuse transcends national borders.

The stance adopted in EU policy has been consistent with that of member countries; indeed, the structure of EU competition policy has informed UK legislation. With expanding globalisation, it may be important to coordinate policy still more widely, but this is likely to be problematic. For example, Microsoft went on trial in the USA for alleged predatory action in the way that it had launched its internet browser; although initially the judgment went against it, there followed a lengthy appeal. The EU then launched its own court action against Microsoft, making similar allegations about the way it marketed its media player.

Summary

- Competition policy in the UK is implemented through the Competition and Markets Authority, which replaced the Office of Fair Trading and the Competition Commission in April 2014.
- The main pillars of policy are legislation dealing with agreements between firms and the abuse of a dominant position.
- A key step in any investigation is to define the relevant market.
- The CMA carries out a preliminary investigation of mergers that meet the criteria in terms of market share and size of assets.
- It then decides whether to initiate a thorough investigation.
- Some mergers are allowed to proceed without referral.
- The CMA may permit the merger to go ahead, may impose conditions on the firm, or may prohibit it.

Regulation of privatised industries

Chapter 2 noted the case of the natural monopoly, and hinted that this poses particular problems with regard to allocative efficiency. Figure 6.5 involves an industry with substantial economies of scale relative to market demand — indeed, the minimum efficient scale is beyond the market demand curve. (In other words, long-run average cost is still falling beyond market demand.)

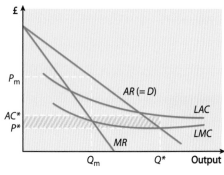

Figure 6.5 A natural monopoly

This market is almost bound to end up as a monopoly because the largest firm is always able to dominate the market and undercut smaller competitors, as it has a natural cost leadership position. If the monopoly chooses to maximise profits, it will set marginal revenue equal to marginal cost, choose output Q_m and set price at P_m.

Such industries tend to have large fixed costs relative to marginal costs. Railway systems, water or gas supply and electricity generation are all examples of natural monopolies.

The key problem is that, if such firms were forced to set a price equal to marginal cost, they would make a loss. If the firm in Figure 6.5 were required to set price equal to marginal cost (i.e. at $P\star$) then it would not be viable: average cost would be $AC\star$, with losses represented by the shaded area on the diagram.

In the past, one response to this situation would have been to nationalise the industry (i.e. take it into state ownership), since no private sector firm would be prepared to operate at a loss, and the government would not allow firms running such natural monopolies to act as profit-maximising monopolists making supernormal profits.

In order to prevent the losses from becoming too substantial, many utilities such as gas and electricity supply adopted a pricing system known as a *two-part tariff system*, under which all consumers paid a monthly charge for being connected to the supply, and on top of that a variable amount based on usage. In terms of Figure 6.5, the connection charge would cover the difference between $AC^\star$ and $P^\star$, spread across all consumers, and the variable charge would reflect marginal cost.

However, as time went by this sort of system came to be heavily criticised. In particular, it was argued that the managers of the nationalised industries were insufficiently accountable. The situation could be regarded as an extreme form of the principal–agent problem, in which the consumers (the principals) had very little control over the actions of the managers (their agents), a situation leading to considerable X-inefficiency and waste.

In the 1980s such criticism led to widespread privatisation (i.e. the transfer of nationalised industries into private ownership), one central argument being that now at least the managers would have to be accountable to their shareholders, which would encourage an increase in efficiency.

However, this did not remove the original problem: that these industries were natural monopolies. Therefore, wherever possible, privatisation was also accompanied by measures to encourage competition, which was seen as an even better way to ensure efficiency improvements. This proved to be more feasible in some industries than in others because of the nature of economies of scale — there is little to be gained by requiring that there must be several firms in a market where the economies of scale can be reaped only by one large firm. However, the changing technology in some of the industries did allow some competition to be encouraged, especially in telecommunications.

Where it was not possible, or feasible, to encourage competition, regulation was seen as the solution. Attention of the regulatory bodies focused on price, and the key control method was to allow price increases each year at a rate that was a set amount below changes in the retail price index (RPI). This became known as the $(RPI - X)$

Electricity generation is an example of a natural monopoly

contracting out a situation in which the public sector places activities in the hands of a private firm and pays for the provision

competitive tendering a process by which the public sector calls for private firms to bid for a contract to provide a good or service

public–private partnership (PPP) an arrangement by which a government service or private business venture is funded and operated through a partnership of government and the private sector

Private Finance Initiative (PFI) a funding arrangement under which the private sector designs, builds, finances and operates an asset and associated services for the public sector in return for an annual payment linked to its performance in delivering the service

The simplest form of this is **contracting out**. Under such an arrangement, the public sector issues a contract to a private firm for the supply of some good or service. One example is waste disposal, where a local authority may issue a contract for a firm to provide the necessary waste disposal service. Competition between firms can be encouraged by a **competitive tendering** process. In other words, the contract would be announced and firms invited to put in bids specifying the quality of service they are prepared to provide, and at what price. The local authority would then be in a position to look for efficiency in choosing the most competitive bid.

More complex models of cooperation between public and private sectors have been developed, involving various kinds of **public–private partnership** (PPP). A PPP is 'an arrangement by which a government service or private business venture is funded and operated through a partnership of government and the private sector' (National Audit Office). The most common partnership model is the **Private Finance Initiative** (PFI).

The Private Finance Initiative

The PFI was launched in 1992 as a way of trying to increase the involvement of the private sector in the provision of public services. This established a partnership between the public and private sectors. The public sector specifies, perhaps in broad terms, the services that it requires, and then invites tenders from the private sector to design, build, finance and operate the scheme. In some cases, it may be that the project would be entirely free-standing — for example, the government may initiate a project such as a new bridge, which is then taken up by a private firm that will recover its costs entirely through user charges such as tolls. In some other cases, the project may be a joint venture between the public and private sectors. The public sector could get involved with such a venture in order to secure wider social benefits, perhaps through reductions in traffic congestion that would not be reflected in market prices, and thus would not be fully taken into account by the private sector. In other cases, it may be that the private sector undertakes a project and then sells the services to the public sector, often over a period of 25 or 30 years.

Figure 6.6 shows the range of PFI deals that were signed during the first 10 years of the scheme: you can see that a sizeable proportion of these were in transport. These included projects involving road construction, street lighting, bridges and rail projects. The largest project in this period was the Channel Tunnel Rail Link (£4,178 million), signed in 2000. Subsequently, projects involving the London Underground were signed in 2003, totalling £10,695 million. The pattern changed over the years, and Figure 6.7 shows the government departments involved in current PFI projects as at March 2013. These projects included the funding of new schools and hospitals, for example.

The aim of the PFI is to improve the financing of public sector projects. This is partly achieved by introducing a competitive element into the tendering process, but in addition it enables the risk of a project to be shared between the public and private sectors. This was intended to enable efficiency gains to be made.

Ofgem claims that the best way to protect customers' interests is through the promotion of competition between suppliers. A review published in 2004 estimated that around 50% of customers had switched their supplier of gas or electricity. The ease of switching supplier is, of course, crucial if effective competition is to be a way of holding prices at a competitive level. High switching costs are a disincentive to switching.

Research quoted by Ofgem indicates that suppliers lose customers when they increase their prices, and Ofgem claims that this is evidence that competition is working.

A cautionary note is struck by the observation that non-price factors such as brand and marketing methods are increasing in importance, and there have been occasional items on television programmes such as BBC's *Watchdog* about high-pressure door-to-door sales methods used to try to get customers to change supplier. Indeed, Ofgem imposed a £2 million penalty on London Electricity (now EDF Energy) for mis-selling, after which complaints about high-pressure sales methods fell by 60%.

Thus, Ofgem's current strategy is to monitor the energy market and find ways of stimulating greater competition among suppliers. The focus is especially on facilitating switching between suppliers and lowering barriers to the entry of new suppliers.

Summary

- Natural monopolies pose particular problems for policy, as setting price equal to marginal cost forces such firms to make a loss.
- In the past, many such industries were run by the state as nationalised industries.
- However, this led to widespread X-inefficiency.
- Many of these industries were privatised after 1979.
- Regulation was put into place to ensure that the newly privatised firms did not abuse their market positions.
- Prices were controlled through the application of the $(RPI - X)$ rule.
- In some cases, regulatory capture was a problem, whereby the regulators became too close to their industries.

Exercise 6.4

How does the principal-agent argument help to explain why nationalised industries may become inefficient? How does privatisation (with regulation) attempt to remedy this situation?

Other interventions to promote competition

There are other ways in which governments intervene in order to promote competition, reflecting the view that this is the best way of ensuring consumer protection and good resource allocation.

Public–private partnerships

It has been recognised that the same arguments that apply to the impact of competition on private sector efficiency are also relevant for public sector activity. In the case of public goods, there has to be some sort of government involvement as a free market will not ensure the provision of these goods. However, this does not necessarily mean that the public sector has to provide these goods directly. A number of ways in which the public sector can ensure provision through some sort of engagement with the private sector have been developed.

Study tip

Public goods were discussed in Chapter 7 of Book 1.

The simplest form of this is **contracting out**. Under such an arrangement, the public sector issues a contract to a private firm for the supply of some good or service. One example is waste disposal, where a local authority may issue a contract for a firm to provide the necessary waste disposal service. Competition between firms can be encouraged by a **competitive tendering** process. In other words, the contract would be announced and firms invited to put in bids specifying the quality of service they are prepared to provide, and at what price. The local authority would then be in a position to look for efficiency in choosing the most competitive bid.

More complex models of cooperation between public and private sectors have been developed, involving various kinds of **public–private partnership** (PPP). A PPP is 'an arrangement by which a government service or private business venture is funded and operated through a partnership of government and the private sector' (National Audit Office). The most common partnership model is the **Private Finance Initiative** (PFI).

The Private Finance Initiative

The PFI was launched in 1992 as a way of trying to increase the involvement of the private sector in the provision of public services. This established a partnership between the public and private sectors. The public sector specifies, perhaps in broad terms, the services that it requires, and then invites tenders from the private sector to design, build, finance and operate the scheme. In some cases, it may be that the project would be entirely free-standing — for example, the government may initiate a project such as a new bridge, which is then taken up by a private firm that will recover its costs entirely through user charges such as tolls. In some other cases, the project may be a joint venture between the public and private sectors. The public sector could get involved with such a venture in order to secure wider social benefits, perhaps through reductions in traffic congestion that would not be reflected in market prices, and thus would not be fully taken into account by the private sector. In other cases, it may be that the private sector undertakes a project and then sells the services to the public sector, often over a period of 25 or 30 years.

Figure 6.6 shows the range of PFI deals that were signed during the first 10 years of the scheme: you can see that a sizeable proportion of these were in transport. These included projects involving road construction, street lighting, bridges and rail projects. The largest project in this period was the Channel Tunnel Rail Link (£4,178 million), signed in 2000. Subsequently, projects involving the London Underground were signed in 2003, totalling £10,695 million. The pattern changed over the years, and Figure 6.7 shows the government departments involved in current PFI projects as at March 2013. These projects included the funding of new schools and hospitals, for example.

The aim of the PFI is to improve the financing of public sector projects. This is partly achieved by introducing a competitive element into the tendering process, but in addition it enables the risk of a project to be shared between the public and private sectors. This was intended to enable efficiency gains to be made.

In order to prevent the losses from becoming too substantial, many utilities such as gas and electricity supply adopted a pricing system known as a *two-part tariff system*, under which all consumers paid a monthly charge for being connected to the supply, and on top of that a variable amount based on usage. In terms of Figure 6.5, the connection charge would cover the difference between $AC^\star$ and $P^\star$, spread across all consumers, and the variable charge would reflect marginal cost.

However, as time went by this sort of system came to be heavily criticised. In particular, it was argued that the managers of the nationalised industries were insufficiently accountable. The situation could be regarded as an extreme form of the principal–agent problem, in which the consumers (the principals) had very little control over the actions of the managers (their agents), a situation leading to considerable X-inefficiency and waste.

In the 1980s such criticism led to widespread privatisation (i.e. the transfer of nationalised industries into private ownership), one central argument being that now at least the managers would have to be accountable to their shareholders, which would encourage an increase in efficiency.

However, this did not remove the original problem: that these industries were natural monopolies. Therefore, wherever possible, privatisation was also accompanied by measures to encourage competition, which was seen as an even better way to ensure efficiency improvements. This proved to be more feasible in some industries than in others because of the nature of economies of scale — there is little to be gained by requiring that there must be several firms in a market where the economies of scale can be reaped only by one large firm. However, the changing technology in some of the industries did allow some competition to be encouraged, especially in telecommunications.

Where it was not possible, or feasible, to encourage competition, regulation was seen as the solution. Attention of the regulatory bodies focused on price, and the key control method was to allow price increases each year at a rate that was a set amount below changes in the retail price index (RPI). This became known as the $(RPI - X)$

Electricity generation is an example of a natural monopoly

rule, and was widely used, the idea being that it would force companies to look for productivity gains to eliminate the inefficiency that had built up. The X refers to the amount of productivity gain that the regulator believes can be achieved, expressed in terms of the change in average costs. For example, if the regulator believed that it was possible to achieve productivity gains of 5% per year, and if the RPI was increasing at a rate of 10% per year, then the maximum price increase that would be allowed in a year would be $10\% - 5\% = 5\%$.

There are problems inherent in this approach. For example, how does the regulator set X? This is problematic in a situation where the company has better information about costs than the regulator — another instance of the problems caused by the existence of asymmetric information. There is also the possibility that the firm will achieve its productivity gains by reducing the quality of the product, or by neglecting long-term investment for the future and allowing maintenance standards to lapse.

It is also important to realise that as time goes by, if the $(RPI - X)$ system is effective, the inefficiency will be gradually squeezed out, and the X will have to be reduced as it becomes ever more difficult to achieve productivity gains.

In the case of water supply, the regulator Ofwat has adopted a variant of the rule. Water companies must set prices in accordance with $(RPI + k)$, where RPI is the change in the RPI and k is Ofwat's estimate of how much is needed for capital investment.

In some cases, **regulatory capture** is a further problem. This occurs when the regulator becomes so closely involved with the firm it is supposed to be regulating that it begins to champion its cause rather than imposing tough rules where they are needed.

An alternative method of regulation would be to place a limit on the rate of return the firm is permitted to make, thereby preventing it from making supernormal profits. This too may affect the incentive mechanism: the firm may not feel the need to be as efficient as possible, or may fritter away some of the profits in managerial perks to avoid declaring too high a rate of return.

Key term

regulatory capture a situation in which the regulator of an industry comes to represent the industry's interests rather than regulating it

Gas and electricity supply

As an example of regulation, consider the gas and electricity supply sector. British Gas was privatised in 1986, and the electricity sector followed in 1989. These industries have a joint regulator known as Ofgem. They have a joint regulator because together they comprise the energy market.

The energy market in the early twenty-first century is structured as three sub-markets: the wholesale markets, the delivery system and the retail markets.

The delivery sector, which is sometimes referred to as the 'pipes and wires' business, remains a monopoly — or, rather, a sequence of geographical monopolies. These companies run the gas and electricity transportation networks. They are subject to price control using the $(RPI - X)$ rule, and the value of X is reviewed every 5 years.

In the wholesale and retail segments, competition has been encouraged. The retail gas market was opened fully to competition in 1998, and the electricity market followed in 1999 — to the extent that price regulation ended in 2002. The wholesale market is now going through a process of reform.

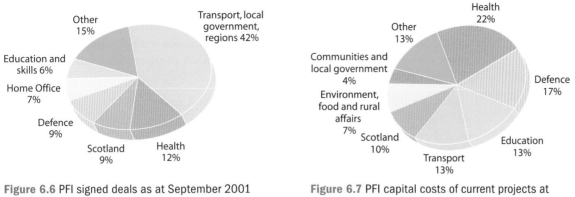

Figure 6.6 PFI signed deals as at September 2001

Source for both figures: HM Treasury

Figure 6.7 PFI capital costs of current projects at March 2013

The PFI has been much debated — and much criticised. One effect of the PFI is to reduce the pressures on public finances by enabling greater private sector involvement in funding. However, it might be argued that this may in fact raise the cost of borrowing, if the public sector would have been able to borrow on more favourable terms than commercial firms. The introduction of a competitive element in the tendering process may be beneficial, but on the other hand it could be argued that the private sector may have less incentive than the public sector to give due attention to health and safety issues. In other words, there may be a concern that private firms will be tempted to sacrifice safety or service standards in the quest for profit. Achieving the appropriate balance between efficiency and quality of service is an inevitable problem to be faced in whatever way transport is financed and provided, for example, but it becomes a more critical issue to the extent that use of the PFI switches the focus more towards efficiency and lower costs.

PFI deals often involve major road construction projects

Encouragement of small businesses

There are measures in place to encourage small businesses. One example of this was in the wake of the financial crisis, a time when the UK government was keen to restore confidence in the economy.

The Department of Business Innovation and Skills (BIS) noted that small and medium-sized enterprises (SMEs) provide 'nearly 60% of our jobs and 50% of GDP'. A new set of measures to help small businesses was launched in 2010/11, including steps to improve access to finance for small businesses and to provide other forms of support. The underlying rationale for these measures was to help small businesses to compete more effectively, and to provide targeted support to small firms with high growth potential.

One of the features of the financial crisis was that banks became reluctant to lend, causing particular problems for small firms in need of funding for investment. Banks faced a severe crisis, and some needed government assistance to bail them out of trouble. This was perhaps one of the largest-scale interventions of recent decades. Its prime aim was not to promote competition, but this was one of its side-effects through the encouragement for banks to lend to small businesses.

> **Synoptic link**
>
> The roots of the financial crisis and its effects are discussed under Theme 4 in Chapters 13 and 14.

The main focus of the work of the CMA is on mergers and markets in which there could potentially be problems with firms gaining a dominant position. In the past, the Competition Commission has also identified issues with competition involving a monopsony, rather than a monopoly position. A high-profile example involved UK supermarkets.

Large supermarkets form a large part of the food industry in the UK, providing consumers with low prices and a wide variety of products. However, issues were raised about the way in which some of the supermarkets were treating their suppliers and farmers. When small farmers are supplying supermarkets that have substantial buying power, there is a possibility of the exploitation of market power. In December 2012, the competition minister announced that the Groceries Code Adjudicator was to be given greater powers to enforce the Groceries Code, providing additional protection for farmers and other suppliers, including the ability to fine supermarkets that transgress the code. In February 2015 it was announced that the Adjudicator was launching an investigation into Tesco following allegations that it had delayed payments to some suppliers and treated payments for shelf promotions unfairly.

The impact of government intervention

It is clear that successive UK governments have taken serious action to promote competition, using a variety of tools and approaches. The assumption underpinning this approach to intervention is that competition encourages firms to be efficient, as firms that fail to reach efficiency in their activities will lose out to their rivals, making lower profits and gaining lower market shares — and perhaps being forced out of the market altogether.

At the same time, competition should also ensure that consumers face reasonable prices, with good-quality products and variety of choice. Indeed, the whole basis of the market system is that the consumer is king, and firms only make profit when they are producing the products that consumers wish to buy.

How effective has all this intervention been in practice? This is difficult to evaluate, as it is not possible to observe how things would look in the absence of intervention. There have been instances where the CMA or its predecessors have stepped in to prohibit a merger or acquisition, or have set conditions that safeguard consumer interests. The number of merger cases that are brought to the attention of the CMA seems high, but many of these are ruled not to be contentious or not meeting the threshold rules for investigation. In any case, it might be argued that the very existence of the CMA with its powers to intervene may act as a deterrent to anti-competitive actions.

Is monopoly always bad? Microsoft reached a position in which it supplied 95% of the global market for operating systems for PCs. It was argued that this was not because of abusing a dominant market position, but because it was very good at what it did. Are firms like Amazon and Google reaching market dominance because they are building market power? Or because they are providing a service that consumers want?

Is competition always good? When a local shop goes out of business because it cannot compete with the prices and variety of choice offered by the supermarkets, do consumers end up with less choice, or with more choice?

There are no simple answers to these questions, but endless possibilities for debate and for watching how markets evolve into the future.

Summary

- Governments intervene in a variety of ways to promote competition.
- The authorities have also attempted to encourage efficiency through the establishment of public–private partnerships, such as the Private Finance Initiative.
- Support has been provided to help small businesses, particularly with access to finance.
- The Groceries Code Adjudicator holds a watching brief to ensure that supermarkets do not abuse their monopsony power.
- Evaluating the impact of intervention is not straightforward, but the existence of legislation and monitoring by the CMA may deter firms from acting against consumer interests.

Case study 6.1

Cinemas in Basingstoke and Edinburgh

In September 2005, the OFT referred to the Competition Commission (CC) a completed takeover of Ster Century by Vue Entertainment Holdings. Before the merger, Vue was the third largest operator of cinemas in the UK, with 42 cinemas and 409 screens; Ster owned and operated 6 cinemas in the UK with 73 screens; these were located in Basingstoke, Cardiff, Edinburgh, Leeds, Norwich and Romford.

In investigating the merger, the CC had first to define what was the relevant market. It decided to restrict the market definition to cinema exhibition, and that the appropriate scale for market investigation was a local geographic area. The main focus was on cinemas within a 20-minute drive-time of the acquired cinemas. Evidence suggested that cinema-goers tend to decide which film they wish to see first of all, and then where to see it as a secondary decision, normally going to the closest cinema, although there may be some variation in the quality of cinema, which may be reflected in ticket prices. It was not thought that the merger would significantly increase Vue's negotiating position with screen advertising contracts, distributors or other suppliers, so there would not be an impact at the national level.

In Basingstoke, the merger meant that Vue owned the only two cinemas within a 20-minute drive of the city. Vue argued that it was in competition with cinemas in Winchester, Alton, Bracknell, Reading and Woking, but the CC did not find this to be a strong argument. As a result, a substantial lessening of competition (SLC) was expected to occur, which was likely to lead to higher prices for cinema tickets and a reduced incentive to maintain quality.

The situation in Edinburgh was quite different. After the merger there were still a 'significant number of competing cinemas and screens' in the city. The CC therefore took the view that there would be no SLC resulting from the merger in this case.

Vue mounted a defence of its position in Basingstoke. One argument put forward related to the market for DVDs, claiming that the DVD market was constraining cinemas in their pricing policy. In addition, Vue offered to agree a price cap, restricting any increase in ticket price in Basingstoke to the average percentage ticket price rise across the whole Vue cinema circuit for each type of ticket. Vue also promised to maintain quality by spending at least as much as the average across its circuit on site maintenance. It also promised to keep both cinemas open, and to offer a broad range of films to ensure consumer choice.

Follow-up questions

a Explain what is meant by 'relevant market' and why it is important for an investigation of this sort.

b Why might it be important to check whether the merger would significantly affect Vue's bargaining power with its suppliers?

c How convincing do you find Vue's defence?

d What decision would you have taken if you had been the CC?

Theme 3 key words

allocative efficiency achieved when society is producing the appropriate bundle of goods and services relative to consumer preferences

arbitrage a process by which prices in two market segments are equalised by the purchase and resale of products by market participants

average cost total cost divided by the quantity produced

backward integration a process under which a firm merges with a firm that is involved in an earlier part of the production chain

barrier to entry a characteristic of a market that prevents new firms from readily joining the market

cartel an agreement between firms on price and output with the intention of maximising their joint profits

competition policy a set of measures designed to promote competition in markets and protect consumers in order to enhance the efficiency of markets

competitive tendering a process by which the public sector calls for private firms to bid for a contract to provide a good or service

conglomerate merger a merger between two firms operating in different markets

constant returns to scale found when long-run average cost remains constant with an increase in output, i.e. when output and costs rise at the same rate

contestable market a market in which the existing firm makes only normal profit, as it cannot set a higher price without attracting entry, owing to the absence of barriers to entry and sunk costs

contracting out a situation in which the public sector places activities in the hands of a private firm and pays for the provision

corporate social responsibility actions that a firm takes in order to demonstrate its commitment to behaving in the public interest

cost-plus pricing a pricing policy whereby firms set their price by adding a mark-up to average cost

derived demand demand for a good or service not for its own sake, but for what it produces, e.g. labour is demanded for the output that it produces

diseconomies of scale occur for a firm when an increase in the scale of production leads to higher long-run average costs

dominant strategy a situation in game theory where a player's best strategy is independent of those chosen by others

dynamic efficiency a view of efficiency that takes into account the effect of innovation and technical progress on productive and allocative efficiency in the long run

economies of scale what happens if an increase in a firm's scale of production leads to production at lower long-run average cost

economies of scope economies arising when average costs fall as a firm increases output across a range of different products

external economies of scale economies of scale that arise from the expansion of the industry in which a firm is operating

firm an organisation that brings together factors of production in order to produce output

fixed costs costs that do not vary with the level of output

forward integration a process under which a firm merges with a firm that is involved in a later part of the production chain

game theory a method of modelling the strategic interaction between firms in an oligopoly

horizontal integration the result of a horizontal merger

horizontal merger a merger between two firms at the same stage of production in the same industry

industry long-run supply curve (*LRS*) under perfect competition, the curve that, for the typical firm in the industry, is horizontal at the minimum point of the long-run average cost curve

internal economies of scale economies of scale that arise from the expansion of a firm

law of diminishing returns a law stating that if a firm increases its inputs of one factor of production while holding inputs of the other factor fixed, it will eventually derive diminishing marginal returns from the variable factor

limit price the highest price that an existing firm can set without enabling new firms to enter the market and make a profit

long run the period over which the firm is able to vary the inputs of all its factors of production

marginal cost the cost of producing an additional unit of output

marginal physical product of labour (*MPP*$_L$) the additional quantity of output produced by an additional unit of labour input

marginal productivity theory a theory which argues that the demand for labour depends upon balancing the revenue that a firm gains from employing an additional unit of labour against the marginal cost of that unit of labour

marginal revenue the additional revenue gained by a firm from selling an additional unit of output

marginal revenue product of labour (*MRP*$_L$) the additional revenue received by a firm as it increases output by using an additional unit of labour input, i.e. the marginal physical product of labour multiplied by the marginal revenue received by the firm

market structure the market environment within which firms operate

minimum efficient scale the level of output at which long-run average cost stops falling as output increases

minimum wage a government-set minimum wage rate below which firms are not allowed to pay

monopolistic competition a market that shares some characteristics of monopoly and some of perfect competition

monopoly a form of market structure in which there is only one seller of a good or service

monopsony a market in which there is a single buyer of a good, service or factor of production

multinational corporation a firm that conducts its operations in a number of countries

n-firm concentration ratio a measure of the market share of the largest *n* firms in an industry

Nash equilibrium a situation occurring within a game when each player's chosen strategy maximises payoffs given the other player's choice, so that no player has an incentive to alter behaviour

natural monopoly monopoly that arises in an industry in which there are such substantial economies of scale that only one firm is viable

non-pecuniary benefits benefits offered to workers by firms that are not financial in nature

normal profit profit that covers the opportunity cost of capital and is just sufficient to keep the firm in the market

oligopoly a market with a few sellers, in which each firm must take account of the behaviour and likely behaviour of rival firms in the industry

oligopsony a market in which there are a few buyers of a good, service or factor of production

overt collusion a situation in which firms openly work together to agree on prices or market shares

participation rate the proportion of the population of working age who are in employment or seeking work

perfect competition a form of market structure that produces allocative and productive efficiency in long-run equilibrium

perfect/first-degree price discrimination a situation arising in a market whereby a monopoly firm is able to charge each consumer a different price

predatory pricing an anti-competitive strategy in which a firm sets price below average variable cost in an attempt to force a rival or rivals out of the market and achieve market dominance

price taker a firm that must accept whatever price is set in the market as a whole

principal–agent (agency) problem a problem arising from conflict between the objectives of the principals and those of the agents who take decisions on their behalf

prisoners' dilemma an example of game theory with a range of applications in oligopoly theory

Private Finance Initiative (PFI) a funding arrangement under which the private sector designs, builds, finances and operates an asset and associated services for the public sector in return for an annual payment linked to its performance in delivering the service

product differentiation a strategy adopted by firms that marks their product as being different from their competitors'

productive efficiency occurs when firms have chosen appropriate combinations of factors of production and produce the maximum output possible from those inputs, thus producing at minimum long-run average cost

public–private partnership (PPP) an arrangement by which a government service or private business venture is funded and operated through a partnership of government and the private sector

regulatory capture a situation in which the regulator of an industry comes to represent the industry's interests rather than regulating it

relevant market a market to be investigated under competition law, defined in such a way that no major substitutes are omitted but no non-substitutes are included

satisficing behaviour under which the managers of firms aim to produce satisfactory results for the firm, e.g. in terms of profits, rather than trying to maximise them

short run the period over which a firm is free to vary the input of one of its factors of production (labour), but faces a fixed input of the other (capital)

short-run supply curve for a firm operating under perfect competition, the curve given by its short-run marginal cost curve above the price at which $MC = SAVC$; for the industry, the horizontal sum of the supply curves of the individual firms

static efficiency efficiency at a particular point in time

sunk costs short-run costs that cannot be recovered if the firm closes down

supernormal profits/abnormal profits/economic profit terms referring to profits that exceed normal profit

tacit collusion a situation occurring when firms refrain from competing on price, but without communication or formal agreement between them

third-degree price discrimination a situation in which a firm is able to charge groups of consumers a different price for the same product

variable costs costs that vary with the level of output

vertical merger a merger between two firms in the same industry, but at different stages of the production process

X-inefficiency a situation arising when a firm is not operating at minimum cost, perhaps because of organisational slack

Theme 3 Practice questions

1 Business growth and objectives

1 In 1999, Exxon, the leading US oil company, paid $81 billion to buy Mobil, another oil company. This deal was approved by the US government following a promise that the two would sell more than 2,400 gasoline (petrol) stations across the country. This takeover is an example of:
 A Vertical integration
 B Diversification
 C Conglomerate integration
 D Horizontal integration

2 A chocolate manufacturer buys a group of cocoa producers. This is an example of:
 A Forward vertical integration
 B Horizontal integration
 C Conglomerate integration
 D Backward vertical integration

3 A rise in long-run average costs necessarily indicates that the firm is experiencing:
 A Diminishing returns
 B Increasing returns to scale
 C Diseconomies of scale
 D Increasing revenues

4 Figure 1 shows the short-run cost curves of a firm.

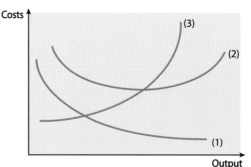

Figure 1 Short-run cost curves of a firm

Which of the following is correct?
 A Curve (1) is the average total cost curve
 B Curve (1) is the total cost curve
 C Curve (2) is the average fixed cost curve
 D Curve (3) is the marginal cost curve

5 X-inefficiency occurs when a firm:
  A Is producing at the lowest marginal cost
  B Is operating above its long-run average cost curve
  C Sets price equal to marginal cost
  D Is producing more goods than are demanded

6 A firm that aims to maximise profits will produce the output at which:
  A The marginal revenue is zero
  B Total cost is equal to total revenue
  C The difference between total revenue and total cost is greatest
  D Average revenue is less than average cost

7 In the short run, a firm will continue in business so long as:
  A Average revenue is greater than marginal cost
  B Average revenue is greater than average variable cost
  C Marginal cost is greater than marginal revenue
  D Average revenue is greater than average fixed cost

2 Market structure: perfect competition and monopoly

1 Which of the following may be found under conditions of perfect competition?
  A Product differentiation
  B Barriers to the entry of new firms
  C Price discrimination
  D An individual firm faces a perfectly elastic demand curve

2 A firm operating in a perfectly competitive market is currently making supernormal profits. In the long run:
  A There will be an increase in the price of the product
  B The firm's output and price will fall
  C The firm will continue to make supernormal profits
  D Firms will leave the industry

3 A perfectly competitive firm's total costs for various levels of output are shown in the table below:

Units of output	1	2	3	4	5	6	7	8	9	10
Total cost (pence)	7	13	18	22	25	29	34	40	47	55

If the market price is 6p, which of the following ranges of output would a profit-maximising firm choose to produce?
  A 1–2
  B 3–4
  C 5–6
  D 7–8

4 A profit-maximising monopolist will produce the output at which:
  A Marginal revenue is zero
  B Price is equal to marginal cost
  C Marginal cost is equal to marginal revenue
  D The difference between marginal revenue and marginal cost is greatest

5 The monopoly power of a business will tend to rise if:
  A Barriers to the entry of new firms increase
  B It diversifies into new product lines
  C There is a rise in monopoly profits
  D There is a reduction in tariffs on similar goods

6 A necessary condition for a monopolist to practise price discrimination is that:

A The price elasticity of demand must be the same in both markets

B The two markets must be geographically separate

C The cost of separating the two markets must be greater than the revenue obtained from charging different prices in the two markets

D The markets must be completely separated

3 Market structure: monopolistic competition and oligopoly

1 A monopolistically competitive firm is in long-run equilibrium. Which of the following applies to such a firm?

	Allocative efficiency	Productive efficiency	Supernormal profit
A	Yes	No	No
B	No	No	Yes
C	No	Yes	Yes
D	No	No	No

2 Which of the following conditions is most likely to explain the small number of firms controlling over 90% of the market for detergents?

A High sunk costs

B Absence of legal barriers

C Low start-up costs

D High contestability

3 Which market structure is characterised by barriers to entry and interdependence between the few firms operating in the market?

A Monopoly

B Perfect competition

C Oligopoly

D Monopolistic competition

4 Mobile phone companies operating in an oligopolistic market usually employ price competition or advertising as means of increasing market share. Use game theory to explain how firms might behave in such a market.

4 Pricing strategies and contestable markets

1 Evaluate pricing and non-pricing strategies that car retailers might employ as means of competing with rival firms.

2 If a firm switches from a policy of profit maximisation to a policy of revenue maximisation, then which of the following will be true?

	Price	Output	Profit
A	Higher	Higher	Higher
B	Lower	Higher	Higher
C	Lower	Higher	Lower
D	Lower	Lower	Lower

3 Increased expenditure on advertising by firms in an industry is likely to:

  A Decrease the concentration ratio in the industry

  B Decrease sunk costs

  C Decrease contestability

  D Reduce the revenues of marketing firms

5 The labour market

1 The demand for workers in the UK vegetable farming industry will decrease if:

  A The price that supermarkets are prepared to pay for vegetables increases

  B The increase in world population causes increased demand for vegetables

  C It becomes cheaper to use machinery to harvest the vegetables

  D More people become vegetarians

2 The demand for labour in a particular industry will be inelastic if:

  A The prices of the products produced by the workers form a large proportion of consumers' incomes

  B It is possible to substitute capital for labour

  C The proportion of total costs accounted for by wage costs is very small

  D The demand for the product is price elastic

3 The National Minimum Wage

The UK government introduced a National Minimum Wage (NMW) in 1999 at a rate of £3.60 and by October 2012 this had been increased to £6.19 for workers over the age 21, with lower rates for younger workers. One aim of this was to prevent the exploitation of workers by firms that paid very low wages.

Some business owners and economists argued that an NMW would cause widespread unemployment, especially in labour-intensive industries such as hotels and catering. However, there is only limited evidence of this because it is difficult to replace workers with machines in this industry. There is a ready supply of workers because only limited qualifications are required and also because of the availability of immigrant workers from eastern Europe.

  (a) Explain **one** reason why the government intervenes in labour markets by imposing a National Minimum Wage.

  (b) Outline **two** factors that influence the demand for labour in the hotel industry.

  (c) To what extent might an increase in the National Minimum Wage lead to job losses in the hotel industry? Illustrate your answer with an appropriate labour market diagram.

  (d) Apart from the National Minimum Wage, discuss the factors that might influence the supply of labour to the hotel industry **or** to another occupation of your choice.

6 Government intervention to promote competition

1 The UK government has agreed many contracts under the Private Finance Initiative (PFI) for the building of new hospitals over the last 10 years. A significant reason for the government's use of PFI contracts is that:

  A It had a budget surplus

  B There was a surplus of building workers

  C The number of people requiring treatment in hospitals was declining

  D PFI enabled hospitals to be built without an immediate increase in the budget deficit

2 Prices charged by companies providing water to UK consumers are regulated by the *RPI* + *k* formula. The *main* purpose of this regulation is to:

   A Ensure water companies have sufficient funds for investment

   B Reduce consumer surplus

   C Prevent an increase in competition

   D Ensure that prices increase more slowly than the rate of inflation

3 The Competition and Markets Authority (CMA) might investigate a proposed merger if it is likely:

   A That the new firm will benefit from economies of scale

   B To result in a substantial reduction in competition

   C To increase contestability

   D To reduce the concentration ratio

4 Discuss the impact on economic efficiency of the regulation of a privatised industry such as water or energy.

5 Assess the impact on economic efficiency of a merger between two airlines such as British Airways and Iberia.

THEME 4

A GLOBAL
PERSPECTIVE

Globalisation and trade

The world economy is becoming increasingly integrated, and it is no longer possible to think of any single economy in isolation. The UK economy is no exception. It relies on international trade, engaging in exporting and importing activity, and many UK firms are increasingly active in global markets. This situation has created opportunities for UK firms to expand and become global players, and for UK consumers to have access to a wider range of goods and services. However, there is also a downside: global shocks, whether caused by oil prices, financial crises or the emergence of China as a world economic force, can reverberate throughout economies in all parts of the world. These are some of the issues that will be explored in this chapter.

Learning objectives

After studying this chapter, you should:
→ appreciate the importance of trade and exchange between nations
→ understand what is meant by globalisation, and be aware of the factors that have given rise to this phenomenon
→ be aware of the role and workings of the World Trade Organization
→ understand the importance of foreign direct investment and the role of multinational corporations
→ be aware of the impact that external shocks can have within the global economy

The importance of international trade

The central importance of international trade for growth and development has been recognised since the days of Adam Smith and David Ricardo. For example, during the Industrial Revolution a key factor was that Britain could bring in raw materials from its colonies for use in manufacturing activity. Today, consumers in the UK are able to buy and consume many goods that simply could not be produced within the domestic economy. From the point of view of economic analysis, Ricardo showed that countries could gain from trade through a process of *specialisation*.

Absolute and comparative advantage

The notion of specialisation was briefly introduced in Book 1, where it was pointed out that the division of labour could enable efficiency gains. This analysis can now be extended to demonstrate the potential gains to be made from specialisation and trade.

Consider an example. Matthew and Sophie try to supplement their incomes by working at weekends. They have both been to evening classes and attended pottery and jewellery-making classes to sell at a local market. Depending upon how they divide their time, they can make differing combinations of these goods; some of the possibilities are shown in Table 7.1.

Table 7.1 Matthew and Sophie's production

Matthew		Sophie	
Pots	**Bracelets**	**Pots**	**Bracelets**
12	0	18	0
9	3	12	12
6	6	6	24
3	9	3	30
0	12	0	36

Notice that Sophie is better than Matthew at both activities; if they each spend all of their time producing one of the goods, Sophie can make 18 pots to Matthew's 12, or 36 bracelets to Matthew's 12. This illustrates **absolute advantage**. Sophie is simply better than Matthew at both activities. Another way of looking at this is that, in order to produce a given quantity of a good, Sophie needs less labour time than Matthew.

There is another significant feature of this table. Although Sophie is better at producing both goods, the difference is much more marked in the case of bracelet production than for pot production. So Sophie is relatively more proficient in bracelet production: in other words, she has a **comparative advantage** in making bracelets. This is reflected in differences in opportunity cost. If Sophie switches from producing pots to producing bracelets, she must forgo 6 pots for every 12 additional bracelets that she makes. The opportunity cost of an additional bracelet is thus $6/12 = 0.5$ pots. For Matthew, there is a one-to-one trade-off between the two, so his opportunity cost of a bracelet is 1 pot.

More interesting is what happens if the same calculation is made for Matthew and pot making. Although Sophie is absolutely better at making pots, if Matthew increases his production of pots, his opportunity cost in terms of bracelets is still 1. But for Sophie the opportunity cost of making pots in terms of bracelets is $12/6 = 2$, so Matthew has the lower opportunity cost. Although Sophie has an *absolute* advantage in pot making, Matthew has a *comparative* advantage. It is this difference in comparative advantage that gives rise to the gains from specialisation.

The **law of comparative advantage** states that overall output can be increased if individuals specialise in producing the goods in which they have a comparative advantage.

Gains from international trade

This same principle can be applied in the context of international trade. Suppose there are two countries, Anywhere and Somewhere, where Anywhere has an absolute advantage in the production of both agricultural and manufactured goods. Assume (for simplicity) that the two countries are of similar size in output terms, although Somewhere uses more resources in production than Anywhere because of the absolute advantage held by Anywhere. However, suppose that Anywhere faces lower opportunity cost in producing manufactured goods, and Somewhere has lower opportunity cost in producing agricultural goods. Their respective *PPF*s are shown in Figure 7.1.

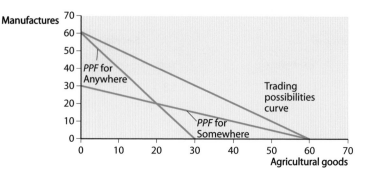

Figure 7.1 Trading possibilities for Anywhere and Somewhere

The pattern of comparative advantage held by the two countries is reflected in the different slopes of the countries' *PPF*s. In the absence of trade, each country is constrained to consume along its *PPF*. For example, if Somewhere wants to consume 20 units of manufactures, it can consume a maximum of 20 units of agricultural goods.

However, suppose that each country were to specialise in producing the product in which it has a comparative advantage. Anywhere could produce 60 units of manufactures and Somewhere could produce 60 units of agricultural goods. If each country were to specialise completely in this way, and if trade were to take place on a one-to-one basis (i.e. if one unit of manufactures is exchanged for one unit of agricultural goods), then it can be seen that this expands the consumption possibilities for both countries. The **trading possibilities curve** in Figure 7.1 shows the potential consumption points for each country in this situation.

Quantitative skills 7.1

Calculating opportunity cost ratios

The key to comparative advantage is the difference in the opportunity costs faced by each country in the production of these goods. This can be calculated. First notice that if Anywhere chooses to increase output of agricultural goods by 10 units, it must sacrifice 20 units of manufactures, so the opportunity cost ratio is 2:1, meaning that for every extra unit of agricultural goods it must sacrifice 2 units of manufactures. However, for Somewhere 10 units of manufactures are sacrificed if 10 more units of agricultural goods are to be produced, so the opportunity cost ratio is 1:1. Similarly, the opportunity cost ratios for manufactured goods are 0.5 for Anywhere and 1 for Somewhere.

Exercise 7.1

Figure 7.2 shows production possibility curves for two countries, each of which produces both coats and scooters. The countries are called 'Here' and 'There'.

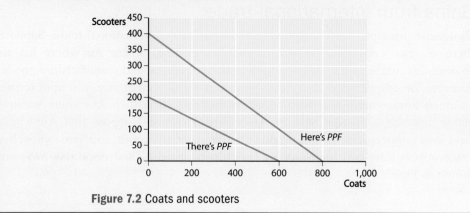

Figure 7.2 Coats and scooters

a Suppose that Here produces 200 scooters and There produces 100: how many coats are produced in each country?

b Now suppose that 300 scooters and 200 coats are produced by Here, and that There produces only coats. What has happened to total production of coats and scooters?

In the above examples and exercises, specialisation and trade are seen to lead to higher overall production of goods. Although the examples have related to goods, you should be equally aware that services too may be a source of specialisation and trade. This is potentially important for an economy such as the UK's, where there is a comparative advantage in the provision of financial services.

Who gains from international trade?

Specialisation can result in an overall increase in total production. However, one of the fundamental questions of economics in Chapter 1 of Book 1 was 'for whom?' It is *possible* that exchange can take place between countries in such a way that both countries are better off. But whether this will actually happen in practice depends on the prices at which exchange takes place.

In particular, specialisation may bring dangers and risks, as well as benefits. One obvious way in which this may be relevant is that, by specialising, a country allows some sectors to run down. For example, suppose a country came to rely on imported food, and allowed its agricultural sector to waste away. If the country then became involved in a war, or for some other reason was unable to import its food, there would clearly be serious consequences if it could no longer grow its own foodstuffs. For this reason, many countries have in place measures designed to protect their agricultural sectors — or other sectors that are seen to be strategic in nature.

Over-reliance on some commodities may also be risky. For example, the development of artificial substitutes for rubber had an enormous impact on the demand for natural rubber; this was reflected in falls in its price and caused difficulties for countries that had specialised in producing rubber.

The terms of trade

One of the key factors that determines who gains from international trade is the **terms of trade**, defined simply as the ratio of export prices to import prices.

Suppose that both export and import prices are rising through time, but import prices are rising more rapidly than export prices. This means that the ratio of export to import prices will fall — which in turn means that a country must export a greater volume of its goods in order to acquire the same volume of imports.

Study tip

Don't forget these three fundamental questions of economics that were introduced in Chapter 1, Book 1: what, how and for whom. They underpin economic analysis.

Key term

terms of trade the ratio of export prices to import prices

Quantitative skills 7.2

Calculating and interpreting the terms of trade

Export and import prices are expressed as index numbers, based on a particular year. Suppose we want to know how the terms of trade have changed in October 2014 relative to 2000. This can be done using the data in Table 7.2, which shows price indexes for exports and imports based on 2011=100.

Table 7.2

Date	Price index of exports	Price index of imports
2000	72.1	74.4
October 2014	94.8	95.7

Source: ONS

First calculate the price index number for October 2014 based on 2000 = 100. The rebased price index for exports is $100 \times 94.8/72.1 = 131.5$. For the price of imports, the index is 128.6 (check this calculation to make sure you understand how to do it). These calculations show that prices of both exported and imported goods have risen over the period.

The terms of trade represent the relative price change over the period, so for October 2014 we calculate the ratio of the price of exports to the price of imports. This is normally expressed as a percentage (i.e. as an index number), so the calculation is $100 \times 131.5/128.6 = 102.3$. The terms of trade increased by 2.3% between 2000 and October 2014. This indicates that the same volume of exports will purchase a greater volume of imports than in 2000.

A fall in the terms of trade indicates that the same volume of exports will purchase a smaller volume of imports than before. A downward movement in the terms of trade is thus unfavourable for an economy. Figure 7.3 shows the terms of trade for the UK economy since 1963. The substantial fall that is seen in 1973 and 1974 is due to the adverse oil price shock that occurred at that time. However, it would seem from this figure that the terms of trade have remained fairly constant since the early 1980s, even through the financial crisis.

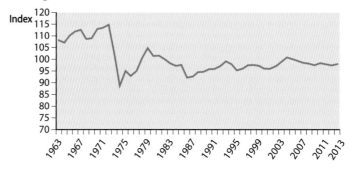

Figure 7.3 The UK terms of trade, 1963–2013 (2005 = 100)

Source: ONS

The terms of trade are calculated purely with respect to prices, and take no account of changing volumes of trade. In other words, a deterioration in the terms of trade does not necessarily mean that an economy is worse off, so long as the volume of trade is increasing sufficiently rapidly.

Extension material

The terms of trade

The terms of trade described in the text are known more formally as the *net barter terms of trade*. As noted, the net barter terms of trade relate solely to the relative prices of exports and imports, so do not take into account changes in the volume of exports and imports. The *income terms of trade* take the volume of trade into account, being defined as the value of a country's exports divided by the price of imports. In other words, this measures the purchasing power of a country's exports in terms of the price of its imports. It is possible for all countries to experience an increase in the income terms of trade simultaneously.

In recent years, concerns have been raised about the effect of changes in the terms of trade for less developed countries (LDCs). One problem faced by LDCs that export primary products is that they are each too small as individual exporters to be able to influence the world price of their products. They must accept the prices that are set in world commodity markets.

Short-run volatility

In the case of agricultural goods, demand tends to be relatively stable over time, but supply can be volatile, varying with weather and climatic conditions from season to season. Figure 7.4 shows a typical market in two periods. In period 1 the global harvest of this commodity is poor, with supply given by S_1: equilibrium is achieved with price at P_1 and quantity traded at Q_1. In period 2 the global harvest is high at S_2, so that prices plummet to P_2 and quantity traded rises to Q_2.

Notice that in this case the movement of prices is relatively strong compared with the variation in quantity. This reflects the price elasticity of demand, which is expected to be relatively inelastic for many primary products. From the consumers' point of view, the demand for foodstuffs and other agricultural goods will tend to be inelastic, as demand will not be expected to respond strongly to changes in prices.

For many minerals and raw materials, however, the picture is different. For such commodities, supply tends to be stable over time, but demand fluctuates with the economic cycle in developed countries, which are the importers of raw materials. Figure 7.5 illustrates this. At the trough of the economic cycle, demand is low, at D_1, and so the equilibrium price will also be low, at P_1. At the peak of the cycle, demand is more buoyant, at D_2, and price is relatively high, at P_2.

From an individual country's point of view, the result is the same: the country faces volatility in the prices of its exports. From this perspective it does not matter whether the instability arises from the supply side of the market or from the demand side. The problem is that prices can rise and fall quite independently of conditions within the domestic economy.

Instability of prices also means instability of export revenues, so if the country is relying on export earnings to fund its development path, to import capital equipment or to meet its debt repayments, such volatility in earnings can constitute a severe problem — for example, if export earnings fall such that a country is unable to meet its commitments to repaying debt.

Long-run deterioration

The nature of the demand for primary products may be expected to influence the long-run path of relative prices. In particular, the income elasticity of demand is an important consideration. As real incomes rise in the developed countries, the demand for agricultural goods can be expected to rise relatively slowly. Ernst Engel pointed out that at relatively high income levels, the proportion of expenditure devoted to foodstuffs tends to fall and the demand for luxury goods rises. This suggests that the demand for agricultural goods shifts relatively slowly through time.

Exercise 7.2

In 2013, the terms of trade index for Venezuela was 254.6 (based on 2000 = 100). For Togo it was 28.9, and for Malaysia it was 100.5. Explain what is implied by these statistics.

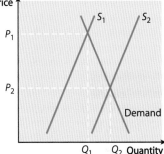

Figure 7.4 Volatility in supply

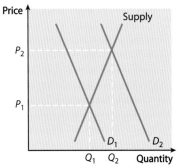

Figure 7.5 Volatility in demand

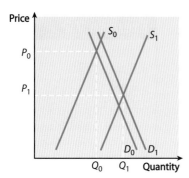

Price

S_0 S_1

P_0

P_1

D_0 D_1

Q_0 Q_1 Quantity

Figure 7.6 Long-term movements of demand and supply

In the case of raw materials, there have been advances in the development of artificial substitutes for many commodities used in manufacturing. Furthermore, technology has changed over time, improving the efficiency with which inputs can be converted into outputs. This has weakened the demand for raw materials produced by LDCs.

Furthermore, if some LDCs are successful in boosting output of these goods, there will be an increase in supply over time. Figure 7.6 shows the result of such an increase. Suppose that the market begins with demand at D_0 and supply at S_0. Market equilibrium results in a price of P_0 and quantity of Q_0. As time goes by, demand moves to the right a little to D_1, and supply shifts to S_1. The result is a fall in the price of the commodity to P_1.

It is thus clear that, not only may LDCs experience short-run volatility in prices, but the terms of trade may also deteriorate in the long run.

Pattern of comparative advantage

In the light of these twin problems, it is perhaps no surprise that many LDCs see themselves as trapped by their pattern of comparative advantage, rather than being in a position to exploit it. They are therefore reluctant to continue in such a state of dependency on primary products, but the process of diversification into a wide range of products has been difficult to achieve.

A potential change in this pattern was seen in 2007 and 2008, with food prices rising rapidly. This included the prices of some staple commodities such as maize and rice. The net effect of this on LDCs was not clear. Countries in a position to export these commodities would benefit from the rise in prices — that is, an increase in their terms of trade. However, there are many LDCs that need to import these staple commodities and for them the terms of trade deteriorated. These trends were interrupted by the onset of recession in many developed countries in 2008.

The degree to which a country or region engages in trade depends upon several factors. One important influence is the extent to which a country has the resources needed to trade — in other words, whether it can produce the sorts of goods that other countries wish to buy. However, it also depends upon the policy stance adopted by a country. Some countries have been very open to international trade. For example, a number of countries in South East Asia built success in economic growth on the basis of promoting exports. In contrast, there are countries such as India that in the past have been less eager to trade, and introduced policies that have hindered their engagement with trade.

Two Swedish economists, Eli Heckscher and Bertil Ohlin, argued that a country's comparative advantage would depend crucially on its relative endowments of factors of production. They argued that the optimal techniques for producing different commodities varied. Some commodities are most efficiently produced using labour-intensive techniques, whereas others could be more efficiently produced using relatively capital-intensive methods. This then suggests that if a country has abundant labour but scarce capital, then its natural comparative advantage would lie in the production of goods that require little capital but lots of labour. In contrast, a country with access to capital but facing a labour shortage would tend to have a comparative advantage in capital-intensive goods or services.

Changes in the price of staple commodities such as maize and rice could change the pattern of comparative advantage for many LDCs

Labour- or land-intensive techniques

Under these arguments, it would seem to make sense for LDCs to specialise in labour- or land-intensive activities such as agriculture or other primary production. Countries like the UK and the USA could then specialise in more capital-intensive activities such as manufacturing activity and financial services. By and large, this describes the way in which the pattern of world trade developed. However, the pattern is not static and there have been changes over time. For example, countries in South East Asia, such as Hong Kong, Singapore or Taiwan, encouraged the structure of their economies to change over time, switching away from labour-intensive activities as the access to capital goods improved. Their success then induced changes in the structure of activity in more developed countries as the availability of imported manufactured goods allowed the expansion of service sector activity. In more recent years, China's economy has been undergoing even faster structural change, with the rapid expansion of the manufacturing sector, supported by an exchange rate policy that made its exports highly competitive in global markets.

Whether it is good for countries to rely on this pattern of natural comparative advantage is a different matter — for example, in the light of the changing patterns of relative prices reflected in the evolution of the terms of trade over time. This suggests that there may be potential for countries to seek to alter the pattern of their comparative advantage by diversifying their economies and developing new specialisms in the face of changing patterns of global consumer demand. This is not an easy path for an economy to travel, and it may be tempting to turn instead to a more inward-looking protectionist strategy. There is a choice to be made between seeking to exploit this natural comparative advantage, or diversifying the economy in an attempt to develop new specialisms.

Summary

- Specialisation opens up the possibility of gains from trade.
- The theory of comparative advantage shows that even if one country has an absolute advantage in the production of goods and services, trade may still increase total output if each country specialises in the production of goods and services in which it has a comparative advantage.
- Who gains from specialisation and trade depends crucially on the prices at which exchange takes place.
- The terms of trade are measured as the ratio of export prices to import prices.
- When the terms of trade deteriorate for a country, it needs to export a greater volume of goods to be able to maintain the same volume of imports.
- The terms of trade have tended to be volatile in the short run, and to deteriorate over the longer term for countries that rely heavily on non-fuel primary production.
- The pattern of comparative advantage that characterises a country may depend upon the relative endowments of the factors of production.

Globalisation

Key term

globalisation a process by which the world's economies are becoming more closely integrated

The term **globalisation** has been much used in recent years, not least by the protest groups that have demonstrated against it. It is therefore important to be clear about what the term means before seeking to evaluate the strengths and weaknesses of the phenomenon.

Ann Krueger, the first deputy managing director of the IMF, defined globalisation as 'a phenomenon by which economic agents in any given part of the world are much more affected by events elsewhere in the world' than before. Joseph Stiglitz, the Nobel Laureate and former Chief Economist at the World Bank, defined it as follows:

Fundamentally, [globalisation] is the closer integration of countries and peoples of the world which has been brought about by the enormous reduction of costs of transportation and communication, and the breaking down of artificial barriers to the flows of goods, services, capital, knowledge, and (to a lesser extent) people across borders.

Source: *Globalization and its Discontents* (Penguin, 2004)

On this basis, globalisation is crucially about the closer integration of the world's economies. Critics have focused partly on the environmental effects of rapid global economic growth, and partly on the opportunities that powerful nations and large corporations have for exploiting the weak. Some of these arguments will be evaluated after a more careful exploration of the topic.

The quotation from the book by Joseph Stiglitz not only defines what is meant by globalisation, but also offers some reasons for its occurrence.

Transportation and communication costs

One of the contributory factors to the spread of globalisation has undoubtedly been the rapid advances in the technology of transportation and communications.

Improvements in transportation have enabled firms to fragment their production process to take advantage of varying cost conditions in different parts of the world.

For example, it is now possible to site labour-intensive parts of a production process in parts of the world where labour is relatively plentiful, and thus relatively cheap. This is one way in which **multinational corporations (MNCs)** arise, in some cases operating across a wide range of countries.

Furthermore, communications technology has developed rapidly with the growth of the internet and e-commerce, enabling firms to compete more easily in global markets. The importance of email and other forms of communication such as video-conferencing and Skype should not be underestimated. It is now taken for granted that there can be instant communication across the globe. This has made it very much easier for firms to communicate within their organisations and with other firms, and has certainly fuelled the closer integration of firms and economies.

These technological changes have augmented the existing economies of scale and scope, enabling firms to grow. If the size of firms were measured by their gross turnover, many of them would be found to be larger in size than a lot of the countries in which they operate (when size is measured by GDP): for example, on this basis General Motors is bigger than Hong Kong or Norway.

Reduction of trade barriers

A second factor that has contributed to globalisation has been the successive reduction in trade barriers during the period since the Second World War, first under the auspices of the **General Agreement on Tariffs and Trade (GATT)**, and later under the **World Trade Organization (WTO)** which replaced it.

In addition to these trade-liberalising measures, there has been a trend towards the establishment of free trade areas and customs unions in various parts of the world, with the European Union being just one example. The appearance of China on the world stage has also been of crucial importance. China has the largest population of any country in the world, and has experienced economic growth at an unprecedented and consistent rate in recent decades. It joined the WTO in 2001, and has had a major impact on global markets. By joining the WTO, China agreed to abide by its rules, thus affecting the confidence with which other countries could view trade with, and investment in, China.

By facilitating the process of international trade, such developments have encouraged firms to become more active in trade, and thus have added to the impetus towards globalisation.

Deregulation of financial markets

Hand in hand with these developments, there have been moves towards removing restrictions on the movement of financial capital between countries. Many countries have removed capital controls, thereby making it much easier for firms to operate globally. This has been reinforced by developments in technology that enable financial transactions to be undertaken more quickly and efficiently.

Globalisation and sustainability

Critics of globalisation have pointed to the impact that the increase in trade associated with globalisation may be having on the environment, especially in the context of climate change and global warming. This is bound up with the notion of **sustainable development**, which refers to the effect that economic growth and increased trade may have on future generations.

The core of the argument is that increased trade means increased emissions of greenhouse gases because of the need to transport goods over long distances. For example, if you check the country of origin of the fruit and vegetables in your local supermarket, you will find that these are imported from far and wide. This is the case even for some produce that can be grown in the UK. On this basis it is argued that increasing such trade damages the environment. However, the case is not fully accepted by everyone. For example, a study by DEFRA showed that importing tomatoes from Spain into the UK (especially by sea) causes less environmental damage than growing them at home because of the difference in climate between the two countries. This enables tomatoes to be grown in a more environmentally friendly manner in Spain, where no heat is needed to encourage growth and ripening. Nonetheless, this is an aspect of globalisation that needs to be considered and taken into account.

The World Trade Organization

A famous conference was held at Bretton Woods in the USA at the end of the Second World War to agree on a set of rules under which international trade would be conducted. This conference established an exchange rate system under which countries agreed to set the price of their currencies relative to the US dollar (see Chapter 9). In addition, the conference set up three institutions to oversee matters. The International Monetary Fund (IMF) would provide assistance (and advice) to countries experiencing balance of payments difficulties and the World Bank would provide assistance (and advice) on long-term development issues. However, it was also recognised that the conduct of trade would need some oversight. Initially, this role was fulfilled by the General Agreement on Tariffs and Trade (GATT), under the auspices of which there was a sequence of 'rounds' of reductions in tariffs, together with a significant reduction in quotas and voluntary export restraints. The last of these was the Uruguay Round, which covered the period 1986–94 and led to the formation of the World Trade Organization (WTO), which replaced the GATT in 1995.

While continuing to pursue reductions in barriers to trade, the WTO has also taken on the role of providing a framework for the settlement of trade disputes. You will appreciate that, with all the moves towards regional integration and protectionism, such a role is very important. Indeed, the WTO reports that around 300 cases for settlement of disputes were brought to the WTO in its first 8 years — about the same number that were dealt with over the entire life of the GATT from 1947 to 1994.

In 2000 new talks started, covering agriculture and services. The fourth WTO Ministerial Conference in Doha in November 2001 incorporated these discussions into a broader work programme, the Doha Development Agenda. According to the WTO website, this agenda includes:

work on non-agricultural tariffs, trade and environment, WTO rules such as anti-dumping and subsidies, investment, competition policy, trade facilitation, transparency in government procurement, intellectual property, and a range of issues raised by developing countries.

Progress on the Doha agenda has been far from smooth. This is partly because agriculture is an especially contentious area, with the USA, the EU and Japan having large-scale policies in place to support their agricultural sectors. In the case

Activists protest against the
WTO in Bali in 2013

of the EU's Single Market, some moves have been made towards reforming the Common Agricultural Policy, but progress has not been as rapid as developing countries would like — remembering that agriculture is especially important for many of the less developed countries. Reluctance on the part of the rich nations to provide concessions in these key areas, combined with determination on the part of LDCs to make genuine progress, results in a seeming deadlock.

The so-called 'Bali package' of measures was agreed in 2013, amidst great optimism amongst ministers, but the crucial issues surrounding agriculture remained, and the future of the Doha Round remains uncertain.

Trading blocs and the WTO

There has been a proliferation of regional trade agreements in recent years — as at January 2013 the WTO had received 536 notifications of regional trade agreements, of which 354 were in force. There has been much debate as to whether these agreements are stepping stones to further global cooperation, or whether they may turn out to be obstacles to that process. If nations establish individual agreements with other nations or groups of nations, this may militate against reaching agreement on a more global scale, especially if the groupings of nations establish stronger barriers against trade with nations that are not part of the blocs. In other words, such regional agreements may be divisive rather than advancing globally freer trade. These issues are discussed in Chapter 8.

Summary

- The World Trade Organization (WTO) has a responsibility to promote trade by pursuing reductions in tariffs and other barriers to trade, and also discharges a role in dispute settlement between nations.

more began to rise. Notice that the scale of the vertical axis has had to be changed in order to accommodate the rise in price, which became even more severe in 2007–08. When the price of oil began to fall again, the Organization of the Petroleum Exporting Countries (OPEC) met to discuss whether to reduce supply in order to maintain the oil price at its high level.

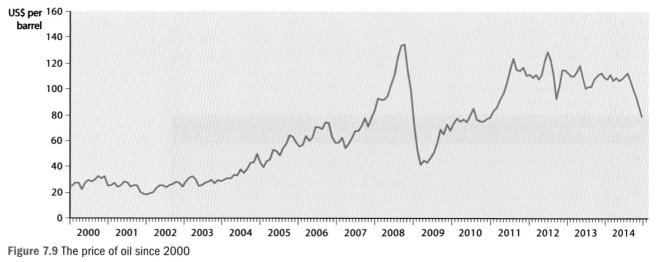

Figure 7.9 The price of oil since 2000

Source: IMF

Arguably, economies were better equipped to withstand the increase than they had been in the 1970s. The UK was partly able to weather the storm because of its position as an oil producer, although by this time, reserves were becoming depleted.

Another difference was that the price rises in 1973–74 and 1979–80 had been primarily supply-side changes, caused by disruptions to supply following the actions of the OPEC cartel. In the 2000s part of the upward pressure on price was coming from demand, with China's demand for oil being especially strong. In the event, the pressures of falling demand as the global recession began to unfold brought the price of oil tumbling.

Financial crises

Given the increasing integration of financial markets, a further concern is whether globalisation increases the chances that a financial crisis will spread rapidly between countries, rather than being contained within a country or region. The 1997 Asian financial crisis provides some evidence on this issue.

This crisis began in Thailand and South Korea. Both countries had been the recipients of large flows of FDI. In the case of Thailand, a significant part of this had been investment in property, rather than in productive investment. The Thai currency (the baht) came under speculative pressure early in 1997, and eventually the authorities had to allow a devaluation. This sparked a crisis of confidence in the region, and foreign investors began to withdraw funds, not only from Thailand but from other countries too. As far as globalisation was concerned, the key questions were how far the crisis would spread, and how long it would last.

In the event, five countries bore the main burden of the crisis: Indonesia, Malaysia, the Philippines, South Korea and Thailand. Beyond this grouping there were some knock-on effects because of trade linkages, but arguably these were not too severe, and were probably dominated by other events taking place in the period. At the time of the crisis, Indonesia and the Philippines had been at a somewhat lower

FDI can have positive and negative effects on the host country. On the positive side, it is hoped that FDI will bring potential gains in employment, tax revenue, capital and technology, with consequent beneficial impact on economic growth. This may be seen as especially important for less developed countries that may especially lack capital and technology or the ability to raise tax revenue. However, there is a downside, as these potential benefits may not always be as strong as had been hoped. In particular, if profits are repatriated to shareholders elsewhere in the world, then the long-term impact of FDI may be diluted, rather than feeding back into economic growth. For less developed countries, the tax concessions negotiated by foreign multinational firms may reduce the benefits, and the technology may not be appropriate, or not disseminated.

Summary

- An important part of globalisation has been the spread of foreign direct investment (FDI) by multinational corporations.
- Motivations for FDI include market-seeking, resource-seeking and efficiency-seeking reasons.
- Cross-border mergers and acquisitions have tended to follow a cyclical pattern over time, with a peak in 2000.

Globalisation and external shocks

One of the issues concerning a more closely integrated global economy is the question of how robust the global economy will be to shocks. In other words, globalisation may be fine when the world economy is booming, as all nations may be able to share in the success. But if the global economy goes into recession, will all nations suffer the consequences? There are a number of situations that might cause the global economy to take a downturn.

Oil prices

Oil prices seem to provide one possible threat. In the past, sudden changes in oil prices have caused widespread disruption — for example, in 1973–74 and in 1979–80.

Figure 7.8 shows the historical time path of the price of oil from 1964 to 2004, measured in US dollars. In 1973–74 the sudden increase in the price of oil took most people by surprise. Oil prices had been steady for several years, and many economies had become dependent upon oil as an energy source, not only for running cars but for other uses such as domestic central heating. The sudden increases in the price in 1973–74 and again in 1979–80 caused widespread problems because demand in the short run was highly inelastic, and oil-importing countries faced sudden deficits on their balance of payments current accounts. However, in time people switched away from oil for heating, firms developed more energy-efficient cars, and demand was able to adjust. Arguably, national economies in the twenty-first century are less vulnerable to changes in the price of oil than they were in 1973.

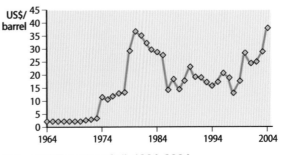

Figure 7.8 The price of oil, 1964–2004

Source: IMF

Figure 7.9 shows how the price of oil changed on a monthly basis after 2000, causing concern in late 2004 when it once more began to rise. Notice that the scale of the vertical axis has had to be changed in order to accommodate the rise in price, which became even more severe in 2007–08. When the price of oil began to fall again, the Organization of the Petroleum Exporting Countries (OPEC) met to discuss whether to reduce supply in order to maintain the oil price at its high level.

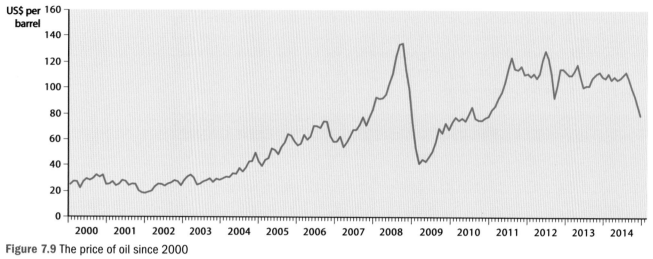

Figure 7.9 The price of oil since 2000

Source: IMF

Arguably, economies were better equipped to withstand the increase than they had been in the 1970s. The UK was partly able to weather the storm because of its position as an oil producer, although by this time, reserves were becoming depleted.

Another difference was that the price rises in 1973–74 and 1979–80 had been primarily supply-side changes, caused by disruptions to supply following the actions of the OPEC cartel. In the 2000s part of the upward pressure on price was coming from demand, with China's demand for oil being especially strong. In the event, the pressures of falling demand as the global recession began to unfold brought the price of oil tumbling.

Financial crises

Given the increasing integration of financial markets, a further concern is whether globalisation increases the chances that a financial crisis will spread rapidly between countries, rather than being contained within a country or region. The 1997 Asian financial crisis provides some evidence on this issue.

This crisis began in Thailand and South Korea. Both countries had been the recipients of large flows of FDI. In the case of Thailand, a significant part of this had been investment in property, rather than in productive investment. The Thai currency (the baht) came under speculative pressure early in 1997, and eventually the authorities had to allow a devaluation. This sparked a crisis of confidence in the region, and foreign investors began to withdraw funds, not only from Thailand but from other countries too. As far as globalisation was concerned, the key questions were how far the crisis would spread, and how long it would last.

In the event, five countries bore the main burden of the crisis: Indonesia, Malaysia, the Philippines, South Korea and Thailand. Beyond this grouping there were some knock-on effects because of trade linkages, but arguably these were not too severe, and were probably dominated by other events taking place in the period. At the time of the crisis, Indonesia and the Philippines had been at a somewhat lower

Activists protest against the WTO in Bali in 2013

of the EU's Single Market, some moves have been made towards reforming the Common Agricultural Policy, but progress has not been as rapid as developing countries would like — remembering that agriculture is especially important for many of the less developed countries. Reluctance on the part of the rich nations to provide concessions in these key areas, combined with determination on the part of LDCs to make genuine progress, results in a seeming deadlock.

The so-called 'Bali package' of measures was agreed in 2013, amidst great optimism amongst ministers, but the crucial issues surrounding agriculture remained, and the future of the Doha Round remains uncertain.

Trading blocs and the WTO

There has been a proliferation of regional trade agreements in recent years — as at January 2013 the WTO had received 536 notifications of regional trade agreements, of which 354 were in force. There has been much debate as to whether these agreements are stepping stones to further global cooperation, or whether they may turn out to be obstacles to that process. If nations establish individual agreements with other nations or groups of nations, this may militate against reaching agreement on a more global scale, especially if the groupings of nations establish stronger barriers against trade with nations that are not part of the blocs. In other words, such regional agreements may be divisive rather than advancing globally freer trade. These issues are discussed in Chapter 8.

Summary

- The World Trade Organization (WTO) has a responsibility to promote trade by pursuing reductions in tariffs and other barriers to trade, and also discharges a role in dispute settlement between nations.

Foreign direct investment

Key term

foreign direct investment (FDI) investment undertaken in one country by companies based in other countries

An important aspect of globalisation has been the spread of **foreign direct investment (FDI)** by MNCs. UNCTAD has identified three main reasons for such activity:

1 market seeking

2 resource seeking

3 efficiency seeking

Some MNCs may engage in FDI because they want to sell their products within a particular market, and find it preferable to produce within the market rather than elsewhere: such FDI is *market seeking*. Second, MNCs may undertake investment in a country in order to take advantage of some key resource. This might be a natural resource such as oil or natural gas, or a labour force with certain skills, or simply cheap unskilled labour: such FDI is *resource seeking*. Third, MNCs may simply review their options globally, and decide that they can produce most efficiently in a particular location. This might entail locating just part of their production chain in a certain country. Such FDI is *efficiency seeking*.

Market-seeking FDI has been important in some regions in particular. The opening up of China to foreign investment has proved a magnet for MNCs wanting to gain access to this large and growing market. In addition, non-European firms have been keen to gain entry to the EU's Single Market, which has encouraged substantial flows of FDI into Europe.

For the UK, there has been a two-way flow of direct investment. In other words, foreign investors have invested in the UK, and UK investors have invested abroad. Figure 7.7 shows the inward and outward flows, expressed as a percentage of GDP. Both inward and outward flows peaked in 2000, a year in which outward direct investment reached more than 16% of GDP. This reflected intense merger and acquisition activity at that time. The largest outward acquisitions were by Vodafone Airtouch, which invested in Mannesmann AG to the tune of £100 billion, and BP Amoco plc, which purchased the Atlantic Richfield Company for a reported £18 billion. After 2000, merger and acquisition activity slowed down, partly following the terrorist attacks in September 2001. Figure 7.7 shows that it was some time before FDI activity began to pick up again. You can also see how the flows were affected by the financial crisis of the late 2000s and the recession that followed.

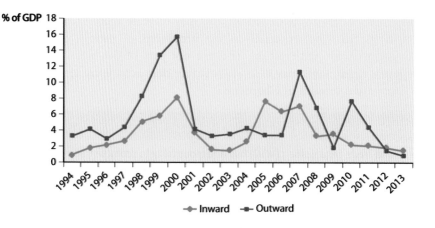

Figure 7.7 UK foreign direct investment, 1994–2013

Source: Pink Book

stage of development than the other countries involved, and thus suffered more deeply in terms of recession. However, with the benefit of hindsight, it seems that the region showed resilience in recovering from the crisis. Indeed, it can be argued that South Korea and Thailand especially emerged as stronger economies, through the weeding out of some relatively inefficient firms and institutions, and through a heightened awareness of the importance of sound financial regulation.

China and the USA

An important question in the early to mid-2000s was how the global economy would cope with two seemingly distant but related phenomena: the rapid growth of the Chinese economy, and the deficit on the US current account of the balance of payments. The US current account deficit arose partly from the heavy public expenditure programme of the Bush administration. However, the deficit grew to unprecedented levels partly through the actions of China and other East Asian economies that had chosen to peg their currencies to the US dollar. Effectively, this meant that those economies were buying US government securities as a way of maintaining their currencies against the dollar, thereby keeping US interest rates relatively low and allowing the American public to borrow to finance high consumer spending.

Who gains from this situation? The USA is able to spend, and China is able to sell, fuelling its rapid rate of economic growth. For how long the situation can be sustained remains to be seen.

The credit crunch

Another example of the dangers of close interdependence began to unfold in 2007–08, when the so-called 'credit crunch' began to bite, and commercial banks in several countries found themselves in financial crisis. This followed a period in which relatively low interest rates had allowed a bubble of borrowing. When house prices began to slide, many banks in several countries found that they had overextended themselves, and had to cut back on lending, in some cases threatening their viability. This affected a number of countries simultaneously, and there was a danger that the financial crisis would affect the real economy, leading to a recession. This was a recession that would affect countries all around the globe because of the new interconnectedness of economies. It became apparent that no single country could tackle the problem alone, as measures taken to support the banks in one economy had rapid knock-on effects elsewhere. Once this was realised, coordinated action was taken, and in October 2008 the central banks of several countries reduced their bank rates together. This was followed by action aiming to salvage the situation and avoid a full-blooded recession.

By early 2009, the UK economy was officially in recession, the bank rate had been driven down to an unprecedented 0.5%, and the Bank of England was introducing quantitative easing to try to stimulate the economy. One of the problems was that the commercial banks had become reluctant to lend, so firms that wanted to invest were finding it difficult to obtain funds. Attempts were made to coordinate the efforts of governments of key countries around the world — for example, at the G20 Summit held in London in April 2009. As time went by and the recession deepened, a number of countries in the euro zone faced crises with the level of public debt. This affected Ireland, Greece and Portugal in particular, all of which needed bailouts. The financial crisis will be discussed in Chapters 13 and 14.

The emerging economies

Industrialisation and economic growth began in the UK and other countries in Western Europe and North America, and by the 1960s there was a divide between those countries that had gone through the development and growth process and those that had not. Since the 1960s, relatively few countries have managed to bridge the gap in living standards.

There was a group of countries that became known as the *newly industrialised countries* (NICs) that made the transition. These included some countries in South East Asia, such as Singapore, South Korea, Taiwan and Hong Kong, and some Latin American countries, although the latter group fell foul of hyperinflation, which interrupted their progress.

More recently, some other countries have accelerated in terms of economic growth and human development; they have become known as the **emerging economies**. This group has included the so-called *BRIC countries* (Brazil, Russia, India and China), and a less defined group including Thailand, Malaysia, Turkey and South Africa, among others. These economies (especially China) have had a significant effect on the global economy.

The BRIC countries

In the early 2000s, a group of countries — Brazil, Russia, India and China — were identified as experiencing rapid economic growth and closing the gap on the developed economies. The BRIC economies were originally just a set of countries identified as having some characteristics in common. However, they began forming a political group and having summit meetings, and in 2011 they invited South Africa to join them. At this point in time, the BRICs accounted for about 18% of world GDP and 15% of world trade, and contained about 40% of the world's population. If economic growth continues at current rates, the group will gain increasing economic and political influence relative to the G7.

Figure 7.10 shows economic growth in the original four BRIC countries since 1999, with the growth rate for the world as a whole to provide context. The consistency and rapidity of growth during the 2000s reveals why these countries were singled out for attention, although Brazil was perhaps rather less successful in terms of its growth rates. What makes this performance more startling is the size of these economies, both in population and in the size of GDP. The achievements of the economies of China and India are especially impressive, in each case starting from a relatively low base — and for these two economies, the growth seemed relatively robust in the face of the global recession. China in particular has shown very little sign of slowing down. However, the factors underlying the growth performance were different in each case, as these economies are all at very different stages in terms of average incomes and display different characteristics, both politically and economically.

These countries, together with some other rapid-growth economies, have had a significant impact on the global economy, most obviously in the case of China, which in 2014 overtook the USA as the world's biggest economy. This is based on GDP in PPP$.

Key term

emerging economies economies that have experienced rapid economic growth with some industrialisation and characteristics of developed markets

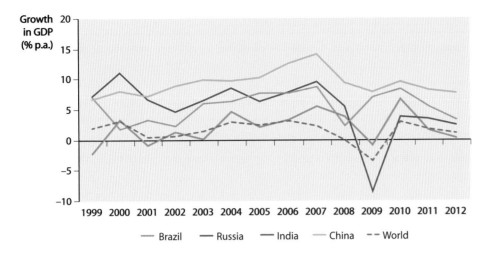

Figure 7.10 Growth in the BRIC countries since 1999

Source: World Bank

The impact on the global economy has been evident in many ways. China's growth was built upon rapid growth of exports, which for at least part of the period was bolstered by China's exchange rate, maintained at a level that made China's exports highly competitive overseas. A number of the Asian emerging economies also accumulated reserves of US Treasury securities during the 2000s, which had the effect of allowing lower US interest rates than would otherwise have been. This in turn encouraged consumer borrowing, and may have contributed to the financial crisis. Of course, China also had to import goods that it needed to fuel its production process, with a consequent impact on commodity prices in global markets. The net effect of these factors is quite difficult to evaluate, but it could be argued that without China's continuing growth through the period of recession following the financial crisis, the slowdown would have been longer-lived.

China's exports are highly competitive in global markets

Globalisation evaluated

The economic arguments in favour of allowing freer trade are strong, in the sense that there are potential gains to be made from countries specialising in the production of goods and services in which they have a comparative advantage. Globalisation facilitates and accelerates this process. And yet, there have sometimes been violent protests against globalisation, directed in particular at the WTO, whose meeting at Seattle in 1999 ended in chaos following demonstrations in the streets.

Tension has always been present during moves towards freer trade. Even if the economic arguments appear to be compelling, nations are cautious about opening up to free trade. In particular, there has been concern about jobs in the domestic economy. This is partly because there are transitional costs involved in liberalising trade, as some economic activities must contract to allow others to expand. Vested interests can then lead to lobbying and political pressure, as was apparent in the USA in the early part of the twenty-first century. There is also the question of whether globalisation will allow recession to spread more quickly between countries.

In many ways, the WTO gets caught in the middle. It has the responsibility of encouraging moves towards free trade, and thus comes under pressure from nations that want to keep some degree of protection because they are unwilling to undergo the transitional costs of structural change. The WTO thus has the unpalatable job of protecting countries from themselves, enforcing short-term costs in the interests of long-term gains.

However, the anti-globalisation protests are based on rather different arguments. One concern is that economic growth can proceed only at some cost to the environment. It has been argued that, by fragmenting the production process across countries, the cost to the environment is high. This is partly because the need to transport goods around the world uses up valuable resources. It is also argued that nations have an incentive to lower their environmental standards in order to attract MNCs by enabling low-cost production. This is not so much an argument against globalisation as an argument that an international agency is required to monitor global environmental standards.

It has also been suggested that it is the rich countries of the world that stand to gain most from increasing global trade, as they have the market power to ensure that trading conditions work in their favour. Again, the WTO may have a role here in monitoring the conditions under which trade takes place. At the end of the day, trade allows an overall increase in global production and more choice for consumers. The challenge is to ensure that these gains are equitably distributed, and that the environment can be conserved.

Summary

- Although closer integration may bring benefits in terms of increased global production and trade, it may also create vulnerability by allowing adverse shocks to spread more rapidly between countries.
- Such shocks include oil price changes and financial crises. However, the integrated global economy may turn out to be more resilient in reacting to adverse circumstances.
- Globalisation facilitates and accelerates the process by which gains from trade may be tapped.
- However, the transitional costs for individual economies in terms of the need for structural change have encouraged politicians to turn to protectionist measures.
- Critics of globalisation have pointed to the environmental costs of rapid global economic growth and the expansion of trade, and have argued that it is the rich countries and the multinational corporations that gain the most, rather than the less developed countries.

Exercise 7.3

Examine the economic arguments for and against globalisation.

More than just exports

The UK imports a great many products, from Audi cars to Hollywood blockbusters, from other European countries and overseas. At the same time, companies based in the UK, from Vauxhall to the BBC, sell their products to customers abroad.

As the Nobel prize-winning economist Paul Krugman argued in an interview to the BBC, international trade matters as it helps firms to specialise and produce in large quantities. At the same time, it expands everyone's choice. Indeed, if you walk down the cookie aisle in a UK supermarket you will see that it has cookies from Denmark, Britain and the United States, as people enjoy variety. This, of course, applies to both exports and imports: the BBC exports the *Sherlock Holmes* series to Europe and the USA, while BBC4 has taken to showing Scandinavian and other European subtitled crime drama; Cadbury exports chocolate to the USA and Germany, while British supermarkets import Milka from Germany and Belgian Godiva chocolate.

International trade in goods is an important and integral part of any economy. As well as material goods, firms may trade in services such as banking and consultancy, invest directly in other companies abroad or contract a foreign company to produce a specific good exclusively for them. Business people understand the importance of these various international activities, while governments often focus on exports of goods. But why do governments focus on firms' export activities?

One reason is the ease of observation — income statements submitted by companies will detail revenues from domestic and foreign sources separately. Exports are simply revenues from abroad. However, observing other types of involvement in international markets, such as investments and outsourcing, is substantially more difficult.

The BBC exports the *Sherlock Holmes* series to Europe

Internationalisation

A recent survey of European firms allowed researchers to look into firms' international activities in seven European countries, including the UK. One observation is that it is very common for European manufacturing firms to have contacts with firms beyond country borders. Almost 80% of firms with at least ten employees engage in some form of international activity.

Exporting is the most frequent mode of internationalisation, with about two-thirds of firms shipping some products abroad. However, many other modes are also popular. About half the firms import directly — that is, they do not just buy foreign-made goods from an intermediary. Working with foreign customers based on contracts is quite widespread, as a quarter of firms have outsourced some of their production, using foreign inputs made specifically for them. Almost 40% of firms provide outsourcing for other firms. Foreign ownership is not rare, as about 10% of firms own or are owned by foreign firms. So, while exports are important, firms are likely to get involved in several modes of internationalisation at once.

Some of the most competitive companies are engaged in several modes of internationalisation. Consider Armstrong, a specialist mid-sized company making acoustic and metal ceilings in the UK. This company makes metal and glass ceilings for theatres, shopping malls and tube stations, and exports them worldwide. However, to be globally competitive, it uses a large amount of tools, materials and semi-finished products made in other countries. Part of the labour-intensive work is contracted out to eastern Europe. Moreover, it is part of a global network owned by a US global player designing and manufacturing floors and ceilings.

Often, several modes of internationalisation are interrelated, with one activity leading to another. For instance, when Kraft took over Cadbury, it started to produce Oreo biscuits, previously imported into the UK, at a plant in Sheffield and then exported the biscuits to other countries.

International activities are found to be related to overall firm performance: companies that are tied into global business are likely to be more efficient and do better in their home market. In some cases, this is the result of learning from foreign business practices. However, it is often the case that a higher level of performance has been achieved before starting to trade: due to fixed trade costs, only the most productive firms may be competitive on export markets.

Source: adapted from Gábor Békés, 'More than just exports', *Economic Review*, November 2013

Follow-up question

Discuss the range of ways in which firms engage in internationalisation, and whether this activity yields net benefits to economies.

8 Trading blocs and restrictions on trade

Although the economic analysis of specialisation suggests that there are potential gains to be made from engaging in international trade, there has been a continuing debate about trade liberalisation and protectionism. Furthermore, the economic landscape of Europe since the Second World War has been shaped by the move towards ever-closer economic integration. Regional trading blocs have also proliferated in other parts of the world. This chapter explores these issues.

Learning objectives

After studying this chapter, you should:
→ be familiar with the general pattern of world trade and the trade of the UK
→ be aware of the different forms that economic integration may take: free trade areas, customs unions, common markets and economic and monetary union
→ know the features of these alternative forms of integration and understand the distinctions between them
→ understand the significance of the Single European Market (SEM)
→ evaluate the costs and benefits of membership of a single currency area
→ be aware of the role and effectiveness of monetary and fiscal policy within a single currency area
→ be aware of the ways in which protectionist policies have been implemented
→ be able to evaluate the case for and against protectionism

The pattern of world trade

In order to provide the context for a discussion of the effect of globalisation on trade, and the place of the UK economy in the global economy, it is helpful to examine the pattern of world trade.

Table 8.1 presents some data on this pattern. It shows the size of trade flows between regions. The rows of the table show the exports from each of the regions to each other region, while the columns show the pattern of imports from each region. The numbers on the 'diagonal' of the table (in bold type) show the trade flows *within* regions. One remarkable feature of the table is the high involvement of the EU in world trade, accounting for 36% of imports and 34% of exports. Of course, this includes substantial flows within Europe. In contrast, Africa shows very little involvement in world trade, in spite of the fact that, in population terms, it is far larger.

Indeed, trade flows between the developed countries — and with the more advanced developing countries — have tended to dominate world trade, with the flows between developing countries being relatively minor. This is not surprising, given that by definition the richer countries have greater purchasing power. However, the

Table 8.1 Intra- and interregional merchandise trade, 2011 (US$bn)

	Destination								
Origin	North America	South and Central America	European Union	Other Europe	CIS	Africa	Middle East	Asia	World
North America	**1,103**	201	328	54	15	37	63	476	2,278
South and Central America	181	**200**	120	17	8	21	18	169	736
European Union	433	109	**3,906**	388	211	183	159	575	5,965
Other Europe	47	9	352	**22**	23	16	35	63	567
CIS	43	11	356	53	**154**	12	24	117	770
Africa	102	19	182	23	2	**77**	21	146	572
Middle East	107	10	133	25	6	38	**110**	660	1,089
Asia	906	189	847	75	110	152	242	**2,926**	5,447
World	2,923	749	6,223	658	530	538	672	5,133	**17,425**

Note: world totals have been calculated from the table.

Source: World Trade Organization

degree of openness to trade of economies around the world varies also as a result of conscious policy decisions. Some countries, especially in East Asia, have adopted very open policies towards trade, promoting exports in order to achieve export-led growth. In contrast, some countries (including a number in Latin America) have been much more reluctant to become dependent on international trade, and have adopted a more closed attitude towards trade. In more recent years, both China and India have been experiencing economic growth at a very high rate indeed, and have become significant trading nations. This has had repercussions for other countries around the world.

Quantitative skills 8.1

Using percentages

In Table 8.1, origin countries are shown in the rows, and destination countries in the columns. For example, to identify the exports from (say) the EU to Asia, you need to look in the EU row and the Asia column, which is $575 bn. The world column shows total exports from each of the row regions, so the total of EU exports is $5,965 bn. The share of EU exports going to Asia is thus $100 \times 575/5,965 = 9.64\%$. In similar fashion, the share of EU imports coming from Asia is $100 \times 847/6,223 = 13.61\%$. Make sure you understand why this is the case.

The pattern of UK trade

Figures 8.1(a) and (b) show the destination of UK exports of goods and services to major regional groupings in the world. The most striking feature of this graph is the extent to which the UK relies on Europe and the USA for nearly three-quarters of its exports. Figures 8.2(a) and (b) reveal a similar pattern for the UK's imports of goods and services. Notice also that imports of goods from China (including Hong Kong) have become significant — and comprise a much larger share in imports than in exports.

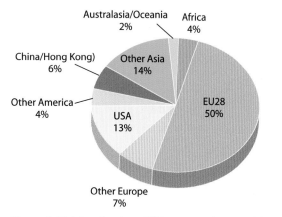

Figure 8.1(a) Destination of UK exports of goods, 2013

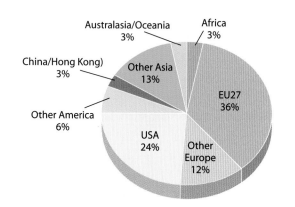

Figure 8.1(b) Destination of UK exports of services, 2013

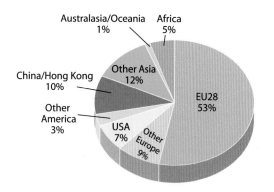

Figure 8.2(a) Source of UK imports of goods, 2013

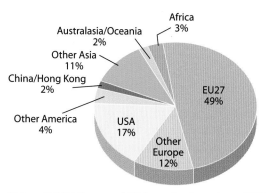

Figure 8.2(b) Source of UK imports of services, 2013

Source for both figures: Pink Book

The proportion of UK trade (both exports and imports) that is with Europe has undergone substantial change over the past 50 years. In 1960, when the Commonwealth was still thriving and the UK was ambivalent about the idea of European integration, less than a quarter of UK exports of goods went to other European countries (23% in 1960). However, this has changed as the UK has grown closer to Europe, reaching 57% in 1990 and remaining at 50% in 2013.

Exercise 8.1

a Using the data provided in Table 8.1, calculate the share of each region in world exports and imports. Think about the factors that might influence the contrasting performance of the EU and Africa. Also, for each region calculate the share of exports and imports that are within the region and comment on any significant differences that you find.

b Are there any aspects of the pattern of world trade that took you by surprise? Can you find reasons for these?

Summary

- There are substantial differences in the degree to which countries trade: trade with and within the EU accounts for an appreciable proportion of world trade, whereas Africa shows very little involvement.
- About three-quarters of UK exports go to Europe and the USA.
- The share of UK trade with the rest of Europe has increased substantially over the past 40 years.

Trading blocs

An important influence on the pattern of world trade has been the establishment of trading blocs in different parts of the world. These are intended to encourage trade among groups of nations, normally on a regional basis, in order to tap the gains from trade. Examples are ASEAN (an organisation of ten countries in South East Asia), MERCOSUR (five countries in Latin America), NAFTA (Canada, the USA and Mexico) and, of course, the European Union. These groupings are at very different stages of integration and cooperation.

Regional trade integration can take on a variety of forms, representing differing degrees of closeness. The underlying motivation for integration is to allow trading partners to take advantage of the potential gains from international trade, as illustrated by the law of comparative advantage. By reducing the barriers to trade, this specialisation can be encouraged, and there should be gains from the process. In practice, there may be other economic and political forces at work that affect the nature of the gains, and the extent to which integration will be possible — and beneficial.

Free trade areas

A **free trade area** is a group of countries that agree to trade without barriers between themselves, but maintain their own individual barriers with countries outside the area. The North American Free Trade Area (NAFTA) is one such grouping. The Association of Southeast Asian Nations (ASEAN) has the aim of establishing a free trade area by the year 2020.

Customs unions

A **customs union** goes further than a free trade area, not only eliminating barriers to trade between the member countries, but also having a common tariff barrier against the rest of the world. Notice that a customs union does not need to have a common currency.

Evaluation

An important question in evaluating both free trade areas and customs unions is the extent to which they are able to generate increased trade and improved efficiency in production.

By creating a free trade area or customs union (i.e. without or with common barriers against the rest of the world), it is possible that the member nations will trade with each other instead of with the rest of the world: in other words, it is possible that trade will simply be diverted from the rest of the world to the partners in the agreement. Such **trade diversion** does not necessarily mean that gains from trade are being fully exploited, as ideally there should be **trade creation** as well as trade diversion.

> ### Key terms
>
> **free trade area** a group of countries that agree to trade without barriers between themselves, but having their own individual barriers with countries outside the area
>
> **customs union** a group of countries that agree to trade without barriers between them, and with a common tariff barrier against the rest of the world
>
> **trade creation** the replacement of more expensive domestic production or imports with cheaper output from a partner within the trading bloc
>
> **trade diversion** the replacement of cheaper imported goods by goods from a less efficient trading partner within a bloc

Extension material

The effects of trade creation and trade diversion

Figure 8.3 illustrates the effects of trade creation. It shows the demand and supply of a good in a certain country that joins a customs union. Before joining the union, the price of the good is T, which includes a tariff element. Domestic demand is D_0, of which S_0 comes from domestic producers, and the remainder is imported. When the country joins the customs union, the tariff is removed and the domestic price falls to P. Consumers benefit from additional consumer surplus, given by the area $PTBG$. However, notice that not all of this is pure gain to the country. The area $PTAC$ was formerly part of producer surplus, so there has been a redistribution from domestic firms to consumers. $ABFE$ was formerly tariff revenue collected by the government, so this represents effectively a redistribution from government to consumers. The area ACE is a net gain for the country, as this represents resources that were previously used up in the production of the good, but which can now be used for other purposes. The area BFG also represents a welfare gain to the country.

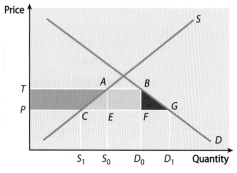

Figure 8.3 The effects of trade creation

Figure 8.4 helps to show the effects of trade diversion. Here, D represents the demand curve for a commodity that is initially imported from a country outside the customs union. It is assumed that the supply of the good from the non-member is perfectly elastic, as shown by S_n. However, the importing country imposes a tariff of the amount T, so the quantity imported is given by Q_n, and the price charged is $P_n + T$.

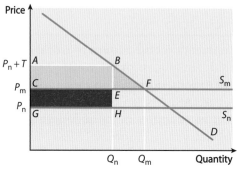

Figure 8.4 The effects of trade diversion

After the importing country joins the customs union, the tariff is removed, but the good is now imported from a less efficient producer within the union. The supply from this member country is assumed to be elastic at S_m, so the new price is P_m and the quantity is Q_m.

In examining the welfare effects, there are two issues to consider. First, notice that consumer surplus has increased by the area $ABFC$. However, this is not pure gain to the economy because, in the original position, the government was collecting tariff revenue of the amount $ABHG$. In other words, the increase in consumer surplus comes partly as a pure gain (the triangle BFE), but partly at the expense of the government ($ABEC$). This is not all, because the area $CEHG$ was also formerly part of tariff revenue, but now is a payment by domestic consumers to producers in the other (member) country. This means that whether the country is better or worse off depends upon the relative size of the areas BFE (which is a gain) and $CEHG$ (which is a loss).

It is to be hoped that a trading agreement such as a free trade area or customs union would generate efficiency gains. If firms are able to service a larger overall market, it should be possible to exploit economies of scale and scope, which would reduce average production costs. This may require countries to alter their pattern of specialisation to take full advantage of the enlarged market. For example, within the European Union there is a wide range of countries having different patterns of comparative advantage, ranging from countries like the UK, France and Germany to the new members from eastern Europe and the Baltic. The relative endowment of labour and capital among the member states can be expected to be very different.

This diversity is important for the success of a trade grouping. Remember that it is the *difference* in relative opportunity costs of production that drives the comparative advantage process and creates the potential gains from trade. However, it is clear that there also tends to be a strong political dimension affecting the outcome of such trade agreements.

Common markets

It may be that the countries within a customs union wish to move to closer integration, by extending the degree of cooperation between the member nations. A **common market** adds to the features of a customs union by harmonising some aspects of the economic environment between them. In a pure common market, this would entail adopting common tax rates across the member states, and a common framework for the laws and regulations that provide the environment for production, employment and trade. A common market would also allow for the free movement of factors of production between the member nations, especially in terms of labour and capital (land is less mobile by its nature!). Given the importance of the public sector in a modern economy, a common market would also set common procurement policies across member governments, so that individual governments did not favour their own domestic firms when purchasing goods and services. The Single European Market has encompassed most of these features, although tax rates have not been harmonised across the countries that are included.

Economic and monetary union

An alternative form of integration is where countries choose to share a common currency, but without the degree of cooperation that is involved with a free trade area or common market. Such an arrangement is known as a **monetary union** or a *currency union*. Full **economic and monetary union** combines the common market arrangements with a shared currency (or permanently fixed exchange rates between the members countries). This requires member states to follow a common monetary policy, and it is also seen as desirable to harmonise other aspects of macroeconomic policy across the union.

The adoption of permanently fixed exchange rates is a contentious aspect of proposals for economic and monetary union, as governments are no longer able to use monetary policy for internal domestic purposes. This is because monetary variables become subservient to the need to maintain the exchange rate, and it is not possible to set independent targets for the rate of interest or money supply if the government has to maintain the value of the currency on the foreign exchange market. This is all very well if all countries in the union are following a similar economic cycle, but if one country becomes poorly synchronised with the others, there may be major problems.

For example, it could be that the union as a whole is enjoying a boom, and setting interest rates accordingly. For an individual member country suffering a recession, this could mean deepening and prolonging the recession, as it would not be possible to relax interest rates in order to allow aggregate demand to recover.

A successful economic and monetary union therefore requires careful policy coordination across the member nations. Notice that economic and monetary union involves fixed exchange rates between the member countries, but does not necessarily entail the adoption of a common currency, although this may follow at some stage.

Key terms

common market a set of trading arrangements in which a group of countries remove barriers to trade among them, adopt a common set of barriers against external trade, establish common tax rates and laws regulating economic activity, allow free movement of factors of production between members and have common public sector procurement policies

monetary union a situation in which countries adopt a common currency

economic and monetary union a set of trading arrangements the same as for a common market, but in addition having a common currency (or permanently fixed exchange rates between the member countries) and a common monetary policy

Summary

- Economic integration can take a variety of forms, of differing degrees of closeness.
- A free trade area is where a group of countries agree to remove restrictions on trade between them, but without having a common external tariff.
- A customs union is a free trade area with an agreed common set of restrictions on trade with non-members.
- A customs union can entail trade creation, in which member countries benefit from increased trade and specialisation.
- However, there may also be trade diversion, in which countries divert their trading activity from external trade partners to countries within the union.
- Trade diversion does not always bring gains, as the producers within the union are not necessarily more efficient than external producers.
- A common market is a customs union in which the member countries also agree to harmonise their policies in a number of key respects.
- Economic and monetary union entails fixed exchange rates between member countries, but not necessarily agreement to adopt a common currency.

The European Union

The European Union is one of the most prominent examples of regional trade integration, and has progressed further than most in evolving towards economic and monetary integration. Figure 8.5 shows the population size of EU member countries in 2012, and the dates at which they joined.

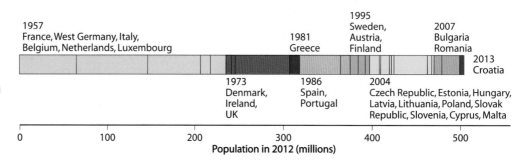

Figure 8.5 Population of EU28, 2012

Source: data from the *World Development Report*, 2014

Bulgaria and Romania had been judged not to be ready to join in 2004, but joined in 2007; Croatia joined in 2013. Negotiations with Turkey began in 2005, but quickly ran into problems. If Turkey were to join, this would add a massive 74 million citizens to the EU.

Notice that the 15 pre-2004 member countries of the EU (the 'EU15') already contained more people than the USA; the combined population of the EU28 member states in 2012 was 510 million, compared with 314 million in the USA.

The Single European Market (SEM)

From the moment of formation of the European Economic Community (EEC) in 1957, the member countries began working towards the creation of a single market in which there would be free movement of goods, services, people and capital. In other words, the idea was to create a *common market* in which there would be no barriers to trade. The EEC was a *customs union* in which internal tariffs and non-tariff barriers were to be removed and a common tariff was to be set against the rest of the world.

A package of measures that came into effect in January 1993 might be seen as the final stages in the evolution of the SEM. The key measures were the removal (or reduction) of border controls and the winding down of non-tariff barriers to trade within the EU. In this way, physical, technical and fiscal barriers were removed. It has also become increasingly easy for people to move around within the EU, with passport and customs checks being abolished at most internal borders. Associated with these measures were a number of expected benefits.

The Single Market package came into effect in 1993, bringing a number of benefits to the EU countries

Transaction costs

Tariff barriers between EU countries were abolished under the Treaty of Rome, but a range of non-tariff barriers had built up over the years as countries sought to protect domestic employment. It was expected that the removal of these obstacles to trade, combined with the removal of border controls, would reduce the costs of trade within the EU. However, it is difficult to gauge the significance of these transaction cost savings, as it is not easy to quantify them.

Economies of scale

As trade increases, firms will find that they are operating in a larger market. This should allow them to exploit more fully the economies of large-scale production. From society's point of view, this should lead to a more efficient use of resources, as long as the resulting trade creation effects are stronger than any trade diversion that may take place.

It seems that the nature of technological change in recent years has favoured the growth of large-scale enterprises. Improved transport and communications have contributed to this process. The SEM has enabled firms in Europe to take advantage of these developments.

Intensified competition

Firms will find that they are facing more intense competition within that larger market from firms in other parts of the EU. This then brings up the same arguments that are used to justify privatisation — that intensified competition will cause firms or their managers to seek more efficient production techniques, perhaps through the elimination of X-inefficiencies. This again is beneficial for society as a whole.

From the perspective of individual countries, there has been a divergence of views concerning the large firms that have been created through mergers and acquisitions. In some countries, large firms have been seen as 'national champions'. These have been protected (or even subsidised) by domestic governments, based on the argument that they will then be better prepared to compete in the broader European market. Elsewhere, governments have taken the view that the only way to ensure that domestic firms are lean enough to be competitive in overseas markets is to face intense competition at home, as an inducement to efficiency.

Who gains most from the SEM?

As trade within Europe becomes freer, two groups of countries stand to gain the most. First, the pattern of comparative advantage between countries will be important. Many EU countries are advanced industrial nations, where labour is expensive relative to capital. These countries tend to specialise in manufacturing or capital-intensive service activities, and already have fairly similar structures. It is thus possible that the relatively labour-abundant countries of southern Europe may gain more from closer integration and an expansion of trade. This is because they have a pattern of comparative advantage that is significantly different from existing members. This diversity was reinforced by the new entrants who joined in May 2004.

Second, if the main effect of integration is to remove barriers to trade, the countries with the most to gain may be those that begin with relatively high barriers.

How important is this to the UK?

An important piece of background information is that, over the years, UK trade has become increasingly focused on Europe. This means that the UK depends heavily on trade with other countries in the EU, so successful economic performance cannot be seen in isolation from events in the broader market.

The single currency area

The establishment of the SEM was seen by some as an end in itself, but others regarded it as a step towards full monetary integration, in which all member states would adopt a single currency, thereby reducing the transaction costs of international trade even more. However, full monetary union and the adoption of a common currency is about much more than transaction costs and has raised considerable debate, not least because of the political dimension. Critics of closer integration are concerned about the loss of sovereignty by individual countries. This concern is partly an economic one, focusing on the loss of separate currencies and (perhaps more significantly) the loss of control over national economic policy.

The European Monetary System

The foundations for monetary union began to be laid down in 1979, with the launch of the European Monetary System (EMS). One aspect of the EMS was the Exchange Rate Mechanism (ERM), which can be seen as a precursor of the single currency. Those countries that chose to opt into the ERM agreed to maintain their exchange rates within a band of plus or minus 2.25% against the average of their currencies — known as the European Currency Unit (ECU). The UK remained outside the ERM except for a brief flirtation between September 1990 and September 1992. During this period, the UK was operating within a slightly wider (6%) band.

During the period of the EMS/ERM, it was recognised that occasional realignment of currencies might be needed, and in fact there were 11 realignments between 1979 and 1987. However, the conditions under which such realignments were permitted were gradually tightened, so that they became less frequent as time went by.

Another key feature of the EMS period was the removal of capital controls. During the early part of this period, most of the member nations restricted the movement of financial capital across borders. This gave them some scope for using monetary policy independently of other countries. However, it was agreed that such capital controls would be phased out.

The Delors Plan, issued in 1989, set out proposals for creating European economic and monetary union (EMU), together with plans for a single currency and a European central bank. It was crucial to establish a European central bank because, with a single currency, a central bank is needed to administer monetary policy throughout the EU.

Treaty of Maastricht

The next major step was the Maastricht Treaty, which created the European Union (EU). This treaty encompassed not only economic issues, such as the introduction of the single currency, but also aspects of social policy, steps towards creating a common foreign, security and defence policy, and the development of a notion of European 'citizenship'.

It was considered that, if a single currency was to be established, the participating nations would need to have converged in their economic characteristics. If the countries were too diverse in their economic conditions, the transition to a single currency would be costly. For example, if they had very different inflation rates, interest rates or levels of outstanding government debt, the tensions of union might be too great to sustain. Strong countries would be dragged down, and weak countries would be unable to cope. The Maastricht Treaty therefore set out the *convergence criteria* by which countries would be eligible to join the single currency area. These criteria covered aspects of both monetary and fiscal policy.

Monetary policy

This is obviously important, as monetary union entails the centralisation of monetary policy within the EU. If there is to be a single currency and a single central bank to control interest rates or money supply, the monetary conditions of the economies concerned need to be reasonably close before union takes place. It was thus important to evaluate whether countries were sufficiently close to be able to join with minimal tension.

Inflation

Could countries with widely different inflation rates successfully join in a monetary union? One view is that it would be unreasonable to expect a country with 10% or 20% inflation to join a monetary union along with a country experiencing inflation at just 1%. An alternative view is that it is equally unreasonable to expect a country to cure its inflation before joining a union when one of the alleged benefits of joining is that it will cure inflation by enforcing financial discipline and removing discretion over monetary policy from individual states. However, the first criterion specified by the treaty was that countries joining the union should be experiencing low and similar inflation rates — defined as inflation no more than 1.5% above the average of the three countries in the EMS with the lowest rate.

Interest and exchange rates

Given that financial capital tends to follow high interest rates, it is argued that diversity of interest rates before union may be undesirable, as this would imply instability of capital movements. Similarly, it has been argued that a period of exchange rate stability before union would be some indication that countries have been following mutually consistent policies, and would indicate that union is plausible.

The criteria set out in the treaty required that long-term interest rates be no more than 2% above the average of the three EMS countries with the lowest rate, and that each joining country should have been in the narrow band of the ERM for a period of 2 years without the need for realignment.

Fiscal policy

Should there also be conformity in fiscal stance between countries? Would there be severe problems if countries embarked upon union and policy coordination in conditions in which unemployment rates differed markedly? These are separate but related questions. If unemployment is high, this will be connected (via social security payments) with the fiscal stance adopted by the government — as judged in terms of the government budget deficit.

The reason why unemployment rates are relevant is that there may need to be fiscal transfers between member states in order to reduce the differentials. This will clearly be politically significant in the context of a monetary union, and is an issue that will affect the long-term viability of the union. However, although unemployment rates are potentially important for this reason, the convergence criteria did not refer to unemployment directly. Instead, the criteria included a reference to fiscal policy. In practice, the divergence in unemployment rates was substantial.

Two areas are critical in judging the distance between countries in terms of fiscal policy. First, there is the question of the short-term fiscal stance, which can be measured by the budget deficit. Second, it is important to consider some indication of a longer-term commitment to stability in fiscal policy, in terms of achieving sustainable levels of outstanding government debt. Thus, the treaty required that the budget deficit be no larger than 3% of GDP, and that the national debt be no more than 60% of GDP.

Economic and monetary union

The final stage of the transition towards the single currency was European Economic and Monetary Union (EMU). Under EMU, exchange rates between participating countries were permanently locked together: in other words, no further realignments

Euro notes and coins began to circulate in the euro zone in 2002

were allowed. Furthermore, the financial markets of the countries were integrated, with the European Central Bank setting a common interest rate across the union. This was achieved in 1999.

Formation of the euro area

In the event, 11 countries were judged to have met the Maastricht criteria (Belgium, Germany, Spain, France, Ireland, Italy, Luxembourg, the Netherlands, Austria, Portugal and Finland). Together with Greece, these countries formed the single currency area, which came into operation on 1 January 2002. Slovenia joined the euro zone in 2007, followed by Cyprus and Malta in 2008, Slovakia in 2009, Estonia in 2011 and Latvia in 2014.

Costs and benefits of a single currency

Some of the arguments for and against a single currency area such as the euro zone are similar to those used in evaluating a fixed exchange rate system against a flexible one, which will be discussed in the next chapter. This is because a common currency is effectively creating an area in which exchange rates between member nations are fixed for ever, even if that common currency varies relative to the rest of the world. The question of whether such an arrangement is beneficial overall for the member states rests on an evaluation of the benefits and costs of joining together. An *optimal currency area* occurs when a group of countries are better off with a single currency.

Benefits

The main benefits of a single currency area come in the form of a *monetary efficiency gain*, which has the effect of encouraging more trade between member countries. The hope is that this will bring further gains from exploiting comparative advantage between countries and enabling firms to reap the benefits of economies of scale.

The efficiency gain comes from two main sources. First, there are gains from reducing *transaction costs*, if there is no longer the need to convert from one currency into another. Second, there are gains from the reduction in *uncertainty*, in the sense that there is no longer a need to forecast future movements in exchange rates — at least between participating countries. This is similar to the gains from a fixed exchange rate system, but it goes further, as there is no longer a risk of occasional devaluation or revaluation of currencies.

The extent to which these gains are significant will depend upon the degree of integration between the participating nations. If most of the trade that takes place is between the participants, the gains will clearly be much more significant than if member nations are also trading extensively with countries outside the single currency area.

Costs

The costs come in the conduct and effectiveness of policy. Within the single currency area, individual countries can no longer have recourse to monetary policy in order to stabilise the macroeconomy. As with the fixed exchange rate system, one key question then is how well individual economies are able to adjust to external shocks. Thus, it is important for each economy to have flexibility. In addition, individual countries have to be aware that, once in the single currency area, it is impossible to use monetary policy to smooth out fluctuations in output and employment.

In this context, it is very important that the economic cycles of participating economies are well synchronised. If one economy is out of phase with the rest, it may find itself facing an inappropriate policy situation. For example, suppose that most of the countries within the euro zone are in the boom phase of the economic cycle, and are wanting to raise the interest rate in order to control aggregate demand: if one country within the zone is in recession, then the last thing it will want is rising interest rates, as this will deepen the recession and delay recovery. These arguments came to the fore during the recession of the late 2000s.

Evaluation

Paul Krugman suggested a helpful way of using cost–benefit analysis to evaluate these aspects of a single currency area. He argues that both the costs and the benefits from a single currency area will vary with the degree to which member countries are integrated. Thus the benefits from joining such a currency area would rise as the closeness of integration increased, whereas the costs would fall.

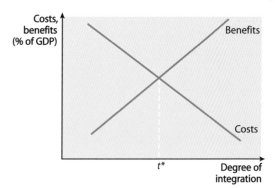

Figure 8.6 Costs and benefits of a single currency area

Figure 8.6 illustrates the balance between costs and benefits. For countries that are not very closely integrated (that is, if 'integration' is less than $t\star$), the costs from joining the union exceed the benefits, so it would not be in the country's interest to join. However, as the degree of integration increases, so the benefits increase, and the costs decrease, so for any country beyond $t\star$, the benefits exceed the costs, and it is thus worth joining.

For an individual country considering whether or not to join the euro area, a first step is to reach a judgement on whether the country is to the left or to the right of $t\star$. There may be other issues to consider in addition to the costs and benefits, but unless the country has at least reached $t\star$, it could be argued that entry into the union should not be considered.

One way of viewing the situation is that the costs are mainly macroeconomic, but the benefits are microeconomic. This complicates the evaluation process. Some research published in 2006 argued that most of the boost to trade within the euro area occurred during the initial period, and would not continue to build up over time. It was also suggested that the EU countries that decided not to join the euro (the UK, Sweden and Denmark) gained almost as much as the countries that had joined.

The experience of some European countries during and in the aftermath of the financial crisis has cast doubt on whether the euro zone could be viewed as an optimal currency area. In particular, some countries faced problems because they could not pursue independent monetary or fiscal policies.

From a UK perspective, the debate has shifted substantially. There was a time when the key issue was whether the UK should join the euro, and the 1997 Labour government went to great lengths to set out the conditions that would need to be met for this to be seen as the best way forward. This debate has now been supplanted by views expressed by some pressure groups that not only should the UK not join the euro, but it should withdraw entirely from the EU, in spite of the importance of trade with Europe in terms of both exports and imports.

> ### Study tip
>
> Note that feelings can run high on issues like the euro and the EU, but you need to stay objective as far as possible, and advance economic arguments, not personal views.

Exercise 8.3

Identify the costs and benefits that would be associated with the UK's entry into the euro single currency group of countries, and discuss whether you believe that the UK should join if conditions favour it. Do you consider that the UK should remain in the EU?

Structural change

A feature that all of these forms of integration have in common is that they involve the removal of barriers to trade amongst member countries. It is important to be aware that this will not be perceived as a good thing by all the parties involved. In order to benefit from increased specialisation and trade, countries need to allow the pattern of their production to change. The benefits to the expanding sectors are apparent, but it is also the case that industries that formerly enjoyed protection from competition will become exposed to competition, and will need to decline in order to allow resources to be transferred into the expanding sectors. This can be a painful process for firms that need to close down, or move into new markets, and for workers who may need to undergo retraining before they are ready for employment in the newly expanding parts of the economy.

An especially contentious area of debate in the UK concerns the structural change that has taken place in recent decades, in which manufacturing activity has declined and financial services have expanded. This seems to reflect the changing pattern of the UK's comparative advantage, in which banking, finance and insurance have become a major strength of the economy, whereas the manufacturing sector has found it more difficult to compete with the host of new entrants into this market from elsewhere in the world.

Trading blocs and the WTO

To some extent there might be seen to be a conflict between the establishment of trading blocs and the operations of the WTO. Trading blocs encourage trade within regional groupings, but may also impose restrictions on trade from non-member nations. On the other hand, the WTO has the objective of promoting freer trade amongst countries.

The WTO monitors the establishment and operations of trading blocs, and performs an important role in arbitrating in the case of disputes between countries that arise in relation to the conditions under which trade takes place.

Summary

- The first step towards monetary union was the launch of the European Monetary System (EMS) in 1979.
- An important part of this was the Exchange Rate Mechanism (ERM), under which participating countries (which did not include the UK) agreed to keep their currencies within a narrow band (2.25%) against the average of their currencies.
- The Maastricht Treaty created the European Union (EU), and set out the route towards closer integration.
- The treaty also set out the convergence criteria, to be used to judge which countries were ready to join in monetary union. These criteria covered financial and fiscal aspects.
- Twelve countries adopted the euro as their common currency in January 2002.
- The main benefit of a common currency area is that it encourages trade by reducing transaction costs and reducing foreign exchange risk.
- However, the downside is that individual countries have less autonomy in controlling their macroeconomies. Adjusting to external shocks and smoothing short-term fluctuations in output and employment become more difficult with a common monetary policy that may not always be set in ways that are appropriate for all participating countries.
- There are many other examples of regional trade agreements that have reached various stages of integration, such as NAFTA and ASEAN.

Trade liberalisation or protectionism?

Comparative advantage is just one of many reasons for countries to engage in international trade. Trade enables consumers in a country to have access to products that could not be produced at home, and enables producers to have access to new markets and resources. In some cases it allows producers to take advantage of economies of scale that would not be possible if they had to rely only on selling to the domestic market. From the country's perspective, export-led growth may be possible, and there are countries such as China and other countries in South East Asia that have benefited from this. It is also possible that exposure to competition from foreign firms provides a good incentive for domestic firms to become more efficient, raising the quality of their goods or the efficiency with which they are produced. Consumers may then gain from wider variety of available products, improved quality and lower prices.

In spite of these potential gains from trade, countries have often seemed reluctant to open their economies fully to international trade, and have tended to intervene in various ways to protect their domestic producers. Many reasons have been given for this, not all of which have a grounding in economic analysis.

There may be political reasons for wanting to protect domestic industries. For example, there may be strategic arguments that a country should always maintain an agricultural sector so as not to be over-dependent on imported foodstuffs, as this could be disastrous in the event of war. Such arguments were used in setting up the Common Agricultural Policy in Europe. Some have also argued that domestic industries should be protected because of the impact of high unemployment among workers displaced from declining sectors. This is really an argument about the period of transition to more open trade, as it could also be noted that workers released from those declining sectors could, in time, be redeployed in sectors that are more efficient in comparative advantage terms.

A common line of argument is about the need to protect so-called *infant industries*. This may be especially important in the context of less developed countries wanting to develop their manufacturing sectors. The argument is that protecting a domestic industry from international competition will allow the new activities to become familiar with the market so that in the longer term they will be able to compete.

When recession began to threaten in 2008, there was strong lobbying from pressure groups in the USA and elsewhere in favour of introducing protectionist measures. Indeed, in the lead-up to the G20 Summit in April 2009, the World Bank reported that 17 members of that group had taken a total of 47 trade-restricting steps in the previous months. However, the drive towards globalisation had created a more integrated global economy, in which many firms relied on a global supply chain. With the production process fragmented between different parts of the world, the dangers of protectionism become more severe, and the possibilities of rapid contagion from a crisis become acute.

Tariffs

A policy instrument commonly used in the past to give protection to domestic producers is the imposition of a **tariff**. Tariff rates in the developed countries have been considerably reduced in the period since the Second World War, but nonetheless are still in place.

Key term
tariff a tax imposed on imported goods

Figure 8.7 shows how a tariff is expected to operate. D represents the domestic demand for a commodity, and S_{dom} shows how much domestic producers are prepared to supply at any given price. The price at which the good can be imported from world markets is given by P_{w}. If dealing with a global market, it is reasonable to assume that the supply at the world price is perfectly elastic, especially for a small economy that is unable to influence the world price. Another way of thinking about this is that supply is perfectly elastic in the sense that the country can import as much as it wishes at the going world price. So in the absence of a tariff, domestic demand is given by D_0, of which S_0 is supplied within the domestic economy and the remainder $(D_0 - S_0)$ is imported. If the government wishes to protect this industry within the domestic economy, it needs to find a way of restricting imports and encouraging home producers to expand their capacity.

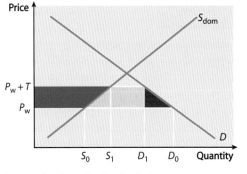

Figure 8.7 The effects of a tariff

By imposing a tariff, the domestic price rises to $P_{\text{w}} + T$, where T is the amount of the tariff. This has two key effects. One is to reduce the demand for the good from D_0 to D_1; the second is to encourage domestic producers to expand their output of this good from S_0 to S_1. As a consequence imports fall substantially, to $(D_1 - S_1)$. On the face of it, the policy has achieved its objective. Furthermore, the government has been able to raise some tax revenue (given by the yellow rectangle).

However, not all the effects of the tariff are favourable for the economy. Consumers are certainly worse off, as they have to pay a higher price for the good; they therefore consume less, and there is a loss of consumer surplus, represented in the figure by the sum of the shaded areas. Some of what was formerly consumer surplus has been redistributed to others in society. The government has gained the tariff revenue, as mentioned. In addition, producers gain producer surplus, shown by the dark blue coloured area. There is also a deadweight loss to society, represented by the red and pale blue triangles. These areas were formerly part of consumer surplus, but are now lost. In other words, overall society is worse off as a result of the imposition of the tariff. Notice that the impact of the tariff will depend upon the elasticity of demand and supply in the domestic market.

Effectively, the government is subsidising inefficient local producers, and forcing domestic consumers to pay a price that is above that of similar goods imported from abroad.

Some would defend this policy on the grounds that it allows the country to protect an industry, thus saving jobs that would otherwise be lost. However, this goes against comparative advantage and in the longer term it may delay structural change. For an economy to develop new specialisations and new sources of comparative advantage, there needs to be a transitional process in which old industries contract and new ones emerge. Although this process may be painful, it is necessary in the long run if the economy is to remain competitive. Furthermore, the protection which firms enjoy that allows them to reap producer surplus from the tariff may foster complacency and an inward-looking attitude. This is likely to lead to X-inefficiency, and an inability to compete in the global market.

Even worse is the situation that develops where nations respond to tariffs raised by competitors by putting up tariffs of their own. This has the effect of further reducing the trade between countries, and everyone ends up worse off, as the gains from trade are sacrificed.

> **Synoptic link**
>
> Notice that the notions of consumer and producer surplus turn up again here. These were first discussed in Book 1, Chapter 4.

Key term

voluntary export restraint (VER) an agreement by a country to limit its exports to another country to a given quantity or quota

Quotas

An alternative policy that a country may adopt is to limit the imports of a commodity to a given volume. For example, a country may come to an agreement with another country that only a certain quantity of imports will be accepted by the importing country. Such arrangements are sometimes known as **voluntary export restraints (VERs)** or as *quotas*.

Figure 8.8 illustrates the effects of such a quota. D represents the domestic demand for this commodity, and S_{dom} is the quantity that domestic producers are prepared to supply at any given price. Suppose that without any agreement, producers from country A would be prepared to supply any amount of the product at a price P_a. If the product is sold at this price, D_0 represents domestic demand, of which S_0 is supplied by domestic producers and the remainder $(D_0 - S_0)$ is imported from country A.

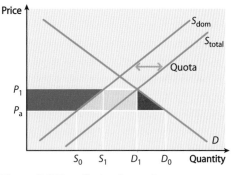

Figure 8.8 The effects of a quota

By imposing a quota, total supply is now given by S_{total}, which is domestic supply plus the quota of imports allowed into the economy from country A. The market equilibrium price rises to P_1 and demand falls to D_1, of which S_1 is supplied by domestic producers and the remainder is the agreed quota of imports.

Figure 8.8 shows who gains and who loses by this policy. Domestic producers gain by being able to sell at the higher price, so (as in the case of the tariff) they receive additional economic rent given by the dark blue area. Furthermore, the producers exporting from country A also gain, receiving the yellow rectangle (which, in the case of the tariff, was tax revenue received by the government). As in the case of the tariff, the two triangles (red and pale blue) represent the deadweight loss of welfare suffered by the importing country. Such an arrangement effectively subsidises the foreign producers by allowing them to charge a higher price than they would have been prepared to accept. Furthermore, although domestic producers are encouraged to produce more, the protection offered to them is likely to lead to X-inefficiency and weak attitudes towards competition.

Study tip

Notice that the diagram for a quota is very like the diagram for a tariff. Make sure you do not confuse the two, as they differ in terms of who gains and who loses from the measure.

There are a number of examples of such agreements, especially in the textile industry. For example, the USA and China have long-standing agreements on quotas for a range of textile products. Ninety-one such quotas expired at the end of 2004 as part of China's accession to the WTO. As you might expect, this led to extensive lobbying by producers in the USA, especially during the run-up to the 2004 presidential election. Notice that it could be argued that the removal of the quotas would allow domestic consumers to benefit from lower prices, and would allow American textile workers to be released for employment in higher-productivity sectors, where the USA maintains a competitive advantage.

An export subsidy

Another way in which a country may attempt to restrict trade is by subsidising domestic producers to enable them to compete more effectively with imports. Figure 8.9 illustrates a possible scenario.

This shows domestic demand and supply for a product that can be imported at the world price P_w. If the government decides to pay a subsidy of an amount Sub to domestic producers, this affects the supply curve such that it is horizontal up to S_1 in Figure 8.9.

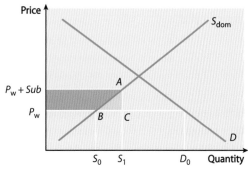

Figure 8.9 The effects of an export subsidy

The USA has tried to curtail the growth of the highly competitive Chinese textile industry through the use of import quotas

This encourages domestic firms to increase production up to S_1, but unlike the case of the tariff, domestic consumers are still able to buy the good at the world price, so there is not the same impact on consumer surplus.

Producers gain from this, receiving the additional producer surplus given by the dark blue shaded area. However, this needs to be covered by the government, as does the area ABC in the figure, which represents the production inefficiency that was a deadweight loss in the case of the tariff.

The total cost to the government of providing the subsidy is thus the sum of the dark and light blue areas. The downside of this approach is that these funds need to be raised from elsewhere in the economy, thus distorting the allocation of resources in other markets. Although consumers are better off in respect of this product with the subsidy than with a tariff, as taxpayers they may pay the price in other ways. Furthermore, it is not clear that subsidising exports in this way provides any better incentives for efficiency than the tariff approach. If governments wish to encourage firms to become more efficient in order to compete, a better approach might be to subsidise education and training, or research and development to improve production techniques, and thus tackle the problem more directly. Of course, this would depend on what was causing the inefficiency in the first place.

Non-tariff barriers

There are other ways in which trade can be hampered, one example being the use of what are known as **non-tariff barriers**. These often comprise rules and regulations that control the standard of products that can be sold in a country.

This is a grey area, as some of the rules and regulations may seem entirely sensible and apply equally to domestic and foreign producers. For example, laws that prohibit the sale of refrigerators that contain CFCs are designed to protect the ozone layer, and may be seen as wholly appropriate. In this case, the regulation is for purposes other than trade restriction. However, there may be other situations in which a regulation is more clearly designed to limit trade: for example, by making it more difficult for foreign firms to meet technical or quality standards.

Such rules and regulations may operate especially against producers in less developed countries, who may find it especially difficult to meet demanding standards of production. This applies in particular where such countries are trying to develop new skills and specialisations to enable them to diversify their exports and engage more actively in international trade.

Exercise 8.4

Figure 8.10 illustrates the impact of a tariff. S_{dom} represents the quantity supplied by domestic producers, and D_{dom} shows the demand curve of domestic consumers. The world price is OE, and the country can import as much of the good at that price as it wishes.

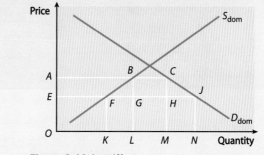

Figure 8.10 A tariff

a In the absence of government intervention, identify domestic demand and supply, and the quantity of imports.

b Suppose now that a tariff is imposed on imports of this product. Identify the price that will be charged in the domestic market.

c What will be the quantity demanded, the quantity supplied by home producers, and the quantity imported?

d Which area represents government revenue from the tariff?

e Identify the additional producer surplus received by domestic producers.

f Identify and explain the deadweight loss of the tariff.

g Discuss whether a tariff can be beneficial for society.

h Suppose that a tariff has been in place on this commodity, but that the government proposes to remove it. Discuss the effects that the removal of the tariff will have, and the difficulties a government might face in removing it.

Summary

- The law of comparative advantage shows that countries can gain from international trade by specialising in the production of goods or services in which they have a lower opportunity cost of production.
- In spite of these possible gains, countries have often introduced protectionist measures to restrict trade, including tariffs, quotas and non-tariff barriers.

Free trade and protectionism

Some early economic thinkers such as Adam Smith and David Ricardo drew attention to the possible benefits that nations could derive from engaging in international trade. These arguments were developed from notions of specialisation and division of labour, and Ricardo's law of comparative advantage. In spite of these potential economic gains, nations have always been tempted to introduce protectionist measures that interfere with free trade.

Specialisation

The arguments in favour of free trade stem from the observation that if countries specialise in the production of goods (or services) in which they have a comparative advantage, then it is possible for overall economic welfare to be increased through engaging in international trade. At the heart of this is the issue that countries face different patterns of potential specialisation – in other words, differing opportunity costs in production of goods. For example, an industrialised country is likely to have a comparative advantage in the production of manufactured goods relative to agricultural commodities, whereas a less developed country may have a comparative advantage in agricultural goods. Another way of putting this is that the opportunity cost of producing agricultural goods is higher for the industrial country than for the less developed country. Because of this, if each country specialises in producing the good in which it has a comparative advantage, total production of the goods can be increased.

One very important point to notice is that it cannot be guaranteed that both countries actually *will* be better off with trade. Some of the critics of globalisation have argued that many less developed countries today find themselves in a position in which they are encouraged to open up to more trade – but then find that the gains are being pre-empted by others.

Trade liberalisation

One of the hopes for a trade liberalisation policy is that resources may be released from inefficient domestic production into more productive employment in the export sector. For many less developed countries, it may turn out that the export sector is unable to expand, so that the only effect of liberalisation is to release workers and other resources into unemployment.

Another political or strategic issue arises in this situation. Suppose that a country agrees to specialise completely in producing manufactures at the expense of agricultural goods, and then finds itself unable to engage in trade because of a war. How does it then feed its people? Following two world wars, many European countries in the 1950s may have seen this possibility as a real threat, and felt that maintaining some form of protection of their agricultural sectors was strategically crucial. This was one of the stated motivations behind the development of Europe's Common Agricultural Policy, which remains one of the world's prime examples of a protectionist policy.

Globalisation has given an added impetus to world trade, but has also highlighted problem areas. The rapid rise of China's economy and its success in export activity has been seen as threatening by some, and a protectionist lobby in the USA put trade policy on the US election agenda. The developed countries are eager to persuade developing countries to open up their economies to services and manufactured goods, but a sticking point has been the reluctance of the developed countries to reduce their high farm subsidies, which make it difficult for developing countries to market the produce in which they have a natural comparative advantage. If an agreement is to be reached, it is likely that concessions will be needed on both sides.

Follow-up questions

a Explain the difference between absolute advantage and comparative advantage. Which of these notions gives rise to the potential gains from trade?

b Discuss why these gains may not always be shared equally among the trading partners.

c Examine the arguments for and against the use of tariffs.

The North American Free Trade Agreement (NAFTA)

NAFTA is a trilateral agreement between the USA, Canada and Mexico that was launched on 1 January 1994, with the aim of removing tariff barriers between the countries. These provisions were fully implemented on 1 January 2008. Although NAFTA is primarily about trade in goods and services between the three countries, there are also side agreements dealing with environmental and labour issues.

The US Department of Agriculture claims that NAFTA is 'one of the most successful trade agreements in history', having stimulated 'significant increases in agricultural trade and investment' between the three member countries.

Whether all partners have gained equally remains an open question. There is a strong protectionist lobby in the USA that has argued that jobs have been lost as a result of the agreement. Some commentators in Mexico have argued that NAFTA has damaged Mexico's agricultural sector, as it has faced subsidised imports from the USA. Labour issues have also been highly contentious, and the proposal from the USA to erect new fences to stem the flow of migrants from Mexico into the USA has aroused substantial debate.

It is important to treat these arguments with great care, as there are sensitive political issues that can sometimes override economic analysis. The law of comparative advantage suggests that there are potential gains from engaging in trade, but the process of liberalising trade entails short-run costs.

These may be expected to be transitional, especially for economic activities that are forced into decline in the face of expanding imports from partner countries. The existence of these costs should not prevent trade liberalisation if the long-term gains are sufficient to overcome them eventually. There must be a balancing of the costs against the benefits.

Whether Mexico's agricultural sector has benefited from NAFTA is open to debate

Follow-up questions

a What do you think might have motivated the members of NAFTA to join together in a free trade agreement?

b Which countries do you think would have most to gain from NAFTA?

c What factors would you need to take into account in evaluating the potential benefits of trade liberalisation in the context of an agreement such as NAFTA?

9 The balance of payments and exchange rates

For an individual economy, the potential gains from international trade in a globalised economy depend on the pattern of comparative advantage and on the competitiveness of domestic economic activity compared with the rest of the world. The ultimate health of the economy also requires long-term external balance. This chapter explores these issues. For any economy that is open to international trade, the exchange rate is a crucial variable, as it influences the competitiveness of domestic firms in international markets. The way in which the exchange rate is determined has wide-reaching effects on the conduct and effectiveness of macroeconomic policy. From the end of the Second World War until the early 1970s, a system of fixed exchange rates was in operation, whereby economies set the value of their currency relative to the US dollar. After this system broke down, most developed countries allowed their currencies to 'float', finding their own market levels, although at times governments have been tempted to intervene in this market. Some countries continue to peg their exchange rates to the US dollar. This chapter thus also investigates why the exchange rate is so important, and how the various systems for determining its value work.

Learning objectives

After studying this chapter, you should:

→ understand the role and significance of the balance of payments and the need to maintain external balance in the long run
→ be familiar with the use of alternative policy measures to manage the balance of payments
→ understand what is meant by the market for foreign exchange
→ understand the operation of a fixed exchange rate system
→ be familiar with a floating exchange rate system
→ be aware of the major determinants of exchange rates within a floating exchange rate system
→ understand the way in which macroeconomic policy influences the exchange rate, and vice versa
→ understand how changes in exchange rates can affect the level of economic activity in a country
→ be familiar with measures of international competitiveness and their significance

The balance of payments

For an economy like the UK that is open to international trade, it is important to monitor the trade that takes place. Book 1, Chapter 10 introduced the balance of payments, a set of accounts that monitors the transactions that take place between UK residents and the rest of the world. For an individual household it is important to monitor incomings and outgoings, as items purchased must be paid for in some way — either by using income or savings, or by borrowing. In a similar way, a country has to pay for goods, services or assets that are bought from other countries. The balance of payments accounts enable the analysis of such international transactions.

As with the household, transactions can be categorised as being either incoming or outgoing items. For example, if a car made in the UK is exported (i.e. purchased by a non-resident of the UK), this is an 'incoming' item, as the payment for the car is a credit to the UK. On the other hand, the purchase of a bottle of Italian wine (an import) is a debit item.

Similarly, all other transactions entered into the balance of payments accounts can be identified as credit or debit items, depending upon the direction of the payment. In other words, when money flows into the country as the result of a transaction, that is a credit; if money flows out, it is a debit. As all items have to be paid for in some way, the overall balance of payments when everything is added together must be zero. However, individual components can be positive or negative.

In line with international standards, the accounts are divided into three categories. The **current account** identifies transactions in goods and services, together with income payments and international transfers. Income payments here include the earnings of UK nationals from employment abroad and payments of investment income. Transfers are mainly transactions between governments: for example, between the British government and EU institutions, which make up the largest component. Also included here are flows of bilateral aid and social security payments abroad.

The **financial account** measures transactions in financial assets, including investment flows and central government transactions in foreign exchange reserves.

The **capital account** is relatively small. It contains capital transfers, the largest item of which is associated with migrants. When a person changes status from non-resident to resident of the UK, then any assets owned by that person are transferred to being British-owned.

Figure 9.1 shows the relative size of the balances on the main accounts since 1950, expressed as a percentage of GDP. As the total balance of payments must always be zero, the surplus (positive) components above the line must always exactly match the deficit (negative) items below the line. What this means is that any deficit on the current account must be matched by a surplus on the financial and other accounts. The relative magnitudes of the three major accounts vary through time.

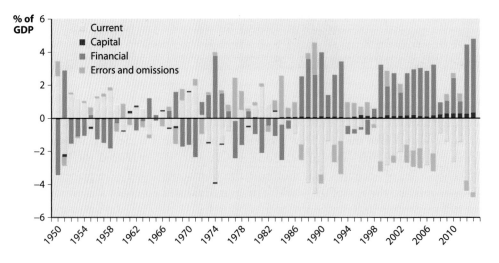

Figure 9.1 The UK balance of payments, 1950–2013
Source: ONS

The current account

The current account has been in deficit every year since 1984. The recorded current account surpluses in 1980–83 were associated with North Sea oil, which was then just coming on stream. There followed a phase in which the deficit grew to record levels, peaking in 1989. During the 1990s, the deficit fell until 1999, at which time the UK economy entered a period in which the current account has been consistently in substantial deficit, and the financial account in surplus. During the financial crisis of the late 2000s the current account deficit fell, as the recession resulted in a drop in the volume of international trade.

Figure 9.2 shows the components of the current account. You can see that until the early 1990s the overall balance on the current account (CBAL) tracked closely the trade in goods. More recently, however, the trade in goods has moved further into deficit, although this has been partially offset by a gradual increase in the trade in services and (except in 1999) by an increase in income — which is made up mainly of investment income.

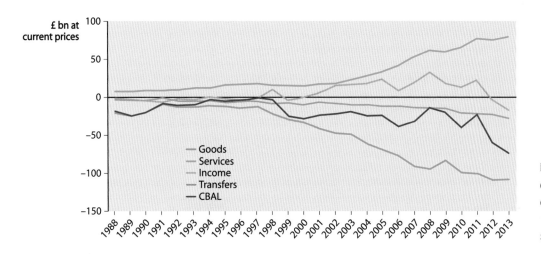

Figure 9.2 The composition of the current account, 1980–2013 (balances)
Source: ONS

Quantitative skills 9.1

Calculate the balance of an item in the balance of payments accounts

In 2013, the exports of goods amounted to £299.5 billion and imports were £407.4 billion. The balance of trade in goods was thus total exports minus imports: that is, 299.5 − 407.4 = −£107.9 billion.

Trade in goods (formerly known as **visible trade**) has traditionally shown a deficit for the UK — it has shown a surplus in only 6 years since 1950. As reserves of oil in the North Sea have run down, the UK has become a net importer of oil, although up to 2004 the UK had been a net exporter: in other words, the oil part of the trade in goods was in surplus. However, imports of cars and other consumer goods have persistently exceeded exports. A summary for 2007 (just before the financial crisis set in) is presented in Table 9.1, with data for 1997 as well to show how the pattern has changed. You should be aware that these data are in current prices, so you need to focus on the relative sizes rather than the absolute values.

Table 9.1 UK trade in goods (balances), 1997 and 2007 (£m in current prices)

Item	1997	2007
Food, beverages and tobacco	−5,808	−15,018
Basic materials	−3,520	−4,052
Oil	4,560	−4,047
Coal, gas and electricity	−368	−3,202
Semi-manufactured goods:		
Chemicals	4,496	4,180
Precious stones and silver	−318	−406
Other	−5,014	−10,069
Finished manufactured goods:		
Motor cars	−4,465	−7,230
Other consumer goods	−6,683	−24,734
Intermediate goods	−625	−11,112
Capital goods	3,753	−11,563
Ships and aircraft	1,646	−894
Commodities not classified	184	−1,105
Total	**−12,342**	**−89,252**

Source: Pink Book

Table 9.2 UK trade in services (balances), 1997 and 2007 (£m in current prices)

Item	1997	2007
Transportation	−2,092	−2,189
Travel	−3,638	−17,332
Communications	−185	346
Construction	98	154
Insurance	2,597	4,513
Financial	11,145	31,045
Computer and information	952	4,009
Royalties and licence fees	503	1,539
Other business	8,018	18,859
Personal cultural and recreational	274	1,128
Government	−769	−1,013
Total	**16,801**	**41,772**

Source: Pink Book

Key term

invisible trade trade in services

In contrast, trade in services has recorded a surplus in every year since 1966. This was formerly known as **invisible trade**. Table 9.2 shows the component items in 1997 and 2007 — again, measured in current prices, so that no allowance has been made for the effects of inflation.

As you can see, the largest deficit items in trade in services are transportation (especially air transport services, which has shown a deficit every year since the mid-1980s) and travel, where again the deficit has grown significantly since the late 1980s. The main reason for this is the increasing number of UK residents travelling aboard. However, these negative items are more than compensated for by the surplus components, especially financial services, which has grown steadily, as have computer and information services. You can see that 'Other business' also makes a significant contribution. This category includes trade-related services such as merchanting, consultancy services such as advertising, engineering and legal services, and operational leasing.

An important item on the current account is investment income, which represents earnings on past investment abroad. This item has shown strong growth since 1999 (when there was a deficit). The largest item in this part of the account is earnings from direct investment, although there is also an element of portfolio investment — earnings from holdings of bonds and other securities. If UK assets are sold abroad, this generates a credit item on the financial account. However, the investment income that accrues in the future would be a debit item on the current account. For example, when BAA (now Heathrow Holdings Ltd) was taken over by a consortium led by the Spanish firm Ferrioval in 2006, this generated a positive item on the financial account, but the profits generated by the company flow out of the UK to Spain, and constitute a negative item on the current account.

The final category is current transfers. These include taxes and social contributions received from non-resident workers and businesses, bilateral aid flows and military grants. However, the largest item is transfers with EU institutions, which has been in persistent deficit.

The financial account

The trend towards globalisation means that both inward and outward investment increased substantially during the 1990s, although there was a dip after 2000. However, Figure 9.1 shows that the financial account has been in strong surplus in the early part of the twenty-first century. This is in part forced by the deficit on the current account. In other words, if an economy runs a current account deficit, it can do so only by running a surplus on the financial account. Effectively, what is happening is that, in order to fund the current account deficit, the UK is selling assets to foreign investors and borrowing abroad.

An important question is whether this practice is sustainable in the long run. Selling assets or borrowing abroad has future implications for the current account, as there will be outflows of investment income, and debt repayments in the future following today's financial surplus. It also has implications for interest rate policy. If the authorities hold interest rates high relative to the rest of the world, this will tend to attract inflows of investment, again with future implications for the current account.

The capital account

The capital account is relatively small. The largest item relates to the flows of capital associated with migration. If someone migrates to the UK, that person's status changes from being a non-resident to being a resident. His or her property then becomes part of the UK's assets, and a transaction has to be entered in the balance of payments accounts. There are also some items relating to various EU transactions. This account has been in surplus for 20 years.

Study tip

Remember that it is important to have a general feel for trends in the data over the recent past, but it is not necessary to spend time learning detailed data about the economy.

Summary

● The balance of payments is a set of accounts that contains details of the transactions that take place between the residents of an economy and the rest of the world.
● The accounts are divided into three sections: the current, financial and capital accounts.
● The current account identifies transactions in goods and services, together with some income payments and international transfers.
● The financial account measures transactions in financial assets, including investment flows and central government transactions in foreign reserves.
● The capital account, which is relatively small, contains capital transfers.
● The overall balance of payments must always be zero.
● The current account has been in persistent deficit since 1984, reflecting a deficit in trade in goods that is partly offset by a surplus in invisible trade.
● The financial account has been in strong surplus — as is required to balance the current account deficit.

Exercise 9.1

Allocate each of the following items to either the current, financial or capital account, and calculate the balances for each account. Check that (together with errors and omissions) the total is zero. All data refer to 2011, at current prices in £ billion.

a	Trade in goods	−100.34
b	Migrants' transfers	+3.18
c	Total net direct investment	−33.17
d	Investment income	+17.31
e	Current transfers	−22.22
f	Transactions in reserve assets	−4.95
g	Trade in services	+76.38
h	Other capital transfers	+0.26
i	Compensation of employees	−0.17
j	Total net portfolio investment	−40.62
k	Other transactions in financial assets	+94.60
l	Errors and omissions	+9.73

The foreign exchange market

Book 1 introduced the foreign exchange market, and argued that it could be regarded as involving demand and supply, just like any normal market. A foreign exchange transaction is needed whenever trade takes place. If, as a UK resident, you buy goods from abroad, you need to purchase foreign exchange — say, euros — and you have to supply pounds in order to buy euros. Similarly, if a French tourist in the UK buys UK goods or services, the transaction needs to be carried out in pounds, so there is a demand for pounds.

This market is shown in Figure 9.3. The demand curve is downward sloping because when the €/£ rate is low, UK goods, services and assets are relatively cheap in terms of euros, so demand is relatively high. On the other hand, when the €/£ rate is relatively high, Europeans receive fewer pounds for their euros, so the demand will be relatively low.

The supply curve of pounds is upward sloping. When the €/£ rate is relatively high, the supply of pounds will be relatively strong, as UK residents will get plenty of euros for their pounds and thus will demand European goods, services and assets, supplying pounds in order to buy the foreign exchange needed for the transactions. When the €/£ rate is low, European goods, services and assets will be relatively expensive for UK residents, so fewer pounds will be supplied.

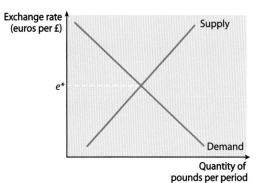

Figure 9.3 The market for pounds

The market is in equilibrium at $e^\star$, where the demand for pounds is just matched by the supply of pounds. This position has a direct connection with the balance of payments. If the demand for pounds exactly matches the supply of pounds, this implies that there is a balance between the demand from Europeans for UK goods, services and assets and the demand by UK residents for European goods, services and assets. In other words, the balance of payments is in overall balance. The key question for consideration is how the market reaches $e^\star$ — in particular, do the authorities allow the exchange rate to find its own way to $e^\star$, or do they intervene to ensure that it gets there?

Summary

- The foreign exchange market can be seen as operating according to the laws of demand and supply.
- The demand for pounds arises when non-residents want to buy UK goods, services or assets.
- The supply of pounds arises when UK residents wish to buy foreign goods, services or assets.
- When the exchange rate is at its equilibrium level, this automatically ensures that the overall balance of payments is zero.

A fixed exchange rate system

In the Bretton Woods conference at the end of the Second World War, it was agreed to establish a **fixed exchange rate** system, under which countries would commit to maintaining the price of their currencies in terms of the US dollar. This system remained in place until the early 1970s. For example, from 1950 until 1967 the sterling exchange rate was set at $2.80, and the UK government was committed to making sure that it stayed at this rate. This system became known as the Dollar Standard. Occasional changes in exchange rates were permitted after consultation if a currency was seen to be substantially out of line — as happened for the UK in 1967.

> **Key term**
>
> **fixed exchange rate** a system in which the government of a country agrees to fix the value of its currency in terms of that of another country

Figure 9.4 illustrates how this works. Suppose the authorities announce that the exchange rate will be set at e_f. Given that this level is set independently by the government, it cannot be guaranteed to correspond to the market equilibrium, and in Figure 9.4 it is set above the equilibrium level. At this exchange rate the supply of pounds exceeds the demand for pounds. This can be interpreted in terms of the overall balance of payments.

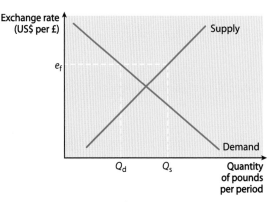

Figure 9.4 Maintaining a fixed exchange rate

John Maynard Keynes played a leading role in the Bretton Woods conference

Key term

foreign exchange reserves stocks of foreign currency and gold owned by the central bank of a country to enable it to meet any mismatch between the demand and supply of the country's currency

If there is an excess supply of pounds, the implication is that UK residents are trying to buy more American goods, services and assets than Americans are trying to buy British: in other words, there is an overall deficit on the balance of payments.

In a free market, you would expect the exchange rate to adjust until the demand and supply of pounds came back into equilibrium. As the authorities are committed to maintaining the exchange rate at e_f, such adjustment cannot take place. However, the UK owes the USA for the excess goods, services and assets that its residents have purchased, so the authorities then have to sell **foreign exchange reserves** in order to make the books balance.

In terms of Figure 9.4, Q_d represents the demand for pounds at e_f and Q_s represents the supply. The difference represents the amount of foreign exchange reserves that the authorities have to sell to preserve the balance of payments. Such transactions are known as 'official financing', and are incorporated into the financial account of the balance of payments.

Notice that the *position* of the demand and supply curves depends on factors other than the exchange rate that can affect the demand for UK and American goods, services and assets in the respective countries. It is likely that, through time, these will shift in position. For example, if the preference of Americans for UK goods changes through time, this will affect the demand for pounds.

Consider Figure 9.5. For simplicity, suppose that the supply curve remains fixed but demand shifts through time. Let e_f be the value of the exchange rate that the UK monetary authorities have undertaken to maintain. If the demand for pounds is at D_1, the chosen exchange rate corresponds to the market equilibrium, and no action by the authorities is needed. If demand is at D_0, then with the exchange rate at e_f there is an excess supply of pounds (as shown in Figure 9.4). The monetary

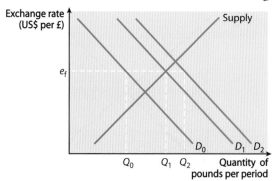

Figure 9.5 Maintaining a fixed exchange rate in the face of changing demand for pounds

authorities in the UK need to buy up the excess supply by selling foreign exchange reserves. Conversely, if the demand for pounds is strong, say because Americans have developed a preference for Scotch whisky, then demand could be at D_2. There is now excess demand for pounds, and the UK monetary authorities supply additional pounds in return for US dollars. Foreign exchange reserves thus accumulate.

In the long term, the system will operate successfully for the country so long as the chosen exchange rate is close to the average equilibrium value over time, so that the central bank is neither running down its foreign exchange reserves nor accumulating them.

A country that tries to hold its currency away from equilibrium indefinitely will find this problematic in the long run. For example, in the early years of the twenty-first century China and some other Asian economies were pegging their currencies against the US dollar at such a low level that they were accumulating foreign exchange. In the case of China, it was accumulating substantial amounts of US government stock. The low exchange rate had the effect of keeping the exports of these countries highly competitive in world markets. However, such a strategy relies on being able to continue to expand domestic production to meet the high demand; otherwise inflationary pressure will begin to build.

During the period of the Dollar Standard, the pound was probably set at too high a level, which meant that UK exports were relatively uncompetitive, and in 1967 the UK government announced a **devaluation** of the pound from \$2.80 to \$2.40.

During the Dollar Standard period, the UK economy went through what became known as a 'stop–go' cycle of growth. When the government tried to stimulate economic growth, the effect was to suck in imports, as the marginal propensity to import was high. The effect of this was to generate a deficit on the current account of the balance of payments, which then needed to be financed by selling foreign exchange reserves.

This process has two effects. First of all, in selling foreign exchange reserves, domestic money supply increases, which then puts upward pressure on prices, threatening inflation. In addition, the Bank of England has finite foreign exchange reserves, and cannot allow them to be run down indefinitely. This meant that the government had to rein in the economy, thereby slowing the rate of growth again; hence the label 'stop–go'.

An important point emerges from this discussion. The fact that intervention to maintain the exchange rate affects domestic money supply means that under a fixed exchange rate regime the monetary authorities are unable to pursue an independent monetary policy. In other words, money supply and the exchange rate cannot be controlled independently of one another. Effectively, the money supply has to be targeted to maintain the value of the currency. Governments may be tempted to use tariffs or non-tariff barriers to reduce a current account deficit, but this has been shown to be distortionary.

The effects of devaluation

During the stop–go period there were many debates about whether there should be a devaluation. The effect of devaluation is to improve competitiveness. At a lower value of the pound, you would expect an increase in the demand for exports and a fall in the demand for imports, *ceteris paribus*.

However, this does not necessarily mean that there will be an improvement in the current account. One reason for this concerns the elasticity of supply of exports and import substitutes. If domestic producers do not have spare capacity, or if there are time lags before production for export can be increased, then exports will not expand quickly in the short run, and so the impact of this action on exports will be limited. Furthermore, similar arguments apply to producers of goods that are potential substitutes for imported products, which reinforces the sluggishness of adjustment. In the short run, therefore, it may be that the current account will worsen rather than improve, in spite of the change in the competitiveness of domestic firms.

This is known as the *J-curve effect*, and is shown in Figure 9.6. Time is measured on the horizontal axis, and the current account is initially in deficit. A devaluation at time *A* initially pushes the current account further into deficit because of the inelasticity of domestic supply. Only after time *B*, when domestic firms have had time to expand their output to meet the demand for exports, does the current account move into surplus.

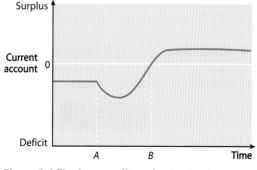

Figure 9.6 The J-curve effect of a devaluation

A second consideration relates to the elasticity of demand for exports and imports. Again, if competitiveness improves but demand does not respond strongly, there may be a negative impact on the current account. If the demand for exports is price inelastic, a fall in price will lead to a fall in revenue. There is reason to expect that the demand for exports is relatively inelastic in the short run. In many cases, exports may be supplied under contracts that cannot be immediately renegotiated. Furthermore, people and firms may wait to see whether the devaluation is permanent or temporary, and thus not revise their spending plans in the short run.

The *Marshall–Lerner condition* states that devaluation will have a positive effect on the current account only if the sum of the elasticities of demand for exports and imports is negative and numerically greater than 1. If there is a devaluation, there will be a quantity effect and a price effect. At the new exchange rate, the quantity effect on the trade balance will be positive because exports tend to increase and imports to decrease. However, there is also a negative price effect, because export prices in terms of foreign currency have fallen and import prices in domestic currency have risen. The trade balance (measured in revenue terms) will improve only if the quantity effect fully offsets the price effect — in other words, if the Marshall–Lerner condition holds true.

The Bretton Woods Dollar Standard broke down in the early 1970s. Part of the reason for this was that such a system depends critically on the stability of the base currency (i.e. the US dollar). During the 1960s the USA's need to finance the Vietnam War meant that the supply of dollar currency began to expand, one result of which was accelerating inflation in the countries that were fixing their currency in terms of the US dollar. It then became increasingly difficult to sustain exchange rates at fixed levels. The UK withdrew from the Dollar Standard in June 1972.

Summary

- After the Bretton Woods conference at the end of the Second World War, the Dollar Standard was established, under which countries agreed to maintain the value of their currencies in terms of US dollars.
- In order to achieve this, the monetary authorities engaged in foreign currency transactions to ensure that the exchange rate was maintained at the agreed level, accumulating foreign exchange reserves to accommodate a balance of payments surplus and running down the reserves to fund a deficit.
- Occasional realignments were permitted, such as the devaluation of sterling in 1967.
- Under a fixed exchange rate system, monetary policy can be used only to achieve the exchange rate target.
- A devaluation has the effect of improving international competitiveness, but the effect on the current account depends upon the elasticity of demand for exports and imports.
- The current account may deteriorate in the short run if the supply response is sluggish.
- The Bretton Woods system broke down in the early 1970s.

Exercise 9.2

A firm wants to purchase a machine tool which is obtainable in the UK for a price of £125,000, or from a US supplier for $300,000. Suppose that the exchange rate is fixed at £1 = $3.

a What is the sterling price of the machine tool if the firm chooses to buy in the USA?

b From which supplier would the firm be likely to purchase?

c Suppose that, between ordering the machine tool and its delivery, the UK government announces a devaluation of sterling, so that when the time comes for the firm to pay up the exchange rate is £1 = $2. What is the sterling price of the machine tool bought from the USA?

d Comment on how the competitiveness of UK goods has been affected.

e Discuss the effects that the devaluation is likely to have on the economy as a whole.

Floating exchange rates

Under a **floating exchange rate** system, the value of the currency is allowed to find its own way to equilibrium. This means that the overall balance of payments is automatically assured, and the monetary authorities do not need to intervene to make sure it happens. In practice, however, governments have tended to be wary of leaving the exchange rate entirely to market forces, and there have been occasional periods in which intervention has been used to affect the market rate.

An example of this was the **Exchange Rate Mechanism (ERM)**, which was set up by a group of European countries in 1979 with the objective of keeping member countries' currencies relatively stable against each other. This was part of the European Monetary System (EMS). Each member nation agreed to keep its currency within 2.25% of a weighted average of the members' currencies, known as the European Currency Unit (ECU). This was an *adjustable peg* system. Eleven realignments were permitted between 1979 and 1987.

Key terms

floating exchange rate a system in which the exchange rate is permitted to find its own level in the market

Exchange Rate Mechanism (ERM) a system that was set up by a group of European countries in 1979 with the objective of keeping member countries' currencies relatively stable against each other

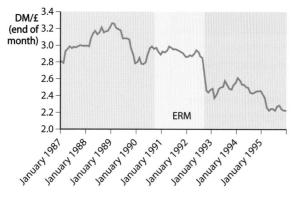

Figure 9.7 The nominal DM/£ exchange rate, 1987–95
Source: Bank of England

The UK opted not to join the ERM when it was first set up, but started shadowing the Deutschmark in the mid-1980s, aiming to keep the rate at around DM3 to the pound, as you can see in Figure 9.7. The UK finally decided to become a full member of the ERM in September 1990. However, the rate at which sterling had been set against the Deutschmark was relatively high, and the situation was worsened by the effects of German reunification, which led to substantial capital flows into Germany, reinforcing the overvaluation of sterling. Once it became apparent that sterling was overvalued, speculative attacks began, and the Bank of England's foreign exchange reserves were depleted; in 1992 the pound left the ERM. You can see in Figure 9.7 that the value of the pound fell rapidly after exit.

What determines exchange rates?

If the foreign exchange market is left free to find its own way to equilibrium, it becomes important to consider what factors will influence the level of the exchange rate. In particular, will the exchange rate resulting from market equilibrium be consistent with the government's domestic policy objectives?

Exchange rate equilibrium also implies a zero overall balance of payments. If the exchange rate always adjusts to the level that ensures this, it might be argued that the long-run state of the economy is one in which the competitiveness of domestic firms remains constant over time. In other words, you would expect the exchange rate to adjust through time to offset any differences in inflation rates between countries. The **purchasing power parity theory of exchange rates** argues that this is exactly what should be expected in the long run. The nominal exchange rate should adjust in such a way as to offset changes in relative prices between countries.

However, in the short run the exchange rate may diverge from its long-run equilibrium. An important influence on the exchange rate in the short run is speculation. So far, the discussion of the exchange rate has stressed mainly the current account of the balance of payments. But the financial account is also significant, especially since regulation of the movement of financial capital was removed. Some of these capital movements are associated with direct investment, which was discussed in Chapter 7. However, sometimes there are also substantial movements of what has come to be known as **hot money**: that is, stocks of funds that are moved around the globe from country to country in search of the best return. The size of the stocks of hot money is enormous, and can significantly affect exchange rates in the short run. The returns to be gained from such capital flows depend on the relative interest rate in the country targeted, and on the expected exchange rate in the future, which in turn may depend on expectations about inflation.

Suppose you are an investor holding assets denominated in US dollars, and the UK interest rate is 2% higher than that in the USA. You may be tempted to shift the funds into the UK in order to take advantage of the higher interest rate. However, if you believe that the exchange rate is above its long-run equilibrium, and therefore is

In financial markets, 'hot money' moves swiftly around the world in search of the best return

likely to fall, this will affect your expected return on holding a UK asset. Indeed, if investors holding UK assets expect the exchange rate to fall, they are likely to shift their funds out of the country as soon as possible — which may then have the effect of pushing down the exchange rate. In other words, this may be a self-fulfilling prophecy. However, speculators may react to news in an unpredictable way, so not all speculative capital movements act to influence the exchange rate towards its long-run equilibrium value.

Speculation was a key contributing factor in the unfolding of the Asian financial crisis of 1997. Substantial flows of capital had moved into Thailand in search of high returns, and speculators came to believe that the Thai currency (the baht) was overvalued. Outward capital flows put pressure on the exchange rate, and although the Thai central bank tried to resist, it eventually ran down its reserves to the point where it had to devalue. This then sparked off capital flows from other countries in the region, including South Korea.

Summary

- Under a floating exchange rate system, the value of a currency is allowed to find its own way to equilibrium without government intervention.
- This means that an overall balance of payments of zero is automatically achieved.
- The purchasing power parity theory argues that the exchange rate will adjust in the long run to maintain international competitiveness, by offsetting differences in inflation rates between countries.
- In the short run, the exchange rate may diverge from this long-run level, particularly because of speculation.
- The exchange rate is thus influenced by relative interest rates and expected inflation, as well as by news about the economic environment.

Fixed or floating?

In evaluating whether a fixed or a floating regime is to be preferred, there are many factors to be taken into account; this section will consider three of them. First, it is important to examine the extent to which the respective systems can accommodate and adjust to external shocks that push the economy out of equilibrium. Second, it is important to consider the stability of each of the systems. Finally, there is the question of which system best encourages governments to adopt sound macroeconomic policies.

Adjustment to shocks

Every economy has to cope with external shocks that occur for reasons outside the control of the country. A key question in evaluating exchange rate systems is whether there is an effective mechanism that allows the economy to return to equilibrium after an external shock.

Under a floating exchange rate system, much of the burden of adjustment is taken up by changes in the exchange rate. For example, if an economy finds itself experiencing faster inflation than other countries, perhaps because those other countries have introduced policies to reduce inflation, then the exchange rate will adjust automatically to restore competitiveness.

However, if the country is operating a fixed exchange rate system, the authorities are committed to maintaining the exchange rate, and this has to take precedence. Thus, the only way to restore competitiveness is by deflating the economy in order to bring inflation into line with other countries. This is likely to bring with it a transitional cost in terms of higher unemployment and slower economic growth. In other words, the burden of adjustment is on the real economy, rather than on allowing the exchange rate to adjust.

The Bretton Woods system operated for more than 20 years in a period in which many economies enjoyed steady economic growth. However, in the UK the system brought about a stop–go cycle, in which the need to maintain the exchange rate hampered economic growth, because of the tendency for growth to lead to an increase in imports and thus to a current account deficit. The increasing differences between inflation rates in different countries led to the final collapse of the system, suggesting that it was unable to cope with such variation.

Furthermore, a flexible exchange rate system allows the authorities to utilise monetary policy in order to stabilise the economy — remember that under a fixed exchange rate system, monetary policy has to be devoted to the exchange rate target.

Stability

When it comes to stability, a fixed exchange rate system has much to commend it. After all, if firms know that the government is committed to maintaining the exchange rate at a given level, they can agree future contracts with some confidence. Under a floating exchange rate system, trading takes place in an environment in which the future exchange rate has to be predicted. If the exchange rate moves adversely, firms then face potential losses from trading. This foreign exchange risk is reduced under a fixed rate regime.

In a climate where speculative activity creates volatility in exchange rates, international trade may be discouraged because of the exchange rate risk. The effects of such volatility can be mitigated to some extent by the existence of **futures markets**. In such a market, it is possible to buy foreign exchange at a fixed price for delivery at a specified future date.

For example, suppose a firm is negotiating a deal to buy component parts for a manufacturing process that will be delivered in 3 months' time. The firm can buy the foreign exchange needed to close the deal in the futures market, and then knows that the contract will be viable, having negotiated a price for the components based on the known exchange rate, rather than on the unpredictable rate that will apply at that future date. The firm may, of course, have to pay a price for the foreign currency that is below the current (*spot*) exchange rate, but as the future rate has been built into the terms of the contract, that will not affect the viability of the deal. The process by which a firm avoids losses by buying forward is known as *hedging*.

However, even with the use of hedging to reduce the risk, it is costly to engage in international trade when exchange rates are potentially volatile, so world trade is unlikely to be encouraged under such a system. Of course, it might be argued that the risk to firms is still present under a fixed exchange rate system, in the sense that a government may choose to realign its currency, with even greater costs to firms that are tied into contracts. However, such realignments were rare under Bretton Woods, and are more predictable than the volatility that can occur on a day-to-day basis in the foreign exchange market.

It is important also to realise that flows of foreign direct investment may be influenced by the exchange rate — and by expectations about future movements of the exchange rate. This will be one of the key factors that a foreign firm takes into account when deciding where to locate its investment.

Macroeconomic policy

Critics of the flexible exchange rate system argue that it is too flexible for its own good. If governments know that the exchange rate will always adjust to maintain international competitiveness, they may have no incentive to behave responsibly in designing macroeconomic policy. Thus, they may be tempted to adopt an inflationary domestic policy, secure in the knowledge that the exchange rate will bear the burden of adjustment. In other words, a flexible exchange rate system does not impose financial discipline on individual countries.

An example of this was seen in the UK in the early 1970s when the country first moved to a floating exchange rate regime. Money supply was allowed to expand rapidly, and inflation increased to almost 25%, aided by the oil price shock. Other examples are evident in Latin America, where hyperinflation affected many countries during the 1980s and early 1990s. For the country itself, such policies are costly in the long run, as reducing inflation under flexible exchange rates is costly. If interest rates are increased in order to reduce domestic aggregate demand and thus reduce inflationary pressure (see Chapter 14), the high return on domestic assets encourages an inflow of hot money, thereby putting upward pressure on the exchange rate. This reduces the international competitiveness of domestic goods and services, and deepens the recession.

There may also be spillover effects on other countries. Suppose that two countries have been experiencing rapid inflation, and one of them decides to tackle the problem. It raises interest rates to dampen domestic aggregate demand, which leads to an **appreciation** of its currency. For the other country, the effect is a **depreciation**

Key term

futures market a market in which it is possible to buy a commodity at a fixed price for delivery at a specified future date; such a market exists for foreign exchange

Study tip

When a government under a fixed exchange rate system chooses to lower the exchange rate, this is known as a devaluation; if the exchange rate falls under a floating exchange rate system, it is known as a depreciation. Similarly, an increase in the exchange rate initiated by the authorities under a fixed exchange rate system is known as a revaluation, whereas under a floating rate system a rise in the exchange rate is known as an appreciation.

Key terms

appreciation a rise in the exchange rate within a floating exchange rate system

depreciation a fall in the exchange rate within a floating exchange rate system

of the currency. (If one currency appreciates, the other must depreciate.) The other country thus finds that its competitive position has improved, and it faces inflationary pressure in the short run. It may then also choose to tackle inflation, which in turn will affect the other country. These spillover effects could be minimised if the countries were to harmonise their policy action.

The exchange rate and macroeconomic policy

The discussion above has shown that the relationship between the exchange rate and macroeconomic policy is an important one. Under a fixed exchange rate system, the need to maintain the value of the currency is a constraint on macroeconomic policy, and forces the economy to adjust to disequilibrium through the real economy. On the other hand, it does have the benefit of imposing financial discipline on governments.

Under floating exchange rates the relationship with policy is less obvious. With a flexible exchange rate, the authorities can use monetary policy to stabilise the economy, knowing that there will be overall balance on the balance of payments. Nonetheless, the government needs to monitor the structure of the balance of payments. When interest rates are set at a relatively high level compared with other countries, the financial account will tend to be in surplus because of capital inflows, with a corresponding deficit on the current account. This may not be sustainable in the long run.

Summary

- There are strengths and weaknesses with both fixed and floating exchange rate systems.
- A floating exchange rate system is more robust in enabling economies to adjust following external shocks, but it can lead to volatility and thus discourage international trade.
- Under a floating exchange rate system, much of the burden of adjustment to external shocks is borne by changes in the exchange rate, rather than by variations in the level of economic activity, which may be affected more under a fixed exchange rate system.
- A fixed exchange rate system offers stability, in the sense that firms know the future value of the currency, whereas under a floating rate regime there is more volatility.
- A fixed exchange rate system imposes discipline upon governments, and may facilitate international policy harmonisation.

Exercise 9.3

Critically evaluate the following statements, and discuss whether you regard fixed or floating exchange rates as the better system.

a A flexible exchange rate regime is better able to cope with external shocks.

b A fixed exchange rate system provides a more stable trading environment and minimises risk.

c Floating exchange rates enable individual countries to follow independent policies.

d A fixed exchange rate system may encourage governments to adopt distortionary policies, such as tariffs and non-tariff barriers, in order to control imports.

International competitiveness

In analysing the UK's position within Europe and with its other trading partners, the relative competitiveness of UK goods and services is an important issue. The UK has persistently shown a deficit on the current account over a long period of time, but especially in the 2000s. Does that imply that UK goods are uncompetitive in international markets? In order to investigate this, and to evaluate its importance, it is first necessary to examine how competitiveness can be measured, and the factors that affect it.

The demand for UK exports in world markets depends upon a number of factors. In some ways, it is similar to the demand for a good. In general, the demand for a good depends on its price, on the prices of other goods, and on consumer incomes and preferences. In a similar way, you can think of the demand for UK exports as depending on the price of UK goods, on the price of other countries' goods, and on incomes in the rest of the world and foreigners' preferences for UK goods over those produced elsewhere. However, in the case of international transactions the exchange rate is also relevant, as this determines the purchasing power of UK incomes in the rest of the world. Similarly, the demand for imports into the UK will depend upon the relative price of domestic and foreign goods, incomes in the UK, preferences for foreign and domestically produced goods and the exchange rate. These factors will all come together to determine the balance of demand for exports and imports.

The exchange rate plays a key role in influencing the levels of both imports and exports. Figure 9.8 shows the time path of the US$/£ exchange rate since 1971. It shows some fluctuations between 1971 and the late 1980s, although around a declining trend. However, since then the exchange rate seems to have remained fairly steady.

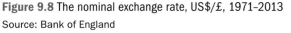

Figure 9.8 The nominal exchange rate, US$/£, 1971–2013
Source: Bank of England

Nonetheless, there was a fall from a peak of $2.50 to the pound in 1972 to $1.56, 40 years later. Other things being equal, this would suggest an improvement in the competitiveness of UK products. In other words, Americans wanting to buy UK goods got more pounds for their dollars in 2013 than in 1972, and thus would tend to find UK goods more attractive.

However, some care is needed because other things do not remain equal. In particular, remember that the competitiveness of UK goods in the US market depends not only on the exchange rate, but also on movements in the prices of goods over time, so this needs to be taken into account — which is why Figure 9.8 refers to the *nominal exchange rate*. In other words, if the prices of UK goods have risen more rapidly than prices in the USA, this will partly offset the downward movement in the exchange rate.

Figure 9.9 shows the nominal exchange rate again, but also the ratio of UK/US consumer prices. This reveals that between 1971 and 1977 UK prices rose much more steeply than those in the USA, and continued to rise relative to the USA until the 1990s. Thus, the early decline in the nominal exchange rate was offset by the movement in relative prices.

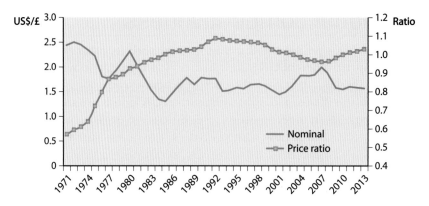

Figure 9.9 The nominal exchange rate, US$/£, and the ratio of UK/US prices, 1971–2013

Sources: Bank of England, OECD

Key term

real exchange rate the nominal exchange rate adjusted for differences in relative inflation rates between countries

In order to assess the overall competitiveness of UK goods compared with the USA's, it is necessary to calculate the **real exchange rate**, which is defined as the nominal exchange rate multiplied by the ratio of relative prices.

The real exchange rate is shown in Figure 9.10. The real exchange rate also shows some fluctuations, especially between about 1977 and 1989. However, there does not seem to be any strong trend to the series, although the real rate was higher at the end of the period than at the beginning.

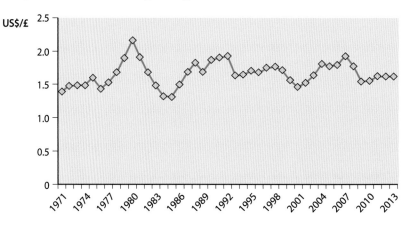

Figure 9.10 The real exchange rate, US$/£, 1971–2013

Source: calculated from data in Figure 9.9

Notice that this series relates only to competitiveness relative to the USA, as it is the real US$/£ exchange rate. An alternative measure is the *sterling effective exchange rate*, shown in Figure 9.11. This shows the strength of sterling relative to a weighted average of exchange rates of the UK's trading partners. Notice the fall in the effective rate that occurred towards the end of 2008 at the time of the financial crisis.

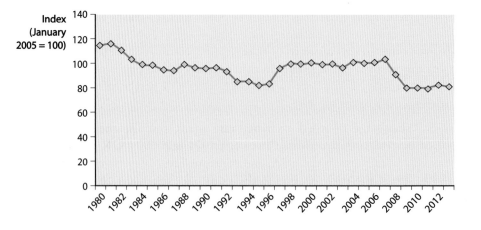

Figure 9.11 The sterling effective exchange rate, 1980–2013 (2005 = 100)

Source: Bank of England

The real exchange rate

Table 9.3 provides data for the €/£ exchange rate, together with the consumer price index for the euro area and for the UK for the period from 2005 to 2013. These data can be used to calculate the real exchange rate.

Table 9.3 Competitiveness of the UK compared to the euro zone

	Nominal exchange rate (€/£)	Consumer price index (2005 = 100)	
		UK	Euro zone
2005	1.4629	100.0	100.0
2006	1.4670	102.4	102.2
2007	1.4619	104.8	104.4
2008	1.2588	108.6	107.8
2009	1.1233	110.9	108.1
2010	1.1664	114.5	109.9
2011	1.1527	119.7	112.9
2012	1.2337	123.0	115.7
2013	1.1776	126.2	117.3

Sources: based on data from OECD and Bank of England

To calculate the real exchange rate for 2013, the nominal exchange rate must be multiplied by the ratio of prices in the UK to prices in the euro area. This is $1.1776 \times 126.2 \div 117.3 = 1.267$. Thus the real exchange rate had not fallen by as much as the nominal rate, because prices in the UK had risen by more than in the euro zone over the period.

Study tip

The distinction between real and nominal values is important, not only in relation to the exchange rate but in many other macroeconomic variables. Make sure that you are clear about the difference between real and nominal, and why it matters.

Exercise 9.4

Use the data in Quantitative skills 9.2 to calculate the real exchange rate for each year in the period, plot the results against time and comment on the effect that any movement will have had on the competitiveness of UK goods and services relative to the euro zone.

The terms of trade

A final indicator to consider is the *terms of trade*, which were discussed in Chapter 7. They are defined as the ratio of export prices to import prices, and provide information about the purchasing power of exports in terms of imports.

A fall in the terms of trade indicates that the same volume of exports will purchase a smaller volume of imports than before. A downward movement in the terms of trade is thus unfavourable for an economy. Figure 7.3 showed the terms of trade for the UK economy since 1963. The substantial fall seen in 1973 and 1974 was due to the adverse oil price shock that occurred at that time. However, it would seem from this figure that the terms of trade have remained fairly constant since the early 1980s, even during the financial crisis.

The terms of trade are calculated purely with respect to prices, and take no account of changing volumes of trade. In other words, a deterioration in the terms of trade does not necessarily mean that an economy is worse off, so long as the volume of trade is increasing sufficiently rapidly.

Summary

- Relative prices and the exchange rate are an important influence on the competitiveness of goods and services in the international market.
- The real exchange rate adjusts the nominal exchange rate to allow for differing inflation rates between countries.
- The terms of trade are measured by the ratio of export prices to import prices.

International differences in productivity

Key term

labour productivity a measure of output per worker, or output per hour worked

From a different angle, competitiveness also depends upon relative costs of production in different countries, which influence the prices that firms can charge. In particular, if UK firms face higher unit labour cost than their trading partners, this puts them at a disadvantage in terms of costs. This reflects different levels of productivity across countries. Remember that productivity is a measure of productive efficiency: for example, **labour productivity** is output per unit of labour input. Different countries show appreciable differences in efficiency by this measure.

However, international comparisons of productivity are not straightforward, as measurements are subject to differences in data collection and differences in work practices. One approach might be to compare data on GDP per head of population. As a measure of productivity levels, however, this is a misleading indicator. In particular, working hours are longer in the UK than in many other countries (especially within Europe), so differences in GDP per head partly reflect differences in the quantity of labour input.

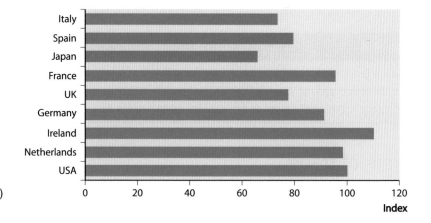

Figure 9.12 GDP per hour worked, selected countries, 2011 (USA = 100)
Sources: OECD, ONS

For this reason, GDP per hour worked is often seen as a more reliable indicator of relative productivity levels. This measure is graphed in Figure 9.12. The UK does not perform especially well on this measure, with the USA, Ireland and the Netherlands in particular showing higher productivity.

Figure 9.13 gives the time path for an index of GDP per hour worked, based on 1991 = 100. This puts the UK in a very different light, as it outperformed the other countries shown in terms of the growth of productivity on this measure, indicated by the steepness of the time path. The UK's productivity increased by about 58% between 1991 and 2011, compared with 43% in the USA over the same period.

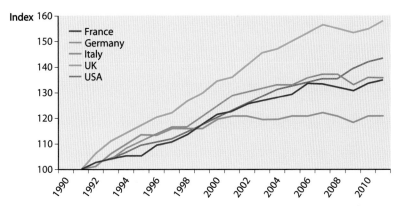

Figure 9.13 Index of GDP per hour worked, selected countries, 1991–2011 (1991 = 100)
Sources: OECD, ONS

It is also important to realise that labour productivity is not the only relevant measure, as countries may also differ in their use of capital. **Total factor productivity** is more difficult to measure, as the measurement of capital stock is especially prone to error and misinterpretation. However, some estimates of multifactor productivity growth are shown in Figure 9.14.

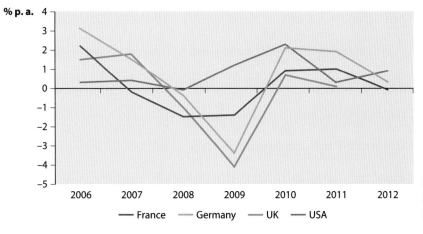

Figure 9.14 Multifactor productivity growth, selected countries, 2006–12
Source: OECD

Exercise 9.5

Table 9.4 provides data on two labour productivity measures, based on 2000 = 100. Discuss whether the UK's position improved or deteriorated between 2000 and 2014. How well has the UK performed relative to the other countries in the table? Explain your answer, and discuss why this might be important for the UK economy.

Table 9.4 Productivity measures

	GDP per worker (2000 = 100)					GDP per hour worked (2000 = 100)				
	UK	France	Germany	Japan	USA	UK	France	Germany	Japan	USA
2000	100	100	100	100	100	100	100	100	100	100
2002	103.4	101.1	102.1	103.3	103.3	103.5	103.3	104.4	103.4	104.5
2004	108.0	104.3	104.3	106.7	107.8	109.3	105.5	106.6	107.9	110.2
2006	111.5	106.5	105.3	108.9	110.0	114.0	109.9	108.8	110.1	112.5
2008	112.6	106.5	106.4	110.0	111.1	115.1	108.8	109.9	112.4	113.6
2010	110.3	106.5	104.3	111.1	115.6	114.0	108.8	108.8	115.7	119.3
2012	110.3	107.5	104.3	113.3	117.8	114.0	111.0	109.9	116.9	121.6

Source: calculated from ONS data

Productivity and competitiveness

Countries gain from trade by exploiting their comparative advantage, so maintaining that comparative advantage seems desirable. If productivity in the UK grows more slowly than in countries such as the USA or Germany, this implies a loss of competitiveness over time. This in turn may mean that the UK gains less strongly from its exporting activity in world markets. International competitiveness may also be lost if the UK experiences inflation at a more rapid rate than its trading rivals.

These arguments seem to suggest that there are significant benefits to be gained from maintaining international competitiveness by improving productivity and keeping inflation under control.

If the UK finds that its exports have become less competitive, and that imports have become more competitive with domestic goods, then this could result in a fall in aggregate demand, and a possible increase in unemployment, magnified by multiplier effects.

Furthermore, if the UK experiences a deficit on the current account of the balance of payments, there will also be a corresponding surplus on the financial account, so essentially the UK funds the deficit by selling financial assets to economic agents overseas. In the long run, the income paid out on foreign investment feeds through to reinforce the deficit on the current account.

The benefits of engaging in trade have been widely discussed, but is there a downside to this? When world trade is booming, the gains from trade can help to maintain the economy at or close to full employment. However, suppose there is a global recession? If the economy is committed to trade, and reliant on export revenues, a sudden fall in export demand could deepen the recession in the domestic economy, and this is the risk of being export-biased in economic activity. however, in normal times, it seems better to be competitive in international markets than to be uncompetitive.

Summary

- Competitiveness can depend upon the relative costs of production in different countries, which in turn partly reflects differences in productivity.
- Data for international comparison of productivity differences need to be treated with some care, but GDP per hour worked is a helpful indicator.
- Labour productivity is not a sufficient measure, given that countries differ in their relative endowments of labour, capital and other factors of production.

Balancing the balance of payments

There are many ways in which the overall 'balance' of the balance of payments can be achieved — which sometimes becomes controversial.

One way in which the balance of payments is made to balance is through allowing the exchange rate to respond to the relative levels of supply and demand in the foreign exchange market. In other words, if the exchange rate is free to find its market level, it will tend to move to equalise the demand and supply of currency.

However, the balance of payments depends not only on trade in goods and services, but also on transactions in financial assets. The demand for a country's financial assets depends not only on the exchange rate, but also on the relative rate of interest in different countries. If UK interest rates are high compared with those elsewhere in the world, there will tend to be an inflow of financial capital. The resulting financial surplus will tend to cause the exchange rate to appreciate. This in turn affects the competitiveness of domestic goods and services, so the net result may be that the financial account surplus will be offset by a deficit on the current account.

Some countries have chosen to treat the balance of payments in a different way, by fixing the exchange rate in terms of some other currency, such as the US dollar. What this means is that any surplus or deficit on current or financial accounts must be offset by the purchase or sale of reserve assets (that is, financial assets denominated in terms of US dollars) in order to maintain the price of the currency.

The choice between fixing the exchange rate and allowing it to find its market value has a major effect on the structure of the balance of payments. This is illustrated in Figure 9.15, which shows the structure of the balance of payments for the USA and China in 2003.

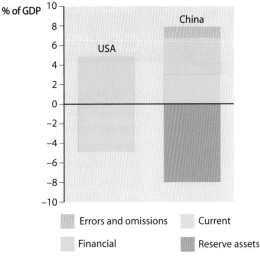

Figure 9.15 The balance of payments, USA and China, in 2003

In the USA, where the exchange rate is allowed to find its own market value, the accounts reveal a substantial current account deficit (amounting to nearly 5% of GDP), balanced by a financial account surplus. In contrast, China shows surpluses on both the current and the financial account, balanced by substantial transactions in reserve assets, indicating that the Chinese authorities have been artificially holding the value of their currency away from its equilibrium value.

Why should they want to do this? One reason is that the policy has allowed China to maintain rapid growth in exports, by keeping its goods highly competitive in international markets, while at the same time attracting flows of inward foreign direct investment. In order to do this, it has had to purchase US dollar-denominated assets — such as US Treasury bills. In turn, this allowed the USA to maintain its current account deficit, funded partly by the sale of Treasury bills.

Follow-up questions

a Discuss this from the perspective of China. What are the benefits of this strategy — and what are the risks?

b Now view the strategy from the USA's viewpoint. Why do you think that the USA tried to persuade China to revalue its currency?

10 Poverty and inequality in developed and developing countries

In all societies there is some inequality in the distribution of income and wealth, although the extent of inequality varies between countries. Indeed, one of the gravest economic challenges facing the world today is the global inequity in the distribution of resources. Worldwide, it is estimated that in 2011 more than a billion people were living in what the United Nations regards as absolute poverty. Furthermore, there were an estimated 57 million primary-age children who were not enrolled for school, more than a billion people without access to safe water, and 2.5 billion without access to sanitation. This chapter explores ways of measuring inequality and poverty in both developed and developing countries, looks at some of the causes of inequality and discusses some of the policies that are used to affect the distribution of income and wealth.

Learning objectives

After studying this chapter, you should:
→ understand what is meant by economic and human development
→ be familiar with the most important economic and social indicators that can help to evaluate the standard of living in different societies
→ be aware of significant differences between regions of the world in terms of their level and pace of development
→ recognise the strengths and limitations of economic and social indicators in providing a profile of a country's stage of development
→ be familiar with ways of identifying and monitoring inequality, including Lorenz curves and the Gini coefficient (index)
→ be familiar with ways of measuring relative and absolute poverty
→ be aware of the changing pattern of inequality in the UK
→ understand the main causes of inequality and poverty
→ be familiar with policies designed to affect the distribution of income and wealth

Developed and developing countries

In considering the global economy, it is apparent that there is a divide; there are some countries that have gone through a process of economic and human development to reach a high standard of living, but there are many other countries that have failed to make progress in this way. In seeking to analyse inequality, there are therefore two crucial dimensions that need to be taken into account. On the one hand, it is important to be aware of inequality between nations, and the gap in living standards that exists between different regions of the world. However, it is also important to be aware that there is inequality within societies — even within the most developed economies in the world. The first step in examining these issues is to identify the developed and developing countries in the world.

Defining development

What is meant by 'development'? You might think that it is about economic growth — if a society can expand its productive capacity, surely that is development? But development means much more than this. Economic growth may well be an *essential* ingredient, since development cannot take place without an expansion of the resources available in a society; however, it is not a *sufficient* ingredient, because those additional resources must be used wisely, and the growth that results must be the 'right' sort of growth.

Wrapped up with development are issues concerning the alleviation of poverty — no country can be considered to be 'developed' if a substantial portion of its population is living in absolute poverty. Development also requires structural change, and possibly changes in institutions and, in some cases, cultural and political attitudes.

The Millennium Development Goals

In September 2000, the 189 member states of the United Nations met at what became known as the *Millennium Summit*. They agreed the following declaration:

We will spare no effort to free our fellow men, women and children from the abject and dehumanising conditions of extreme poverty to which more than a billion of them are currently subjected.

This was a global recognition of the extreme inequality that is a feature of the world distribution of resources. Before beginning to analyse these important questions, it is important to identify what is meant by 'development', and to recognise the symptoms of underdevelopment. Once the symptoms have been identified, explanations can be sought.

As part of the Millennium Summit, it was agreed to set quantifiable targets for a number of dimensions of development, in order to monitor progress. These are known as the **Millennium Development Goals (MDGs)**, and will be the starting point for learning to recognise the symptoms of underdevelopment.

There are eight goals, each of which has specific targets associated with it.

> ### Key term
>
> **Millennium Development Goals (MDGs)** targets set for each less developed country, reflecting a range of development objectives to be monitored each year to evaluate progress

Goal 1: Eradicate extreme poverty and hunger

The headline target for goal 1 is to halve the proportion of people whose income is less than $1.25 per day, and to halve the proportion of people suffering from hunger, between 1990 and 2015. The alleviation of such extreme poverty is essential for development to take place. In addition, it was aimed to 'achieve full and productive employment and decent work for all, including women and young people'. However, the outbreak of the Ebora virus in West Africa in 2014 was a grim reminder of the fragility of public health in Africa.

Globally, the headline target was met 5 years ahead of the 2015 deadline, and there were 700 million fewer people living in extreme poverty in 2010 than there had been in 1990. However, at the 2015 deadline there were still more than a billion people worldwide living in extreme poverty, many of them in sub-Saharan Africa. On the other hand, the rapid rate of economic growth in China has enabled millions of people to escape from poverty.

Goal 2: Achieve universal primary education

The target here is to ensure that by 2015 all children everywhere will be able to complete a full course of primary schooling. Education is seen as an essential feature of the process of development, as it provides the knowledge that is needed for people to use resources effectively. In 2011, there were still 57 million primary school age children who were not in school.

Goal 3: Promote gender equality and empower women

This target aims to eliminate gender disparity in primary and secondary education. Gender inequality is widespread in less developed countries, and means that large numbers of women are disadvantaged. Although progress has been made towards equalising primary school enrolments, inequality persists at higher levels.

Goal 4: Reduce child mortality

This target is to reduce the under-5 mortality rate by two-thirds between 1990 and 2015. Here again, there has been progress, but sub-Saharan Africa lags behind.

Goal 5: Improve maternal health

The target is to reduce the maternal mortality ratio by three-quarters between 1990 and 2015. All regions have made some progress, but as the 2015 deadline approached it seemed unlikely that the target would be fully met.

Goal 6: Combat HIV/AIDS, malaria and other diseases

The target is to have halted, and begun to reverse, the spread of HIV/AIDS and the incidence of malaria and other major diseases by 2015. The impact of HIV/AIDS and other diseases has been felt especially in sub-Saharan Africa, and has had adverse effects on the age structure of the population in many less developed countries. New HIV infections have declined in most parts of the world, and access to treatment for HIV/AIDS is spreading. The global incidence of malaria is estimated to have decreased significantly. However, the outbreak of the Ebola virus in West Africa in 2014 was a grim reminder of the fragility of public health in Africa.

Goal 7: Ensure environmental sustainability

The targets here are to integrate the principles of sustainable development into national policies and programmes and to reverse the loss of environmental resources, to halve the proportion of people without sustainable access to safe drinking water by 2015, and to have achieved a significant improvement in the lives of at least 100 million slum dwellers by 2020. Development must be *sustainable*, in the sense that the foundations for future development need to be laid in such a way that they do not endanger the resources available for future generations.

There is still work to be done to safeguard the environment, but some progress has been made in improving the proportion of people in the world with sustainable access to safe drinking water and basic sanitation, and in improving the lives of slum dwellers.

Goal 8: Develop a global partnership for development

The target here is to develop further an open, rule-based, predictable, non-discriminatory trading and financial system, including a commitment to good governance, development and poverty reduction, both nationally and internationally.

One of the Millennium Development Goals is to achieve universal primary education

A wide range of indicators will be used to monitor this goal in relation to *official development assistance* (ODA), *market access*, *debt sustainability* and some other targets. The need for international cooperation in ensuring development is pressing and will be a recurring theme in the following chapters — it is crucial if globalisation is to be beneficial to all nations.

This final goal is less focused than the other seven, but no less important. There is a widespread view that less developed countries have been disadvantaged by the international trading system, and that richer countries have been insufficiently cooperative — partly in terms of the amount of ODA that has been provided, but also in terms of a reluctance of some developed countries to open their markets to products from less developed countries.

ODA was the subject of an earlier UN summit in the 1970s, at which the more developed countries promised to provide overseas assistance. Indeed, there was a specific commitment that 0.7% of developed countries' GDP would be devoted to this purpose.

'Market access' refers to the difficulty experienced by developing countries in seeking to increase exports to the developed world in order to earn more foreign exchange. This target is aimed especially at landlocked and small island developing states, but market access is not a problem for these countries alone.

'Debt sustainability' refers to the difficulties that many countries experienced in paying off their accumulated debt. This became a major problem, especially in sub-Saharan Africa, where some countries were devoting more resources to paying off debts than to providing education and healthcare for their people. The issue was tackled by the HIPC (Heavily Indebted Poor Countries) initiative, which has made progress in this important area.

Other targets relate to youth unemployment, access to affordable essential medical drugs and access to new technology, especially in the fields of information and communications.

These eight goals represent the key facets of development that need to be addressed, and they constitute an enormous challenge, especially as progress was slow and uneven. The United Nations has worked with governments, civil society and other partners to create an ambitious post-2015 agenda to build on the progress that was made up to 2015.

In thinking about these goals, you can begin to understand the various dimensions of development, and realise that development is about much more than economic growth — although growth may be seen as a prerequisite for the achievement of the goals. At the same time, failure to achieve these goals will retard economic growth.

Summary

- Economic growth is one aspect of economic development, in that it provides an increase in the resources available to members of society in less developed countries.
- However, in addition, development requires that the resources made available through economic growth are used appropriately to meet development objectives.
- The Millennium Development Goals were set by the Millennium Summit of the United Nations in September 2000.
- These goals comprised a set of targets for each less developed country, to be achieved by 2015.

Exercise 10.1

Choose two or three less developed countries in different regions of the world. Visit the Millennium Development Goals website at **www.un.org/ millenniumgoals/**. Discuss the extent to which progress is being made towards the goals for your chosen countries.

Identifying the less developed countries

It is difficult to find an agreed definition of what constitutes a less developed country. A less developed country cannot be defined solely in terms of average incomes because the notion of development encompasses a wide variety of different dimensions. A country may have relatively high average incomes, but yet be characterised by high poverty or inequality, or be weak in the provision of education or healthcare. In the discussion that follows, a wide range of countries will be referred to as *less developed countries* (LDCs), and the discussion will be illustrated by examples from a selection of countries from different regions of the world.

In broad terms, the countries regarded as LDCs are concentrated in four major regions: sub-Saharan Africa, Latin America, South Asia and South East Asia. This excludes some countries in the 'less developed' range, but relatively few. For some purposes it may be necessary to treat China separately, rather than including it as part of South East Asia, partly because of its sheer size, and partly because it has followed a rather different development path.

It is very important when discussing economic development to remember that there is wide diversity between the countries that are classified as LDCs, and although it is tempting to generalise, you need to be a little wary of doing so. Different countries have different characteristics, and face different configurations of problems and opportunities. Therefore, a policy that works for one country may fail totally in a different part of the world.

Prior knowledge needed

This section of the chapter builds upon discussion in Book 1, Chapter 9.

Indicators of development

GNI per capita

One measure of the level of development is GNI per capita — the average level of income per person in the population. For reasons outlined in Book 1, Chapter 9, the preferred measure is GNI per capita, measured in purchasing power parity dollars (PPP$). This is important because using official exchange rates to convert from local currency into US dollars can be misleading. The US$ measure understates the *real* purchasing power of income in LDCs, but what is of interest is exactly that — the relative command over resources that people in different countries have.

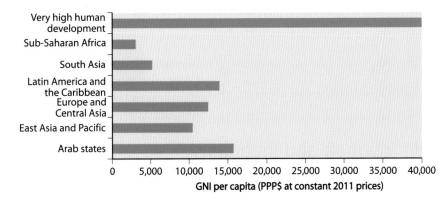

Figure 10.1 GNI per capita, regional groupings, 2013 (PPP$)

Source: *Human Development Report*, 2014

Figure 10.1 shows the relative size of GNI per capita in PPP$ for the regional groupings of countries around the world in 2013. The gap in income levels between the LDCs and the high-income countries shows very clearly in the figure; equally, the gap between the countries of sub-Saharan Africa and South Asia and those in East Asia and Latin America is apparent. The figure also puts into context the position of the transition economies of Europe and the Arab states. The Arab states are rather different in character because of the oil resources that have enabled them to increase their average income levels.

Not all data are available on a regional basis, so in discussing the developing countries, a selected group of countries has been chosen as a focus, with three countries from each of the major four groupings. The GNI per capita (PPP$) levels in 2012 are shown in Figure 10.2. Because of the diversity of countries in each of the regions, such a selection must be treated with some caution. Singapore, South Korea and China have been chosen to represent East Asia and the Pacific in order to highlight three of the countries that have achieved rapid economic growth over a sustained period, and the following discussion will highlight some of the factors that have enabled this to take place.

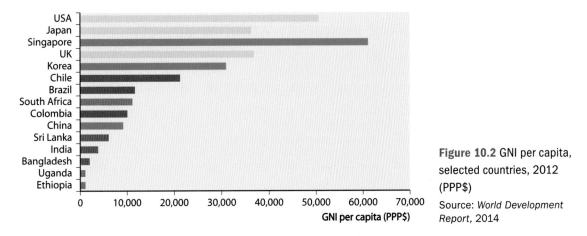

Figure 10.2 GNI per capita, selected countries, 2012 (PPP$)

Source: *World Development Report*, 2014

GNI has some limitations as a measure of living standards, even when measured in PPP$. One limitation that is especially important when considering low-income countries is that in many LDCs there is much *informal economic activity*, which may not be captured by a measure like GNI, based on monetary transactions. Such activity includes subsistence agriculture, which remains important in many countries, especially in sub-Saharan Africa. In other words, GNI may not capture production that is directly used for consumption.

However, the informal sector also encompasses many other forms of activity in both rural and urban areas, from petty traders, shoe-shiners and wayside barbers to small-scale enterprises operating in a wide range of activities. In 1999 the ILO estimated that the informal sector accounted for 50.2% of total employment in Ethiopia; in 2000 it was thought to account for 45.8% of total employment in India. This suggests the need for some caution in the use of GNI per capita data.

Income distribution and inequality

Another important limitation of GNI per capita as a measure of living standards is that it is an average measure, and so does not reveal information about how income is distributed among groups in society. One way of presenting data on this topic is to rank households in order of their incomes, and then calculate the share of total household income that goes to the poorest 10%, the poorest 20% and so on.

Quantitative skills 10.1

Deciles and quintiles

When the groups are divided into tenths in this way, they are referred to as *deciles*; thus, the poorest 10% is the first decile, the next 10% is the second decile and so on. Similarly, the poorest 20% is the first *quintile*. This is useful in trying to explore the pattern of the distribution of income because it quantifies the difference between income going to low-income and high-income households.

According to the World Bank, the top decile (richest 10%) of households in Brazil receive 55.8 times higher income than the lowest decile (poorest 10%). In Belarus, on the other hand, the ratio was only 5.5. These are extreme examples of the degree of inequality in the distribution of income within countries.

Evaluating inequality within a society

Inequality is present in all societies, and always will be. However, the degree of inequality varies from one country to another; and before exploring the causes of inequality, and the policies that might be used to influence how income and wealth are distributed within society, it is necessary to be able to characterise and measure inequality. This is important in order to be able to judge relative standards of living in different countries or different periods.

Table 10.1 presents some data for three developed countries. Notice that the unit of measurement is normally the household rather than the individual, on the presumption that members of a household tend to share their resources — a millionaire's life-partner may not earn any income, but he or she is not usually poor.

Table 10.1 Distribution of income in the USA, the UK and Japan, by quintiles (%)

	UK, 2010	USA, 2010	Japan, 2008
First decile	2	1	3
First quintile	6	5	7
Second quintile	11	10	13
Third quintile	16	16	17
Fourth quintile	23	23	23
Top quintile	44	46	40
Top decile	29	30	25
Ratio top quintile: first quintile	7.3	9.2	3.1

Source: *World Development Indicators*

It can be seen that in the UK households in the top quintile receive 7.3 times more income than those in the poorest quintile. On the basis of these data, inequality in the UK is lower than that in the USA, but higher than that in Japan.

The Lorenz curve

The structure of this information is quite different from the sorts of data that economists normally encounter, and it would be helpful to find an appropriate type of diagram to allow the data to be presented visually. The usual types of graph are not well suited to presenting such data visually, but there is a method of presenting the data visually via the **Lorenz curve**. Some Lorenz curves are shown in Figure 10.3.

> ### Key term
>
> **Lorenz curve** a graphical way of depicting the distribution of income within a country

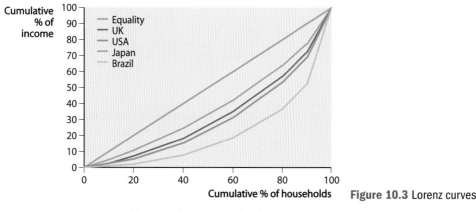

Figure 10.3 Lorenz curves

Lorenz curves are constructed as follows. The curves for the UK, USA and Japan are based on the data in Table 10.1. The first step is to convert the numbers in the table into *cumulative* percentages. In other words (using the UK as an example), the data show that the poorest 20% receive 6.6% of total household income, the poorest 40% receive 6.6% + 11.5% = 18.1%, the poorest 60% receive 18.1% + 16.3% = 34.4%, and so on. It is these cumulative percentages that are plotted to produce the Lorenz curve, as in Figure 10.3. (The figure also plots the lowest and highest deciles.)

Suppose that income were perfectly equally distributed between households. In other words, suppose the poorest 10% of households received exactly 10% of income, the poorest 20% received 20% and so on. The Lorenz curve would then be a straight line going diagonally across the figure.

To interpret the country curves, the closer a country's Lorenz curve is to the diagonal equality line, the more equal is the distribution. You can see from the figure that Japan comes closest to the equality line, bearing out the earlier conclusion that income is more equally distributed in that country. The UK and the US curves are closer together, but there seems to be slightly more inequality in the USA, as its Lorenz curve is further from the equality line. Brazil has also been included on the figure, as an example of a society in which there is substantial inequality.

Exercise 10.2

Use the data provided in Table 10.2 to calculate the ratios of top decile income to bottom decile income, and of top quintile income to bottom quintile income. Then draw Lorenz curves for the two countries, and compare the inequalities shown for Belarus and South Africa with each other and with the countries already discussed.

Table 10.2 Income distribution in Belarus and South Africa

	Percentage share of income or consumption	
	South Africa	**Belarus**
First decile	1	4
First quintile	2	9
Second quintile	4	14
Third quintile	8	18
Fourth quintile	16	23
Top quintile	70	36
Top decile	54	21

Source: *World Development Indicators*

The Gini index

The Lorenz curve is fine for comparing income distribution in just a few countries. However, it would also be helpful to have an index that could summarise the relationship in a numerical way. The **Gini coefficient** does just this. It is a way of trying to quantify the equality of income distribution in a country, and is obtained by calculating the ratio of the area between the equality line and the country's Lorenz curve (area A in Figure 10.4) to the whole area under the equality line (area $A + B$ in Figure 10.4).

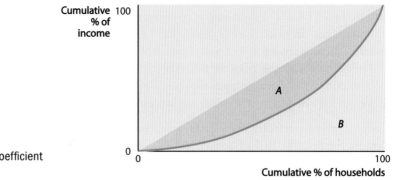

Figure 10.4 The Gini coefficient and the Lorenz curve

In international publications, such as the *World Development Indicators*, published by the World Bank, the indicator is expressed as a percentage, and is known as the *Gini index*. The closer the Gini index is to 100 (or the Gini coefficient to 1), the further the Lorenz curve is from equality, and thus the more unequal is the income distribution. The Gini index values for the countries in Figure 10.3 are shown in Table 10.3.

Table 10.3 The Gini index

Country	Gini index
USA, 2010	41.1
UK, 2010	38.0
Japan, 2008	32.1
Brazil, 2012	52.7

Source: *World Development Indicators*

Study tip

Notice that the Gini coefficient is simply the Gini index divided by 100. This should be treated in the same way as the Gini index: for example, in Table 10.3, the UK would have a Gini coefficient of 0.38.

Some measurement issues

When measuring income inequality, some important measurement issues need to be borne in mind. For example, in talking about the 'poorest' and 'richest' households, you need to be aware that absolute income levels per household may be a misleading indicator, given that households are of different sizes and compositions. Thus, when looking at the income distribution in the UK, it is important to make adjustments for this.

The way this is done is by the use of *equivalence scales*. These allow a household to be judged relative to a 'reference household' made up of a childless couple. It can then be decided that a household with a husband, wife and two young children rates as 1.18 relative to the childless couple with a rating of 1. So if the couple with two children had an income of, say, £40,000 per year, this would be the equivalent of 40,000/1.18 = £33,898. In order to examine the inequality of income, it is these equivalised incomes that need to be considered.

A further question is whether income is the most appropriate indicator. People tend to smooth their consumption over their lifetimes, and it has been argued that it is more important to look at consumption (expenditure) than income when considering inequality.

Then there is the question of housing costs. In the short run, households have no control over their spending on housing. Some measures of inequality therefore choose to exclude housing costs from the calculations in order to focus on the income that households have at their disposal for other expenditures. As housing tends to constitute a higher proportion of the budgets of poor households, measures of inequality that exclude housing costs tend to show greater levels of inequality.

It is also important to bear in mind that the standard of living that households can achieve depends partly on government-provided services, such as health and education. Remember that rich as well as poor households may benefit from these.

Finally, in considering inequality in a society, it may be important to examine inequalities in the distribution of wealth as well as income. Wealth can be regarded as the accumulated stock of assets that households own, and in the UK wealth is more unequally distributed than income.

It is interesting to note that many people remain unaware of where they fit into the income distribution of their country. A survey in the USA in 2000 found that 19% of Americans believed that they were in the top 1% of earners.

Summary

- Less developed countries (LDCs) are largely located in four major regions: sub-Saharan Africa, Latin America, South Asia and Southeast Asia.
- These regions have shown contrasting patterns of growth and development.
- Different countries have different characteristics, and face different configurations of problems and opportunities.
- GNI per capita is one measure of the standard of living in a country, but it has a number of shortcomings for LDCs.
- In particular, it neglects the importance of the informal sector, and fails to take into account inequality in the distribution of income.
- Some degree of inequality in income and wealth is present in every society.
- Inequality is measured by ranking households in order of income, then comparing the income received by the richest decile (or quintile) with that received by the poorest.
- The Lorenz curve gives a visual impression of the income distribution; this can be quantified into the Gini index as a single statistic representing the degree of income inequality.
- Calculations of the income distribution are normally undertaken using equivalised incomes, taking into account the size and composition of households.
- In some cases, consumption (expenditure) provides a more reliable measure of inequality, as people tend to smooth their consumption over time.

Measuring poverty

One aspect of inequality is poverty. If there is a wide gap between the richest and poorest households, it is important to evaluate just how poor those poorest households are, and whether they should be regarded as being 'in poverty'. This requires a definition of poverty.

One way of defining poverty is to specify a basket of goods and services that is regarded as the minimum required to support human life. Households that are seen to have too low an income to allow them to purchase everything in that basic bundle of goods would be regarded as being in **absolute poverty**.

Research published in 2008 by the World Bank claimed that new data on incomes and prices in LDCs revealed that global poverty was more widespread than had been thought previously. It was estimated that households in which people were living on less than $1.25 per person per day (in PPP$) should be regarded as being in absolute poverty. In 2005, about 1.4 billion people in the world were said to be living below this threshold. Figure 10.5 shows a regional distribution of poverty. On a more positive note, the research showed that there had been substantial progress in the preceding years in reducing the number of people in poverty, although sub-Saharan Africa had made less progress than other regions.

> **Key term**
>
> **absolute poverty** the situation of a household whose income is insufficient to allow it to purchase the minimum bundle of goods and services regarded as necessary for survival

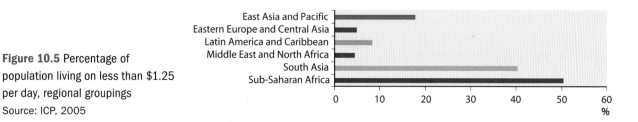

Figure 10.5 Percentage of population living on less than $1.25 per day, regional groupings
Source: ICP, 2005

For a country like the UK, this absolute poverty line is not helpful, as so few people fall below it. Thus poverty is defined in *relative* terms. If a household has insufficient income for its members to participate in the normal social life of the country, it is said to be in **relative poverty**. This too is defined in terms of a poverty line, normally set at 50 or 60% of the median adjusted household disposable income. (The median is the income of the middle-ranked household.)

Figure 10.6 presents some data for a range of developed countries. The proportion of people below the relative poverty line varies substantially across these countries, from 4.9% in the Czech Republic to 18.8% in the Russian Federation.

The percentage falling below the poverty line is not a totally reliable measure on its own: it is also important to know *how far* below the poverty line households are falling. The *income gap* (the distance between household income and the poverty line) is a useful measure of the intensity of poverty as well as of its incidence.

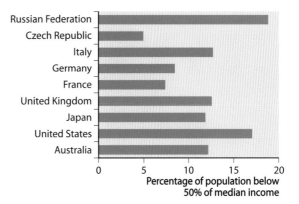

Figure 10.6 Poverty in developed nations

Source: *Human Development Report*, 2007/08

Exercise 10.3

Imagine that you are the Minister for Poverty Alleviation in a country in which the (absolute) poverty line is set at $500. Of the people living below the poverty line, you know that there are two distinct groups, each made up of 50 individuals. The people in group 1 have an income of $450, whereas those in group 2 have only $250. Suppose that your budget for poverty alleviation is $2,500.

a Your prime concern is with the most needy: how would you use your budget?

b Suppose instead that your prime minister instructs you to reduce the percentage of people living below the poverty line: do you adopt the same strategy for using the funds?

c How helpful is the poverty line as a strategic target of policy action?

Changes in inequality and poverty over time

Although the distribution of income does not change rapidly from one year to the next, there have been changes over time. Figure 10.7 graphs the Gini index, calculated for income (after adjusting for housing costs) in the UK since 1977.

Because people can be expected to smooth their consumption through time, expenditure inequality is seen to have been a little steadier than income inequality. However, both show a noticeable increase in inequality during the 1980s, since when there seems to have been no discernible trend.

It is worth noting that this has not been a general trend across all of the developed countries. A study by the OECD in 2002 found no generalised trend in the distribution of household incomes since the mid-1970s, although about half of the countries studied did show an increase between the mid-1980s and mid-1990s.

Study tip

The distinction between absolute and relative poverty is an important one. Absolute poverty is almost entirely confined to the less developed countries, but relative poverty can exist in any society, even the advanced nations, because some individuals may be excluded from normal society.

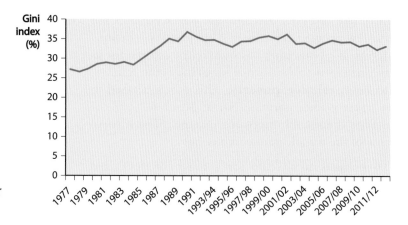

Figure 10.7 The Gini index for the UK, 1977–2012/13

Another study, undertaken by the Institute for Fiscal Studies, analysed trends and noted that there were very different trends identifiable over some 'periods of political interest'. In particular, between 1979 and 1990, with Margaret Thatcher as prime minister, income growth was higher for each successive quintile. The richest quintile saw income growth that was more than eight times that of the poorest. In other words, inequality increased during this period. Under John Major, from 1990 to 1997, growth was sluggish, but the poorest quintile gained relative to higher quintile groups. Under Tony Blair, from 1997 to 2001, income growth was more or less equally divided over the quintile groups.

However, you should not read too much into these differences. The causes of change in income distribution reflect not only the political stance of the government in power, but other changes occurring in society, and in the pattern of employment over time.

Summary

- Absolute poverty measures whether individuals or households have sufficient resources to maintain a reasonable life.
- Relative poverty measures whether individuals or households are able to participate in the life of the country in which they live: this is calculated as 50% of median adjusted household disposable income.
- Income distribution and poverty levels change relatively slowly over time.
- In the UK there has been little change since the mid-1990s, following a decade of increasing inequality.

Causes of inequality and poverty

Inequality arises from a variety of factors, some reflecting patterns in the ownership of assets, some relating to the operation of the labour market and some arising from the actions of governments. Changes in the demographic structure of the population can also be important.

Ownership of assets

Perhaps the most obvious way in which the ownership of assets influences inequality and its changes through time is through inheritance. Wealth that accumulates in a family over time and is then passed down to succeeding generations generates a source of inequality that does not arise from the current state of the economy or the operations of markets.

You need to be aware that income and wealth are not the same. Income is a 'flow' of money that households receive each period, whereas wealth is a 'stock': that is, the accumulation of assets that a household owns. During 2008–10 people in the highest decile were estimated to own 44% of identified wealth in the UK. The Gini index for wealth in 2003 was 67, which is much higher than that for income, indicating that wealth is much less evenly distributed than income.

Notice that, although wealth and income are not the same thing, inequality in wealth can *lead to* inequality in income, as wealth (the ownership of assets) creates an income flow — from rents and profits — which then feeds back into a household's income stream.

A significant change in the pattern of ownership of assets in recent decades has been the increase in home ownership and the rise in house prices. For those who continue to rent their homes, and in particular for those who rent council dwellings, this is a significant source of rising inequality.

For developing countries, there is also considerable inequality in the distribution of ownership of assets. Financial markets in developing countries are much less well developed than in developed countries, and many people, especially in the rural areas, do not have access to the formal financial institutions. This inevitably means a concentration in the ownership of financial assets. Furthermore, the ownership of land is highly concentrated in some countries. This is notably the case in much of Latin America and has contributed to the relatively high levels of inequality that have characterised that region. The situation is further complicated by the fact that property rights are weak in many developing countries, so that even if a household has farmed a piece of land for generations, it may not be able to demonstrate ownership rights over that land. Such inequality in the ownership of assets leads also to inequality in income distribution.

Labour market explanations

As explained in Chapter 5, there are several ways in which the labour market is expected to give rise to inequalities in earnings. Inequality could arise from demand and supply conditions in labour markets, which respond to changes in the pattern of consumer demand for goods and services, and changes in international comparative advantage between countries. Furthermore, differences in the balance between economic rent and transfer earnings between different occupations and economic sectors reinforce income inequalities.

However, a by-product of changes in the structure of the economy may be an increase in inequality between certain groups in society. For example, a change in the structure of employment, away from unskilled jobs and towards occupations requiring a higher level of skills and qualifications, can lead to an increase in inequality, with those workers who lack the skills to adapt to changing labour market conditions being disadvantaged by the changes. In other words, if the premium that employers are prepared to pay in order to hire skilled or well-qualified workers rises as a result of changing technology in the workplace, then those without such skills are likely to suffer.

The decline in the power of the trade unions may have contributed to this situation, as low-paid workers may find that their unions are less likely to be able to offer employment protection. It has been argued that this is a *good* thing if it increases the flexibility of the labour market. But again, a balance is needed between worker protection and free and flexible markets.

Synoptic link

Notice that when we talk about the labour market in the aggregate, we tend to ignore the fact that at the microeconomic level, there are significant differences between individual labour markets. This was discussed under Theme 3, in Chapter 5.

The difference in earnings between female and male workers was also highlighted in Chapter 5. Figure 10.8 provides empirical evidence for some developed countries. In the UK, a female worker with an educational attainment below upper secondary level on average earns 55% of the average male wage. As educational attainment increases, this differential widens somewhat. The pattern varies across this group of countries. For example, in Germany education brings a marked narrowing of the earnings differential between men and women. Overall, the differentials are less for countries like Hungary and Italy than for Germany, the USA and the UK. Some of the earnings differences between men and women can be explained by the fact that when women have to take time out from working to look after children, they lose human capital by missing out on work experience. However, such market explanations may not suffice to explain all the differences in earnings that are observed.

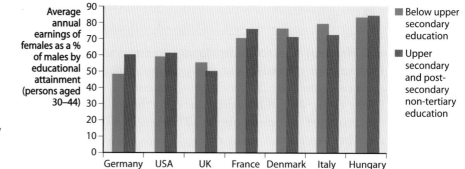

Figure 10.8 Gender inequality in earnings, various countries
Source: OECD

Many LDCs are characterised by inefficient and underdeveloped labour markets, which may give rise to income inequalities. This may in particular contribute to inequality between rural and urban areas. In many countries, rural areas are still highly dependent on subsistence agriculture, with relatively little wage labour. In contrast, the modern sector, located primarily in the urban areas, demonstrates higher wage levels and a more formal sector — but with limited job opportunities. This can create a situation in which there is substantial migration from the rural to the urban areas, attracted by the high wage differentials between the regions.

However, given limited job opportunities in the formal urban sector, the result may be high levels of urban unemployment, together with congestion and overcrowding. The high rate of migration may also give rise to the development of an urban informal sector, so that the labour market is effectively structured in three segmented sections — rural, urban informal and urban formal. The limited linkages between them may then perpetuate inequality.

Demographic change

A feature of many developed countries in recent years has been a change in the age structure of the population. Improved medical drugs and treatments have meant that people are living longer, and this has combined with low fertility rates to bring about an increase in the proportion of the population who are in the older age groups. This has put pressure on the provision of pensions, and increased the vulnerability of this group in society. State pensions have been funded primarily by the contributions of those in work, but if the number of people of working age falls as a proportion of the whole population, then this funding stream comes under pressure.

Many developed countries have seen a change in the age structure of the population

Government intervention

In the developed countries, there are a number of ways in which government intervention influences the distribution of income in a society, although not all of these interventions are expressly intended to do so. Most prominent is the range of transfer payments and taxation that has been implemented.

The overall effect of these measures has a large effect on income distribution. This can be shown using a Lorenz curve, as in Figure 10.9. ('Original income' is income before any adjustment is made for the effect of taxation or benefits.) You can see the extent to which tax and benefit measures bring the Lorenz curve closer to the equality line.

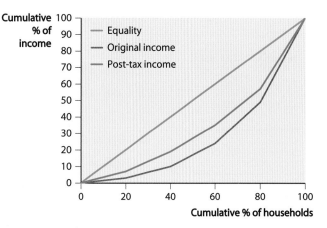

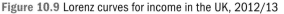

Figure 10.9 Lorenz curves for income in the UK, 2012/13

Benefits

There are two forms of benefit that households can receive to help equalise the income distribution. First, there are various types of cash benefit, such as Income Support, Child Benefit, Incapacity Benefit and Working Tax Credit. These are designed to protect families whose income in certain circumstances would otherwise be very low. Second, there are benefits in kind, such as health and education. These accrue to individual households depending on the number of members of the household and their age and gender. Of these, the cash benefits are far more important in influencing the distribution of income. For the lowest quintile such benefits make up about three-fifths of growth in income; they are also significant for the second quintile.

Key terms

direct tax a tax levied directly on income

progressive tax a tax in which the marginal tax rate rises with income, i.e. a tax bearing most heavily on the relatively well-off members of society

marginal tax rate tax on additional income, defined as the change in tax payments due divided by the change in taxable income

Exercise 10.4

Table 10.5 shows the amount of tax paid by an individual as income increases. Calculate the average and marginal tax rates at each of the income levels. (*Remember the definition of the marginal tax rate provided above.*)

Table 10.5

Income	Tax paid
£1,000	£100
£2,000	£300
£3,000	£600
£4,000	£1,000

Taxation

Direct taxes (taxes on incomes) tend to be progressive. In other words, higher income groups pay tax at a higher rate. In 2010/11, people earning more than £1 million in the year on average paid 44.4% of the income as tax, whereas those in the £15,000–19,999 income range paid 11.3% in tax.

In the UK the main direct taxes are income tax, corporation tax (paid by firms on profits), capital gains tax (paid by individuals who sell assets at a profit), inheritance tax and petroleum revenue tax (paid by firms operating in the North Sea). There is also the council tax, collected by local authorities.

With a tax such as income tax, its **progressive** nature is reflected in the way the tax rate increases as an individual moves into a higher income range. In other words, the **marginal tax rate** increases as income increases. The progressive nature of the tax ensures that it does indeed help to reduce inequality in income distribution — although its effects are less than those of the cash benefits discussed earlier.

Table 10.4 shows average tax rates for taxpayers in different income bands in 2010/11. Notice that the table shows *average* rather than *marginal* tax rates. When average rates are rising, marginal tax rates are higher than the average. Exercise 10.4 illustrates this.

Table 10.4 Income tax payable in the UK by annual income, 2010/11

Income band	Number of taxpayers (m)	Average rate of tax payable (%)	Average amount of tax payable (£)
£6,475–£7,499	0.9	1.3	91
£7,500–£9,999	2.6	4.3	382
£10,000–£14,999	6.4	7.7	956
£15,000–£19,999	5.2	11.3	1,960
£20,000–£29,999	6.9	13.7	3,350
£30,000–£49,999	5.7	15.4	5,800
£50,000–£99,999	2.1	22.3	14,600
£100,000–£199,999	0.3	29.8	35,700
£200,000–£499,999	0.1	37.8	109,000
All incomes	30.5	18.3	5,220

Source: *Social Trends*, no. 41.

The effect of **indirect taxes**, on the other hand, can sometimes be **regressive**: in other words, indirect taxes may impinge more heavily on lower-income households. Indirect taxes are taxes that are paid on items of expenditure, rather than on income.

Examples of indirect taxes are value added tax (VAT), which is charged on most goods and services sold in the UK, tobacco taxes, excise duties on alcohol and oil duties. These specific taxes are levied per unit sold. Book 1 analysed how the incidence of a tax is related to the price elasticity of demand of a good or service. It explained how, where demand is price inelastic, producers are able to pass much of an increase in the tax rate on to consumers, whereas if demand is price elastic they have to absorb most of the increase as part of their costs.

Key terms

indirect tax a tax on expenditure, e.g. VAT

regressive tax a tax bearing more heavily on the relatively poorer members of society

Why should some of these taxes be regressive? Take the tobacco tax. In the first place, the number of smokers is higher among lower-income groups than among the relatively rich — research has shown that only about 10% of people in professional groups now smoke compared with nearly 40% of those in unskilled manual groups. Second, expenditure on tobacco tends to take a lower proportion of income of the rich compared with that of the poor, even for those in the former group who do smoke. Thus, the tobacco tax falls more heavily on lower-income groups than on the better-off. It is estimated that for households in the bottom quintile of the income distribution in 2008/09, indirect taxes accounted for 28.2% of disposable income, compared with 12.8% for households in the top quintile.

Notice that a tax that is simply **proportional** to income would be neither regressive nor progressive, but would be charged at the same rate to all taxpayers.

The balance of taxation

Achieving a balance of taxation between direct and indirect taxes is an important aspect of the government's redistributive policy. A switch in the balance from direct to indirect taxes will tend to increase inequality in a society.

There may be reasons why such a switch is seen as desirable. When Margaret Thatcher came to power back in 1979, one of the first actions of her government was to increase indirect taxes and introduce cuts in income tax. An important part of the rationale was that high marginal tax rates on income can have a disincentive effect: if people know that a large proportion of any additional work they undertake will be taxed away, they may be discouraged from providing more work. In other words, cutting income tax can encourage work effort by reducing marginal tax rates.

This is yet another reminder of the need for a balanced policy, one that recognises that while some income redistribution is needed to protect the vulnerable, disincentive effects may arise if the better-off are over-taxed.

Long-term policy

An economic analysis of the causes of inequality suggests that there are some long-term measures that can be taken to reduce future inequality, although they may take quite a while to become effective. Policies that encourage greater take-up of education, and provide skills retraining, may be important in the long run if the unskilled are not to be excluded from the benefits of economic growth.

To some extent it could be argued that some inequality is inevitable within a free market capitalist society. Indeed, it could be argued that without some inequality, capitalism could not operate, as it is the pursuit of gain that provides firms with the incentive to maximise profits, workers with the incentive to provide labour effort, and consumers with the incentive to maximise their utility. It is the combination of these efforts by economic agents that leads to good resource allocation, through the working of Adam Smith's 'invisible hand'. In a world in which every individual was guaranteed the same income as everyone else, there would be no incentive for anyone to strive to do better. However, few would argue for complete equality of income. More important is that there should be equality of opportunity.

Weak institutions and poor governance in developing countries mean that measures such as taxation and transfers to influence the distribution of income are largely untried or ineffective. The economist Simon Kuznets argued that there is expected to be a relationship between the degree of inequality in the income distribution and the level of development that a country has achieved. He claimed that in the early stages of economic development income is fairly equally distributed, with everyone living at a relatively low income level. However, as development begins to take off there will be some individuals at the forefront of enterprise and development, and their incomes will rise more rapidly. So in this middle phase the income distribution will tend to worsen. At a later stage of development, society will eventually be able to afford to redistribute income to protect the poor, and all will begin to share in the benefits of development.

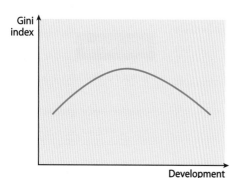

Figure 10.10 The Kuznets curve

This can be portrayed as a relationship between the Gini index and the level of development. The thrust of the Kuznets hypothesis is that this should reveal an inverted U-shaped relationship, as shown in Figure 10.10. Although the data in Table 10.1 do not strongly support this hypothesis, there is some evidence to suggest that the relationship does hold in some regions of the world.

Extension material

The Kuznets curve: empirical evidence

One reason why the empirical support for the Kuznets hypothesis is rather weak is that the relationship may not show up clearly in *cross-section* data — in other words, when the evidence is based on looking at how the relationship varies across countries at a single point in time. Looking at how the relationship changes through time for individual countries might be more revealing, but unfortunately data on inequality are expensive to compile and not collected on a regular basis. Such data would be known as *time series* data.

It is also worth noting that there are substantial regional variations in the degree of inequality. Latin America has been known for wide inequality between groups in society, whereas eastern Europe has shown much lower levels of inequality, partly because inequality was low across the Soviet bloc. This may also conceal the underlying Kuznets relationship.

Exercise 10.5

Using appropriate economic analysis, discuss the various policy measures available to a government wishing to ensure an equitable distribution of income without damaging incentives to work.

Exercise 10.6

Discuss the extent to which LDCs would benefit from introducing policies attempting to reduce income inequality.

Summary

- Inequality arises from a range of factors.
- The distribution of wealth is strongly influenced by the pattern of inheritance, but in recent years changing patterns of home ownership, coupled with rises in house prices, have also been significant.
- The natural operation of labour markets gives rise to some inequality in income.
- The skills premium resulting from technological change has widened the wage gap between skilled and educated workers on the one hand, and the unskilled on the other.
- Gender differences in pay persist, in spite of successive policies intended to root out discrimination.
- Government action influences the pattern of income distribution, with the net effect being a reduction in inequality.
- Most effective in this is the provision of cash benefits to low-income households.
- Direct taxes tend to be progressive, and help to redistribute income towards poorer households.
- Some indirect taxes, however, can be regressive in their impact.
- It is important to keep a balance between protecting the low-paid and providing incentives for those in work.

Inequality and economic growth

If you visit Rio de Janeiro, you may be surprised to see high metal fences in front of many of the luxurious multi-storey buildings along the lovely beaches of Copacabana. However, it is not really surprising, given that Rio has one of the highest crime rates in Brazil, exacerbated by the high level of income inequality.

It is not uncommon to find a substantial gap between the rich and the poor in many societies. Inequality exists in both developing and developed countries. For example, Paul Krugman has noted that the 13,000 richest families in the USA have almost as much income as the 20 million poorest households; those 13,000 families have incomes 300 times that of average families. Thus, it is important to examine the effects of such income inequality not only on crime rate and social behaviour, but also on the economy.

In Rio de Janerio, the slum areas or 'favelas' sit alongside middle-class districts reflecting the high level of income inequality in Brazil

Level of income inequality

The level of income inequality depends primarily on the distribution of assets and wages as well as on government policy. First, an important factor is the distribution of productive assets such as land. If land ownership is concentrated among a few owners, which is typical of many agriculture-dominated developing economies, then income inequality tends to be high in such countries. In addition, if the ownership of minerals and natural resources is concentrated among the elite, then countries well endowed with natural resources — especially mineral resources such as oil, diamonds, copper and so on — tend also to have higher asset and income inequality than other types of economy. Another factor that explains variations across countries is the rural-urban inequality within developing countries, which is the result of urban bias.

Overall, income inequality depends to a large extent on earnings inequality, as in many countries earnings account for 60–70% of total income. In some countries, rising wage inequality has often been ascribed to technological change. New technologies generate a demand for skills. This favours higher-skilled workers over lower-skilled ones and leads to increasing wage differentials between skilled and unskilled workers. In addition, education tends to play an important role in reducing income inequality.

Thus, if some groups in a society do not have access to education, this leads to higher earnings inequality and therefore higher income inequality. Thus, earnings inequality is clearly an important contributor to the increases in overall income inequality witnessed in many countries recently.

Economic performance and output

But how does inequality influence economic performance and output? More unequal societies tend to develop larger groups of people who are excluded from opportunities that others enjoy. Poor people may not have the same chances in life as richer people, and may thus never quite realise their full productive potential. This may be because they do not get as good an education as those afforded by richer families, or because they can't get loans to start up a business as easily, or because they can't afford the insurance they would require to undertake some risky — but productive — venture. An income distribution with lots of poor people, or unequally distributed opportunities, would under-utilise its aggregate productive potential to a greater degree than a distribution with relatively fewer poor people, or one where opportunities were more equitably distributed. Both theory and empirical evidence

→

suggest that these incomplete realisations of economic potential are not of concern only to those who care about equity *per se*. They also affect aggregate economic potential, and therefore aggregate output and its rate of growth.

The impact on growth may also be negative when the gap between the rich and the poor widens excessively. For instance, rural economies with very high land concentration in a few hands and landlessness for the majority face very high shirking and supervision costs. For these reasons, these economies tend to be less efficient (e.g. to have lower yields per hectare) than more equitable agrarian systems, even when accounting for the economies of scale in marketing, processing and shipping which benefit larger farms.

Political instability and social problems

Finally, high levels of income inequality can also create political instability and social problems and very negatively affect growth over both the short and long term. There is increasing evidence of a strong relation between inequality and the crime rate. Income differences between households also create *psychological stress* for the relatively poor that may explain higher morbidity, mortality and violence rates. Social tensions, in turn, erode the security of property rights, augment the threat of expropriation, drive away domestic and foreign investment and increase the cost of business security and contract enforcement.

Follow-up questions

a Identify the key causes of inequality in a society.

b In your own words, outline the main ways in which inequality may have an impact on economic growth.

Emerging and developing economies

One of the greatest challenges faced by the world economy is the enormous gap in living standards that has built up as the process of economic growth and development has left many countries far behind. Development is not about economic growth alone, but growth is a vital prerequisite if progress in development is to be achieved. This chapter examines some models of economic growth that are of special significance for less developed countries, and highlights some of their limitations. In particular, it evaluates some of the factors that may be thought to contribute to the process of economic growth — and some of the obstacles to growth that have hindered progress, especially in sub-Saharan Africa. This will be illustrated with reference to the experience of the emerging economies that have begun to close the gap in living standards.

Learning outcomes

After studying this chapter, you should:

→ be familiar with ways of measuring and monitoring human development
→ understand the importance of economic growth for less developed countries
→ be familiar with the Harrod–Domar model of economic growth, and its relevance for less developed countries
→ understand the importance of factors that can contribute to economic growth, such as capital, technology and human capital
→ be aware of the World Bank model of market-friendly economic development and the role of Structural Adjustment Programmes
→ realise the importance of sustainability in development
→ be familiar with the contrasting patterns of development in different regions of the world
→ understand the causes and significance of rapid population growth
→ appreciate the importance of missing markets, especially financial markets
→ be aware of the importance of social capital in promoting long-term development
→ appreciate the significance of relationships with more developed countries

Measuring development

Chapter 10 noted that the notion of '**development**' goes beyond economic growth. It encompasses many more aspects of the quality of people's lives. In other words, although expanding the resources available to a society through economic growth is an essential ingredient of development, the way in which those resources are used is also crucial.

How do we recognise that a country is undergoing development? The discussion in this chapter will be illustrated using indicators for a selection of countries from different regions of the world, but try to remember the wide diversity among the countries that are classified as less developed countries (LDCs). There are some countries that have undergone a process of economic growth, and have started to

> **Key term**
>
> **development** a process by which real per capita incomes are increased and the inhabitants of a country are able to benefit from improved living conditions, i.e. lower poverty and enhanced standards of education, health, nutrition and other essentials of life

close the gap on the developed countries. This group includes the **tiger economies** of South East Asia (Hong Kong, South Korea, Singapore and Taiwan) and more recently a group of **emerging economies**, including the **BRIC countries** (Brazil, Russia, India and China). However, there are also LDCs, especially in sub-Saharan Africa, that have made relatively little progress.

How can the less developed countries be identified? An obvious first indicator to consider would be GNI per capita, but the problems entailed in using this measure for international comparisons are well known.

Figure 11.1 shows levels of GNI per capita (measured in PPP$) for selected countries from different regions of the world. Notice that the countries here have been ranked in descending order of GNI per capita in US$. The data points for each country have been colour-coded by region.

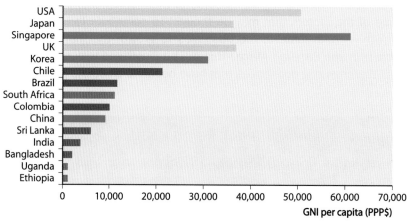

Figure 11.1 GNI per capita, selected countries, 2012 (PPP$)

Source: *World Development Report*, 2014

The figure underlines the gap in income levels between countries, but there are other dimensions of development that need to be taken into account.

> ### Study tip
>
> Do not be tempted to learn by heart lots of statistics about individual countries, as this will not be expected of you. Being aware of the general differences in the stage of development reached by countries in different regions may be helpful, but the detail is not necessary.

The Human Development Index

To deal with the criticism that GNI per capita fails to take account of other dimensions of the quality of life, in 1990 UNDP devised an alternative indicator, known as the **Human Development Index** (HDI). This was designed to provide a broader measure of the stage of development that a country had reached. It has since become a widely used indicator.

The basis for this measure is that there are three key aspects of human development: resources, knowledge of how to make good use of those resources, and a reasonable life span in which to make use of those resources (see Figure 11.2). The three components are measured by, respectively, GNI per capita in PPP$, indicators of education (mean years of schooling and expected years of schooling) and life expectancy. The measurements are then combined to produce a composite index ranging between 0 and 1, with higher values reflecting higher human development.

Prior knowledge needed

GNI per capita was introduced in Book 1, Chapter 9, which also investigated some of the problems in its use. You may find it helpful to review this material.

Key terms

tiger economies a group of economies in South East Asia (Hong Kong, South Korea, Singapore and Taiwan) that enjoyed rapid economic growth from the 1960s

emerging economies economies that have experienced rapid economic growth with some industrialisation and characteristics of developed markets

BRIC countries a group of countries comprising Brazil, Russia, India and China that have made rapid progress in recent years (South Africa is also included in this group)

Human Development Index a composite indicator of the level of a country's development, varying between 0 and 1

Values of the HDI for 2013 are charted in Figure 11.3 for the selected countries. You can see that the broad ranking of the countries in Figure 11.1 is preserved, but the gap between low and high human development is less marked. Exceptions are South Africa and Brazil, which are ranked lower on the basis of the HDI than on GNI per capita: what this suggests is that these countries have achieved relatively high income levels, but other aspects of human development have not kept pace. There are other countries in the world that share this feature. You will see that there are also countries that seem to perform better on HDI grounds than on GNI per capita — for example, China and Sri Lanka.

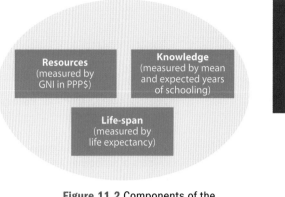

Figure 11.2 Components of the Human Development Index

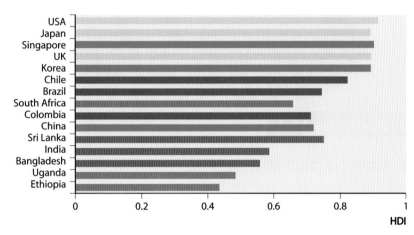

Figure 11.3 The Human Development Index, selected countries

Source: *Human Development Report*, 2014

Figures 11.4 and 11.5 show the levels of two of the measures that enter into the HDI: life expectancy and mean years of schooling. It would seem that life expectancy is primarily responsible for the low ranking of South Africa in the HDI, as its level of life expectancy is out of kilter with its average income level and mean years of schooling. In contrast, Bangladesh and India perform quite well in terms of lifespan, but relatively poorly in terms of education. By comparing these data, you can get some idea of the diversity between countries that was mentioned earlier.

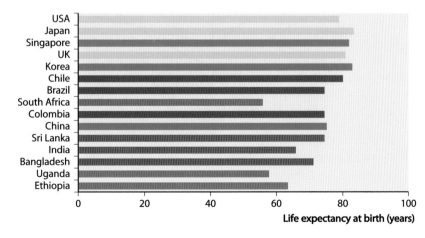

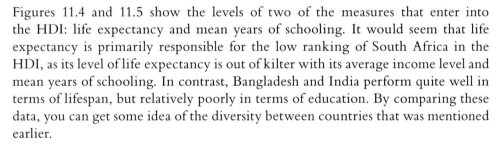

Figure 11.4 Life expectancy at birth (years), selected countries

Source: *Human Development Report*, 2014

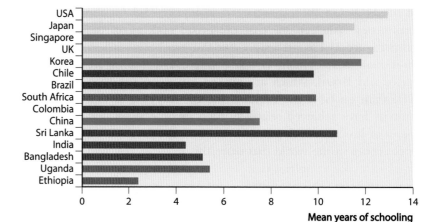

Figure 11.5 Mean years of schooling, selected countries

Source: *Human Development Report,* 2014

In part, this diversity reflects differing priorities that governments have given to different aspects of development. Countries such as Brazil have aimed primarily at achieving economic growth, while those such as Sri Lanka have given greater priority to promoting education and healthcare.

Quantitative skills 11.1

A development diamond

Another way of putting a country into perspective is to construct a *development diamond*. An example is shown in Figure 11.6. This compares Ethiopia's performance with the average for countries in its region: sub-Saharan Africa. On each axis, the value of the variable achieved by Ethiopia is expressed as a proportion of the value for sub-Saharan Africa. In this instance, Ethiopia is seen to have low life expectancy, relatively much lower GNI per capita but shows stronger achievement on mean years of schooling. These combined with other indicators contribute to the HDI value, which is lower than the average for sub-Saharan Africa.

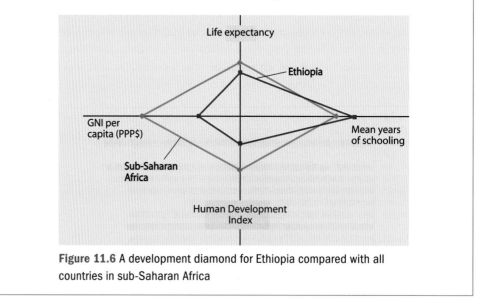

Figure 11.6 A development diamond for Ethiopia compared with all countries in sub-Saharan Africa

---

There is a view that growth should be the prime objective for development, since by expanding the resources available, the benefits can begin to trickle down through the population. An opposing view claims that, by providing first for basic needs, more rapid economic growth can be facilitated. The problem in some cases is that growth has not resulted in the trickle-down effect, and inequality remains. It may be significant that countries such as Brazil and South Africa, where the GNI per capita ranking is high relative to the HDI ranking, are countries in which there remain high levels of inequality in the distribution of income.

The HDI may be preferred to GNI per capita as a measure of development on the grounds that it reflects the key dimensions of development as opposed to growth. However, it will always be difficult to reduce a complex concept such as development to a single statistic. The diverse characteristics of LDCs demand the use of a range of alternative measures in order to identify the configuration of circumstances and problems facing a particular country. In the area of healthcare it is useful to look at the number of doctors relative to population, or levels of infant mortality. Access to improved water, sanitation or electricity is informative about the level of infrastructure, as is the access to a mobile phone.

Extension material

Beyond the HDI

The UNDP has recognised that the HDI does not encompass all the dimensions of human development that should be taken into account when evaluating the state of development in an LDC. It now produces some additional indicators intended to capture other key facets of the quality of life. These include indicators that adjust the HDI to take into account inequality in societies. For example, it produces indicators to highlight gender inequality, which is an important feature of many LDCs, where females receive less education than men, and are more exposed to health risks.

The UNDP also produces an index that tries to capture poverty. This is based on the idea that what we mean by poverty is best reflected in deprivations. In other words, people may be considered poor if they lack access to key components of what makes for a good life. In constructing this index, the UNDP consider indicators that include poor nutrition, high child mortality, years of schooling and lack of access to clean water, sanitation, electricity and so on.

Summary

- Less developed countries (LDCs) are largely located in four major regions: sub-Saharan Africa, Latin America, South Asia and South East Asia.
- These regions have shown contrasting patterns of growth and development.
- The Human Development Index (HDI) recognises that human development depends upon resources, knowledge and health, and therefore combines indicators of these key aspects.
- Different countries have different characteristics, and face different configurations of problems and opportunities.

Economic growth

Although development is about more than economic growth, growth is a crucial part of any process of economic and human development. It provides the increase in resources necessary to enable a country to provide for the basic needs of its citizens and to expand its choices in the future, and it lays the foundations for future development.

For a less developed country (LDC), one important problem is the inability to produce capital goods. In many LDCs the capacity to produce capital goods is limited because they lack the necessary technical knowledge and resources. Furthermore, a country

Prior knowledge needed

Economic growth was discussed in Book 1, Chapter 14. The following sections build upon that discussion, extending the analysis to incorporate the particular problems faced by less developed countries.

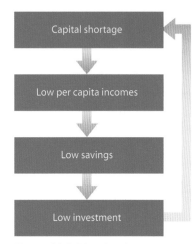

Figure 11.7 A low-level equilibrium trap

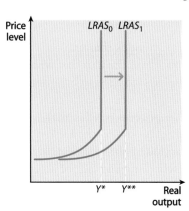

Figure 11.8 Economic growth as a shift in aggregate supply

in which there are high levels of poverty, and in which many households face low income-earning opportunities, needs to devote much of its resources to consumption. The question for LDCs is thus how to overcome this problem in order to kick-start a process of economic growth.

Figure 11.7 illustrates the problem. A shortage of capital means low per capita income, which means low savings, which in turn means low investment, limited capital, and hence low per capita incomes. In this way a country can get trapped in a *low-level equilibrium* situation.

Another view of economic growth sees it in terms of a shift in the aggregate supply curve. It was argued in Book 1, Chapter 14 that investment is critical to the process of expanding the productive capacity of the economy. This is illustrated in Figure 11.8, where the long-run aggregate supply curve shifts from $LRAS_0$ to $LRAS_1$. Book 1 explained that the aggregate supply curve could move to the right either following investment, which would expand the stock of capital, or following an improvement in the effectiveness of markets. All of this suggests that the first focus for LDCs must be on savings and investment.

For both developed and developing countries, the potential productive capacity of the economy depends fundamentally on two things: the quantity of factors of production available within the economy, and the efficiency with which they are utilised. By increasing the quantity and/or quality of the factors of production and their productivity, the aggregate supply curve can be shifted to the right.

For the developing countries, the problem is magnified because of lack of resources. In many cases, human capital is low, and there are limited resources to devote to education, training and improving health. Capital tends to be scarce, and the flows of foreign direct investment — especially to the poorest LDCs — are relatively low. Markets do not operate effectively to allocate resources efficiently. There are thus many obstacles to be overcome in seeking to promote growth and development.

Stages of economic growth

Key term

stages of economic growth a process described by economic historian Walt Rostow, which set out five stages through which he claimed that all developing countries would pass

The economic historian Walt Rostow examined the pattern of development that had been followed in history. He argued in 1960 that all of the more developed countries could be seen to have passed through five **stages of economic growth**. Figure 11.9 gives a general impression of how income per capita changes through these stages.

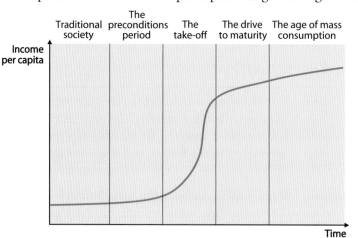

Figure 11.9 The stages of economic growth

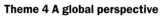

In the first stage — the *traditional society* — land is the basis of wealth, most of the production that takes place is in agriculture, and investment is low. Some societies can remain in this stage or get trapped in it. This may correspond to the low-level equilibrium trap that was referred to above. Income per capita is static in this phase.

In order to escape from this situation, Rostow argued that a country must establish the *preconditions* for economic growth. In this period, agricultural productivity begins to increase. This enables resources to be released from the agricultural sector so that some diversification can take place: for example, into manufacturing activity. Such changes are typically accompanied by a range of social and political changes. It is also important in this stage that some resources are devoted to the provision of the infrastructure that is needed for industrialisation to take place, especially in terms of transport and communications and market facilities.

In the *take-off* stage the economy passes through a 20–30-year period of accelerated growth, with investment rising relative to GDP. Barriers that held back economic growth are overcome. The process of growth in this period tends to be driven by a few leading sectors. A key element of this period is the emergence of entrepreneurs — people who are able to recognise opportunities for productive investment, and who are willing to accept the risk of carrying out that investment. A flow of funds for investment is also needed. Such funds may come from domestic savings, but it may also be necessary to draw in funds from external sources.

The *drive to maturity* stage is a period of self-sustaining growth. New sectors begin to emerge to complement the leading sectors that emerged during the take-off, so that the economy becomes more diversified and balanced. In this period, investment continues to take a relatively high proportion of GDP.

The final period is the *age of mass consumption*, in which the economy is now fully diversified, output per head continues to rise, but consumption now takes a higher proportion of GDP. Countries in this stage have effectively become developed.

Rostow's discussion has been much criticised. For example, it has been suggested that, as an economic historian, Rostow was more concerned with describing the way in which economies had developed in the past than with providing an explanation of *why* they had developed in this way. Nor does his approach provide much helpful guidance for designing policy that would stimulate development in those countries that are still stuck in the 'traditional society' stage, except insofar as countries could study the preconditions and try to replicate them. For example, he offers no explanation of how the barriers to growth disappear in the take-off stage, although it is helpful to be aware that there may be such barriers, and that they need to be overcome.

Industrialisation

So what are the prospects for a country in the traditional stage wanting to move towards **industrialisation**, and to reduce its reliance on primary production?

In an influential paper in 1954, Sir Arthur Lewis argued that agriculture in many LDCs was characterised by surplus labour. Perhaps farms were operated on a household basis, with the work and the crop being shared out between members of the household. If there was not enough work to be done by all the members of the household, then, although all seemed to be employed, there would in fact be *hidden unemployment*, or *under-employment*. Given the size of the rural population and its rapid growth, there could be almost unlimited *surplus labour* existing in this way.

> **Key term**
>
> **industrialisation**
> a process of transforming an economy by expanding manufacturing and other industrial activity

Lewis model a model developed by Sir Arthur Lewis which argued that less developed countries could be seen as being typified by two sectors, traditional and modern, and that labour could be transferred from the traditional to the modern sector in order to bring about growth and development

Harrod–Domar model a model of economic growth that emphasises the importance of savings and investment

Lewis then pointed out that because the marginal product of labour in agriculture was zero, it would be possible to transfer such surplus labour into the industrial sector without a loss of agricultural output, as the remaining labour would be able to take up the slack. All that would be necessary is for the industrial sector to set a wage sufficiently higher than the rural wage to persuade workers to transfer. Industry could then reap profits that could be reinvested to allow industry to expand, without any need for the industrial wage to be pulled upwards to cause inflation.

Unfortunately, the process did not prove to be as smooth as Lewis suggested. One reason relates to *human capital* levels. Agricultural workers do not have the skills or training that prepares them for employment in the industrial sector, so it is not straightforward to transfer them from agricultural to industrial work, especially if it is the least productive workers who choose to migrate. Furthermore, if migration to the cities is rapid, the urban infrastructure may not be able to cope, perhaps resulting in the development of shanty towns, which might be seen as a form of negative externality.

It is also the case that the expanding industry did not always reinvest the surplus in order to enable continuous expansion of the industrial sector. Foreign firms tended to repatriate the profits (as will be seen later in this chapter), and in any case tended to use modern, relatively capital-intensive technology that did not require a large pool of unskilled labour.

Perhaps more seriously, the **Lewis model** encouraged governments to think in terms of industry-led growth, and to neglect the rural sector. This meant that agricultural productivity often remained low, and inequality between urban and rural areas grew.

The Harrod–Domar model

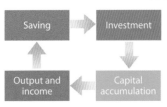

Figure 11.10 The Harrod–Domar process of economic development

The idea that the initial focus for LDCs should be on savings and investment is supported by the **Harrod–Domar model** of economic growth, which first appeared in separate articles by Roy Harrod in the UK and Evsey Domar in the USA in 1939. This model was to become significant in influencing LDCs' attitudes towards the process of economic growth. It was developed in an attempt to determine how equilibrium could be achieved in a growing economy.

The basic finding of this model was that an economy can remain in equilibrium through time only if it grows at a particular rate, given by the ratio of the savings rate to the capital–output ratio (s/k). This unique stable growth path is thus seen to depend on the savings ratio and the productivity of capital. Any deviation from the path will cause the economy to become unstable. This finding emphasised the importance of savings in the process of economic growth, and led to the conclusion that a country wishing to achieve economic growth must first increase its flow of savings. For many LDCs, there may be a savings gap, in the sense that domestic savings may not be sufficient to enable investment to take place.

Study tip

This is quite a useful schematic diagram describing the process of economic growth, as long as you remember all the ways in which it may fail to work smoothly.

Figure 11.10 illustrates the process that leads to growth in a Harrod–Domar world. Savings are crucial in enabling investment to be undertaken — always remembering that some investment will have to be used to replace existing capital that has worn out. Investment then enables capital to accumulate and technology to be improved. The accumulation of capital leads to an increase in output and incomes, which leads to a further flow of savings, and the cycle is back where it started from.

The algebra of the Harrod–Domar model

The algebra of the Harrod–Domar model can be revealing.

Suppose there is a closed economy with no government. If there is equilibrium in the goods market, then planned saving (S) equals planned investment (I):

$$S = I$$

Assume that there is no depreciation, so investment results in capital accumulation (ΔK, where Δ means 'change in'):

$$I = \Delta K$$

Assume also that the capital–output ratio (k) remains constant over time. Then:

$$k = \Delta K / \Delta Y$$

where Y is income and/or output.

If savings are a proportion (s) of income, then for equilibrium to be maintained:

$$sY = \Delta K = k\Delta Y$$

Rearranging, this implies that the growth rate of output ($\Delta Y/Y$) must be equal to s/k.

This then provides a simple rule. If a government wishes to achieve a growth rate of, say, 5%, and knows that the capital–output ratio is 3, then the saving ratio needs to be $3 \times 5 = 15\%$. This is a simple rule, but deceptive. There are many reasons why it is not enough to generate a flow of saving and then sit back and wait for results, especially in the context of less developed countries.

The key question is whether this process can allow an LDC to break out of the low-level equilibrium trap. Figure 11.10 can be used to identify a number of problems that may prevent the Harrod–Domar process from being effective for LDCs.

It has already been argued that generating a flow of savings in an LDC may be problematic. When incomes are low, households may have to devote most of their resources to consumption, and so there may be a lack of savings. Nonetheless, some savings have proved possible. For example, in the early 1960s South Korea had an average income level that was not too different from that of countries like Sudan and Afghanistan, but it managed to build up the savings rate during that decade.

Setting aside the problem of low savings for the moment, what happens next?

Will savings lead to investment and the accumulation of capital?

If a flow of savings can be generated, the next important step is to transform the savings into investment. This is the process by which the sacrifice of current consumption leads to an increase in productive capacity in the future.

Some important preconditions must be met if savings are to be transformed into investment. If the funds that have been saved are to be mobilised for investment, there must be a way for potential borrowers to get access to the funds. In developed countries this takes place through the medium of financial markets. For example, it may be that households save by putting their money into a savings account at the bank; then with this money the bank can make loans to entrepreneurs, enabling them to undertake investment.

In many LDCs, however, financial markets are undeveloped, so it is much more difficult for funds to be recycled in this way. For example, a study conducted in 1997 by the Bank of Uganda found that almost 30% of households interviewed in rural Ugandan villages had undertaken savings at some time. However, almost none of these had done so through formal financial institutions, which did not reach into the rural areas. Instead, the saving that took place tended to be in the form of fixed assets, or money kept under the bed. Such savings cannot readily be transformed into productive investment.

In addition, governments in some periods have made matters worse by holding down interest rates in the hope of encouraging firms to borrow. The idea here is that a low interest rate means a low cost of borrowing, which should make borrowing more attractive. However, this ignores the fact that if interest rates are very low there is little incentive to save, since the return on saving is so low. In this case, firms may wish to invest but may not be able to obtain the funds to do so.

The other prerequisite for savings to be converted into investment is that there must be entrepreneurs with the ability to identify investment possibilities, the skill to carry them through and the willingness to bear the risk. Such entrepreneurs are in limited supply in many LDCs.

This worked effectively for Hong Kong, one of the so-called tiger economies. During its period of rapid development after the 1950s, Hong Kong benefited from a wave of immigrant entrepreneurs, especially from Shanghai, who provided the impetus for rapid development. In Singapore the entrepreneurship came primarily from the government, and from multinational corporations that were encouraged to become established in the country. Singapore and South Korea also adopted policies that ensured a steady flow of savings, so that, for example, in Singapore gross domestic savings amounted to 52% of GDP in 1999.

Singapore city — gross savings in Singapore amounted to almost half of GDP in 2012

Will investment lead to higher output and income?

For investment to be productive in terms of raising output and incomes in the economy, some further conditions need to be met. In particular, it is crucial for firms to have access to physical capital, which will raise production capacity. Given the limited capability of producing capital goods in many LDCs, they have to rely on capital imported from the more developed countries. This may be beneficial in terms of upgrading home technology, but such equipment can be imported only if the country has earned the foreign exchange to pay for it.

One of the most pressing problems for many LDCs is that they face a **foreign currency gap** — in other words, they find it difficult to earn sufficient foreign exchange with which to purchase the crucial imports required to allow manufacturing activity to expand. In order to do this, physical capital is needed, together with key inputs to the production process. Indeed, many LDCs need to import food and medical supplies in order to develop their human capital. A shortage of foreign exchange may therefore make it difficult for the country to accumulate capital.

The tiger economies were all very open to international trade, and focused on promoting exports in order to earn the foreign exchange needed to import capital goods. This strategy worked very effectively, and the economies were able to widen their access to capital and move to higher value-added activities as they developed their capabilities.

The importance of human capital

If the capital *can* be obtained, there is then a need for skilled labour with which to operate the capital goods. In other words, human capital in the form of skilled, healthy and well-trained workers is as important as physical capital if investment is to be productive.

In principle, it could be thought that today's LDCs have an advantage over the countries that developed in earlier periods. In particular, they can learn from earlier mistakes, and import technology that has already been developed, rather than having to develop it anew. This suggests that a convergence process should be going on, whereby LDCs are able to adopt technology that has already been produced, and thereby grow more rapidly and begin to close the gap with the more developed countries.

However, by and large this has not been happening, and a lack of human capital has been suggested as one of the key reasons for the failure. This underlines the importance of education in laying the foundations for economic growth as well as contributing directly to the quality of life.

In the case of the tiger economies, their education systems had been well established, either through the British colonial legacy (in the case of Singapore and Hong Kong) or through past Japanese occupation periods (in Taiwan and South Korea). In all of these countries, education received high priority, and cultural influences encouraged a high demand for education. The tiger economies thus benefited from having highly skilled and well-disciplined labour forces that were able to make effective use of the capital goods that had been acquired.

Harrod–Domar and external resources

Figure 11.11 extends the earlier schematic presentation of the process underlying the Harrod–Domar model of economic growth. This has been amended to underline the importance of access to technology and human capital.

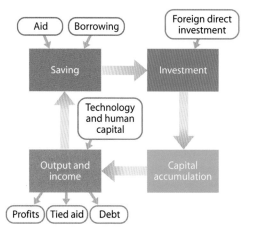

Figure 11.11 The Harrod-Domar process of economic development augmented

The discussion above has emphasised the difficulty of mobilising domestic savings, both in generating a sufficient flow of savings and in translating such savings into productive investment.

The question arises as to whether an LDC could supplement its domestic savings with a flow of funds from abroad. Figure 11.11 identifies three possible injections into the Harrod–Domar process. First, it might be possible to attract flows of overseas assistance from higher-income countries. Secondly, perhaps the amount of investment could be augmented directly by persuading multinational corporations to engage in foreign direct investment. Thirdly, perhaps the LDC could borrow on international capital markets to finance its domestic investment. It is worth noting that the tiger economies took full advantage of these external sources of funds.

Each of these ways of attracting external resources has a downside associated with it. As far as overseas assistance is concerned, in the past such flows have been seen by some donor countries as part of trade policy, and have brought less benefit to LDCs than had been hoped. In the case of the multinational corporations, there is a tendency for the profits to be repatriated out of the LDC, rather than recycled into the economy. Finally, international borrowing has to be repaid at some future date, and many LDCs have found themselves burdened by debt that they can ill afford to repay.

Summary

- Although development is a broader concept than economic growth, growth is a key ingredient of development.
- Economic growth can be seen in terms of a shift in the production possibility frontier, or a shift in long-run aggregate supply.
- The Harrod-Domar model of economic growth highlights the importance of savings, and of transforming savings into productive investment.
- However, where markets are underdeveloped, this transformation may be impeded.
- Human capital is also a critical ingredient of economic growth.
- If resources cannot be generated within the domestic economy, a country may need to have recourse to external sources of funding.

Market-friendly growth

Key term

market-friendly growth an approach to economic growth in which governments are recommended to intervene less where markets can operate effectively, but to intervene more strongly where markets are seen to fail

An alternative way of viewing the process of economic growth has been put forward by the World Bank. The core argument here is that markets should be allowed to work without government intervention wherever possible, and that the government should intervene only where markets cannot operate effectively. This is called a **market-friendly growth** strategy. The World Bank has argued that there are four areas that should be of high priority to LDCs looking to stimulate development: *people*, *microeconomic markets*, *macroeconomic stability* and *global linkages*.

At the core of this approach is the argument that, if markets can be made to work effectively, this will lead to more efficient resource allocation. Furthermore, governments should intervene only where markets themselves cannot operate effectively because of some sort of market failure. If the four components can be made to work together, it will lay the foundations for economic growth and development.

People

The importance of human capital formation has already been stressed. The need for skilled and disciplined labour to complement capital accumulation is critical for development. However, this is an area in which market failure is widespread.

Synoptic link

Market failure was discussed as part of Theme 1, particularly in Chapters 6 and 7 of Book 1.

If people do not fully perceive the future benefits to be gained from educating their children, they will demand less education than is desirable for society. In the rural areas of many LDCs, it is common for education to be undervalued in this way, and for drop-out rates from schooling to be high. This may arise both from a failure to perceive the potential future benefits that children will derive from education, and from the high opportunity cost of education in villages where child labour is widespread.

The situation in many LDCs has been worsened in the past by poor curriculum design, whereby the legacy of colonial rule was a school system and curriculum not well directed at providing the sort of education likely to be of most benefit within the context of an LDC. Furthermore, there tended to be a bias towards providing funds to the tertiary sector (which benefits mainly the rich elites within society) rather than trying to ensure that all children received at least primary education.

The benefits from developing people as resources may overflow into other component areas: for example, through an increase in labour productivity — if healthy and educated people are able to work better — or by ensuring that products are better able to meet international standards, thereby reinforcing linkages with the rest of the world.

Microeconomic markets

The World Bank has also argued that LDCs need to encourage competitive and effective microeconomic markets in order to ensure that their resources are well allocated.

It is important that prices can act as signals to guide resource allocation. This can then create a climate for enterprise, enabling people to exploit their capabilities. In the past, many governments in LDCs have tended to intervene strongly in markets, distorting prices away from market equilibrium values — especially food prices, which were kept artificially low in urban areas, thus damaging farmers' incentives. In addition, it is important to encourage the development of financial markets that will act to channel savings into productive investment.

Again, there are likely to be overflow effects from this. First, if microeconomic markets can be made to operate effectively, this will ensure that people get a good return on the education that they undertake, which will encourage a greater demand for education in the future. Second, foreign direct investment is more likely to be attracted into a country in which there are effective operational domestic markets. And the existence of effective financial markets creates a financial discipline that encourages stability at the macroeconomic level.

Macroeconomic stability

It is argued that stability in the macroeconomy is important in order to encourage investment. If the macroeconomic environment is unstable, firms will not be sufficiently confident of the future to want to risk investing in projects. In addition, if the government becomes overactive in the economy, this may starve the private sector of resources.

A key aim for an LDC should be to ensure that prices can act as effective signals in guiding resource allocation. If overall inflation is allowed to get out of hand, then clearly allocative efficiency cannot be expected. On the other hand, a stable macroeconomy should serve to improve the operation of microeconomic markets. An economy that is stable should also be better able to withstand external shocks.

Global linkages

The domestic markets of most LDCs are limited in terms of effective demand. For LDC producers to be able to benefit from economies of scale, they need to be exporting in sufficient quantities — which clearly means being involved in and committed to international trade. Global linkages are therefore important. Furthermore, LDCs can gain access to technology only from abroad, as they do not have the capacity to produce it themselves. As mentioned above, LDCs need to find some way of closing their foreign currency gap — which can only be achieved by developing better global linkages.

Again, there are likely to be spillover effects. The availability of physical and financial capital may help the stability of the macroeconomy; participation in world markets may help domestic markets to operate; and global linkages can provide the knowledge and technology that will improve human capital in the domestic economy.

It is important to notice that establishing global links is a two-way process. On the one hand, it is important for an LDC to be in a strong enough position to form links with more developed countries without creating a vulnerability to outside influence that may damage it: for example, in reaching trade agreements. On the other hand, the more developed countries need to be willing to accept such linkages. This has not always been the case in the past.

So there is an interdependent system in which the four aspects of potential intervention interact. The self-reinforcing aspect of these four components not only provides a focus for analysis, but also highlights the fact that if any one of the elements is lacking, there may be problems.

Whether these aspects are sufficient to encourage development is an important issue. In most LDCs two additional matters will need to be tackled. First, there is the question of **infrastructure**. Infrastructure here covers a range of important facilities needed to support the development process. Transport and communications networks are needed to allow trading activity, as are market facilities. Schools, clinics and hospitals are needed if education and health care is to be provided to the population. The *public good* aspects of some types of infrastructure need to be borne in mind. The provision of transport and communications systems, or the improvement of market facilities to enable trading to take place, may be crucial for the smooth development of an LDC, but will be under-provided if left to the free market.

In sub-Saharan Africa, in particular, there have been further problems resulting from civil or international conflicts. These have often had the effect of diverting resources away from development priorities. If the government of a country does not expect to be in power for very long, it has little incentive to develop policies to stimulate development in the long term, but will concentrate on gaining short-run popularity in the hope of hanging onto power. In some cases in Africa, civil conflict has lasted for decades, and this also may discourage firms and individuals from undertaking much-needed investment.

Key term

infrastructure the complex of physical capital goods needed to support development in the form of roads, communication networks, market, education and healthcare facilities etc.

Road construction in
Congo — good transport
links will enable trading to
take place

Political stability can promote development by encouraging leaders to take a
long-term view. This was the case for Singapore, where Lee Kuan Yu, who was
prime minister from 1957 until 1991, guided the economy through a period of
rapid growth and development. However, political stability by itself does not
guarantee success — as demonstrated by the case of Zimbabwe, where Robert
Mugabe has enjoyed a long period of rule, but has demolished rather than built
up the economy.

In the case of the tiger economies, the government did have a strong influence —
although less so in the case of Hong Kong. In Singapore the government kept a tight
rein on the macroeconomy, encouraged savings, nurtured the education system,
guided the development of key strategic sectors in the economy and provided good
infrastructure for trade and industry, as well as maintaining an open economy. In
South Korea the government subsidised the development of large conglomerate
firms that provided the foundations for economic growth.

The tiger economies offer a good illustration of how markets can be enabled to
bring about rapid growth and development. Indeed, the World Bank model is based
partly on its observation of the experience of these and some other economies.
Although in some cases (especially Singapore and South Korea) the governments
played an active role in encouraging economic growth and influencing the pattern
of economic activity, nonetheless, markets were nurtured and encouraged to play a
role in resource allocation.

As the World Bank has adopted the market-friendly ideal, it has embedded its central
ideas in a set of policies that LDCs have been encouraged to follow.

Summary

- The World Bank has advocated a market-friendly approach to economic growth and
  development.
- Four key elements are seen as crucial to the process: investment in people, properly
  functioning microeconomic markets, macroeconomic stability and international linkages.
- These elements reinforce one another.

Sustainable development

Economic growth may have important effects on the environment, and care needs to be taken to ensure that, in pursuing growth, countries bear in mind the importance of future generations as well as the needs of the present. In other words, it is necessary to ensure sustainable development, which was discussed in Chapter 7.

These issues are equally important for LDCs. Deforestation has been a problem for many LDCs with areas of rainforest. In some cases, logging for timber has destroyed much valuable land; in other cases, land has been cleared for unsuitable agricultural use. This sort of activity creates relatively little present value, and leaves a poorer environment for future generations.

Another aspect of environmental degradation concerns *biodiversity*. This refers to the way in which misuse of the environment is contributing to the loss of plant species — not to mention those of birds, insects and mammals — which are becoming extinct as their natural habitat is destroyed. In some cases the loss is of species that have not even been discovered yet. Given the natural healing properties of many plants, this could mean the destruction of plants that could provide significant new drugs for use in medicine. But how can something be valued when its very existence is as yet unknown?

One way of viewing the environment is as a factor of production that needs to be used effectively, just like any other factor of production. In other words, each country has a stock of *environmental* capital that needs to be utilised in the best possible way.

However, if the environmental capital is to be used appropriately, it must be given an appropriate value. This can be problematic: if property rights are not firmly established — as they are not in many LDCs — it is difficult to enforce legislation to protect the environment. Furthermore, if the environment (as a factor of production) is underpriced, then 'too much' of it will be used by firms.

There are externality effects at work here too, in the sense that the loss of biodiversity is a global loss, and not just something affecting the local economy. In some cases there have been international externality effects of a more direct kind, such as when forest fires in Indonesia caused widespread pollution in Singapore and Malaysia in 2013.

China has been one of the fastest-growing economies in the world since 1978. This persistently rapid growth has had consequences for the quality of the environment. Figure 11.12 shows one aspect of this — emissions of carbon dioxide, which is one of the key greenhouse gases that contribute to the process of global warming.

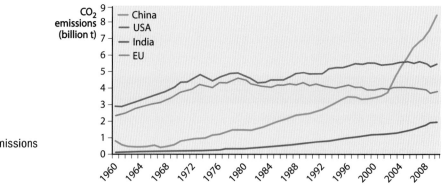

Figure 11.12 Carbon dioxide emissions in selected countries

Source: World Bank

The acceleration of emissions in China in the early years of the twenty-first century is very apparent in the figure, and China overtook the USA to become the largest emitter of CO_2 in the early 2000s.

The link between economic growth and environmental degradation is a clear one. In the case of China, there are several aspects to notice. During the process of industrialisation, it is crucial to ensure that energy supplies keep pace with the demand, as factories cannot operate effectively without reliable electricity and other energy sources. China has become the world's second biggest oil importer (behind the USA), and is the world's largest producer of coal, which accounts for some 80% of its total energy use — and is not the cleanest of energy technologies. It is also possible that inadequate regulation will add to environmental degradation: for example, an explosion at a chemical plant caused pollution in the Songhua river, which not only affected the city of Harbin, but also affected part of Russia, which was downstream from the incident.

For economic growth to be sustainable, these environmental effects must be taken into account, or there is a real danger that the improved standard of living that flows from the growth process will be obtained only at the expense of the quality of life of future generations. This may require growth to be slowed in the short run in order to devote resources to the development of renewable and cleaner energy sources. However, it is difficult to impose this on newly emerging societies in which there is widespread poverty, especially when the richer nations of the world continue to enjoy high standards of living whilst causing pollution of their own.

There are many aspects to this issue, of which protecting the environment is just one. Sustainable development also entails taking account of the depletion rates of non-renewable resources, and ensuring that renewable resources *are* renewed in the process of economic growth. So, although economic growth is important to a society, the drive for growth must be tempered by an awareness of the possible trade-offs with other important objectives.

There may be limits to which a government can influence the growth process. Infrastructure can be put in place, and markets encouraged to operate, but there may be limits to what can be done — especially as, with low levels of income in the LDC and inefficient tax collection, the government itself may have inadequate resources at its disposal.

Summary

- In pursuing economic growth, governments must remain aware of the potential costs of such growth.
- These may be seen especially in terms of possible damage to the environment.
- In this connection, deforestation and the loss of biodiversity are critical areas of concern.
- There are many international externality effects at work in the process of economic growth in LDCs.
- The recent rapid economic growth achieved in the Chinese economy has highlighted some of the environmental costs associated with growth.
- Given low per capita incomes and limited resources, LDC governments may not be able to influence growth very readily.

Contrasting patterns of development

The East Asian experience

The rapid growth achieved by the East Asian tiger economies was undoubtedly impressive, and held out hope that other less developed countries could begin to close the gap in living standards. Indeed, the term 'East Asian miracle' was coined to describe how quickly these economies had been able to develop. At the heart of the success were four countries: Hong Kong, Singapore, South Korea and Taiwan; others, such as Malaysia and Thailand, were not far behind.

How was their success achieved?

None of these countries enjoys a rich supply of natural resources. Indeed, Hong Kong and Singapore are small city-states whose only natural resources are their excellent harbours and good positions; they both have small populations.

The tigers soon realised that to develop manufacturing industry it would be crucial to tap into economies of scale. This meant producing on a scale that would far outstrip the size of their domestic markets — which meant that they would have to rely on international trade.

Key term

export-led growth
a situation in which economic growth is achieved through the exploitation of economies of scale, made possible by focusing on exports and so reaching a wider market than would be available within the domestic economy

By being very open to international trade and focusing on export markets, the tigers were able to sell to a larger market, and thereby improve their efficiency through economies of scale. This enabled them to enjoy a period of **export-led growth**. In other words, the tiger economies expanded by selling their exports to the rest of the world, and building a reputation for high-quality merchandise. This was helped by their judicious choice of markets on which to focus: they chose to move into areas of economic activity that were being vacated by the more developed nations, which were moving up to new sorts of product.

The export-led growth hypothesis explains part of the success of the tiger economies, but there were other contributing factors. The tiger economies nurtured their human capital and attracted foreign investment. Their governments intervened to influence

Hong Kong harbour — by being open to international trade and focusing on export markets, the tiger economies were able to sell to a larger market

the direction of the economies but also encouraged markets to operate effectively, fostering macroeconomic and political stability and developing good infrastructure. Moreover, these countries embarked on their growth period at a time when world trade overall was buoyant.

Sub-Saharan Africa

The experience of countries in sub-Saharan Africa is in total contrast to the success story of the tiger economies. Even accepting the limitations of the GNI per capita measure, the fact that GNI per capita was lower in the region as a whole in 2000 than it had been in 1975 (or even earlier) paints a depressing picture. Can sub-Saharan Africa learn from the experience of the tiger economies?

Part of the explanation for the failure of growth in this region lies in the fact that sub-Saharan Africa lacks many of the positive features that enabled the tiger economies to grow. Export-led growth is less easy for countries that have specialised in the production of goods for which demand is not buoyant. Furthermore, it is not straightforward to develop new specialisations if human and physical capital levels are low, the skills for new activities are lacking and poverty is rife. Encouraging development when there is political instability, and when markets do not operate effectively, is a major challenge.

Latin America

Countries in Latin America followed yet another path. There was a period in which the economies of Argentina, Brazil and Mexico, among others, were able to grow rapidly, enabling them to qualify as 'newly industrialised economies'. However, such growth could not be sustained in the face of the high rates of inflation that afflicted many of the countries in this region, especially during the 1980s. Indeed, many of them experienced bouts of hyperinflation, inhibiting economic growth.

In part this reflected fiscal indiscipline, with governments undertaking high levels of expenditure which they financed by printing money. In many cases, countries in this region have tended to be relatively closed to international trade. International debt reached unsustainable levels, and continued to haunt countries such as Argentina, which in 2005 offered its creditors about 33% of the value of its outstanding debt. Around three-quarters of the creditors accepted the deal, knowing that otherwise they would probably get nothing at all.

The emerging economies

More recently, some countries in different parts of the world have experienced accelerating economic growth and human development. This includes the BRIC countries, which were discussed in the context of globalisation in Chapter 7.

Summary

- A small group of countries in South East Asia, known as the East Asian tiger economies, underwent a period of rapid economic growth, closing the gap on the more developed countries.
- This success arose from a combination of circumstances, including a high degree of openness to international trade, which was seen as crucial if economies of scale were to be reaped.
- However, the tigers are also characterised by high levels of human capital and political and macroeconomic stability.
- In contrast, countries in sub-Saharan Africa have stagnated; in some cases, real per capita incomes were lower in 2000 than they had been in 1975.
- Countries in Latin America began well, experiencing growth for a period, but then ran into economic difficulties.
- The BRIC countries have enjoyed recent success in economic growth.

Population growth

Early writers on development were pessimists. For example, Thomas Malthus argued that real wages would never rise above a bare subsistence level. This was based on his ideas about the relationship between population growth and real incomes.

Malthus, having come under the influence of David Ricardo, believed that there would always be *diminishing returns to labour*. This led him to believe that as the population of a country increased, the average wage would fall, since a larger labour force would be inherently less productive. Furthermore, Malthus argued that the birth rate would rise with the real wage, because if families had more resources they would have more children; at the same time, the death rate would fall with an increase in the real wage, as people would be better fed and therefore healthier.

Extension material

Figure 11.13 shows one way of looking at the relationship between population growth and real wages. The left-hand panel illustrates the relationship between population size and the real wage rate, reflecting diminishing returns to labour in agriculture. The right-hand panel shows the birth rate (B) and death rate (D) functions. When the wage is relatively high, say at W_1, the birth rate (B_1) exceeds the death rate (D_1), which in turn means that the population will grow. However, as population grows, the real wage must fall (as shown in the left-hand panel), so eventually the wage converges on $W\star$, which is an equilibrium situation.

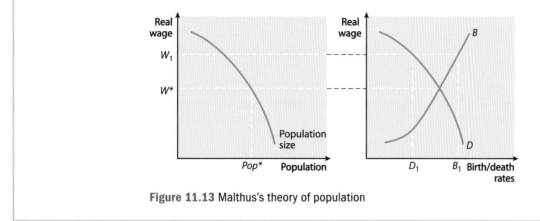

Figure 11.13 Malthus's theory of population

For these reasons, Malthus believed that it was not possible for a society to experience sustained increases in real wages, basically because the population was capable of exponential growth, while the food supply was capable of only arithmetic growth because of diminishing returns.

Although he was proved wrong (he had not anticipated the improvements in agricultural productivity that were to come), the question of whether population growth constitutes an obstacle to growth and development remains. At the heart of this is the debate about whether people should be regarded as key contributors to development, in their role as a factor of production, or as a drain on resources, consuming food, shelter, education and so on. Ultimately, the answer depends upon the quantity of resources available relative to the population size.

In global terms, world population is growing at a rapid rate, by more than 80 million people per year. In November 1999 global population went through the 6 billion mark, and in October 2013 it reached 7 billion — that is, about seven times as many people as in 1800. But the growth is very unevenly distributed: countries like Germany and Japan are expected to experience declining populations in the period 2015–25, while sub-Saharan Africa's population continues to grow by 2.5% per annum. A country whose population is growing at 2.5% per annum will see a doubling in just 28 years, so the growing pressure on resources to provide education and healthcare is considerable. The proportion of the population aged below 15 is very high for much of sub-Saharan Africa.

It has been observed that developed countries seem to have gone through a common pattern of population growth as their development progressed. This pattern has become known as the **demographic transition**, and is illustrated in Figure 11.14 for England and Wales between 1750 and 2000. This shows the birth rate and death rate for various years over this period. Remember that the natural rate of increase in population is given by the difference between these: the birth rate minus the death rate. (This ignores net migration.)

Key term

demographic transition a process through which many countries have been observed to pass whereby improved health lowers the death rate, and the birth rate subsequently also falls, leading to a low and stable population growth

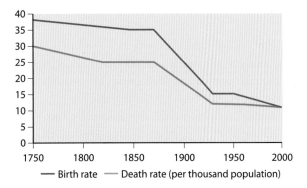

Figure 11.14 The demographic transition in England and Wales, 1750-2000

Source: D. Perkins et al., *The Economics of Development*, Norton/World Bank

Notice that between 1750 and 1820 the death rate fell more steeply than the birth rate, which means that the population growth rate accelerated in this period. This was the time when Britain was embarking on the Industrial Revolution, and corresponds to the early 'take-off' period of economic growth. At this stage the birth rate remains high. However, after 1870 there is a further fall in the death rate, accompanied by an even steeper fall in the birth rate, such that population growth slows down. You can see that by 2000 the natural population growth has shrunk to zero.

This demographic transition process has been displayed in most of the developed countries. The supporting story is that when the development process begins, death rates tend to fall as incomes begin to rise. In time families adapt to the change, and new social norms emerge in which the typical family size tends to get smaller. For example, as more women join the workforce, the opportunity cost of having children rises — by taking time out from careers to have children, their forgone earnings are now higher. This process has led to stability in population growth.

However, for countries that have undergone the demographic transition in a later period things have not been so smooth. Figure 11.15 shows the pattern of the demographic transition for Sri Lanka, which is one of the countries that have achieved some stability in the rate of population growth. Here, it is not until after about 1920 that the death rate begins to fall — and it falls more steeply than it did in the early stages of economic growth in England and Wales. After 1950 it falls even more steeply, partly because methods of hygiene and modern medicine were able to bring the death rate down more rapidly.

Perhaps more crucially, the birth rate in Sri Lanka remained high for much longer — in other words, households' decisions about family size do not seem to have adjusted as rapidly as they did in England and Wales. This led to a period of relatively rapid population growth.

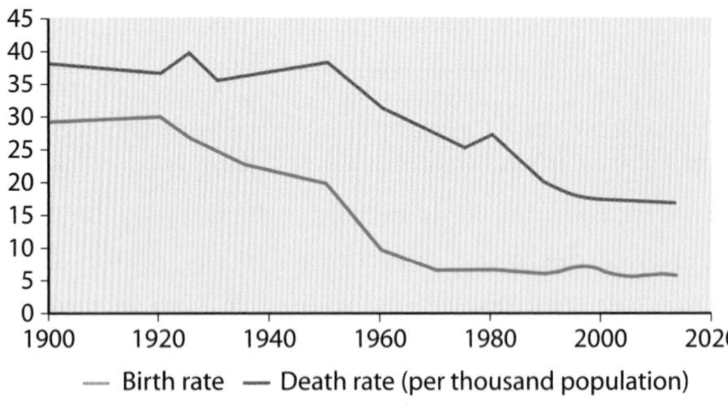

Figure 11.15 The demographic transition in Sri Lanka, 1900-2012

Source: as Figure 11.14; data after 1999 from the World Bank

For a number of countries in sub-Saharan Africa, death rates have fallen, but birth rates remain high, so the natural rate of population growth is also high. For example, in Malawi, the death rate fell from just over 18 per 1,000 people in 1990 to less than 12 in 2012, whilst the birth rate fell from 50 per 1,000 to 40, meaning that the natural population growth rate at the end of the period was 3.8% per annum.

Extension material

The microeconomics of fertility

To some extent, a household's choice of family size might be viewed as an externality issue. Figure 11.16 illustrates this. MPB (= MSB) represents the marginal benefit that the household receives from having different numbers of children (which is assumed to equal the marginal social benefit), and MPC represents the marginal private costs that are incurred. If education is subsidised, or if the household does not perceive the costs inflicted on society by having many children, then the marginal social cost of children (MSC) is higher than the marginal private cost.

Households will thus choose to have C_1 children, rather than the $C\star$ that is optimal for society. In other words, a choice of large family size might be

interpreted as being a market failure. Note that this discussion assumes that the household has the ability to choose its desired family size by having access to, and knowledge of, methods of contraception.

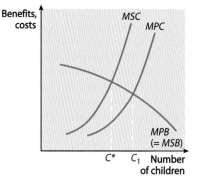

Figure 11.16 The microeconomics of fertility

Figure 11.17 shows fertility rates for the group of countries used earlier. Remember that the countries are in rank order of GDP measured in PPP$. The fertility rate records the average number of births per woman. Thus, in Uganda the average number of births per woman is 6. Of course, this does not mean that the average number of *children* per family is so high, as not all the babies survive.

This pattern of high fertility has implications for the age structure of the population, leading to a high proportion of young dependants in the population. This creates a strain on an LDC's limited resources, because of the need to provide education and healthcare for so many children, and in this sense high population growth can prove an obstacle to development.

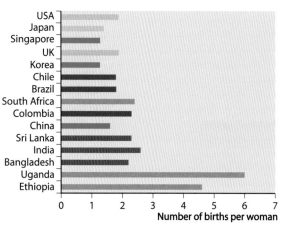

Figure 11.17 Total fertility rates, selected countries

Source: *World Development Indicators*

This argument might be countered by pointing out that people themselves are a resource for the country. However, it is a question of the balance between population and the availability of resources.

Summary

- Early writers such as Malthus were pessimistic about the prospects for sustained development, believing that diminishing returns to labour would constrain economic growth.
- Globally, population is growing rapidly, with most of the increase taking place in less developed countries.
- Developed countries and some LDCs have been seen to have passed through a demographic transition, such that population growth stabilises following decreases in death and birth rates.
- However, many LDCs have not completed the transition, remaining in the rapid population growth phase.
- Coupled with the age structure of the population, rapid population growth can create difficulties for LDCs because of the pressure on resources.

Exercise 11.2

Discuss the way in which the age structure of a population may influence the rate of economic growth and development.

Dependence on primary production

Many LDCs, especially in sub-Saharan Africa, continue to rely heavily on the agricultural sector to provide employment and incomes. Because labour productivity in agriculture tends to be relatively low, this may keep rural incomes low.

It is worth remembering that one of the driving forces behind the Industrial Revolution in Britain was an increase in agricultural productivity, enabling more workers to shift into manufacturing activity. In an LDC context, this transition may run into a number of problems. It is thus important to examine if there are obstacles to increasing agricultural productivity.

In some LDCs the problem stems from the form of land tenancy agreements, which can lead to inefficiency. In other cases, problems arise because of insecure property rights and the inheritance laws that pertain.

Land tenancy

One characteristic of many LDCs is that land is unequally distributed. If a landowner has more land than can be farmed as a single unit, it is likely that he will hire out parcels of land to small farmers. The way in which this is done turns out to be important for productivity and incentives.

One common form of land tenancy agreement in LDCs is that of **sharecropping**. In this system a tenant-farmer and a landlord of a piece of land have an agreement to share the resulting crop. The tenant-farmers in this case act as *agents*, farming the land on behalf of the landlord (the *principal*). The landlord would like the farmers to maximise returns from the land. However, the tenants will set out to balance the return received with the cost of producing the crop in terms of work effort. A *principal–agent problem* arises here, since if tenants receive only a portion of the crop, their incentive will be to supply less effort than is optimal for the landlord. There is also an asymmetric information problem, in the sense that the landlord cannot easily monitor the amount of effort being provided by a tenant. The tenants know how much of the low output results from low effort, and how much from unfavourable weather conditions — but the landlord does not. The problems that can arise from *asymmetric information* were discussed in Book 1.

> ### Key term
>
> **sharecropping** a form of land tenure system in which the landlord and tenant share the crop

Notice that, under a sharecropping contract, tenants have little incentive to invest in improving the land or the production methods, because part of the reward for innovation goes to the landlord. On the other hand, the risk of the venture is shared between the landlord and the tenant, as well as the returns.

An alternative would be for the landlord to charge the tenants a fixed rent for farming the land. This would provide better incentives for them to work hard, as they now receive all of the returns. However, it would also mean that they carry all the risk involved — if the harvest is poor, it is the tenants who will suffer, having paid a fixed rent for the land.

Yet another possibility would be for the landlord to hire tenants on a wage contract, and pay a fixed wage for their farming the land. This again would provide little incentive for the tenants to supply effort, as the wage would be paid regardless. As the landlord may not be able to monitor the supply of effort, this would create a problem. Furthermore, the landlord would now face all of the risk.

Thus, for these forms of tenancy, careful consideration needs to be given to the incentives for work effort, the incentives for innovation and investment, and the sharing of risk.

Land ownership

In other circumstances, inheritance laws can damage agricultural productivity: for example, where land is divided between sons on the death of the household head, which means that average plot size declines in successive generations. In some societies, property rights are inadequate: for example, women may not be permitted to own land, which can bring problems given that much of the agricultural labour is provided by women. Furthermore, in an attempt to make the best of adverse circumstances, over-farming and a lack of crop rotation practices can mean that soil becomes less productive over time. All of this makes it more difficult to achieve improvements in productivity in the agricultural sector.

Poverty is thus perpetuated over time; and with limited resources available for survival, farmers have no chance to adopt new or innovative farming practices. The very fact that people are struggling to make the best of the resources and arrangements available may make it difficult for them to step back and look for broader improvements that would allow the reform of economic and social institutions.

It was pointed out earlier that financial markets in many LDCs are relatively underdeveloped. This is especially so in the rural areas, where the lack of formal financial markets makes borrowing to invest in agricultural improvements almost impossible.

One of the problems here is that the cost of establishing rural branches of financial institutions in remote areas is high; the fixed costs of making loans for relatively small-scale projects are similarly high. This is intensified by the difficulty that banks have in obtaining information about the creditworthiness of small borrowers, who typically may have no collateral to offer.

Notice the importance of property rights in this discussion. In many LDCs, property rights over land and other assets may not be firmly established. Documentation of the rights to plots of land may not exist, or may not be formally and legally recognised. This means that although a plot of land may have been farmed by the same family over many generations, the current incumbent may have no way of proving their ownership of the land. In this case, it is not possible to borrow against the security of that land — in other words, if the individual cannot prove ownership of land, it cannot be used as collateral.

Trade in primary goods

The difficulty of improving agricultural productivity does not make it easy for LDCs to engage in active international trade, but in practice some have little choice but to rely on primary production in their export activity. For many LDCs, the share of primary goods in exports remains extremely high. Chapter 7 highlighted some of the dangers in this, with volatility of prices causing potential problems in the short run, and deterioration of the terms of trade a possible long-run issue.

In LDCs, even small enterprises may be involved in exporting activity. For example, many small farmers even in remote villages in Uganda grow some coffee for export. However, they rely on traders travelling around the rural areas to buy the coffee and sell it on to the exporters. This creates difficulties for the farmers, who may not be able to check up readily on the prices being charged in the cities, and who do not have the storage or market facilities to produce on a larger scale. If they do not have the communication links with which to determine what a good price for their crop is, the traders have an information advantage that may be exploited. The spread of mobile phones is helping to tackle this issue, by enabling farmers to keep in touch with market conditions, thus improving the information available to them in negotiating a fair price for their produce, and in taking decisions about what crops they should produce.

Small coffee farmers in Uganda may not have access to up-to-date market information

The Green Revolution

Given that agricultural productivity is much higher in developed countries than in LDCs, why is it not possible for them to learn from the experience of the more developed countries, and bring in new technology and farming practices?

Part of the reason why this does not work is that the balance between capital and labour is very different in the two groups of countries. In the more developed countries, productivity is high because of very intensive cultivation methods and the heavy use of capital and chemical inputs, which are neither available in, nor suitable for, LDCs. For example, given that there is already a surplus of agricultural labour in many LDCs, the introduction of labour-saving machinery would not seem to make sense — especially where running and servicing the machines would be difficult, and where field sizes tend to be too small for effective mechanisation.

In this context, the Green Revolution that began in the 1970s seemed to offer great promise. The Green Revolution was associated with the development of new, improved, *high-yielding varieties* (HYVs) of certain crops. Techniques for using these HYVs tended to be labour-intensive, and they promised greatly improved yields. They also involved food crops such as rice and wheat, which were attractive even to small-scale farmers. In addition they were fast growing, so that in some countries it was possible to increase the number of harvests per year.

These HYVs were widely adopted in Asia, and led to substantial increases in productivity, with some countries switching from being importers to exporters of the crops. Some regions (e.g. Bali in Indonesia) already had the associated infrastructure that was required, such as irrigation systems, and this enabled their quick adoption of the new techniques. In some regions it was the richer farmers who were able to make best use of the new seeds, having had more education and thus understanding better how to grow them.

In Africa, however, the Green Revolution had a much lower impact, partly because the main crops for which HYVs were developed (rice and wheat) were not widely grown staple crops in sub-Saharan Africa. So again, Africa seemed left behind. Only relatively recently have HYVs for crops such as maize been developed. Moreover, if the Green Revolution is to be successful in Africa, education levels need to be improved (because farmers need to be able to read and interpret instructions), and the necessary infrastructure provided. In the early part of the twenty-first century, the potential for improving productivity by the introduction of genetically modified crops is under debate, although this is opposed by many people.

The impact of HIV/AIDS

The HIV/AIDS epidemic has had a major impact on LDCs, especially in sub-Saharan Africa. There are countries in sub-Saharan Africa where the prevalence of the disease became unimaginably high: for example, in Botswana it was estimated that in 2003 some 37.3% of the population aged 15–49 were affected; and in Swaziland the prevalence rate was 38.8%. The repercussions of the disease are especially marked because of its impact on people of working age. This affected the size of the labour force, and left many orphans with little hope of receiving an education, which in turn has implications for the productivity of future generations.

Governments reacted to the disease in very different ways. In countries where the government was open about the onset of the disease and has striven to promote safe sex, the chances of keeping the disease under control are much higher. For example, in 1990 the incidence of HIV/AIDS amongst adults in Thailand and South Africa was similar, at about 1%. Thailand confronted the problem through a widespread public campaign such that, by 2001, the incidence was still about 1%. South Africa did little to stop the spread of the disease, with the president choosing to downplay the problem and the minister of health recommending beetroot as a treatment. In 2005 the incidence of the disease in South Africa was estimated to be nearly 20%. Some other governments have also kept silent, perhaps not wanting to admit that it is a problem, and here the disease has run rampant. There may also have been problems in measuring the incidence of HIV/AIDS accurately, as individuals may be hesitant to seek treatment or to report that they have the disease for fear of social stigma. The incidence of the disease has been in decline, but in the early 2010s the incidence of HIV/AIDS amongst adults aged 15–49 in the developing countries of sub-Saharan Africa was still about 5%.

Summary

- Many LDCs continue to rely heavily on primary production as a source of employment, incomes and export revenues.
- The agricultural sector exhibits low productivity, partly arising from inefficiencies in land tenure systems and inequality in land ownership.
- Inadequacies in financial markets, especially in rural areas, make it difficult for farmers to obtain credit for improving productivity.
- The Green Revolution had a large impact on productivity in Asia, but was slow to reach sub-Saharan Africa.
- HIV/AIDS has been a significant obstacle to development in recent years, especially in sub-Saharan Africa, where the prevalence of the disease is higher than in other regions.

Can governments influence growth?

Faced with these and other obstacles to economic growth, how much can LDC governments do to encourage a more rapid rate of growth and development? A major factor to remember is the limitations in terms of resources. Where average incomes are low and tax collection systems are undeveloped, governments have difficulty in generating a flow of revenue domestically, which is needed in order to launch policies encouraging growth and development.

In some cases, governments have tended to rely on taxes on international trade, which are relatively easy to administer, rather than on domestic direct or indirect taxes. This has not helped to stimulate international trade, of course.

Some LDC governments have responded to this problem by borrowing funds from abroad. However, in many cases such funds have not been best used. Funds have sometimes been employed for prestige projects, which impress lenders (or donors) but do little to further development. Other funds have been diverted into private use by government officials, and there are well-documented examples of politicians, officials and civil servants who have accumulated personal fortunes at the expense of the development of their countries. Figure 11.18 presents a Corruption Perception Index, produced regularly by the non-governmental organisation Transparency International since 1995. Notice again how Singapore and South Korea, the tiger economies, score as being 'highly clean' — indeed, on this index Singapore was the seventh least corrupt nation in the world.

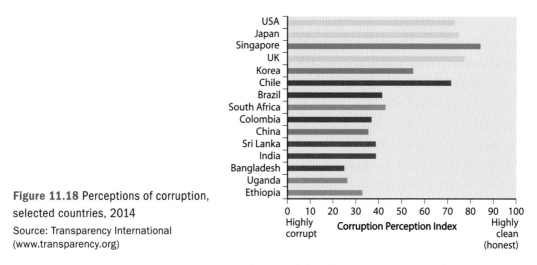

Figure 11.18 Perceptions of corruption, selected countries, 2014

Source: Transparency International (www.transparency.org)

There is a need to be careful with such indicators, for by its nature corruption is difficult to identify and to measure. Corruption may be disguised more successfully in some countries than in others. Nonetheless, the way in which firms and governments perceive the relative state of corruption in different countries may affect their decisions on where to locate foreign direct investment or provide overseas assistance.

Tendencies towards corruption are likely to be more significant in countries where there is relatively little political stability, so that the government knows it will not remain in power for long. Even in the absence of corruption, this discourages such governments from taking a long-term perspective.

Where borrowed funds have not been used wisely, problems inevitably follow when it is time to make repayments on outstanding debt. The debt burden that accumulated for some countries became unsustainable and will be discussed in Chapter 12. Here it suffices to say that the need to repay debt may further limit the resources available for governments to spend on development priorities such as education, healthcare and infrastructure.

Relationships with more developed countries

In the past, the now more developed countries benefited from the resources of today's LDCs. For example, Britain's early success was built partly on the resources of its colonies, and on protecting its own industry at the expense of those colonies. One of the main dangers for LDCs in the twenty-first century is that the more developed countries will continue to protect their own industries and will not allow the LDCs to develop theirs. It seems clear that sub-Saharan Africa at least will not be able to promote development without the cooperation of richer countries.

Summary

- Governments in LDCs have limited resources with which to encourage a more rapid rate of economic growth and development.
- Corruption and poor governance have meant that some of the resources that have been available have not been used wisely in some LDCs.
- For LDCs to develop, more cooperation is needed from the more developed countries.

Exercise 11.3

Looking back over the nature of the economic growth process and the obstacles to growth that have been outlined, discuss the extent to which countries in sub-Saharan Africa may be able to use the pattern of development that was used so successfully in East Asia to promote growth.

Study tip

This chapter has outlined some of the common obstacles to economic growth and development. However, always remember that all countries are different, so you need to avoid making broad generalisations that assume that all LDCs are the same. Each faces a different profile of problems and characteristics.

Case study 11.1

HIV/AIDS and the macroeconomy

At the end of 2014, the World Health Organization (WHO) announced that there were approximately 35 million people (including more than 3 million children) living with HIV at the end of 2013, with 2.1 million people becoming newly infected in 2013 globally, including 199,000 children.

The overall number of people living with HIV continued to increase, partly because of the ongoing number of new infections, but also because antiretroviral therapy was having beneficial effects in keeping those infected alive for longer. However, only 33% of pregnant women living with HIV in low- and middle-income countries received medicine to prevent transmission of HIV to their babies.

The geographic concentration of the disease was high, with some two-thirds of all people living with HIV in sub-Saharan Africa. As many as 68% of new infections are in sub-Saharan Africa.

HIV has a number of macroeconomic effects, and it has been estimated that the disease is likely to reduce growth in high prevalence countries by between 0.5% and 1.5% over 10–20 years. It can also widen economic inequality.

In part, this reflects the fact that HIV/AIDS reduces life expectancy, which in turn may reduce economic growth, through its effects on education, saving and fertility.

There are also likely to be direct effects. Most obviously, there is an effect on the productivity of those affected, especially on unskilled workers in labouring jobs. The disease also affects the rate of absenteeism. Furthermore, HIV/AIDS does not affect all age groups in society equally, which has an effect on the dependency ratio (that is, the percentage of the population who depend upon those who are in work). If productivity falls, then this reduces the rate of return on investment in both human and physical capital, and a high prevalence rate may deter foreign investment.

A concern for the future is that in 2013 young people between the ages of 15 and 24 accounted for some 33% of all new HIV infections, and survey data from 64 countries in the late 2000s indicated that only 40% of males and 38% of females had accurate and comprehensive knowledge about HIV and how to avoid its transmission. This information failure may be viewed as a form of market failure, but all too often the policy response in some countries has failed to address it.

An AIDS awareness billboard in Malawi

Follow-up questions

a The passage indicates that HIV/AIDS reduces life expectancy, and that this has three economic effects. Using the following hints, explain how these effects occur.
Hint 1 (education): the decision to invest in education depends partly on the expected rate of return in terms of future expected income. What effect does a fall in life expectancy have on the expected future stream of income?
Hint 2 (saving): think about the motivation to save. This may include precautionary saving for old age.
Hint 3 (fertility): one of the main ways in which HIV is transmitted is from mother to child; if more children are expected not to survive, how would this affect fertility?

b Explain the macroeconomic effects of lower education and savings, and higher fertility.

c Explain why a fall in productivity may have detrimental economic effects.

d Explain how policy could be better designed to combat information failure.

12 Promoting growth and development

The previous chapter dealing with economic development referred to the limited resources that are available within less developed countries (LDCs), which have constrained attempts to stimulate economic growth and development. If domestic resources are lacking, it is important to consider the possibility of mobilising resources from outside the country. This can be done by attracting foreign direct investment, accepting overseas assistance or borrowing on international capital markets. This chapter reviews these possibilities, and other ways of promoting growth and development.

Learning outcomes

After studying this chapter, you should:

→ be aware of the need for less developed countries to mobilise external resources for development

→ understand the benefits and costs associated with foreign direct investment

→ be familiar with the potential use of overseas assistance for promoting development, and the effectiveness of such flows of funds in the past

→ be aware of the possible use of borrowing to obtain funds for development and its dangers

→ understand the role of the Bretton Woods institutions in international development

→ be familiar with Structural Adjustment Programmes and the HIPC Initiative

→ understand the importance of human capital in the development process

→ be familiar with ways in which market failure may justify intervention in the economy to promote growth and development, and various ways in which this may be attempted

▍Market-friendly growth revisited

Chapter 11 introduced the notion of a market-friendly growth strategy. The core idea of this is that markets should be allowed to work without government intervention wherever this is possible, but that governments should intervene when there is a need to correct market failure. One way of looking at this is that **market-oriented strategies** should be adopted in situations when it is possible for markets to work effectively. However, there may be situations in which markets cannot be expected to be effective, and in such circumstances **interventionist strategies** will be required.

A starting point is to consider global linkages. It is clear that many LDCs have found it very difficult to mobilise resources from domestic sources. Capital tends to be scarce; labour resources are underdeveloped and underutilised; low incomes can mean low savings, and thus limited funds for investment. A natural question is whether an LDC can mobilise external resources in order to trigger the development process, through either market-oriented or interventionist strategies.

Key terms

market-oriented strategy
a strategy for encouraging development that relies on enabling markets to work effectively

interventionist strategy
a strategy for stimulating development that focuses on addressing market failure

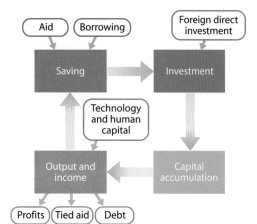

Figure 12.1 The Harrod-Domar process of economic development

In all of this discussion, it is important to remember that LDCs have diverse characteristics, so that a one-size-fits-all approach is not likely to be successful. Different countries face different configurations of obstacles and opportunities, so need different policies and strategies. Indeed, some of the models discussed in earlier chapters may be more applicable to some countries than to others.

The shortage of resources in many LDCs has been a severe obstacle to their economic growth and development. This was emphasised by the Harrod–Domar model of economic growth, which was introduced in Chapter 11. Figure 12.1 offers a reminder of the process, showing possible external inflows of funds.

The underlying process by which growth can take place requires the generation of a flow of savings that can be transformed into investment in order to generate an increase in capital, which in turn enlarges the productive capacity of the economy. This then enables output and incomes to grow, which in turn feeds back into savings and allows the process to become self-sustaining.

However, the process will break down if savings are inadequate, or if markets do not operate sufficiently well to maintain the chain. This chapter begins by considering the possibility that the process could be initiated by an inflow of resources from outside the economy. There are three possible routes to be examined: foreign direct investment, overseas aid and international borrowing. As Figure 12.1 indicates, associated with each of these inflows there are likely to be some costs, and potential leakages from the system.

Market-oriented strategies for development

Many markets in LDCs are seen to be missing or underdeveloped. These include some parts of the economy, such as financial markets, which are crucial in ensuring a flow of funds to the sectors that need to invest in order to allow economic growth to take place. Internal product markets may also be ineffective, not to mention the markets that facilitate international trade and thus allow an LDC to earn much-needed foreign exchange.

Trade liberalisation

A contentious issue over many years has been that of trade liberalisation — whether countries should remove barriers to international trade in order to look for potential gains, as was discussed in Chapter 8. It is important for LDCs to be able to adopt an appropriate trade policy if they are to reap these potential gains. In turn, trade is important because LDCs need to be able to obtain foreign exchange with which to import the capital and technology that is needed to transform the structure of the domestic economy.

If a country is short of foreign exchange, there are two broad approaches that it can take in drawing up its trade policy to deal with the problem. One is to reduce its reliance on imports in order to economise on the need for foreign currency — in other words, to produce goods at home that it previously imported. This is known as an *import substitution policy*.

An alternative possibility is to try to earn more foreign exchange through *export promotion*.

Import substitution

The import substitution strategy has had some appeal for a number of countries. The idea is to boost domestic production of goods that were previously imported, thereby saving foreign exchange. A typical policy instrument used to achieve this is the imposition of a tariff. Tariffs were discussed in Chapter 8.

However, not all the effects of a tariff are favourable for the economy. Look back at Figure 8.7 to remind yourself of how a tariff operates. Consumers are certainly worse off, as they have to pay a higher price for the good. They will therefore consume less, so there will be a loss of consumer surplus. Some of what was formerly consumer surplus will now be redistributed to others in society. The government gains the tariff revenue, as mentioned. In addition, producers gain additional producer surplus, given by the dark blue area in Figure 8.7. There is also a deadweight loss to society, such that, overall, society is worse off as a result of the tariff. Effectively, the government is subsidising inefficient local producers, and forcing domestic consumers to pay a price that is above that of the good if imported from abroad.

Some would defend this policy on the grounds that it allows the LDC to protect an infant industry. In other words, through such encouragement and protection, the new industry will eventually become efficient enough to compete in world markets.

There are two key problems with this argument. First, unless the domestic market is sufficiently large for the industry to reap economies of scale, local producers will never be in a position to compete globally. Secondly, because of such protection, domestic firms are never exposed to international competition, and so will not have an incentive to improve their efficiency. In other words, tariff protection fosters an inward-looking attitude among local producers that discourages them from trying to compete in world markets. They remain happy with the protection that provides them with producer surplus.

Export promotion

Export promotion requires a more dynamic and outward-looking approach, as domestic producers need to be able to compete with producers already established in world markets. The choice of which products to promote is critical, as it is important that the LDC develops a new pattern of comparative advantage if it is to benefit from an export promotion strategy.

For primary producers, a tempting strategy is one that begins with existing products and tries to move along the production chain. For example, in 1997 (under encouragement from the World Bank) Mozambique launched a project whereby, instead of exporting raw cashew nuts, it would establish processing plants that would then allow it to export roasted cashew nuts. In the early 1970s Mozambique was the largest producer of cashew nuts in the world, but by the late 1990s the activity had stagnated, and the country had been overtaken by producers in Brazil and India.

Moving along the cashew nut production chain seemed to be a good idea because it made use of existing products and moved the industry into higher value-added activity. However, the project ran into a series of problems. On the one hand, there were internal constraints: processing the nuts requires capital equipment and skilled labour, neither of which was in plentiful supply in Mozambique. In

By the late 1990s, Brazil and India had overtaken Mozambique in cashew nut production

addition, tariff rates on processed commodities are higher than on raw materials, so the producers faced more barriers to trade. They also found that they were trying to break into a market that was dominated by a few large existing producers which were reluctant to share the market. Furthermore, the technical standards required to sell processed cashew nuts were beyond the capability of the newly established local firms.

These are just some of the difficulties that face new producers from LDCs wanting to compete in world markets. Indeed, the setting of high technical specifications for imported products is one way in which countries have tried to protect their own domestic producers — it is an example of a *non-tariff barrier* (see Chapter 8).

The East Asian tiger economies pursued export promotion strategies, making sure that their exchange rates supported the competitiveness of their products and that their labour was appropriately priced. However, it must be remembered that the tiger economies expanded into export-led growth at a time when world trade itself was booming, and when the developed countries were beginning to move out of labour-intensive activities, thereby creating a niche to be filled by the tigers. If many other countries had expanded their exports at the same time, it is not at all certain that they could all have been successful.

As time goes by, it becomes more difficult for other countries to follow this policy. It is particularly difficult for countries that originally chose import substitution, because the inward-looking attitudes fostered by such policies become so deeply entrenched.

It should also be remembered that there will always be dangers in trying to develop new kinds of economic activity that may entail sacrificing comparative advantage. This is not to say that LDCs should remain primary producers for ever, but it does suggest that it is important to select the new forms of activity with care in order to exploit a potential comparative advantage.

Summary

- In designing a trade policy, an LDC may choose to go for import substitution, nurturing infant industries behind protectionist barriers in order to allow them to produce domestically goods that were formerly imported.
- However, such infant industries rarely seem to grow up, leaving the LDC with inefficient producers which are unable to compete effectively with world producers.
- Export promotion requires a more dynamic and outward-looking approach, and a careful choice of new activities.

Foreign direct investment

One possible source of external funding that has been attractive to many LDCs is foreign direct investment (FDI). This entails encouraging foreign multinational corporations (MNCs) to set up part of their production in an LDC. MNCs were introduced in Chapter 7 in the discussion of globalisation.

In evaluating the potential impact of MNCs operating in LDCs, it is important to consider the characteristics of such companies. Many operate on a large scale, often having an annual turnover that exceeds the less developed country's GDP. They tend to have their origins in the developed countries, although some LDCs are now beginning to develop their own MNCs.

MNCs are in business to make profits, and it can be assumed that their motivation is to maximise global after-tax profits. While they may operate in globally oligopolistic markets, they may have monopoly power within the LDCs in which they locate. They operate in a wide variety of different product markets — some are in primary production (Geest, Del Monte, BP), some are in manufacturing (General Motors, Mitsubishi) and some are in tertiary activity (McDonald's). These characteristics are important in shaping the analysis of the likely benefits and costs of attracting FDI into an LDC.

Chapter 7 identified three basic motivations for MNCs to locate in another country: looking for markets, resources or efficiency — or some combination of the three, of course.

To set a context for the discussion, Figure 12.2 shows the relative size of net FDI inflows for the set of countries selected previously. This reveals a very uneven pattern, with Bangladesh receiving only 1% of GDP as inflows of FDI and Singapore receiving 21.4%.

In some ways this chart is misleading, as it conceals the true size of FDI inflows into China. Remember that China's GDP is very large, so 3.1% of China's GDP represents a very substantial flow of investment. Some of this is market seeking, as the opening up of China's market of more than 1.3 billion people is a major attraction. However, it may also be partly resource seeking, with MNCs wanting to take advantage of China's resource of labour.

Exercise 12.1

Discuss the possible effects on developed countries if LDCs characterised by low-wage labour become more active in world markets.

Exercise 12.2

Discuss the relative merits of import substitution and export promotion as trade strategies. Under what conditions might import substitution have a chance of success?

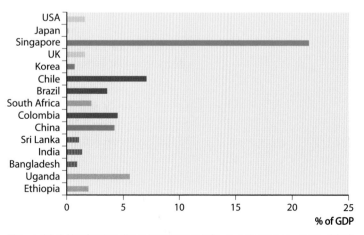

Figure 12.2 Net foreign direct investment inflows, selected countries, 2013
Source: *World Development Indicators*

Potential benefits

Perhaps the prime motivation for LDCs in seeking to attract FDI inflows is the injection they provide into the Harrod–Domar chain of development. In addition to providing investment, MNCs are likely to supply capital and technology, thereby helping to remedy the LDC's limited capacity to produce capital goods. They may also assist with the development of the country's human capital, by providing training and skills development for the workers they employ, together with management expertise and entrepreneurial skills, all of which may be lacking in the LDC.

LDCs may also hope that the MNC will provide much-needed modern sector jobs by employing local workers. Given the rate of migration to the urban areas discussed in Chapter 10, such employment could be invaluable to the LDC, where employment cannot keep up with the rapid growth of the labour force.

The LDC government may also expect to be able to collect tax revenues, both directly from the MNC in the form of a tax on profits and indirectly from taxes on the workers' employment incomes. Moreover, the MNC will export its products, and thus generate a flow of foreign exchange for the LDC.

In time, there may also be spillover effects. As local workers learn new skills and gain management expertise and knowledge about technology, they may be able to benefit local firms if at some stage they leave the MNC and take up jobs with local companies — or use their new-found knowledge to start their own businesses. These externality effects can be significant in some cases.

Potential costs

In evaluating the potential benefits of FDI, however, LDCs may need to temper their enthusiasm a little, as there may be some costs associated with attracting MNCs to locate within their borders. This is certainly the case if the anti-globalisation protesters are to be believed, as they have accused the MNCs of exploiting their strength and market power in order to damage the LDCs in various ways.

In examining such costs, it is important to try to reach a balanced view and to be aware that some of the accusations made by the critics of globalisation may have been overstated. On the other hand, it is also important to remember that MNCs are profit-making firms, and not humanitarian organisations seeking to promote justice and equality.

A first point to note is that, because most MNCs originate in more developed countries, they tend to use technology that suits the conditions with which they are familiar. In many cases these tend to be relatively capital-intensive, which may not be wholly appropriate for LDC factor endowments. One upshot of this is that the employment effects may not be substantial, or may be limited to relatively low-skilled jobs.

It is dangerous to generalise here. The sort of technology that MNCs tend to use may be entirely suitable for a country like Singapore, which has progressed to the stage where it needs high-tech, capital-intensive activity to match its well-trained and disciplined workforce. However, such technology would not be appropriate in much of sub-Saharan Africa. But MNCs are surely aware of such considerations when taking decisions about where to locate. A decision to set up production in China may be partly market oriented, but efficiency considerations will also affect the choice of technology.

An important consideration is whether the MNC will make use of local labour. It might hire local unskilled labour, but use expatriate skilled workers and managers. This would tend to reduce the employment and spillover effects of the MNC presence. Another possibility is that the MNC may pay wages that are higher than necessary in order to maintain a good public image, and to attract the best local workers. This is fine for the workers lucky enough to be employed at a high wage, but it can make life difficult for local firms if they cannot hold on to their best workers.

In addition, the LDC government's desire for tax revenue may not be fully met. In seeking to attract MNCs to locate within their borders, LDCs may find that they need to offer tax holidays or concessions as a 'carrot'. This will clearly limit the tax revenue benefits that the LDC will receive. It is also possible for MNCs to manipulate their balance sheets in order to minimise their tax liability. A high proportion of the transactions undertaken by an MNC are internal to the firm. Thus, it may be possible to set prices for internal transactions that ensure that profits are taken in the locations with the lowest tax. This process is known as *transfer pricing*. It is not strictly legal, but is difficult to monitor.

As far as the foreign exchange earnings are concerned, a key issue is whether the MNC will recycle its surplus within the LDC or repatriate its profits to its shareholders elsewhere in the world. If the latter is the case, this will limit the extent to which the LDC will benefit from the increase in exports. However, at least the MNC will be able to market its products internationally, and if the country becomes better known as a result then, again, there may be spillovers for local firms. Gaining credibility and the knowledge to sell in the global market is problematic for LDCs, and this is one area in which there may be definite benefits from the MNC presence.

The LDC should also be aware that the MNC may use its market power within the country to maximise profits. Local competitors will find it difficult to compete, and the MNC may be able to restrict output and raise price. In addition, MNCs have been accused of taking advantage of more lax environmental regulations, polluting the environment to keep their costs low. The actions of the anti-globalisation protesters in this area may have influenced MNCs to clean up their act somewhat.

Finally, MNCs tend to locate in urban areas in LDCs — unless they are purely resource seeking, in which case they may be forced to locate near the supply of whatever natural resource they are seeking. Locating in the urban areas may increase inequality between the rural and urban areas, which has been a problem in some LDCs.

Given the need to evaluate the benefits and costs of FDI flows, it is important that LDC governments can negotiate good deals with the MNCs. For example, countries such as Indonesia have negotiated conditions on the proportion of local workers who will be employed by the MNC after a period of, say, 5 years. This helps to ensure that the benefits are not entirely dissipated. Of course, it helps if the LDC has some key resource that the MNC cannot readily acquire elsewhere. There is some recent evidence that high levels of human capital help to attract FDI flows, which may help to explain why East Asia and China have been recipients of more FDI inflows than countries in sub-Saharan Africa.

Exercise 12.3

Draw up a list of the benefits and costs of MNC involvement in an LDC, and evaluate the benefits relative to the costs. Remember that many LDCs are enthusiastic about attracting MNCs to locate in their countries. Try to identify which are the most important benefits that they are looking for.

Summary

- Multinational corporations (MNCs) are companies whose production activities are carried out in more than one country.
- Foreign direct investment (FDI) by MNCs is one way in which an LDC may be able to attract external resources.
- MNCs may be motivated by markets, resources or cost effectiveness.
- LDCs hope to benefit from FDI in a wide range of ways, including capital, technology, employment, human capital, tax revenues and foreign exchange. There may also be spillover effects.
- However, MNCs may operate in ways that do not maximise these benefits.

Synoptic link

Notice that the arguments set out in Theme 3, Chapter 6 relating to privatisation are pertinent here in the context of LDCs.

Reducing government involvement

Attracting foreign MNCs to bring investment into an LDC is one way of giving a boost to the working of markets within LDCs. It is also important to ensure that governments themselves do not intervene in ways that distort the working of markets — for example, by subsidising firms in some sectors or controlling prices. This has been a failing in many countries, reflecting the way that governments in the past have tended to intervene inappropriately. For example, many LDC governments have been tempted to try to fix prices of goods, rather than allowing market forces to dictate prices. This can then have unintended effects on incentives. If a government decides to hold food prices down in the urban areas, in order to help the urban poor (or to keep their electorates happy), this then distorts the market and provides insufficient incentive for farmers.

In some LDCs, the government has intervened through subsidising firms or operating state-owned enterprises that have become inefficient and rent-seeking. Privatisation could be one way of improving incentives towards efficiency.

Microfinance

For many LDCs, a particular problem has been the provision of finance for small (but important) projects in rural areas of LDCs. Where a large portion of the population live in the rural areas, the difficulty of raising funds for investment has been an impediment to improving agricultural productivity — in spite of the significance of this sector in many LDCs.

There are elements of market failure in rural credit markets. In particular, there is an information failure. In the absence of branch banking, people in the rural areas do not have access to the formal financial sector. The commercial banks based in the urban areas do not have the information needed to be able to assess loan applications for rural projects. Furthermore, property rights are not secure, so it may be difficult to provide collateral against loans, when ownership of land cannot be proved.

This means that many people in the rural areas are forced to depend upon informal markets for credit, borrowing from local moneylenders or merchants at high, sometimes punitive, interest rates. The rates of interest in the informal sector tend to be much higher than are available in the formal sector, partly because of the risk premium, with it being difficult to assess the probability of default. In addition, local moneylenders may have monopoly power as people in a village may not be able to access other sources of finance.

Attempts have been made to remedy this situation through **microfinance** schemes. This approach was pioneered by the Grameen Bank, which was founded in Bangladesh in 1976. The bank made small-scale loans to groups of women who otherwise would have had no access to credit, and each group was made corporately responsible for paying back the loan. The scheme has claimed great success, both in terms of the constructive use of the funds in getting small-scale projects off the ground and in terms of high pay-back rates.

The Grameen Bank

In 1974 a severe famine afflicted Bangladesh, and a flood of starving people converged on the capital city, Dhaka. Muhammad Yunus was an economics professor at Chittagong University. He tells how he was struck by the extreme contrast between the neat and abstract economic theories that he was teaching, and the plight and suffering of those surviving in bare poverty, and suffering and dying in the famine.

He also tells how he decided to study the problem at first hand, taking his students on field trips into villages near to the campus. On one of these visits they interviewed a woman who was struggling to make a living by making bamboo stools. For each stool that she made, she had to borrow the equivalent of 15p for the raw materials. Once she had paid back the loan, at interest rates of up to 10% per week, her profit margin was just 1p. The woman was never able to escape from her situation because she was trapped by the need to borrow, and the need to pay back at such punitive rates of interest. Her story was by no means unique, and Yunus was keen to find a way of enabling women like her to have access to credit on conditions that would allow them to escape from poverty. He began experimenting by lending out some of his own money to groups in need.

Muhammad Yunus launched the Grameen Bank experiment in 1976. The idea was to provide credit for small-scale income-generating activities. Loans would be provided without the need for collateral, with borrowers being required to form themselves into groups of five with joint responsibility for the repayments. The acceptance of this joint responsibility and the lack of collateral helped to minimise the transaction costs of making and monitoring the loans.

On any criteria, the project proved an enormous success. The repayment record has been impressive, although the Grameen Bank charges interest rates close to those in the formal commercial sector, which are much lower than those of the informal moneylenders. Since the initial launch of the bank, lending has been channelled primarily to women borrowers, who are seen to invest more carefully and to repay more reliably — and to be most in need.

By the end of May 1998 more than $2.4 billion had been loaned by Grameen Bank, including more than 2 million loans for milch cows, nearly 100,000 for rickshaws, 57,000 for sewing machines and many more for processing, agriculture, trading, shop keeping, peddling and other activities. Grameen-type credit programmes are now operating in 59 countries in Africa, Asia, the Americas, Europe and Papua New Guinea. By 2009, more than $8.7 billion had been loaned by Grameen, covering 83,458 villages.

As for the impact of Grameen loans in economic terms, the loans are seen to have generated new employment, to have reduced the number of days workers are inactive, and to have raised income, food consumption and living conditions of Grameen Bank members — not to mention their social impact on the lives of millions of women. Muhammad Yunus and the Grameen Bank were awarded the Nobel Peace Prize in 2006.

ROSCAS

Other schemes have involved groups of households coming together to pool their savings in order to accumulate enough funds to launch small projects. Members of the group take it in turns to use these joint savings, paying the loan back in order for the next person to have a turn. These are known as *rotating savings and credit schemes* (ROSCAS), and they have had some success in providing credit on a small scale. In spite of assisting some successful enterprises, however, such schemes have been found to be less sustainable than Grameen-style arrangements, and have tended to be used to obtain consumer durable goods rather than for productive investment and innovation.

A member from the Grameen bank collects money from the borrowers

Suppose that 12 individuals are saving for a bicycle (a key form of transport in many developing countries). A bicycle costs $130, and each individual saves $10 per month. Simple arithmetic indicates that it would take 13 months for enough funds to have accumulated for the 12 individuals to buy their bicycles. Suppose that the 12 people agree to work together. First, they explain to the bicycle dealer that there is a guaranteed order for 12 bicycles, and they negotiate a discount of $10 per bicycle. They then meet at the end of each month, and each pays $10 into the fund. At the end of the first month, there are sufficient funds for one person to buy a bicycle — usually chosen by a lottery. As a result, even the last person in turn gets the bicycle earlier because of the discount they negotiated. Of course, without the discount, one unfortunate person would have to wait the full period, but clearly this is a very efficient way of making use of small amounts of savings. With more people, or higher contributions, the funds can be used for more substantial projects. Administration costs are minimal, but the schemes do rely on trust, such that the first person to win the lottery does not then stop making payments.

In the absence of such schemes, households may be forced to borrow from local moneylenders, often at very high rates of interest. For example, the Bank of Uganda survey mentioned earlier found that households were paying rates between 0% (when borrowing from family members) and 500%. In part this may reflect a high risk of the borrower's defaulting, but it may also reflect the ability of local moneylenders to use market power. The absence of insurance markets may also deter borrowing for productive investment, especially in rural areas.

There is limited arbitrage between the formal and informal sectors, and institutions in the formal sector may find it difficult to gain information that they would need to make loans available.

How successful has the microfinance movement been? The Grameen Bank has provided finance to many people in many parts of the world. Attempts to replicate the Grameen model have also has some success, but in many cases have struggled to be sustainable in funding terms, needing support from governments or non-governmental organisations (NGOs).

Summary

- The provision of credit in LDCs is problematic, especially in rural areas.
- This is partly due to forms of market failure.
- Microfinance is one way in which attempts have been made to provide credit for small projects in LDCs.
- The Grameen Bank in Bangladesh pioneered such schemes, using group-lending schemes focusing on women.
- Other schemes have included rotating savings and credit schemes.
- In the absence of access to formal credit arrangements, the informal market operates, charging high interest rates relative to the formal sector.

Interventionist strategies

Where markets cannot be made to work effectively, it may be justified for governments to adopt a more interventionist approach.

Human resources

The importance of human resources in the process of growth and development has already been highlighted. For many LDCs, labour is relatively abundant — at least relative to physical capital — but in many cases the potential is not being realised. Investment in human capital is crucial in many LDCs in order to facilitate development.

Investment in human capital comes in many forms. Education and training is one important aspect of such investment. Education and training is needed in order to raise agricultural productivity, and to provide a skilled labour force that enables the growth of modern sector economic activity such as manufacturing industry — and for the increased utilisation of technology. Certainly the absence of skilled labour is a substantial obstacle to economic growth. However, human capital does not only involve education and training, important as that is. For many LDCs, improved provision of nutrition and healthcare can be equally important in raising the productivity of workers — and in contributing directly to the quality of life.

An important question in the context of the market-friendly approach to growth and development is whether markets can be relied upon to ensure the appropriate provision of education and healthcare, or whether there is some form of market failure that requires government intervention.

In the case of both education and healthcare, it can be argued that there are significant externality effects. In the case of education, it has been shown that there are spillover effects, in the sense that a group of educated workers cooperating together becomes more productive because the members of the group interact with each other. This implies that the marginal social benefits of education exceed the marginal private benefits — because society gains from the way in which workers are able to work together.

In terms of healthcare, consider the example of a vaccination programme against a communicable disease. An individual may perceive that the marginal benefit of having their child vaccinated is relatively low, because the probability of becoming infected may be low. However, if everyone thinks in the same way, this increases the likelihood of there being an epidemic of the disease. Thus the social benefits that arise from a vaccination programme may exceed the private benefits — so in the absence of intervention, too few individuals will invest in vaccination.

There may also be information failures in education and healthcare. A poor rural household may not perceive the full benefits of education — especially where uneducated parents are taking decisions on behalf of their children. They may then decide to keep their children out of school, perhaps believing that the benefits to the household from child labour exceed the benefits of sending their children to school. In many LDCs, there has been a tendency to keep female children away from school, as the household may not see any benefit from female education. In healthcare, there may also be situations in which households do not understand the potential benefits from medical treatment (especially preventative treatment), or may not perceive the value of good nutrition.

Given these arguments about market failure, there may be a case for some form of intervention in order to ensure better take-up of education and healthcare. This might take the form of subsidising education, perhaps by providing free primary school education, or it might be through regulation — enforcing a minimum school-leaving age.

The question then arises of how an LDC government can raise the finances needed in order to improve education and healthcare, especially given the problems (discussed in Chapter 11) associated with tax collection systems. For many LDCs, this has proved a major stumbling block. Some progress has been made through the use of overseas assistance. For example, Uganda was able to launch a scheme to encourage primary education by making use of funds provided by the World Bank as part of the Heavily Indebted Poor Countries (HIPC) Initiative. These funds were earmarked for the purpose in the poverty reduction strategy produced by Uganda.

Price stabilisation

It has been noted that in some commodity markets, prices can exhibit volatility over time. This could arise, for example, when the supply of a good varies from period to period because of the varying state of the harvest. In such a market, the supply curve will shift to the right when the harvest is good, but shift to the left in a period when the weather is poor or where crops are affected by some disease or blight. It may also be that the demand curve tends to shift around through time, with demand for some goods reflecting fluctuations in the performance of economies. In other words, demand may shift to the left when recession bites, but to the right in times of boom and prosperity.

Suppose that Figure 12.3 represents a market in which demand is relatively stable between periods, but in which supply varies between S_{poor} when the harvest is poor and S_{glut} when the harvest is good. The price varies between P_p and P_g. This creates a high level of uncertainty for producers, who find it difficult to form good expectations about the future prospects for the commodity. This means that they are less likely to invest in ways of improving productivity because of uncertain future returns. If a way could be found of stabilising the price of the good, then this could encourage producers.

A **buffer stock** is a way of attempting to do this. A scheme is set up whereby excess supply is bought up by the buffer stock in glut years to

Exercise 12.4

Using appropriate diagrams, explain how the provision of education and healthcare may be subject to externality effects. Discuss possible policies to ensure improved healthcare provision in LDCs.

Key term

buffer stock a scheme intended to stabilise the price of a commodity by buying excess supply in periods when supply is high, and selling when supply is low

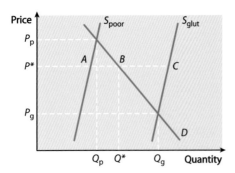

Figure 12.3 A buffer stock

prevent the price from falling too low. In periods when the harvest is poor, stocks of the commodity are released on to the market in order to maintain the price at the agreed level. In terms of Figure 12.3, suppose that it is agreed to maintain the price at $P^\star$. When there is a glut year, with the supply curve located at S_{glut}, there is excess supply at the agreed price of the amount BC, so this amount is bought up by the buffer stock and stored. If the supply is at S_{poor} because of a poor harvest, there is excess demand, so the buffer stock releases the quantity AB on to the market, maintaining the price.

Although this does have the effect of stabilising the price at $P^\star$, there is a downside. If the members of the buffer stock scheme agree to maintain the price at too high a level, relative to the actual average equilibrium price over time, then it will run into difficulties. Notice in Figure 12.3 that to maintain price at $P^\star$, the buffer stock buys up more in the glut year than it has to sell in the poor harvest year. If this pattern is repeated, then the size of stocks to be stored will rise over time. This is costly and will eventually become unsustainable.

Exercise 12.5

Discuss why prices in some markets may be unstable from year to year and evaluate ways in which more stability might be achieved. How effective would you expect such measures to be? What would be the benefits to economic agents of having greater stability in prices?

Other interventionist strategies

There are other ways in which governments have adopted an interventionist approach to promote growth and development. Protectionism has already been discussed, and entails direct intervention to protect infant industries against foreign competition. This has rarely been found to be effective.

Potentially more effective is intervention to provide social infrastructure, by improving transport and communication, or providing market facilities that enable domestic and international markets to work more effectively. One obvious drawback to this approach is that LDC governments rarely have the resources to finance such investment, and have to rely on external sources of funds. How effective has this approach been?

Overseas assistance

If LDCs could enter a phase of economic growth and rising incomes, one result would be an increase in world trade. This would benefit nations around the world, and the more developed industrial countries would be likely to see an increase in the market for their products. This might be a reason for the governments of more developed countries to help LDCs with the growth and development of their economies. Of course, there may also be a humanitarian motive for providing assistance — to reduce global inequality.

Indeed, there may be market failure arguments for providing aid. For example, it may be that governments have better information about the riskiness of projects in LDCs than private firms have. In relation to the provision of education and healthcare, it was argued earlier that there may be externality effects involved. However, LDC governments may not have the resources needed to provide sufficient education for their citizens. Similarly, it was argued that some infrastructure may have public good characteristics that require intervention.

Official aid is known as **official development assistance** (ODA), and is provided through the Development Assistance Committee of the Organisation for Economic Co-operation and Development (OECD). Figure 12.4 shows the relationship between the amount of ODA received (as a percentage of GNI) and GNI per capita in 2010. As there are countries with relatively high levels of GNI per capita that nonetheless receive overseas assistance, there is some suggestion that humanitarian

Key term

official development assistance aid provided to LDCs by countries in the OECD

motives are not the only driver of overseas aid. From a donor's perspective, it might be that the government of a country wishes to demonstrate to its electorate that the aid it is giving is being well used, so it may direct its funds towards countries that are in a position to make good use of the funds. In many cases, this may not be the countries with very low GNI per capita or those facing the greatest development challenges. There may also be political motives for donors to give to certain countries: for instance, if their foreign policy objectives make it desirable to support countries in some regions.

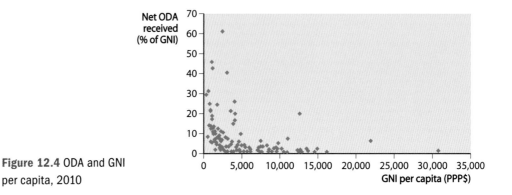

Figure 12.4 ODA and GNI per capita, 2010

At a meeting of the United Nations in 1974, the industrial countries agreed that they would each devote 0.7% of their GNP to ODA. This goal was reiterated at the Millennium Summit as part of the commitment to achieving the Millennium Development Goals. Progress towards this target has not been impressive. Figure 12.5 shows the performance of donor countries relative to this target, and you can see that only five countries had achieved the 0.7% UN target by 2012. The amount of ODA provided by the UK as a percentage of GNI increased after 1997, but the USA's share has fallen. However, it should be borne in mind that in terms of US dollars, the USA is by far the largest contributor.

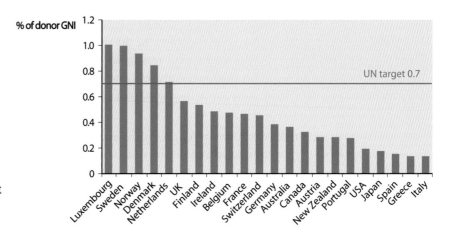

Figure 12.5 Official development assistance in 2012
Source: OECD

An encouraging sign is that total ODA flows increased in the late 1990s and the early years of the new millennium. This seemed to represent an enhanced awareness of the importance of such flows for many LDCs. Indeed, at the G8 summit meeting at Gleneagles in July 2005 the commitment to the UN target for ODA was reiterated. In the UK, the government has expressed its continuing commitment to providing overseas assistance. In the 2013 Budget, official development assistance was one of the areas of spending that was protected by the chancellor, in spite of much criticism from parts of the media. You should be aware that the increase in ODA included funds devoted to debt forgiveness, as brokered by the World Bank under the Heavily Indebted Poor Countries (HIPC) Initiative.

Figure 12.6 shows the relative importance of financial capital flows to low-income countries since 1990. This highlights the importance of overseas assistance relative to other sources, although it also draws attention to the increasing importance of personal remittances, which will be discussed shortly.

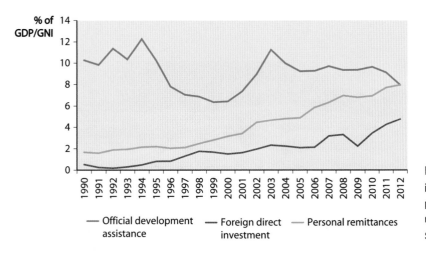

Figure 12.6 Financial flows into low-income countries, 1990–2012

Note: ODA is % of GNI; FDI and remittances are % of GDP

Source: World Bank

There has been much criticism of overseas aid, and its effectiveness has been questioned. There are many possible reasons for the ineffectiveness of aid. It may simply be that providing aid to the poorest countries reduces its effectiveness, in the sense that the resources of such countries are so limited that the funding cannot be efficiently utilised. In some cases it may be related to the fact that aid flows are received by LDC governments, which can be inefficient or corrupt, so there are no guarantees that the funds are used wisely by these governments. Or it might simply be that the flows of aid have not been substantial enough to have made a difference.

There are other explanations, however. For example, some donor countries in the past have regarded aid as part of their own trade policy. By tying aid to trade deals, the net value of the aid to the recipient country is much reduced: for instance, offering aid in this way may commit the recipient country to buying goods from the donor country at inflated prices.

In other cases, aid has been tied to use in specific projects. This may help to assure the donor that the funds are being used for the purpose for which they were intended. However, it is helpful only if appropriate projects were selected in the first place. There may be a temptation for donors to select prestige projects that will be favourably regarded by others, rather than going for the LDC's top-priority development projects. In 1994, 66.1% of total aid was untied (45.8% in the case of aid from the UK), but by 2010 this proportion had increased to 79.4% (99.9% from the UK).

Another distinction is between overseas assistance that is given by one country to another (bilateral aid), and funds that are channelled through organisations such as the World Bank or the United Nations (multilateral aid). Multilateral aid is less likely to be tied to trade agreements, but in some cases may be made conditional on the recipient country implementing certain policies.

An important issue for all sorts of aid is that it should be provided in a way that does not damage incentives for local producers. For example, dumping cheap grain into LDC markets on a regular basis would be likely to damage the incentives for local farmers by depressing prices.

A final issue to notice is that in some cases, the acceptance of foreign aid by a country may result in a phenomenon known as *Dutch disease*. The discovery of a large natural gas field in the Netherlands in the late 1950s resulted in a revaluation of the currency, causing a loss of competitiveness in the manufacturing sector and an acceleration of the deindustrialisation process. It has been argued that a flow of foreign aid into a country can have a similar effect, if the receipt of aid causes the exchange rate to rise, thus reducing the competitiveness of the country's exports.

Aid is not always effective — dumping cheap grain into LDC markets is likely to depress local prices

Summary

- Official development assistance (ODA) comprises grants and concessional funding provided from the OECD countries to LDCs.
- The countries most in need of ODA may not be in a position to use it effectively.
- In some cases the direction of ODA flows is influenced by the political interests of the donor countries.
- The more developed countries have pledged to devote 0.7% of their GNPs to ODA, but few have reached this target.
- Some evidence suggests that aid has been ineffective except in countries that have pursued 'good' economic policies.
- The tying of aid to trade deals or to specific projects can limit the aid's benefits to recipient LDCs.

Exercise 12.6

Examine the arguments for and against providing assistance to those countries in most need of it, as opposed to those best equipped to make good use of it.

International borrowing

Another option for LDCs is to borrow the funds needed for development. This may be on concessional terms from the World Bank or the International Monetary Fund (IMF), or on a commercial basis from international financial markets.

It is important to notice that when countries borrow from the World Bank or the IMF, the loans come with strings attached. In other words, these bodies impose conditions on countries wanting to borrow, typically in relation to the sorts of economic policy that should be adopted. Such policy programmes will be considered below.

As with other forms of external finance, problems have arisen for some LDCs that have tried to borrow internationally. These problems first became apparent in the early 1980s, when Mexico announced that it could not meet its debt repayment commitments. The stock of outstanding debt has been a major issue for many LDCs, especially in sub-Saharan Africa.

Figure 12.7 presents some data about this. It can be seen that in 1990 the debt position for many of these countries was serious indeed. In the case of Uganda, in 1990 more than 80% of the value of exports of goods and services was needed just to service the outstanding debt. For a country with limited resources, this leaves little surplus to use for promoting development. The encouraging aspect of Figure 12.7 is that for most of these countries the situation was considerably improved by 2012 — in some cases dramatically so, as in Uganda, for example.

With so high a proportion of export revenues needed to service outstanding debt, it is to be expected that resources to stimulate economic growth and development would be very limited. But how did countries accumulate such high levels of debt? The story begins in the mid-1970s with the first oil price crisis. In 1973–74 oil prices quadrupled. Countries that were not oil producers were suddenly faced with a deficit on the current account of the balance of payments, as the demand for oil in the short run was highly inelastic.

For LDCs, this was a major problem. They knew that if they went to the IMF for a loan, they would be forced to accept onerous conditions, so they were reluctant to do this. On the other hand, the oil producers were enjoying windfall gains, and their surpluses were lodged with the banks, which were thus keen to lend. LDCs were therefore encouraged to borrow from the banks rather than the IMF, and they took out loans at variable interest rates.

The second oil price crisis came in 1979–80, when prices tripled. Many LDCs were now in deep trouble, carrying a legacy of past debts and needing to borrow still more. Furthermore, countries like the USA and the UK were adopting macroeconomic policies that were pushing interest rates to high levels, making it more difficult for LDCs to meet their existing commitments.

This resulted in the debt crisis of the 1980s, when a number of countries were threatening to default on their debts. A number of plans (including the Baker and Brady Plans) were introduced to safeguard the international financial system, but from the LDC viewpoint these entailed mainly a rescheduling of existing debt: in other words, they were given longer to pay. A consequence was that debt levels continued to grow.

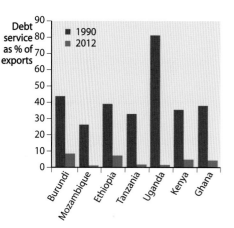

Figure 12.7 Debt servicing in sub-Saharan Africa, 1990 and 2012

Sources: *Human Development Report*, World Bank

The problems were made worse because in some countries the borrowed funds were not used wisely. Development through borrowing is sustainable only if the funds are used to enable exports to grow, so that the funds can be repaid. When they do not lead to increased export earnings, repayment problems will inevitably result.

Before looking at more recent events, this chapter examines the role of the so-called Bretton Woods institutions — the World Bank, the International Monetary Fund and the World Trade Organization.

Summary

- Another way for LDCs to obtain external funds is through borrowing.
- Loans provided by the World Bank and the IMF have conditions attached that are not always palatable for LDCs.
- Many LDCs have borrowed in the past, but have then been unable to meet the repayments.
- In some cases this was because the funds were not well used.

Exercise 12.7

Discuss the extent to which good government within a developing country is a necessary condition for the successful mobilisation of internal and external resources.

The Bretton Woods institutions

At the end of the Second World War in 1945, a conference was held at Bretton Woods, New Hampshire, USA, to establish a system of fixed exchange rates. This became known as the Dollar Standard, as countries agreed to fix their currencies relative to the US dollar. John Maynard Keynes was an influential delegate at the conference. In addition to establishing the exchange rate system that operated until the early 1970s, the conference set up three key institutions with prescribed roles, in support of the international financial system.

International Monetary Fund

The **International Monetary Fund (IMF)** was set up with a specific brief to offer short-term assistance to countries experiencing balance of payments problems. Thus, if a country were running a deficit on the current account, it could borrow from the IMF in order to finance the deficit. However, the IMF would insist that, as a condition of granting the loan, the country put in place policies to deal with the deficit — typically, restrictive monetary and fiscal policies.

World Bank

The International Bank for Reconstruction and Development was the second institution established under the Bretton Woods agreement. It soon became known as the **World Bank**. The role of the World Bank is to provide longer-term funding for projects that will promote development. Much of this funding is provided at commercial interest rates, as the role of the bank was seen to be the channelling of finance to projects that normal commercial banks would perceive as being too risky. However, some concessional lending is also made through the International Development Association (IDA), which is part of the World Bank.

World Trade Organization

Initially, Bretton Woods set up the **General Agreement on Tariffs and Trade (GATT)**, with a brief to oversee international trade. This entailed encouraging countries to reduce tariffs, but the GATT also provided a forum for trade negotiations and for settling disputes between countries. The GATT was replaced

Key terms

International Monetary Fund (IMF) a multilateral institution that provides short-term financing for countries experiencing balance of payments problems

World Bank a multilateral organisation that provides financing for long-term development projects

General Agreement on Tariffs and Trade (GATT) precursor of the WTO, GATT organised a series of 'rounds' of tariff reductions

by the **World Trade Organization (WTO)** in 1995. Between them, these organisations have presided over a significant reduction in the barriers to trade between countries — not only tariffs, but other forms of protection too. The role of the WTO was discussed in Chapter 7.

Heavily Indebted Poor Countries (HIPC) Initiative

In the run-up to the millennium it was clear that many countries' international debt burdens had become unsustainable. Pressure was put on the World Bank and the UN to offer debt forgiveness to LDCs to herald the millennium.

The World Bank was reluctant to consider this route. One of the reasons for its reluctance concerns moral hazard. It is argued that if a country expects to be forgiven its debt, it will have no incentive to behave responsibly. Furthermore, a country that has been forgiven its debt may have no incentive to be more responsible in the future — and other countries too will have less of an incentive to pay off their debts.

The response was the **HIPC Initiative**, which allows for debt forgiveness on condition that the country demonstrates a commitment to 'good' policies over a period of time. The HIPC Initiative was first launched in 1995, but the conditions were so restrictive that few countries were able to benefit. Thus, a number of pressure groups, including Jubilee 2000, lobbied the World Bank to allow the initiative to be more accessible. The original HIPC measures required countries to follow the policy package for a period of 6 years before they would qualify for any debt relief.

The HIPC policy package incorporated four main steps:

1 successful implementation of policies to enhance economic growth (the World Bank's model of market-friendly growth was discussed in Chapter 11)

2 development of a Poverty Reduction Strategy Paper (PRSP)

3 encouragement of private enterprise

4 diversification of the export base

In July 2005 government leaders from the G8 countries met at a summit meeting in Gleneagles. At this meeting the countries present pledged to cancel the debt of the world's most indebted countries — which effectively meant those countries that had qualified under the HIPC Initiative. It remains to be seen how this recommitment will work out in practice. Jubilee 2000 has continued to argue that HIPC remains overly restrictive, and has pointed out that some countries that face heavy debt burdens have been excluded from HIPC, and are therefore also excluded from the Gleneagles statement. This includes such countries as Bangladesh, Cambodia, the Philippines, Nigeria and Peru.

What is not entirely clear is the extent to which improvements in debt service levels can be attributed to the HIPC Initiative. A number of commentators have pointed out that it is not only the HIPC countries that witnessed a reduction in debt service levels.

The Washington Consensus

It has been noted that institutions such as the World Bank and the IMF have tended to impose conditions on countries in return for lending or debt forgiveness. These conditions were based on the prevailing views about how economies would respond to policy changes.

At a conference in 1989, John Williamson drew up a set of ideas about economic policy that he then believed represented accepted views. These ideas became known as the *Washington Consensus*. The ten core policies were:

- fiscal discipline
- reordering public expenditure priorities
- tax reform
- liberalising interest rates
- a competitive exchange rate
- trade liberalisation
- liberalising inward foreign direct investment
- privatisation
- deregulation
- secure property rights

It was argued that countries that adopted these measures would be able to initiate a process of economic development, and the list formed the basis of the conditions imposed on countries. The measures reflect a market-oriented view of how economies operate. Although many countries did adopt some or all of these policies, it became clear that the consensus was not a complete solution. For example, China offered an alternative model, blending the introduction of market reforms with continuing state control.

It has also been argued that the set of measures neglects a number of key issues surrounding governance and the need to establish reliable and robust institutions to underpin the economy. In addition to the consensus measures, successful development also needs attention to be given to improving the way that markets work, especially in terms of the need for flexible labour markets, and there needs to be targeted poverty reduction and social safety nets to bring together macro and micro aspects of the economy. This has led to initiatives centred on the notion of *inclusive growth*. Under this approach, it becomes important to ensure that growth provides genuine benefits for the populace.

Summary

- The Bretton Woods conference in 1945 set up three major multilateral organisations: the IMF, the World Bank and the GATT (which later became the WTO).
- The IMF has the role of providing short-term finance for countries experiencing balance of payments problems.
- The World Bank provides longer-term financing for development projects.
- The WTO oversees the conduct of international trade.
- The HIPC Initiative was designed to address the problems of debt in the poorest countries.
- Under the HIPC Initiative, debt relief is provided to countries that have shown a commitment to World Bank-approved policies and that have implemented a Poverty Reduction Strategy Paper (PRSP).
- The World Bank and IMF encouraged the adoption of policies known as the Washington Consensus, although this proved to be oversimplified in practice.

Other influences on development

Although the flow of finance from FDI, overseas aid and international borrowing is important for the development process, there are many other factors that can be significant influences on the path that an economy takes.

Personal remittances

Looking back at Figure 12.6, the other important source of external financial flows into low-income countries shown in the figure is personal remittances. This has shown a steady increase throughout the period since 1990. Personal remittances here are defined as personal transfers and compensation of employees. In other words, this includes current transfers in cash or in kind to residents of an economy from non-residents, together with incomes of workers who are employed in an economy in which they are not residents. For example, a worker may take a job abroad, but send part of the earnings back to the family in the home country.

The steady increase in such remittances may reflect the effects of globalisation, with more workers being more able to migrate to work abroad and more people being forced to migrate as a result of violence and conflict in the home economy. The World Bank has estimated that more than 215 million people live outside the country of their birth. The extent to which such financial flows can contribute to the process of economic growth and human development is hard to monitor.

Fair trade

Given the relatively weak position that LDCs hold when they try to compete in global markets, there has been increasing interest in the notion of **fair trade schemes**. These had small beginnings, with a number of charities campaigning for small producers in LDCs to be given a 'fair' price for their products. This has flourished and proliferated, to the extent that most supermarkets now stock items labelled as being 'fair trade' — often with a premium price, although this can be difficult to judge because of quality differences between products. If consumers in the rich countries are prepared to pay more for produce in the knowledge that a larger amount goes to the producer, then this may be a way of giving better incentives to farmers in LDCs.

> ### Key term
>
> **fair trade schemes**
> schemes that set out to ensure that small producers in LDCs receive a fair price for their products

However, it is important also to consider the economic arguments that underlie this sort of scheme. There are two key issues. First, are there good economic grounds for intervening by providing subsidies in fair trade schemes? Second, what would be the effect of those subsidies?

The market failure argument in this case is based on the abuse of market power, under which small producers in LDCs are unable to receive a 'fair' price for their output. This may partly reflect information failure as well, as small producers may not always be in a position to discover the going market price for the crops that they produce. The increased use of mobile phones in some countries is helping to overcome this information failure, but there is a long way to go before it is eliminated. The problem is made worse by the time lags involved in responding to changes in market conditions. It takes 3 to 4 years for a newly planted coffee plant to produce marketable coffee, so it is impossible to respond quickly to an increase in price. Indeed, given that prices are set in world markets, and are subject to fluctuations, it is possible that a farmer may manage to increase output only to find that prices have plummeted.

Exercise 12.8

Discuss the economic arguments for and against fair trade schemes, and come to a view about whether you regard them as benefiting LDC producers.

If the issue is one of market power, then using the power of the consumer to affect the bargaining power of the small producer could potentially improve the distribution of the gains from production and provide improved incentives for the producer. If the issue is one of information failure, then the appropriate targeted response would be to take steps to resolve that failure by providing better information to the producers. A fair trade scheme may be able to help by providing advice and guidance to farmers. If the issue is with price fluctuations, then it is not clear how a fair trade scheme by itself can deal with the problems of gestation lags.

In the longer term, there are a number of unanswered questions to be addressed. Some critics have argued that providing subsidies to small producers can produce some anomalous and unintended defects. One danger is that farmers may be subsidised to continue production in a market in which prices may already be on a downward spiral, rather than switching to alternative commodities with better long-term prospects.

Macroeconomic stability

In the context of LDCs, a stable macroeconomic environment may be seen as a prerequisite for encouraging investment — in particular, for attracting foreign direct investment. At times, some LDCs have struggled to achieve such stability, notably in Latin America where inflation became a major problem that interfered with the growth process. More recently, one of the symptoms of economic disaster in Zimbabwe was the hyperinflation that officially reached 231 million per cent, but was thought unofficially to be in the billions: one estimate put the peak inflation rate at 6.5 sextillion per cent. This effectively meant that some 80% of the population were relying on subsistence and barter, and the currency was abandoned in 2009 to be replaced as the country's main currency by the US dollar.

Without macroeconomic stability, the other components of a market-friendly strategy cannot operate. As microeconomic markets will fail when price signals are not clear, people will be reluctant to invest in human capital, and MNCs and governments will be reluctant to invest in the country. Indeed, when domestic markets do not operate effectively, and where financial markets do not pervade the whole economy, then traditional methods of achieving macroeconomic stability will not work.

Industrialisation and structural change

What are the prospects for a country wanting to move towards industrialisation, and to reduce its reliance on primary production? If the Lewis model were valid (see Chapter 11), then a small wage differential would be sufficient to encourage the growth of the modern sector. Unfortunately, the process did not prove to be as smooth as Lewis suggested. One reason relates to human capital levels. Agricultural workers do not have the skills or training that prepare them for employment in the industrial sector, so it is not so straightforward to transfer them from agricultural to industrial work.

Furthermore, to the extent that they were able to transfer, the expanding industry did not always reinvest the surplus in order to enable continuous expansion of the industrial sector. Foreign firms tended to repatriate the profits, and in any case tended to use modern, relatively capital-intensive technology that did not require a large pool of unskilled labour.

Perhaps more importantly, Lewis's model encouraged governments to think in terms of industry-led growth, and to neglect the rural sector. This meant that agricultural productivity often remained low, and inequality between urban and rural areas grew.

Urbanisation

A natural result of the perceived disparity in living conditions between urban and rural areas was to encourage migration from the villages to the town — a process known as *urbanisation*.

Migration occurs in response to a number of factors. One is the attraction of the 'bright lights' of the cities — people in rural areas perceive urban areas as offering better access to education and healthcare facilities, and better recreational opportunities. Perhaps more important are the economic gains to be made from migrating to the cities, in terms of the wage differential between urban and rural areas.

Urban wages tend to be higher for a number of reasons. Employment in the manufacturing or service sectors typically offers higher wages, in contrast to the low productivity and wages in the agricultural sector. Furthermore, labour in the urban areas tends to be better organised, and governments have often introduced minimum wage legislation and social protection for workers in the urban areas — especially where they rely on them for electoral support.

Such wage differentials attract a flow of migrants to the cities. However, in practice there may not be sufficient jobs available, as the new and growing sectors typically do not expand sufficiently quickly to absorb all the migrating workers. The net result of this is that rural workers exchange poor living conditions in the rural areas for unemployment in the urban environment.

Furthermore, as employment in the newer sectors cannot expand at such a rate, the result is an expansion of the informal sector. Migrants to the city who cannot find work are forced to find other forms of employment, as most LDCs do not have well-developed social security protection. The cities of many LDCs are therefore characterised by substantial amounts of informal activity.

A township on the outskirts of Cape Town — urbanisation results when rural populations are lured to cities in search of work

Tourism

The analysis so far suggests that LDCs need to diversify away from primary production and into new activities that do not require large amounts of capital, preferably involving the production of goods or services that can earn foreign exchange and that have a high income elasticity of demand. On the face of it, tourism would seem to fit the bill.

In the first place, the income elasticity of demand for tourism is strongly positive. This means that, as real incomes rise in the more developed countries, there will be an increase in the demand for tourism. Within the domestic economy in the LDC, the development of the tourist sector will have an impact on employment. In the early stages there will be a demand for construction workers, and later there will be jobs in hotels and in transport and other services. Tourism is also the sort of activity that is likely to have large multiplier effects on the domestic economy. The World Bank has reported that visitor expenditures outside the hotel sector can range from half to nearly double the in-hotel spending. In addition, there is likely to be scope for small labour-intensive, craft-based activities to sell goods to foreigners without actually having to go into the export business — because the tourists come to the producers. Tourism may also attract foreign direct investment if international hotel chains move in to cater for the visiting tourists.

Tourism will require an improvement in the country's infrastructure. For example, it may require road improvements, and upgraded transport and communications facilities. However, such facilities not only help the tourist sector, but also generate externality effects, in the sense that local businesses (and residents) benefit from the improvements as well.

Another potentially important aspect of tourism from the government's perspective is that it may generate a flow of tax revenue. This may come partly from taxes on goods and services, but also from airport taxes and landing fees.

As usual, however, there is a potential downside as well. Tourists will also demand goods that cannot be produced locally, so there may be a need to increase imports, adding to the current account deficit on the balance of payments. This may be reinforced by the outflow of profits from the foreign direct investment. In addition, there may be negative externality effects arising from the erosion of the environment. And tourists exhibit different lifestyles, which may alter the aspirations of the local population, and encourage the consumption of inappropriate (and perhaps imported) products.

It is also important to keep opportunity costs in mind. The development of any new activity entails the sacrifice of some alternative. In deciding to develop tourism, some other option will have to be forgone. For example, resources that are used to improve the transport and communications infrastructure cannot be used to improve education or healthcare. Of course, tourism may prove to be so successful that it will generate resources that can be devoted to education or healthcare, but opportunity costs are not an issue that can be ignored in the present.

Summary

- Personal remittances have become an important source of financial inflows to LDCs, but it is difficult to track their impact.
- Fair trade schemes have been mooted as a way of improving the prices paid to farmers in LDCs.
- Sir Arthur Lewis argued that the agricultural sectors in many LDCs are characterised by surplus labour, which could be transferred into the manufacturing and service sectors and thus generate structural change and economic growth.
- However, this process has not been as smooth as Lewis predicted, and in some cases has led to rural neglect and a bias of resources towards the urban areas.
- Migration to the cities has been a feature of many LDCs in recent years, bringing negative externality effects.
- Tourism has been recommended as a potentially profitable area for LDCs to develop, but here again there may be costs as well as benefits.

Exercise 12.9

Identify the factors that an LDC should take into account if planning to change its pattern of comparative advantage by developing new economic activities.

Prospects for the future

This analysis of the situation facing LDCs does not seem to give many grounds for optimism, especially in sub-Saharan Africa, where so many countries seem to have stagnated, and where the combination of problems to be overcome seems so great. The early years of the twenty-first century showed some promise, with some signs of economic growth. The global recession that afflicted many of the industrial economies may have interrupted the progress that LDCs had begun to enjoy. However, it is to be hoped that this will just be a temporary interruption, so that countries around the world and their citizens can become full partners in the global economy.

Case study 12.1

Tourism in Tanzania

Tanzania is among the lowest-income countries in the world. It is located in sub-Saharan Africa, and relies heavily on agriculture for employment, income and export earnings. In 2001, 84% of its merchandise exports consisted of primary goods, and the terms of trade had declined to 44 based on 1980 = 100. Could Tanzania benefit from tourism?

In its favour, Tanzania has a rich wildlife and the potential to offer safari holidays, so there are resources that could attract foreign visitors. However, how widespread would the benefits from tourism be in Tanzania's society?

Traditionally, the farmers who work the fields on the outskirts of Tanzania's capital city, Dar es Salaam, sold their produce in the outdoor markets in the city. This entailed an early start to the day, and a trek to the city over poor paths and roads, with the farm produce loaded on to bicycles. In 2001 the Royal Palm Hotel in Dar es Salaam was taken over by new management, which needed a regular supply of fresh vegetables and flowers to serve its guests. It was decided to obtain these by sending a truck into the villages to buy produce directly from the farmers. This meant that the hotel got its produce fresh from the fields, and that the farmers had a new and more convenient market in which to sell their produce. This is one example of how the multiplier effect can extend the benefits from tourism beyond those directly affected.

Source: the story about the farmers was taken from a World Bank website, www.miga.org

Follow-up question

Discuss the potential benefits and costs of developing tourism as part of a development strategy.

13 The financial sector

This chapter explores the role of the financial sector and the way in which it relates to the real economy. It has often been argued that the quantity of money in the economy — and its rate of growth — are crucial in influencing the rate of inflation, and hence the overall performance of the economy. However, it has also been noted that money stock is difficult to define, measure, monitor and control. This chapter explains why this is the case, setting out the various sources of money and credit creation in a modern economy. It also discusses the main theories that seek to explain the importance of money in the macroeconomy and outlines the role of the banking sector and the patterns of lending and borrowing.

> ## Learning objectives
>
> After studying this chapter, you should:
> → appreciate the importance of the financial sector in the macroeconomy
> → be familiar with the sources of money in the economy, in particular noting the actions of commercial banks, the government and the stock and bond markets, and the impact of international financial transactions
> → be aware of the determinants of the demand for money
> → understand the way in which interest rates are determined in different money markets
> → be familiar with the liquidity preference theory and the loanable funds approach
> → be able to evaluate the role of the financial sector in the real economy

The role of the financial sector

The modern economy relies heavily on the effective working of financial markets. In particular, it is important that a sufficient flow of money and credit is available if product markets are to operate and transactions are to be smooth.

Individuals need to undertake saving, and businesses and individuals need to be able to borrow. This was highlighted in the discussion of the Harrod–Domar model in the context of less developed countries, but is equally important for an advanced economy. It is through financial markets that savings can be mobilised for the investment that raises the productive capacity of the economy, resulting in economic growth.

Financial markets that operate in the modern economy also enable transactions to be conducted on the basis of contracts for future delivery — these are known as *forward* or *futures markets*. These are especially important in relation to transactions in certain commodities and in foreign exchange.

The market for equities is also an important part of the modern financial system, by which firms can obtain funds through the stock market for their investment plans. The whole business of insurance and pension funds is based on the existence of stock markets.

Monetary policy is a key way in which the authorities seek to stabilise the macroeconomy, and it cannot be implemented without there being an efficient and effective financial sector.

For all these reasons, it is important to study how financial markets work. Indeed, if there was any doubt about the importance of the financial sector, this was dispelled by the financial crisis that hit the global economy in the late 2000s. The crisis had far-reaching effects on the stability of the financial system, and worked through into the real economy, resulting in recession and rising unemployment. The recovery from this crisis was slow. In order to understand the reasons for the financial crisis, and the steps needed to deal with it, it is important first to understand how the financial system works, and the extent to which it may be subject to market failure. The analysis begins with money.

Money in the modern economy

Money plays an important role in the modern economy. However, it turns out that the monetary authorities find it difficult to measure and monitor the amount of money in the economy — let alone trying to control it directly. Why should this be? Part of the explanation is that there are many sources of money in a modern, open economy. In other words, it is not simply a question of measuring, monitoring and controlling the quantity of banknotes and coins in circulation.

This partly stems from the functions of money, which were discussed back in Book 1, Chapter 1. Money performs four key roles — as a medium of exchange, a store of value, a unit of account and a standard of deferred payment.

In order to fulfil these functions, money needs to have certain characteristics:

- *Portability*: money must be easy to carry.
- *Divisibility*: money needs to be readily divided into small parts in order to undertake transactions.
- *Acceptability*: money must be generally acceptable if it is to act as a medium of exchange.
- *Scarcity*: money cannot be in unlimited supply, nor should it be able to be counterfeited.
- *Durability*: money needs to be able to withstand wear and tear in use.
- *Stability in value*: the value of money must remain reasonably stable over time if it is to act as a store of value.

Many commodities have acted as money at various times in various circumstances. For example, cigarettes acted as money in prisoner-of-war camps during the Second World War. In parts of West Africa, slaves were used as money in the past — slaves were portable, but were neither divisible nor durable. There is a range of assets that can fulfil some or all of these roles, and this helps to explain why it is difficult to measure and monitor the amount of money in the economy.

An important characteristic of money is **liquidity**. This refers to the ease with which an asset can be spent. Cash is the most liquid asset, as it can be used for transactions. However, if you are holding funds in a savings account whereby you must either give notice of withdrawal or forfeit some return to withdraw it instantly, then such funds are regarded as being less liquid, as they cannot costlessly or instantly be used for transactions.

Prior knowledge needed

The role of money was first introduced in Book 1, Chapter 1, but will now be examined more carefully. The working of monetary policy was explained under Theme 2 in Book 1, Chapter 16, and parts of this chapter build upon that analysis. This chapter will also make use of the *AD/AS* model, which was introduced in Book 1, Chapters 11–13.

Key term

liquidity the extent to which an asset can be converted in the short term and without the holder incurring a cost

Key terms

narrow money (M0) notes and coins in circulation and as commercial banks' deposits at the Bank of England

broad money (M4) M0 plus sterling wholesale and retail deposits with monetary financial institutions such as banks and building societies

Study tip

Notice that it is bank deposits that count as money, not the cheques drawn on them.

One traditional way of measuring the money stock was from the *monetary base*, which comprised all notes and coins in circulation. Together with the commercial banks' deposits at the Bank of England, this was known as **M0** or **narrow money**. This was intended to measure the amount of money held for transactions purposes. However, with the increased use of electronic means of payment, M0 has become less meaningful as a measure, and the Bank of England stopped issuing data for M0 in 2005.

However, there are many assets that are 'near-money', such as interest-bearing current account deposits at banks. These are highly liquid and can readily be converted into cash for transactions. **M4** or **broad money** is a measure of the money stock that includes M0 together with sterling wholesale and retail deposits with monetary financial institutions such as banks. In other words, it includes all bank deposits that can be used for transactions, even though some of these deposits may require a period of notice for withdrawal. However, M4 is held not only for transactions purposes, but also partly as a store of wealth.

Cash and banknotes are the most liquid assets as they can be used for transactions directly. Current (chequing) accounts are almost as liquid, but although savings accounts in banks may also be quite quickly converted to cash, there may be a time delay or a cost involved. Shares or government bonds are much less liquid as it takes time to convert them into cash. Nonetheless, they are several types of asset that can be regarded as near-money. The central bank can control the quantities of some of these assets, but not all.

The commercial banks and credit creation

The operations of commercial banks can influence the quantity of money. Banks accept deposits from their customers, and issue loans. The way in which they undertake lending has an impact on the quantity of money.

The credit creation multiplier

Think first of all about the way in which the money supply is created. You might think that this is simply a question of controlling the amount of notes and coin

The notes and coins in circulation are known as 'narrow money'

issued by the central bank. However, because there are many different assets that act as near-money in a modern economy, the real picture is more complicated. The actions of the commercial banks also have implications for the size of money supply.

One of the reasons why it is difficult for a central bank to control the supply of money is the way that the commercial banks are able to create credit. Consider the way that commercial banks operate. They accept deposits from customers, and supply them with banking services. However, they also provide loans — and this is how they make profits. Suppose that the government undertakes a piece of expenditure, and finances it by issuing money. The firms receiving the payment from the government are likely to bank the money they receive, so bank deposits increase. From the perspective of the commercial banks, they know that it is unlikely that all their customers will want to withdraw their money simultaneously, so they will lend out some of the additional deposits to borrowers, who are likely to undertake expenditure on goods or services. As their expenditures work their way back into the banking system, the commercial banks will find that they can lend out even more, and so the process continues. In other words, an increase in the amount of money in the economy has a multiplied effect on the amount of credit created by the banks. This process is known as the **credit multiplier**.

Key term

credit multiplier
a process by which an increase in money supply can have a multiplied effect on the amount of credit in an economy

Consider an arithmetic example illustrated in Figure 13.1. Suppose that the commercial banks always act such as to hold 10% of their assets in liquid form — that is, as cash in the tills. If an extra £100 is lodged as deposits, the commercial banks will add £10 to the cash in tills, and lend out the remaining £90. When that £90 finds its way back into the hands of the bank, it will keep £9 as cash, and lend out the remaining £81. And so on. The process will stop when the bank is back to a cash ratio of 10%. The original extra £100 will have been converted into £100 in cash, and £900 in loans!

The value of the multiplier is given by 1 divided by the desired cash ratio that the commercial banks decide to hold. The smaller is this ratio, the larger is the credit multiplier. If the commercial banks want to hold only 5% of their assets in the form of cash, then the credit multiplier will be $1/0.05 = 20$.

The significance of this relationship is that changes in the supply of cash have a multiplied impact on the amount of credit in the economy. This makes monetary control through money supply a highly imprecise business, especially if the central bank does not know exactly what the commercial banks' desired liquidity ratio is. In the past, one way that the monetary authorities tried to control money supply was to impose requirements on the proportion of assets that banks held in liquid form. However, this is also imprecise, as banks need not hold exactly the proportion required, in order to give themselves some leeway in the short run. This method of control was abandoned long ago, although the commercial banks are required to keep a small portion of their assets as cash at the Bank of England. This is purely for operational reasons.

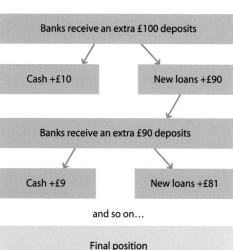

Figure 13.1 Credit creation

Exercise 13.1

Suppose that the commercial banks in a country follow a rule such that they always aim to hold one-tenth of their assets in liquid form (i.e. as cash). Calculate the total increase in bank lending that would follow if government action leads to an extra £200 being lodged as bank deposits. Explain your answer.

Summary

- Money plays an important role in the macroeconomy, fulfilling functions as a medium of exchange, a store of value and a standard of deferred payment.
- There are several different sorts of asset that have the necessary characteristics to fulfil these functions.
- Money supply is difficult to measure or control because money can be generated from a range of sources.
- Commercial banks can influence money supply through their lending policy via the credit multiplier.

The determination of interest rates

Book 1, Chapter 16 introduced the idea that the equilibrium interest rate could be seen as being determined by the intersection of the demand for and the supply of money. This now needs to be explored a bit more closely.

The demand for money

There are three key motives for holding money, which between them determine the demand for money. However, it is important to notice first that the decision to hold money balances carries an opportunity cost.

The opportunity cost of holding money

If a firm or household chooses to hold money, it forgoes the possibility of using the money to purchase some other financial asset, such as a bond, that would yield a rate of return.

This means that the interest rate can be regarded as the opportunity cost of holding money: put another way, it is the price of holding money. At high rates of interest, people can be expected to hold less money, as the opportunity cost of doing so is high.

The transactions demand for money

The first motive for holding money is clear — people and firms will hold money in order to undertake transactions. This is related to the need to use money when buying goods and services, and is closely associated with the functions of money as a medium of exchange and a unit of account. The demand for money for this purpose will most likely be determined by the level of income, because it is the level of income that will determine how many transactions people will wish to undertake. The rate of interest (the opportunity cost of holding money) may be less important than income in this instance.

The precautionary demand for money

People and firms may also hold money for precautionary reasons. They may wish to have liquid assets available in order to guard against a sudden need to cover an emergency payment or to take advantage of a spending opportunity at some point in the future. The opportunity cost of holding money may come into play here, as if the return on financial assets is high, then people may be less inclined to hold money in a relatively liquid form.

The speculative demand for money

The rate of interest may affect the demand for money through another route. If share (or bond) prices are low (and the rate of interest paid is therefore high), then the opportunity cost of holding money is high, and people and firms will tend to hold shares. On the other hand, when the interest rate is low, and share prices are high, people will be more likely to hold money. This effect will be especially strong when people and firms see share prices as unreasonably high, so that they expect them to fall. In this case, they may speculate by selling bonds in order to hold money, in anticipation of taking advantage of future expected falls in the price of bonds.

Liquidity preference

If the interest rate may be regarded as the opportunity cost of holding money, it can be argued that economic agents, whether households or firms, will display a demand for money, arising from the functions that money fulfils in a modern economy. This theory of **liquidity preference**, as it is known, was noted by Keynes in his *General Theory*. Figure 13.2 illustrates what is implied for the money market. If the rate of interest is the opportunity cost of money, then it is expected that the demand for money will be lower when the rate of interest rate is relatively high, as the opportunity cost of holding money is high. People will be more reluctant to forgo the rate of return that has to be sacrificed by holding money. When the rate of interest is relatively low, this will be less of a concern, so the demand for money will be relatively high. This suggests that the money demand curve (*MD*) will be downward sloping. If money supply is fixed at *M★* in Figure 13.2, then the money market will be in equilibrium at the rate of interest *r★*.

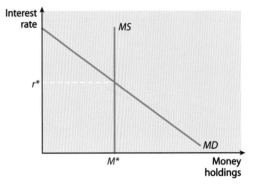

Figure 13.2 The demand for money and the rate of interest

The existence of this relationship means that the monetary authorities have to be aware of the need to maintain (or allow) equilibrium in the money market. Interest rates and money supply cannot be fixed independently. This is a clear constraint on the use of monetary policy. An important question is the extent to which the demand for money is stable. If money demand were to be volatile, moving around from one time period to the next, then it would be virtually impossible for the monetary authorities to have any precise control over the market. The situation is further complicated by the way that interest rates influence behaviour. The degree to which the demand for money is sensitive to the rate of interest is also important. This is reflected in the shape of the *MD* curve. Notice that because the level of income is also important in determining money demand, this will affect the *position* of the *MD* curve in the diagram. An increase in income would lead to a rightward shift in money demand, as people and firms require larger money holdings when incomes are higher.

The market for loanable funds

Although the rate of interest can be interpreted as being the opportunity cost of holding money, this is not the only way of viewing it. From a firm's point of view, it may be seen as the cost of borrowing. For example, suppose that a firm is considering undertaking an investment project. The rate of interest represents the cost of borrowing the funds needed in order to finance the investment. The higher is the rate of interest, the less investment projects will be seen as being profitable. If the firm is intending to finance its investment from past profits, the interest rate is still pertinent, as it then represents the return that the firm could obtain by purchasing a

Exercise 13.2

Analyse the effect on the rate of interest if there is an increase in the supply of money in an economy. Use a diagram such as Figure 13.2 as a starting point.

market for loanable funds
the notion that households
will be influenced by the
rate of interest in making
saving decisions, which
will then determine the
quantity of loanable funds
available for firms to
borrow for investment

financial asset instead of undertaking the investment. Either way, the rate of interest is important in the decision-making process.

The rate of interest is also important to households, to whom it may represent the return on saving. Households may be encouraged to save more if the return on their saving is relatively high, whereas when the rate of interest is low, the incentive to save is correspondingly low. Within the circular flow of income, expenditure and output, it is the flow of saving from households that enables firms to find the funds needed to fund their investment expenditure. It is now apparent that the rate of interest may play an important role in bringing together these flows.

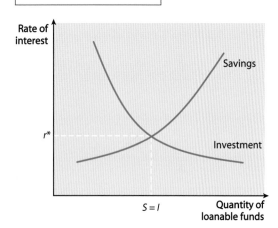

Figure 13.3 The market for loanable funds

The **market for loanable funds** is shown in Figure 13.3. The investment schedule is shown as downward sloping, because firms will find more investment projects to be worthwhile when the rate of interest rate is low. The savings schedule is shown to be upward sloping because a higher rate of interest is expected to encourage households to supply more saving. In other words, the supply of loanable funds will be higher when the rate of interest rate is relatively high.

Keynes believed that this could lead to instability in financial markets. He argued that investment and saving would be relatively insensitive to the rate of interest, such that the schedules in Figure 13.3 would be relatively steep. Investment would depend more crucially on firms' expectations about the future demand for their products, which could be volatile, moving the investment schedule around and thus leading to instability in the rate of interest. He thus came to the conclusion that governments should manage aggregate demand in order to stabilise the economy.

Exercise 13.3

Suppose an economy
begins with equilibrium in
the market for loanable
funds, as was illustrated
in Figure 13.3. Discuss
how the market would be
affected if the government
decided to try to encourage
more investment by holding
the rate of interest below *r**.
Do you think that such a
policy would be effective?

Summary

- People and firms within the economy choose to hold money for certain purposes.
- The demand for money reflects transactions, precautionary and speculative motivations.
- The rate of interest can be regarded as the opportunity cost of holding money.
- Keynes developed liquidity preference theory, showing how the demand for money would be related to the rate of interest.
- It has been argued that both investment and saving depend upon the rate of interest.
- The rate of interest is important in determining equilibrium of saving and investment within the market for loanable funds.

Money and inflation

Why should the quantity of money or credit in circulation be so important?

Classical economists took the view that the overall price level comes to be determined through the mechanism of the quantity theory of money. To explain this requires a new concept: the **velocity of circulation**. If the money stock is defined as the quantity of money (notes and coins) in circulation in the economy, the velocity of circulation is defined as the speed with which that money stock changes hands. It is defined as the volume of transactions divided by the money stock.

Key term

velocity of circulation (V)
the rate at which money
changes hands: the
volume of transactions
divided by money stock

In practice, the volume of transactions is seen as being represented by nominal income, which is the level of real income (Y) multiplied by the average price level (P). If V is the velocity of circulation, and M is the size of the money stock, then the following equation holds:

$$V = PY/M$$

Notice that this is just a definition, sometimes known as the Fisher equation of exchange, after the American economist Irving Fisher. Multiplying both sides of the equation by M gives:

$$MV = PY$$

Quantitative skills 13.1

Theories and definitions

It is important to realise that this is still based on a definition. This is significant because a definition is just a statement about the relationship between the variables that are included. As such it is no more than a statement that always holds true. It only becomes a theory if we introduce some assumptions, which is what is done in the next paragraph.

In a classical world, the velocity of circulation (V) would be constant — or at least would be stable over time. Furthermore, real output would always tend rapidly towards the natural rate. These assumptions together with the $MV = PY$ equation provide us with a direct link between money (M) and the overall price level (P). This relationship suggests that prices can only increase persistently if money stock itself increases persistently, and that money (and prices) have no effect on real output.

How can we interpret this in terms of aggregate demand and aggregate supply? If the money supply increases, then firms and households in the economy find they have excess cash balances — that is, for the given price level they have stronger purchasing power than they had anticipated. Their impulse will thus be to increase spending, which will cause the aggregate demand curve to move to the right. They will probably also save some of the excess, which will tend to result in lower interest rates — which then reinforces the increase in aggregate demand. However, as the AD curve moves to the right, the equilibrium price level will rise, and return the economy to equilibrium.

Prior knowledge needed

Book 1, Chapter 12 discussed the different ways in which the monetarist and Keynesian schools of thought regarded the shape of the long-run aggregate supply curve.

Figure 13.4 illustrates this in the case of a monetarist long-run aggregate supply — recall that the $LRAS$ curve would be vertical at the full employment level under monetarist assumptions. If aggregate demand begins at AD_0, and then shifts to AD_1, the figure shows that price increases from P_0, to P_1, but real output remains unchanged at $Y^\star$.

If money supply continues to increase, the process repeats itself, with price then rising persistently. One danger of this is that people get so accustomed to the process that they speed up their spending decisions, and this accelerates the whole process. Inflation could then accelerate out of control.

To summarise, the analysis suggests that persistent inflation can arise only through persistent excessive growth in the money stock, which can be seen in terms of persistent movements of the aggregate demand curve.

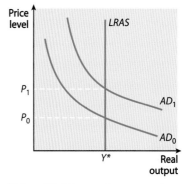

Figure 13.4 A monetary expansion

Quantitative skills 13.2

Real and nominal interest rates

It is worth being aware that when there is inflation in an economy, there is an important distinction between nominal and real interest rates. The stated rate of return on a financial asset represents the nominal return. For example, if you invest £100 now at an annual fixed rate of 5%, you expect to receive £105 in a year's time. However, if inflation has been proceeding at 2% per annum over that year, the value of your investment has been eroded by that 2% increase in prices. The *real rate of interest* is thus the net return after allowing for inflation. This can be approximated as the difference between the nominal rate and the inflation rate. In the above example, the real rate of interest would be 5 − 2 = 3%.

Evaluation

How significant is the quantity theory relationship in understanding the operation of the macroeconomy?

Remember that the equation of exchange is a definition, and only becomes a theory if some assumptions are made. The strength of the theory therefore rests on the validity of those assumptions — namely, that the velocity of circulation is constant and that real output would always tend to the natural rate. This goes back to the debate between the monetarist and Keynesian schools. The former — especially those of the new classical following — argued that the economy would always return to equilibrium rapidly. The stability of the velocity of circulation is closely related to the stability of the demand for money relationship, and the monetarists thought this would be stable — if it existed at all. The Keynesians, on the other hand, did not believe that the economy would always return to equilibrium, and thought that the demand for money (and hence the velocity of circulation) could be quite volatile. Under these assumptions, the direct relationship between money and the price level would be broken.

Either way, the difficulty of identifying money supply makes it difficult to explore the real-world relationship between money and prices. The rapidity of technological progress in financial markets has complicated things even more.

Summary

- The quantity theory suggests that there is a direct relationship between money and the overall price level.
- Persistent inflation can only occur if money supply persistently grows more rapidly than real incomes.
- The validity of the quantity theory relationship depends upon the validity of the underpinning assumptions.

The financial sector and the macroeconomy

The macroeconomy depends heavily on the financial sector to operate effectively. Lending and borrowing underpin the way in which the economy works: firms need to borrow in order to finance their investment, and households borrow for their spending. Insurance markets and pension funds are key features of the financial landscape. The process of globalisation enhances the importance of having an efficient foreign exchange market.

The credit crunch and financial crisis, with their impact on economic growth and unemployment, highlighted the importance of an effective financial sector for the real macroeconomy. To understand how this came about, it is necessary to explore the ways in which the banking sector has developed over time, against a backdrop of deregulation and innovation in types of financial asset.

Financial institutions

Financial institutions provide the key link between borrowers and lenders, and are often referred to as **financial intermediaries**. This term covers banks, building societies and a range of other specialist institutions that provide financial services. Traditionally, the banking sector has been seen as being divided into two main sectors, made up of the **retail banks** and the **wholesale banks**.

The retail banks include the high-street banks that provide banking services to households and small firms, accepting deposits and making loans, mainly on a relatively small scale, and providing a distributed branch banking service. Wholesale banks operate on a larger scale, taking deposits and making loans to companies and other banks. These include the investment banks and other specialist financial institutions. Building societies in the past were distinct institutions providing a specific service, accepting deposits from a range of small depositors and making long-term loans for house purchase, with the property acting as collateral on the debt.

One of the developments of recent years has been the blurring of these distinctions. Deregulation has allowed most building societies to rebrand themselves as retail banks, and the high-street banks have diversified into wholesale banking, becoming **universal banks**, operating in large-scale lending and investment as well as fulfilling their traditional high-street functions. The growth of internet banking has allowed them to reduce the extent of their branch banking networks, thus reducing costs.

Banks operate in order to make profits. They take deposits and make loans, making profit from the return on the loans that they make. The more loans they make, the more profit, but this must be balanced against the need to carry enough liquid

> ### Key terms
>
> **financial intermediaries** institutions such as banks and building societies that channel funds from lenders to borrowers
>
> **retail banks** banks that provide high-street services to depositors
>
> **wholesale banks** banks that deal with companies and other banks on a large scale
>
> **universal banks** banks that operate in both retail and wholesale markets

High-street banks have diversified into wholesale banking, becoming universal banks

assets to meet the demands of depositors who wish to withdraw funds for use in transactions. There is thus a trade-off that the banks need to get right, between making loans and holding enough liquidity to service their customers. The **liquidity ratio** is the ratio of liquid assets to total assets.

In the short run, banks can borrow from each other in order to maintain their liquidity ratio. Such **interbank lending** takes place at a rate of interest that depends upon the amount of liquidity in the market and on the period over which the loan is required. The average rate of interest on loans made in the London interbank market is known as the **LIBOR**, which is set daily. Under normal circumstances, such lending ensures that banks have sufficient liquidity on a day-by-day basis, but problems emerged during the financial crisis.

Another way of accommodating a short-run shortage of funds is to sell financial assets to the central bank (or to other banks), then repurchase them at an agreed date — perhaps two weeks later. These sale and repurchase agreements are known as **repos**, and act like a loan.

Forms of borrowing

Borrowing takes place for various reasons and takes different forms. The nature and characteristics of the borrowing determine the conditions under which borrowing takes place, including the rate of interest to be charged.

The mortgage market is an important form of borrowing. These are long-term loans taken out for house purchase, in which the loan is secured against the value of the property. If the borrower defaults on the loan, the lender takes the property in lieu of the debt. The size of the loan is partly based on the lender's assessment of the ability of the borrower to maintain payments over the life of the loan. This may be related to the income and expected income of the borrower, but also to the expectation that house prices will rise in the future.

Borrowing may also take place without such collateral to cover default. Such unsecured borrowing will carry a higher rate of interest. In recent years, there has been an increase in very short-run loans to provide households with funds to tide them over until the next pay-day. Such pay-day lending comes at a very high rate of interest.

Another form of borrowing comes in the form of overdrafts, an arrangement whereby a bank's customer can spend more than is covered by current deposits at a pre-announced rate of interest. Such borrowing is limited to an amount agreed in advance. Credit cards also allow borrowers to incur debt, and allow ready payment for everyday transactions.

Figure 13.5 shows selected interest rates, before and after the financial crisis, all measured in per cent per annum at the end of the month shown.

The interest rates shown reveal substantial variation. This can be explained with reference to some key characteristics of the form of borrowing to which they relate, particularly the risk involved with lending. The security and length of the loan contribute to the risk. It would be expected that lending with no collateral would carry a risk premium, as the cost of default is high for the borrower. It is also the case that risk may be higher for a long-term loan because of the uncertainty attached to the future. This may be balanced by the nature of collateral — for example, in the case of mortgage lending, where the asset providing the collateral is expected to appreciate in value over time. This was especially true in periods when house prices were rising at a fast rate.

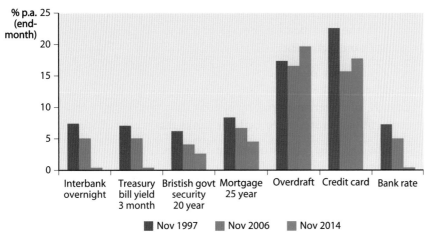

% p.a. (end-month)

Figure 13.5 Selected interest rates in the UK

The figure shows that unsecured loans, such as overdrafts and credit cards, carry significantly higher interest rates than the secured loans such as mortgages, or government securities, which may be perceived as much less risky.

Financial instruments

The development of new financial instruments in recent decades has had a major influence on the way that financial markets operate. Shares are issued by firms in need of finance. Shareholders become part-owners of the company, and may receive dividends from the profits made by the firm. Those holding a large portion of a firm's shares can have a major say in how the firm operates.

When the government needs to borrow, it can do so by issuing bonds. A bond is a financial asset that pays a fixed amount each year and also carries a fixed value payable at a fixed date in the future when the bond matures. Bonds can be bought and sold, and the price of the bond varies with the market valuation at any point in time. The price of a bond varies inversely with the rate of interest.

Certificates of deposit (CDs) are one way in which a financial institution can extend its borrowing. These are certificates issued by banks to customers in return for deposits for a fixed term. For example, a large firm may agree to deposit a sum of money for a fixed period, receiving a CD in return. The CD can be sold on in the secondary market, so if the firm needs liquid funds, it can obtain them in spite of having agreed to the long-term deposit. From the bank's point of view, it knows it does not have to repay the deposit until a fixed point in the future.

Banks have also found ways of selling some of their assets to other financial institutions. For example, suppose a bank has a stock of assets in the form of residential mortgages that generate a regular cash flow. It is possible for the bank to bundle these together and sell them on. This process is known as **securitisation**. This is a device that effectively turns future cash flows into a bond.

One effect of this is that banks find that they need not maintain such a high liquidity ratio in order to meet their obligations, and can thus expand their lending. This is what happened in the lead-up to the financial crisis of the late 2000s. Securitisation altered the balance of bank assets, with a higher proportion now being in the form of bonds rather than equity/shares. There is a key difference between the two, because firms can suspend dividends in a hard year, but the return on bonds has to be paid. It also turned out that some of the securitisation that had taken place had involved

Synoptic link

Notice, however, that when firms are owned by a large and fragmented number of shareholders, the managers who run the firm may not face great accountability, thus giving rise to the principal–agent problem, which was discussed in Chapter 1.

Key term

securitisation a process whereby future cash flows are converted into marketable securities

assets and cash flows that were less secure and more risky than had been thought — for example, the so-called sub-prime mortgage market, where some households began to default on their debts.

This sowed the seeds of the financial crisis, when some banks began to have difficulty in meeting their obligations. Furthermore, with the banks holding lower liquidity ratios, the interbank lending system also came under pressure. In the UK, the government had to step in to bail out banks that were in difficulties.

As public debt rose, the government cut back on spending at the same time that banks were cutting down on lending. In this way, the crisis spread to the real sector of the economy. Recession was here. Chapter 14 will explore the way in which the Bank of England responded to the situation.

The impact was also felt through the stock market, where falling share prices put pressure on insurance and pension funds. It also became apparent that it is not only the liquidity ratio that is important. Partly through securitisation, banks were holding a wider variety of financial assets, carrying varying amounts of risk. Their ability to meet all demands from their depositors and to cover loan defaults would depend upon a bank's capital relative to its current liabilities and assets (weighted by the risk). This is measured by the **capital adequacy ratio**, defined as the ratio of a bank's capital to the value of its risk-weighted assets.

Extension material

The credit creation multiplier in reverse

Recall the credit creation multiplier. This showed that when a bank finds it has an increase in deposits, it can create credit through its lending, and that increase in credit will be multiplied through successive rounds of borrowing. This also applies if a bank considers that its capital adequacy ratio is lower than it needs to be. As banks expanded into ever more inventive types of asset, the capital adequacy ratio became more difficult to monitor. Anyway, the banks were becoming more confident in their ability to reap more profits into the future. When the bubble burst, the danger was that banks would retreat, and stop lending. This would then set the credit creation multiplier into reverse, compounding the problem.

Market failure?

To what extent did market failure contribute to the financial crisis?

Information failure

As securitisation became widespread, there may well have been an information failure, in the sense that the banks were accumulating assets about which they had less than full knowledge. There was information asymmetry here, as the banks had less knowledge about the assets that they were acquiring than the original lenders. This applied in particular to mortgages that were being recycled. They were therefore not in a position to come to an accurate estimate of the risk to which they were becoming exposed.

Speculation

The trend towards securitisation tended to spread through the financial system, building into a sort of speculative bubble, in which increasing numbers of financial institutions sought to join the profit spree in anticipation of future profitability. The problem with such bubbles is that once they burst, all suffer together, and problems spread rapidly through the system. There have also been claims that there was market rigging going on in the early years of the crisis, with some market traders taking deliberate actions to destabilise the system.

Moral hazard

The banks perceived that securitisation was enabling them to have their risks well covered, and were thus prepared to expand their lending beyond what turned out to be reasonable. In other words, the banks thought that they could take on more risk because they were confident that their position was secure. They may even have realised that their position in financial markets meant that if anything did go wrong, they would be bailed out by governments who perceived them to be too big to fail — which, of course, is exactly what transpired.

Externality effects

Once one bank is seen to be failing, the reputation of the whole banking system comes into question, and other banks initially unaffected also come under pressure through externality effects. In this way, contagion can affect the whole financial system and cause lines of credit to dry up as banks become increasingly unwilling to become further exposed by lending.

The next chapter explores the role of the central bank, and the way that the Bank of England and other central banks tackled the crisis.

Summary

- Financial institutions provide the key link between borrowers and lenders.
- The banking sector covers retail and wholesale banking, but the distinction has become blurred over time.
- Banks aim to make profits, and face a trade-off between making loans and retaining sufficient liquidity to service their customers.
- Short-term liquidity requirements are managed through the interbank market.
- Borrowing takes a variety of forms.
- Interest rates payable on loans reflect risk and security.
- New financial instruments developed in recent decades through securitisation have increased the importance of the secondary market.
- Some banks found themselves in difficulties for a variety of reasons.

Exercise 13.5

Discuss what effect the rise of internet banking would have on the financial system.

The financial sector in emerging and developing countries

Less developed countries face particular problems in relation to the financial sector. Formal financial institutions are less well equipped to provide financial services, as was discussed in Chapter 12. Stock markets may not exist, or may not function effectively. The provision of banking services to rural areas is fraught with difficulties. The banks are not readily able to assess the credit-worthiness of potential borrowers. There is a situation of asymmetric information here, as the borrowers have much better information about the riskiness of proposed projects than the banks can obtain, so are likely to be charged high interest rates. Property rights may be weak, so that borrowers cannot provide collateral that the banks would accept. This forces borrowers into the informal market, where local moneylenders have monopoly power, and can charge exorbitant rates of interest.

The Harrod–Domar approach suggests that saving and investment are crucial ingredients for a strategy to promote economic growth and human development. If funds cannot be raised domestically, then an injection of funds from abroad will be necessary, in the form of foreign direct investment, overseas assistance or borrowing on international financial markets.

Whichever approach is adopted, the financial sector is vital as a way of channelling the resources to where they are needed. This needs to be accomplished in a way that addresses areas of market failure. Rural credit markets may need specific attention, but funds also need to be provided for improvements in physical and social infrastructure that will then enable markets to operate effectively. In other words, funds are needed for road and communication links, market facilities and so on. In addition, it is important to be able to invest in human capital, by providing education and healthcare and ensuring adequate nutrition for the population.

All this is challenging for LDCs with limited resources. Where the financial sector has been able to work effectively, countries have been able to show progress on many fronts. This has been evident in the emerging economies. The economies that entered a period of rapid growth in the 1960s found ways of mobilising funds. For example, both Korea and Singapore laid the foundations for rapid growth by finding ways of encouraging saving, the funds from which were then channelled into productive investment and infrastructure. More recently, China's success in mobilising foreign direct investment has been one of the key factors enabling growth.

In sub-Saharan Africa, economic growth has been more elusive. Financial markets have not developed to the same extent as in East Asia, nor have stock markets flourished. Such funds as have been generated — for example, through overseas assistance or international borrowing — have not always been used effectively.

Some progress has also been made in the financial sector, from what may be a surprising source. The use of mobile phones has expanded in many African countries. This has given people in rural areas access to market information, so that they can make better judgements about what is a fair price for their produce. Mobile phone technology has also provided a way of handling transactions previously denied because of lack of access to the formal financial sector. This is in spite of the fact that relatively few people may own their own mobile phones. Entrepreneurs in some villages make a living from renting out their mobile phones or undertaking transactions.

However, to what extent is the relative performance of emerging and less developed countries due to differences in the performance of the financial sector? The emerging economies had other factors working in their favour. The East Asian economies that developed in the 1960s and 1970s all had good social infrastructure to begin with, in the form of education and healthcare sectors that provided the foundations for developing human resources. They also developed in a period that favoured world trade, and when some of the advanced economies were moving towards a service orientation, leaving gaps for newly industrialising nations to fill. In the later wave, China had vast resources and a plentiful supply of labour to be mobilised. It was also able to channel funds into investment and maintain the competitiveness of its exports.

On this basis, the evidence seems to suggest that an effective financial sector is a necessary condition for economic growth and human development to take place, as it enables funds to be channelled to where they are needed. However, this may not be a sufficient condition to guarantee that success will be achieved.

Mobile phones give people in rural areas access to market information

Exercise 13.6

Discuss the importance of the financial sector for economic growth and human development in developing and emerging economies.

Summary

- The financial sector is important for developing and emerging economies to enable funds to be channelled into productive investment.
- Financial markets in such countries are characterised by various forms of market failure.
- The emerging economies have been able to mobilise funds, in contrast to many countries in regions such as sub-Saharan Africa.

Case study 13.1

The history of insurance

Modern insurers charge a premium in exchange for a promise to pay out a larger sum of money if necessary. A risk-averse person will often prefer to pay a small sum today instead of incurring a larger cost later on. Some types of insurance are even mandatory by law. For example, car owners have to buy the basic type of insurance. They are not obliged to buy fully comprehensive insurance. Some choose not to, or 'self-insure'. They undertake to cover certain costs themselves. Most people have insurance even if they also self-insure for some risks. The insurance industry is now an important part of all developed economies.

The basic idea behind an insurance scheme is the pooling of risk. If a number of individuals enter the scheme, then hopefully only a few of them will need to make a claim. As long as the payments into the scheme cover the claims, then the scheme is viable in the long run. The idea of pooling risks

predates private insurers. Many early communities used some form of co-operation (or social insurance) to deal with risks. There was always the possibility that an individual would become unable to work and fall into poverty. There were social and religious reasons to give charity to these people, but there was no guarantee.

The Poor Laws

Under the Elizabethan Poor Laws, communities were obliged to help poor people who were too infirm to support themselves. Taxes were used to raise funds. The Poor Laws required poor people to claim help in the community which they came from. There were good reasons for this, which are also important for private insurance. In a small community, people knew each other very well. They knew who had worked hard and followed social rules, such as attending church. They also knew who had not behaved themselves. Frequently, communities wanted to support only those who followed their rules. Traditionally, these people were called 'the deserving poor'. Other people, who broke social rules, might not be helped. The Poor Laws therefore forced paupers to go to the place where they were known. If they could go anywhere, then liars might claim relief that they were not entitled to. This problem is called an *asymmetry of information*. It means that one party has private information that others do not have. Elizabethan law-makers did not want lazy or deceitful people to exploit others.

Insurers also face the problem of *moral hazard*. This means that after someone has gained insurance, they have an incentive to change their behaviour and take less care. Early social insurance schemes, such as the Poor Laws, took moral hazard problems very seriously. Lawmakers worried that people would not be motivated to avoid poverty if they thought they could claim handouts. Society would be less productive as a result. Strict rules were used to prove that paupers were not merely lazy. If they could work in any way, they were forced to do so or they were not given anything. Payments were kept at a very low level. There was also a social stigma to receiving handouts. These factors helped to minimise the claims on the community.

The shipping industry

The Poor Laws only dealt with the very poorest. Most people had to self-insure. They built up as much wealth as possible and also relied on their relatives to provide for them in old age. Self-insurance was not as easy for merchants, especially those who operated on a large scale. For example, a shipwreck meant the loss of an entire cargo. If a merchant put his entire capital into that one cargo, he was running an enormous risk. But he could spread the risk by sending the cargo by several different ships. Each ship would carry the cargoes of several different merchants. The next step was the development of underwriting. Specialist brokers would offer insurance contracts on ships in exchange for a fee. The marine insurance sector developed well before other types of insurance. One of the most famous insurers, Lloyds of London, initially started as a group of marine underwriters based at the Lloyds coffeehouse in the City of London.

Over time, underwriters began to gather a great deal of information about the shipping industry. They could then assess the risks involved and charge premiums accordingly. Insurers had to worry about going bankrupt if they could not cover all the claims. However, competitive pressures pushed premiums downwards. The problem of setting the right premiums reappeared with the development of both fire and life insurance. Insurers lacked detailed data about the risks of fire or mortality. Without sufficient information, the early firms had trouble estimating the sums needed to cover their claims. In addition, early schemes used a variety of different financial structures. Initially, they did not even charge different premiums to different customers.

The Lloyds of London building in the City of London

Fire insurers

A number of fire insurance schemes were created after the Great Fire of London of 1666. During the massive rebuilding programme, great efforts were made to use stone and other fireproof materials instead of wood. The risks of fire were reduced and fire insurance schemes became more viable. It was not clear whether the government, a monopolist or several private firms should control fire insurance. In the end, a variety of firms competed for customers. Several of the early schemes were mutual funds. In this business model, the insured parties would agree to cover all legitimate claims made. The amount they were charged depended on the total sum of the claims in any one time period, plus running costs. The firm could always call on its members to provide more funds. This was not the case with firms which charged premiums. The premium was fixed in any one time period, even if the firm had to settle large claims. Early firms often set the premium rates far too low. They then found that their outgoings were larger than forecast. The earliest schemes went bust.

The fire insurers tended to restrict their activities to London. They found it very difficult to assess risks outside of the capital because they had less information about provincial areas. Life insurers also had difficulties in judging risks. They had to contend with other problems. Their critics sometimes argued that life insurance was immoral and encouraged gambling. These criticisms might seem surprising today, but there was a link between life insurance and betting. Some people placed bets upon events such as the outcome of a war, or whether the king would die that year.

It was not only the famous who might be insured. People could insure their servants, neighbours or even complete strangers. Many contracts were not an attempt to reduce risks, but to gamble. People were speculating upon how long their acquaintances might live and hoping to benefit from guessing correctly. Life insurance faces the same problems that plague other types of insurance: asymmetric information, adverse selection and moral hazard. Insurers found that many of the people covered by their policies were in worse health than had been expected. Secondly, many worried that after insurance had been issued there was an incentive to kill the insured party. Certainly, there have been plenty of cases of murderers insuring their victims in advance (an example of adverse selection). For example, in the early twentieth century there were the 'Brides in the Bath' murders. George Smith was convicted of murdering three of his wives and claiming on their life insurance policies. Fire insurers also face fraud by deliberate acts of arson. A less dramatic example of moral hazard is the householder who takes less care of the insured property than before. Companies deal with moral hazard by putting clauses into their contracts forcing people to take due care. Otherwise, the contract is void.

Today, insurers charge different premiums to different individuals. However, some early schemes charged the same fee to all. If a single premium is charged then it must be high enough to cover the average claim per person. This is likely to be too high for some who are in good health. They will self-insure. Then too high a proportion of clients will be bad risks (unhealthy) and the scheme may be bankrupted.

Adapted from Helen Paul, 'Insurance: A History', *Economic Review*, September 2010

Follow-up questions

a Explain the meaning of *asymmetric information*, *adverse selection* and *moral hazard*, and why these are examples of market failure.

b Discuss how modern insurance companies address these issues.

14 The role of the central bank

This chapter explores the role of the central bank in the financial system, looking at the functions of the central bank, and the measures it has available to carry out those functions. Of particular importance are the provision of liquidity to the banking system and the role of an independent central bank in meeting targets set by the government. The need for regulation is examined, and the way in which changes in the regulatory framework may have contributed to the financial crisis and its resolution.

Prior knowledge needed

Notice that this chapter builds upon material presented in earlier chapters. In particular, you will need to be familiar with the instruments and operation of monetary policy, which were introduced in Book 1, Chapter 16.

Learning objectives

After studying this chapter, you should:
→ be familiar with the core functions of the central bank
→ be aware of the operations of the Bank of England and their significance
→ be able to explain the rationale for inflation targeting and an independent central bank
→ be familiar with the way in which interest rates can be influenced through open market operations in normal periods
→ appreciate the factors that contributed to the financial crisis that began in the late 2000s
→ understand quantitative easing and why it was necessary to introduce it
→ be able to explain the need for financial regulation
→ be familiar with the way in which financial regulation is administered by the Bank of England
→ be aware of the roles of the BIS, IMF and World Bank in coordinating global financial policies

The functions of the central bank

Key term

central bank the banker to the government, performing a range of functions, which may include issue of coins and banknotes, acting as banker to commercial banks and regulating the financial system

All developed and most developing countries have a **central bank** that fulfils a range of roles, including having the responsibility for issuing currency (banknotes and coins). For example, the UK has the Bank of England to act as the country's central bank. Being the body responsible for issuing notes and coins, the central bank has a direct impact on the quantity of money in circulation in the country. However, this does not mean that it has complete control over the total stock of money, as has been explained in earlier chapters.

The central bank has other important roles to fulfil. The central bank acts as banker to the government, and may manage the government's programme of borrowing and the country's foreign exchange reserves. Furthermore, the central bank may act as a banker for the commercial banks and other financial institutions that operate in the economy. In addition, the central bank may act as the regulator of the financial system, monitoring the behaviour of the commercial banks and financial institutions. In some countries, the central bank has independent authority delegated from the government to pursue targets for inflation through the setting of interest rates or to promote growth and development. However, not all central banks perform all of these various functions.

The central bank in the UK is the Bank of England

The Bank of England operates in sterling money markets — known as the Sterling Monetary Framework (SMF). The Bank's responsibilities include ensuring an adequate supply of liquidity to the SMF participants — that is, the banks and other financial institutions that operate in sterling money markets.

In less developed countries, the central bank may have an important role in establishing and consolidating the domestic financial system in order to build confidence in the currency and financial institutions. It is worth being aware that in parts of sub-Saharan Africa less than 20% of households have an account with a financial institution. This is not only because of the lack of bank branches (although this is clearly important), but is partly due to a lack of confidence in financial institutions. There may also be a developmental role in ensuring that credit can be made available for key development priorities.

In some cases, the central bank may be given responsibility for roles that support other objectives of the government. An example here would be the State Bank of Pakistan, which also has a responsibility for the 'Islamisation' of the banking system, to recognise the importance to the country of developing Islamic forms of financial instrument.

Extension material

Islamic banking

The key difference between banking as it is known in western countries and Islamic banking is that Islam prohibits the use of interest (or usury, as it is known). This means that Islamic banks cannot charge interest on loans or pay interest on savings. Gambling is also prohibited.

A variety of financial instruments have been developed to allow banks to lend to firms or to households without charging interest. For example, a bank may agree a profit-sharing deal with a firm. The bank lends to the firm and then shares in the profits of the project. An alternative is a cost-plus-margin agreement. The bank purchases a given property at an agreed price, and immediately sells it to the buyer, stating the cost plus profit margin. The property is then treated as a commodity sold for money rather than an interest-based loan. The client pays in agreed termly instalments.

The core activities of the Bank of England, the UK's central bank, include acting as banker to the government and financial institutions, managing the country's exchange reserves and supply of currency, and regulating the financial system. These have strong implications for the supply of money and credit in the economy.

Issuing notes and coin

The issuing of notes and coin has long been a core function of the Bank of England, although it does not have a monopoly in the UK (only in England and Wales). Commercial banks in Scotland and Northern Ireland can also issue banknotes, but the issue is regulated by the Bank of England. It is still important to control the issue of banknotes in order to make sure that demands are met without leading to inflation. However, issuing notes and coin does not mean having control of the money supply because of the wide variety of other financial assets that are near-money.

Banker to the government

The Bank of England acts as banker to the government, in the sense that tax revenues and items of government expenditure are handled by the Bank, as are items of government borrowing and lending. In the past, the Bank of England also had responsibility for managing government debt by issuing Treasury bills, but this was transferred to the Debt Management Office (an executive office within the Treasury) when the Bank was given independence to control the interest rate in order to meet the inflation target.

Banker to the commercial banks

The commercial banks and other SMF participants hold deposits at the Bank of England in the form of reserve balances and cash ratio deposits. The reserve balances are used as a stock of liquid assets, but also fulfil a clearing role, in the sense that they are used to equalise any imbalance in transactions between the major banks on a day-by-day basis. In normal times, the Bank agrees an average level of overnight reserves that SMF participants expect to require in the month ahead. If any institution holds reserves out of their agreed range, this attracts a charge. In other words, if a bank needs to borrow beyond its agreed average reserve level, it must pay a rate that is above the bank rate. Deposits above the agreed average are remunerated below bank rate. This encourages institutions to meet their requirements in the interbank market, which helps to keep the interbank rate close to the bank rate.

Managing the exchange rate

The Bank of England manages the UK's gold and foreign currency reserves on behalf of the Treasury. However, interventions have been rare in recent years, with the pound being allowed to find its own level in the foreign exchange market.

Monetary and financial stability

Apart from the functions outlined, the Bank's main mission is 'to promote the good of the people of the United Kingdom by maintaining monetary and financial stability'. **Monetary stability** is interpreted in terms of stability in prices (relative to the government's inflation target). **Financial stability** means an efficient flow of funds in the economy and confidence in UK financial institutions.

Key terms

monetary stability
a situation in which there is stability in prices relative to the government's inflation target

financial stability
a situation in which there is a sufficient and efficient flow of liquidity in the economy

The efficient flow of funds requires that there is sufficient liquidity in the economy. In other words, there must be enough liquidity for the financial institutions to conduct their business. The traditional way in which this was done was by the Bank of England acting as the **lender of last resort**, being prepared to lend to banks if they could not obtain the funds that they needed elsewhere, albeit at a penalty rate. Although this was traditionally seen as a key role, events during the financial crisis made it untenable.

Inflation targeting

In 1997 a significant change in the conduct of monetary policy was introduced by the incoming Labour administration. The Bank of England was given independent responsibility to set interest rates in order to achieve the stated inflation target set by the government. This represented a major change by taking discretion for monetary policy away from the government. An important motivation for this change was to increase the credibility of government policy, in the sense that it could no longer try to use short-run policy measures to create a 'feel-good' factor in the economy. Instead, it was declaring a pre-commitment to controlling inflation, which it hoped would improve expectations about the future course of the macroeconomy.

The **Monetary Policy Committee (MPC)** of the Bank of England has as its primary responsibility the maintenance of monetary stability by meeting the inflation target. However, it also has as a secondary responsibility, as meeting the target for inflation is subject to supporting the economic policy of the government, including the objectives for economic growth and employment. In other words, the MPC cannot pursue the inflation target if this excessively endangers growth or employment.

The challenge of the period of inflation targeting has thus been to balance the needs of monetary stability (meeting the inflation target) with ensuring financial stability (by ensuring the efficient and adequate provision of liquidity).

The advantage of having an independent central bank to pursue the inflation target is to reinforce the credibility of the government's commitment to monetary stability, but the danger is that this could be pursued at the expense of the government's target for economic growth.

Summary

- The central bank of a country fulfils a number of important roles within the financial system to create monetary and financial stability.
- The central bank takes responsibility for issuing notes and coins — or at least for controlling the quantity in circulation.
- It may act as banker to the government and to other financial institutions.
- It also has a role in regulating the foreign exchange market.
- It may manage the government's debt position.
- In some countries, the central bank has been given independent responsibility for meeting a government target — for example, the Bank of England has responsibility for meeting the inflation target.

Key terms

lender of last resort the role of the central bank in guaranteeing sufficient liquidity is available in the monetary system

Monetary Policy Committee (MPC) the body within the Bank of England responsible for the conduct of monetary policy

Study tip

Make sure that you are familiar with the way in which a change in bank rate eventually feeds through to affect aggregate demand and the rate of inflation. This was explained in Book 1, Chapter 16.

Exercise 14.1

Discuss the advantages and disadvantages of having an independent central bank dedicated to meeting an inflation target.

Policy measures available to the Bank of England

There have been significant changes to the operations of the Bank of England in response to the introduction of inflation targeting and the financial crisis that began in the late 2000s. The crisis highlighted the need for closer monitoring of the financial system in order to ensure financial stability.

The pre-crisis period, 1997–2007

In 1997, the incoming Labour government delegated to the Bank of England the responsibility for meeting its inflation target. Specifically, the Bank was to keep inflation within 1 percentage point of the target, which was initially set at 2.5%, as measured by the retail price index (RPI). From January 2004, the target was reset in terms of the consumer price index (CPI), with its rate of change falling within 1 percentage point of 2%. The performance relative to the target from 1997 to 2007 is shown in Figure 14.1.

In the pre-crisis period, the Bank targeted inflation by using the interest rate. As was explained in Chapter 13, there are many different interest rates on financial assets, varying with the degree of risk associated with the asset, the length of loans and so on. However, they are interconnected, so the Bank can influence the rates of interest by changing the rate that it charges on short-term loans to domestic banks. This is known as **bank rate**. You can see how this moved around in Figure 14.1. These changes in bank rate affect the interest rates on other financial assets.

Key terms

bank rate the rate of interest charged by the Bank of England on short-term loans to other banks

open market operations intervention by the central bank to influence short-run interest rates by buying or selling securities

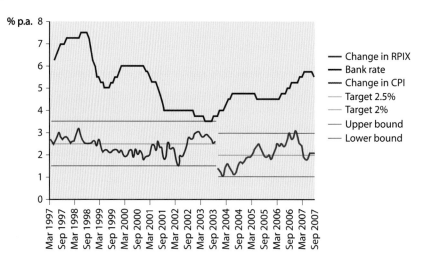

Figure 14.1 UK interest rates and the inflation target, 1997–2007

Sources: ONS, Bank of England

Rates of interest also move around in response to market conditions, and the Bank of England can intervene to make sure that short-run interest rates are kept in line with bank rate. It does this by using **open market operations**, buying or selling securities in order to influence short-run interest rates.

Suppose there is a shortage of liquidity in the financial system. Financial institutions will need to borrow in order to improve their liquidity position. This puts upward pressure on interest rates, so there is a danger that interest rates will move out of line with bank rate. The Bank of England can intervene to prevent this, providing liquidity in the system by buying securities (Treasury bills or gilts) in the open market. Conversely, if there is excess liquidity in the system, interest rates may tend to fall, and the Bank can prevent this by selling securities in the open market.

This was a period in which policy appeared to be working effectively. Inflation remained within the specified one percentage point of its target, apart from one month when it rose to 3.1% (March 2007). Economic growth was steady during this period, and there were no obvious problems with liquidity. This period is sometimes known as the 'Great Moderation'.

Monetary policy from 2008

This period of stability was not to last. Figure 14.2 shows bank rate and inflation (measured by the percentage change in the CPI) from the beginning of 2008. You can see that the pattern is very different from that in the period 1997–2007. Inflation moved out of its target range, and bank rate plummeted to an all-time low.

During 2008, inflation accelerated. This partly reflected increases in food and commodity prices world-wide. The Monetary Policy Committee took the view that this acceleration would not persist. Economic growth was expected to slow, and inflation was expected to move back below 2% per annum. Rather than increasing bank rate in order to put downward pressure on aggregate demand and inflation, the MPC reduced bank rate in August in anticipation of falling growth and inflation. In the following months, the financial crisis began to unfold.

Exercise 14.2

Suppose there is excessive liquidity in the economy. Explain how open market operations would be used to deal with the situation.

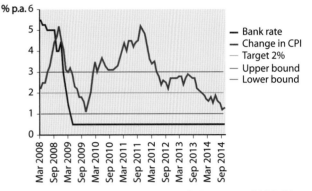
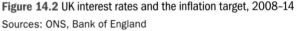

Figure 14.2 UK interest rates and the inflation target, 2008-14
Sources: ONS, Bank of England

Even in 2007, it was becoming clear that a number of banks were facing difficulties, having expanded their borrowing substantially relative to their capital base. The response was to reduce lending, sell assets and look for new capital. Borrowing against property was one of the root causes, as the expectation that house prices would continue to rise had encouraged mortgage lending. When house prices in the USA stalled in 2005/06, defaults began to rise, putting pressure on lenders. The failure of some institutions prompted fears of recession, and one of the side-effects of globalisation was that financial markets were interconnected across national boundaries.

A problem with bank failures is the effect they have on confidence in the financial system. As the crisis developed, it was perceived that some of the banks that were in danger were 'too large' to be allowed to fail. The demise of a large financial institution would have such an effect on expectations that the whole financial system might be called into question. Hence the moves by the UK and other governments to bail out banks that were in difficulties, in spite of the effect that this had on public finances, as shown in Figure 14.3.

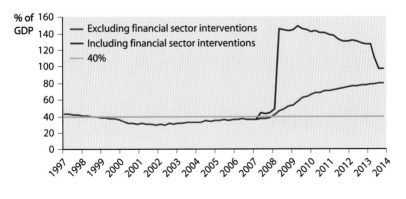

Figure 14.3 Public sector net debt as a percentage of GDP, 1997–2014
Source: ONS

In the UK, the crisis showed up in the interbank market, where a shortage of liquidity put upward pressure on the interbank rate. By March 2009, bank rate had been reduced to 0.5%, and could not feasibly be taken any lower. The Bank of England suspended the reserves averaging regime at this point in time, as it could no longer be effective. Instead, it introduced **quantitative easing**, a policy under which it created central bank reserves, which were used to purchase high-quality financial assets in order to provide additional liquidity. This was financed by creating electronic money, and allowed the Bank to continue to influence credit and interest rates.

Notice that the sudden fall in the public sector net debt (including financial sector interventions) in 2014 resulted from the reclassification of Lloyds Banking Group from the public to the private sector, following sales by the UK government of part of its share holdings in the group.

Quantitative easing is essentially a way of increasing money supply. The foundations for this had been set in January 2009 by establishing the Asset Purchase Facility (APF), a subsidiary company of the Bank of England that carries out the necessary transactions. By the end of 2014, the APF had purchased £375 billion of assets by the creation of central bank reserves. The level of quantitative easing is decided by the MPC as a joint decision with that on bank rate.

The problem faced by the Bank in this situation was that the rate of inflation had to be kept under control, but at the same time, the reluctance of banks to lend would affect investment and the growth of the real economy, which was heading into recession. Expectations were weak, threatening to prolong the recession. The UK was not alone in facing this combination of circumstances, and other central banks were adopting similar strategies to deal with the growing crisis.

Figure 14.4 shows the extent to which some other countries were following a common path for economic growth. Having badged the financial turmoil as being the worst since the 1930s, governments were anxious to avoid a repetition of the mass unemployment that had happened then. This was avoided, but you can see in the figure that the recovery was not rapid. It is difficult to disentangle the extent to which the recovery was a consequence of the policy stance adopted by the government and the Bank of England.

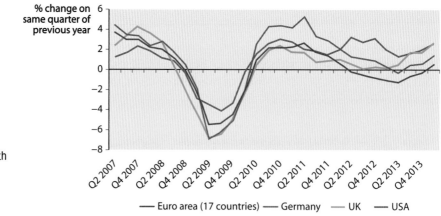

Figure 14.4 Annual growth rate of GDP, 2007-13 (quarterly data)

Source: OECD

Financial regulation

A commonly held view was that one of the key factors leading to the crisis had been the inadequate regulation of financial institutions, which had allowed banks to build up portfolios of lending that carried risk beyond what could be covered by their capital. One way of viewing this is that, although central banks such as the Bank of England had structures to enable them to achieve monetary stability, the regulatory framework had not allowed the same degree of control over financial stability.

A new regulatory framework came into operation in April 2013 to try to remedy this situation, and to avoid repetition of the financial crisis in the future. Two new statutory decision-making bodies were created that are part of the Bank of England. The **Prudential Regulation Authority (PRA)** is responsible for **microprudential regulation**, working at the level of the individual firm to promote the safeness and soundness of deposit-takers, insurers and major investment firms. The **Financial Policy Committee (FPC)** became responsible for **macroprudential regulation**:

> *responsible for identifying, monitoring and taking action to remove or reduce systemic risks with a view to protecting and enhancing the resilience of the UK financial system. And, subject to that, supporting the economic policy of the Government, including its objectives for growth and employment.*
>
> 'Changes to the Bank of England', *Bank of England Quarterly Bulletin*, 2013 Q1

In addition, the **Financial Conduct Authority (FCA)** has been given responsibility for ensuring that relevant markets function well, and has responsibility for financial services firms that are not supervised by the PRA, including asset managers, hedge funds, many broker-dealers and independent financial advisers.

The intention of these arrangements is to improve the resilience and stability of the financial system by filling a perceived regulatory gap that had allowed the seeds of the crisis to develop. The USA and other countries in the EU have also established new bodies to perform similar tasks. This is crucial given the interconnectedness of financial markets following globalisation.

Notice that the FPC has primary responsibility for financial stability, but (like the MPC) it also has secondary responsibility for supporting the government's economic policy. This means that it must keep a balance between taking steps to stabilise the financial system and facilitating economic growth and employment.

The FPC has the power to make recommendations. For example, it can make recommendations to the PRA and FCA to take action to safeguard financial stability. The PRA and FCA need to comply, or to explain why this is not seen to be appropriate. The FPC can use the *countercyclical capital buffer*, under which banks, building societies and large investment firms can be required to hold additional loss-absorbing capital. The FPC can also impose *sectoral capital requirements*, under which firms need to meet additional capital requirements where the FPC perceives a risk to the stability of the financial system as a whole. A further power held by the FPC concerns the scope of regulation, in that it can recommend changes to the boundary between regulated and non-regulated activities.

The aim of these measures is to reduce the likelihood of future financial crises by monitoring activity more closely and having early warning of where problems may be building up. The FPC and PRA between them can then take action to mitigate the risks of a crisis. Given the impact of globalisation, it is recognised that there is a need for international coordination of financial regulation. This is discussed shortly.

Evaluation

The financial crisis highlighted the importance of the financial system for the real economy. Monetary stability is important because low and predictable inflation helps economic agents to form expectations about the future. This encourages firms to

Key terms

Prudential Regulation Authority (PRA) the decision-making body in the Bank of England responsible for microprudential regulation of deposit-takers, insurers and major investment firms

microprudential regulation financial regulation intended to set standards and supervise financial institutions at the level of the individual firm

Financial Policy Committee (FPC) the decision-making body of the Bank of England responsible for macroprudential regulation

macroprudential regulation financial regulation intended to mitigate the risk of the financial system as a whole

Financial Conduct Authority (FCA) a body separate from the Bank of England responsible for conduct regulation of financial services firms

invest and allows households to plan their consumption. This in turn can promote economic growth and improvements in the standard of living. However, the crisis demonstrated that financial stability is also crucial, as this enables the flow of funds needed for firms to finance their investment.

The period before the crisis was characterised by monetary stability, with the inflation target being met, and economic growth proceeding at a steady rate. However, the inadequacy of regulation led to a build-up of pressure which finally erupted in financial instability. This disrupted the financial system and had spillover effects for the real economy, resulting in recession and rising unemployment.

The main manifestations of this were in the failure of liquidity. The interbank market was unable to deliver the liquidity that was needed, and the Bank of England's role as lender of last resort could not be sustained with bank rate at 0.5%. In this situation, the Bank resorted to expansion of the money supply through the process of quantitative easing to supply liquidity whilst still keeping inflation within its target range.

The need for financial stability was tackled by the creation of new decision-making bodies with the responsibility for maintaining financial stability through enhanced regulation of the financial system and by monitoring developments in financial markets.

In seeking to maintain its primary objectives of both monetary and financial stability, the Bank needs also to maintain balance with its secondary objective of supporting the government's overall macroeconomic policy stance. This is no mean feat when the need to bail out failing banks has left a legacy of high public debt.

> **Summary**
>
> - There have been significant changes to the operations of the Bank of England since the financial crisis.
> - The Bank had been given independent responsibility for the conduct of monetary policy in 1997 with a brief to meet the government's inflation target.
> - This was to be accomplished through the Monetary Policy Committee (MPC) setting bank rate.
> - By setting bank rate, the rates of interest in other segments of the money market would also be affected.
> - Open market operations were used to keep short-term interest rates in line with bank rate.
> - In the financial crisis, banks faced shortages of liquidity and the interbank market could not cope.
> - With bank rate at the lowest level that could be sustained, quantitative easing was introduced to supply liquidity to the financial sector.
> - The crisis highlighted the need for greater regulation to maintain financial stability.

The international context

Along with globalisation has come the need to provide coordination of financial markets across countries. Deregulation increased the interconnectedness of financial markets, and the runaway advances in technology and the internet allowed financial transactions to take place smoothly and instantaneously. This improved the efficiency with which markets could operate, but also heightened the possibility for contagion — in other words, it increased the probability that crises could spread rapidly between countries.

> **Study tip**
>
> Be clear in your mind about the distinction between monetary stability (low and predictable inflation) and financial stability (the efficient flow of liquidity). You should also be aware of the primary and secondary objectives of the Bank of England in terms of both monetary and financial stability.

There are three key organisations that contribute to international coordination of financial markets and regulation: the Bank for International Settlements (BIS), the International Monetary Fund (IMF) and the World Bank. Each fulfils a specific function in the global financial system. The BIS was established in 1930 and acts as a banker to central banks. It has also played a key role in financial regulation by brokering international agreements.

At the end of the Second World War in 1945, a conference was held at Bretton Woods, New Hampshire, USA, to establish a system of fixed exchange rates. This became known as the Dollar Standard, as countries agreed to fix their currencies relative to the US dollar. John Maynard Keynes was an influential delegate at the conference. In addition to establishing the exchange rate system that operated until the early 1970s, the conference set up the IMF and World Bank to help to oversee aspects of the international financial system. A third organisation took responsibility for the conduct of international trade. This was the General Agreement on Tariffs and Trade, which was the precursor of the World Trade Organization. The WTO was discussed in Chapter 7.

The Bank for International Settlements

The **Bank for International Settlements (BIS)** was originally set up in 1930 to settle the then-controversial issue of the reparation payments imposed on Germany at the end of the First World War. The onset of the Great Depression changed the focus, which switched to activities involving technical cooperation between central banks. The Bretton Woods conference called for the abolition of the BIS on the grounds that it would be rendered redundant by the IMF and World Bank. However, instead it refocused on European monetary and financial issues, becoming a forum for European monetary cooperation.

After the collapse of the Dollar Standard in the early 1970s, the need for international cooperation in the operation of financial markets became apparent, and in 1982 G10 central bankers created the Basel Committee on Banking Supervision, which was to play a key role in financial regulation. The debt crisis that affected a number of Latin American countries in the early 1980s highlighted the need to have measures in place to provide regulation and avoid the possibility of sovereign default (that is, where nations fail to meet their obligations in international debt).

The Basel Committee established a credit risk measurement framework that became a globally accepted standard. This has since been refined, the latest agreement being the Basel III agreement, which specifies internationally agreed capital adequacy requirements for banks. These are administered by central banks, so in the UK these Basel III capital requirements are built into the Bank of England's regulatory framework. The requirements, which are being phased in, are due to be complete by 2019. This gradual phasing in of the new regulations is intended to avoid slowing the recovery.

In this way, it is hoped that the likelihood of financial instability spreading across countries will be reduced, as central banks will be imposing similar regulation on their respective financial systems.

The International Monetary Fund

The International Monetary Fund (IMF) was set up with a specific brief to offer short-term assistance to countries experiencing balance of payments problems. Thus, if a country was running a deficit on the current account, it could borrow

> **Key term**
>
> **Bank for International Settlements (BIS)** an institution that acts as a bank for central banks and sets standards for regulation of banks that are accepted globally

Christine Lagarde, managing director of the IMF, speaking in 2014

from the IMF in order to finance the deficit. However, the IMF would insist that, as a condition of granting the loan, the country put in place policies to deal with the deficit — typically, restrictive monetary and fiscal policies.

This role was especially important during the period of the Dollar Standard, when countries were agreeing to fix their exchange rates relative to the US dollar. Loans from the IMF could be used to avoid having to go through a devaluation of a currency. The transition to floating exchange rates in the early 1970s was significant in altering the role of the IMF. However, the IMF was still called upon to help countries to support their currencies — for example, Iceland took an IMF loan in 2008 to stabilise the krona.

In the world of the twenty-first century, the IMF continues to play an important role in maintaining the stability of the interconnected global financial system. In particular, it has provided loans to prevent sovereign default. An example is the loan provided to Greece in 2010 (which is discussed in Case study 14.1 at the end of this chapter). The IMF has also provided loans to governments needing to bail out private banks that had become insolvent because of exposure to risky loans. Recent examples include loans to the governments of Ireland, Latvia and Hungary.

The World Bank

The International Bank for Reconstruction and Development was the second institution established under the Bretton Woods agreement and soon became known as the World Bank. The role of the World Bank is to provide longer-term funding for projects that will promote development. Much of this funding is provided at commercial interest rates, as the role of the bank was seen to be the channelling of finance to projects that normal commercial banks would perceive as being too risky. However, some concessional lending is also made through the International Development Association (IDA), which is part of the World Bank.

The role of the World Bank is especially important for less developed countries (LDCs), where internal financial markets are undeveloped or dysfunctional. The World Bank has a presence in most LDCs, being involved a variety of projects to promote development and alleviate poverty. It has also undertaken research into ways of improving access to finance for people and firms in LDCs. Access to finance can be a substantial impediment for firms in LDCs wanting to expand, and for households in need of small loans to improve their income-earning potential. This was discussed in Chapter 12.

Evaluation

Globalisation has increased the interdependence of countries. This allows people around the world to share in economic success and gain mutual advantage through trade. However, it also allows financial crisis to spread more rapidly, and there is a need for international cooperation in regulating financial markets to reduce the likelihood of financial problems occurring.

The BIS, IMF and World Bank have contributed by providing a global framework within which financial markets can be coordinated, and common regulations agreed. However, this has not been enough to prevent crises from occurring, such as the Asian financial crisis of 1997 and the global credit crunch of the late 2000s. In earlier years, the debt crisis of the 1980s gave warning that serious problems could occur when markets are not carefully monitored.

At the time of the 1980s debt crises, there was much criticism that the steps taken in response, such as the rescheduling of the debt of LDCs, were designed to safeguard the global financial system, but not designed to provide a permanent remedy to LDC debt. It was only with the HIPC Initiative that the World Bank agreed to allow debt forgiveness for LDCs — and even then under strict conditions. Failure to deal with the debt problem may have impeded the development of countries, especially in sub-Saharan Africa, where debt was putting such a strain on resources. It is encouraging that some progress has now been made towards promoting growth and development in LDCs, and that measures are now being put in place to improve the stability of the global financial system in the future.

Summary

- The process of globalisation has brought with it the need to coordinate the regulation and operation of financial markets around the world.
- The financial crisis of the late 2000s showed how rapidly a crisis could spread through global markets.
- Three organisations contribute to international coordination in financial markets.
- The Bank for International Settlements has produced standards for the conduct of financial markets that are accepted internationally.
- The IMF has moved on from its traditional role in providing loans for balance of payments purposes, and has made loans to prevent sovereign default. The World Bank provides funds for key projects to promote human and economic development in less developed countries.

The bailout of Greece in 2010

In May 2010 the EU and the IMF announced a €110 billion bailout loan for Greece. Traditionally, the IMF made loans to help a country to overcome a balance of payments problem or to stabilise its currency. But does that apply to this example?

In this case there was only one reason for the IMF to lend money to Greece and that was to prevent a Greek sovereign default. Prior to the credit crunch, highly indebted governments could borrow cheaply. Governments such as the one in Greece took advantage of low borrowing costs by using debt to finance better public services. The recession that followed the crash of 2008 dented confidence. This led to an increase in the cost of borrowing. In Greece, the government debt servicing costs climbed, which created an even bigger fiscal deficit. The government was in a debt spiral, and a Greek sovereign default seemed imminent.

So, this was not a bailout for the people of Greece. Ordinary Greeks did not receive their share of the loan to blow recklessly on imported German BMWs. Instead, the money borrowed was used by the Greek government to pay its bondholders. These bondholders were French and German banks. According to research carried out by the Bank for International Settlements at the end of 2010, 96% of Greek government bonds were held by European banks. German banks alone held €22.7 billion of Greek debt. The Greek 'rescue package' was really designed to save the German and French banking system, which would have collapsed in the event of a Greek sovereign default. Most of the money lent to Greece spent no time in Greece; instead it was paid straight to French and German bankers.

A protester in front of the Greek parliament — the bailout was used by the Greek government to pay its bondholders

Follow-up question

Discuss why it is so important to prevent sovereign default by a country such as Greece.

The role of the state in the macroeconomy

This final chapter focuses on the role of the state in the macroeconomy, especially looking at the relative size of the public and private sectors, and how this depends upon a range of factors, including the stance adopted by the government in its fiscal policy. The chapter draws together material from earlier chapters to explore issues relating to the design of macroeconomic policy, and how this has been handled in different types of economy. After all, the priorities for the government of the UK may be very different from those of an LDC needing to deal with high levels of poverty and inequality.

Learning objectives

After studying this chapter, you should:
- → be familiar with the policy objectives that governments may have at the macroeconomic level and the policy instruments available to them
- → appreciate the importance of the fiscal deficit and its significance for the national debt
- → be familiar with the main categories of public expenditure (current and capital) and the role of transfer payments
- → understand the nature and uses of taxation and be aware of the Laffer curve
- → be able to use the *AD/AS* model under differing assumptions about the long-run aggregate supply curve
- → know what is meant by crowding out and how this affects the relative size of the public and private sectors
- → appreciate the significance of automatic stabilisers and the limitations of discretionary fiscal policy
- → be aware of the arguments surrounding the sustainability of fiscal policy
- → understand that different governments may face different challenges and have differing priorities
- → be familiar with problems that may complicate the process of policy design

Government and the economy

What is the role of the state in the modern macroeconomy?

At the macroeconomic level, the government has a number of key objectives. The most fundamental of these objectives is economic growth, as this allows improvements in the standard of living. However, in order to achieve economic growth, it is crucial to maintain economic stability, thus providing the economic environment within which economic growth can take place. It is also important to be aware of international competitiveness — and to achieve an acceptable distribution of income and wealth. Furthermore, there is a need to ensure that economic growth is sustainable. The government has a range of policy instruments with which to attempt to meet these macroeconomic objectives, including fiscal, monetary and supply-side policies.

Synoptic link

This chapter sets out to draw together material from across the Themes that are pertinent to the design of macroeconomic policy. You may therefore find it helpful to reflect on different parts of the analysis that has been presented, so that you can see linkages between the Themes.

The term 'fiscal policy' covers a range of policy measures that affect government expenditures and revenues through the decisions made by the government on its expenditure, taxation and borrowing. Fiscal policy may be used to influence the level and structure of aggregate demand in an economy. The effectiveness of fiscal policy depends crucially on the whole policy environment in which it is utilised.

Monetary policy entails the use of monetary variables such as money supply and interest rates to influence aggregate demand, and has been discussed earlier. In recent years, the prime use of monetary policy has been in seeking to create a stable macroeconomic environment. By delegating the targeting of inflation to the Bank of England, the UK government has effectively yielded the active use of monetary policy.

Supply-side policies comprise a range of measures intended to have a direct impact on aggregate supply — specifically, on the potential capacity output of the economy. These measures are often microeconomic in character and are designed to increase output and hence economic growth.

The size of the public sector

The way in which fiscal policy is conducted has implications for the overall size of the public sector in the economy. Traditionally, fiscal policy was used to affect the level of aggregate demand in the economy, under the influence of Keynesian thinking. The overall balance between government receipts and outlays affects the position of the aggregate demand curve, which is reinforced by multiplier effects. When government outlays exceed government receipts, the result is a **fiscal deficit**. This occurs when the revenues raised through taxation are not sufficient to cover the government's various types of expenditure. The **national debt** is the accumulation of past borrowing.

> ### Key terms
>
> **fiscal deficit** occurs when government outlays exceed government receipts
>
> **national debt** the total amount of government debt, based on accumulated previous deficits and surpluses

> ### Study tip
>
> Be very careful not to confuse the fiscal deficit with the national debt. The fiscal deficit is a 'flow' concept — the excess of government expenditure over revenues in the current period. The national debt is the 'stock' of accumulated past borrowing.

The overall size of the budget deficit may act as a constraint on the government's actions in terms of fiscal policy. In addition, the overall pattern of revenue and expenditure has a strong effect on the overall balance of activity in the economy. A neutral government budget can be attained either with high expenditure and high revenues, or with relatively low expenditure and revenues. Such decisions affect the overall size of the public sector relative to the private sector. Over the years, different governments in the UK have taken different decisions on this issue — and different countries throughout the world have certainly adopted different approaches.

In part, such issues are determined through the ballot box. In the run-up to an election, each political party presents its overall plans for taxation and spending, and typically they adopt different positions as to the overall balance. It is then up to those voting to give a mandate to whichever party offers a package that most closely resembles their preferences.

Figure 15.1 shows the time path of UK government current expenditure (known in the national accounts as general government final consumption expenditure) as a share of GDP since 1950; it shows minor fluctuations around a downward trend, suggesting that the public sector has been gradually reducing its share of the economy, although it has been fairly constant since the mid-1990s. Notice that this does not give the full picture, as public sector investment is not taken into account in these data. There are one or two periods in the figure where the decline seems to have been especially rapid. In the early 1950s, this partly reflects the winding down of government activity after the rebuilding that followed the Second World War. The decline in the 1980s reflects the privatisation drive of that period, when the government was withdrawing from some parts of the economy.

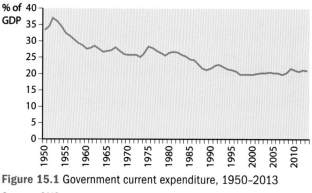

Figure 15.1 Government current expenditure, 1950–2013
Source: ONS

Figure 15.2 provides an international perspective, showing the share of current and capital expenditure by governments in a range of countries. This reveals something of a contrast between, on the one hand, Korea and Switzerland, and on the other hand, many European countries, where governments have been more active in the economy. In part this reflects the greater role that government plays in some countries in providing services such as education and healthcare, whereas in other countries the private sector takes a greater role, often through the insurance market.

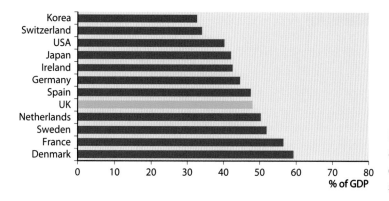

Figure 15.2 Total government spending as a percentage of GDP, selected countries, 2012
Source: OECD

Public expenditure

The figures for the UK discussed above showed **government consumption expenditure**. This is spending on goods and services for current use, such as education and healthcare. The government also undertakes **capital expenditure**, which is spending on infrastructure such as roads and hospitals. This is spending for the future. In addition, the government makes **transfer payments**, such as social security payments. These are payments designed to provide protection for vulnerable households, and may be cash benefits or payments in kind — for example, in the form of education or healthcare provision. These may be universal (paid to everyone) or means-tested (paid to people with low income and capital).

Taxation

Public expenditure must be financed in some way, and the overall position of the public sector relative to the private sector is not only determined by expenditure. The revenue side is also significant. Notice that taxation is not only needed in order to finance expenditure. In addition, taxation remains an important weapon against some forms of market failure, and it also influences the distribution of income. In this context, the choice of using direct or indirect taxes is important.

Direct taxes are taxes levied on income of various kinds, such as personal income tax. Such taxes are designed to be progressive and so can be effective in redistributing income: for example, a higher income tax rate can be charged to those earning high incomes. In contrast, *indirect taxes* — taxes on expenditure, such as VAT and excise duties — tend to be regressive. As poorer households tend to spend a higher proportion of their income on items that are subject to excise duties, a greater share of their income is taken up by indirect taxes. Even VAT can be regressive if higher-income households save a greater proportion of their incomes. The nature of taxes was discussed in Chapter 10.

Margaret Thatcher introduced a switch away from direct taxation towards indirect taxation

When Margaret Thatcher came to power in 1979, one of her first actions was to introduce a switch away from direct taxation towards indirect taxes. VAT was increased and the rate of personal income tax was reduced. In support of this move, it was pointed out that if an income tax scheme becomes too progressive, it can provide a disincentive towards effort. If people feel that a high proportion of their income is being taken in tax, their incentives to provide work effort are weak. Indeed, a switch from direct to indirect taxation is regarded as a sort of supply-side policy intended to influence the position of aggregate supply.

Does an increase in the tax rate necessarily lead to a rise in tax revenue? Arthur Laffer argued that the answer to this was 'no'. He pointed out that changes in tax rates have two effects on tax revenue. The arithmetic says that an increase in the tax rate will increase the tax revenue. However, there is also an economic effect. As tax rates rise, incentive effects come into play, tending to work against the arithmetic effect, as people have less incentive to supply effort at the higher tax rates. The relationship can be captured in the so-called *Laffer curve*, an inverted U-shaped relationship between the tax rate and the amount of revenue raised, as shown in Figure 15.3.

At low rates of tax, revenue increases as the tax rate increases, but beyond $t^\star$, the revenue begins to fall. If an economy has been operating with a tax rate above $t^\star$,

Key terms

government consumption expenditure spending by the government on goods and services

government capital expenditure spending by government on capital projects

transfer payments occur when the government provides benefits (in cash or in kind) to poor households

then a reduction in the tax rate would actually increase the revenue raised by the tax. It is worth noting that Laffer himself pointed out that he had not invented the concept, as it can be found in the writings of Keynes, not to mention Ibn Khaldun, a fourteenth-century Muslim philosopher.

In terms of the impact that fiscal policy can have on aggregate demand, both expenditure and revenue are important, the difference between them being the **government budget deficit (surplus)**. A deficit in this context occurs when expenditure exceeds revenue.

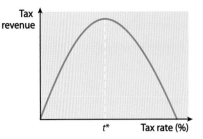

Figure 15.3 The Laffer curve

Aggregate supply revisited

An important question concerns the extent to which a government budget deficit can be used to stabilise the macroeconomy by influencing aggregate demand. In order to explore this, it is first necessary to revisit the aggregate supply curve.

To analyse the impact of public expenditure on aggregate demand, return to the model of aggregate supply and aggregate demand (*AS/AD*). Figure 15.4 shows how a shift in aggregate demand from AD_0 to AD_1 results in an increase in real output and the price level as the economy moves to a new equilibrium — a movement along the short-run aggregate supply curve (*SAS*). However, the *SAS* is called a *short-run* aggregate supply curve for a reason, and there is no guarantee that the equilibrium shown in Figure 15.4 can be sustained. For example, notice that the new equilibrium entails a higher overall price level. In time this will feed back into the costs faced by firms, causing the *SAS* to shift back to the left. Of more importance, therefore, is the long-run aggregate supply curve.

In this connection, it is important to be aware of the debate that developed over the shape of the long-run aggregate supply curve: this is important because it has implications for the conduct and effectiveness of policy options.

During the 1970s, an influential school of macroeconomists, which became known as the **monetarist school**, argued that the economy would always converge on an equilibrium level of output that they referred to as the **natural rate of output**. Associated with this long-run equilibrium was a **natural rate of unemployment**. If this were the case, then the long-run relationship between aggregate supply and the price level would be vertical, as shown in Figure 15.5. Here $Y^\star$ is the natural rate of output: that is, the full-employment level of aggregate output. In other words, a change in the overall price level does not affect aggregate output because the economy always readjusts rapidly back to full employment.

Prior knowledge needed

The *AD/AS* model was first introduced in Book 1, Chapters 11–13; the AS curve was discussed in Book 1, Chapter 12.

Key terms

government budget deficit (surplus) the difference between government expenditure and government revenue

monetarist school a group of economists who believed that the macroeconomy always adjusts rapidly to the full-employment level of output, and that monetary policy should be the prime instrument for stabilising the economy

natural rate of output the long-run equilibrium level of output to which monetarists believe the macroeconomy will always tend

natural rate of unemployment the unemployment rate that exists when the economy is in long-run equilibrium

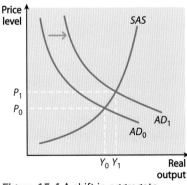

Figure 15.4 A shift in aggregate demand

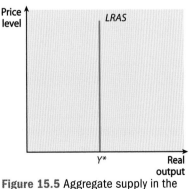

Figure 15.5 Aggregate supply in the long run (the 'monetarist' view)

Key term

Keynesian school a group of economists who believed that the macroeconomy could settle in an equilibrium that was below full employment

An opposing school of thought (often known as the **Keynesian school**) held that the macroeconomy was not sufficiently flexible to enable continuous full employment. They argued that the economy could settle at an equilibrium position below full employment, at least in the medium term. In particular, inflexibilities in labour markets would prevent adjustment. For example, if firms had pessimistic expectations about aggregate demand, and thus reduced their supply of output, this would lead to lower incomes because of the workers being laid off. This would then mean that aggregate demand was indeed deficient, so firms' pessimism was self-fulfilling.

These sorts of argument led to a belief that there would be a range of output over which aggregate supply would be upward sloping. Figure 15.6 illustrates such an aggregate supply curve, and will be familiar from Book 1. In this diagram $Y^\star$ still represents full employment; however, when the economy is operating below this level of output, aggregate supply is somewhat sensitive to the price level, becoming steeper as full employment is approached.

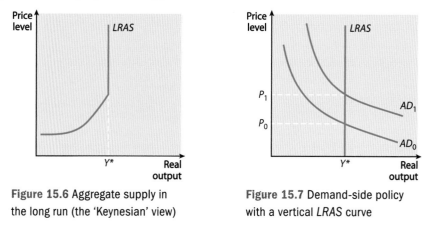

Figure 15.6 Aggregate supply in the long run (the 'Keynesian' view)

Figure 15.7 Demand-side policy with a vertical *LRAS* curve

The policy implications of the monetarist *LRAS* curve are strong. If the economy always converges rapidly on the full-employment level of output, no manipulation of aggregate demand can have any effect except on the price level. This is readily seen in Figure 15.7, where, regardless of the position of the aggregate demand curve, the level of real output remains at $Y^\star$. If aggregate demand is low at AD_0, then the price level is also relatively low, at P_0. An increase in aggregate demand to AD_1 raises the price level to P_1 but leaves real output at $Y^\star$. In such a world, only supply-side policy (which affects the position of the aggregate supply curve) has any effect on real output.

Summary

- Governments pursue a range of policy objectives, including low inflation and low unemployment, a favourable balance of payments position, economic growth, maintenance of a good environment, income redistribution and the correction of market failure.
- In order to pursue these objectives, governments have recourse to fiscal, monetary and supply-side policies.
- In using the *AD/AS* model to analyse policy options, it is useful to distinguish between monetarist and Keynesian views about the shape of aggregate supply.
- Monetarist economists have argued that the economy always converges rapidly on equilibrium at the natural rate of output, implying that policies affecting aggregate demand have an impact only on prices, leaving real output unaffected. Aggregate supply in this world is vertical.
- The Keynesian view is that the economy may settle in an equilibrium that is below full employment, and that there is a range over which aggregate supply slopes upwards.

The impact of a budget deficit

Figure 15.7 shows that shifting the aggregate demand curve affects only the overall price level in the economy when the aggregate supply curve is vertical — and the monetarist school of thought argued that it would always be vertical. Hence a key issue for a government considering the use of fiscal policy is knowing whether there is spare capacity in the economy, because otherwise an expansion in aggregate demand from increased government spending will push up prices but leave real output unchanged.

Under the multiplier, any increase in autonomous spending leads to a multiplied increase in equilibrium output. The idea of the multiplier is that, if there is an increase in (say) government expenditure, this provides income for workers, who will then spend that income and create further expenditure streams. The size of these induced effects will depend upon the marginal propensity to withdraw.

In terms of the *AD/AS* diagram, the existence of the multiplier means that if there is an increase in government expenditure, the *AD* curve moves further to the right than it otherwise would have done, because of the multiplier effects. However, this does not mean that equilibrium income will increase by the full multiplier amount. Looking more closely at what is happening, you can see that there are some forces at work that are acting to weaken the multiplier effect of an increase in government expenditure.

One way in which this happens is through interest rates. If the government finances its deficit through borrowing, a side-effect is to put upward pressure on interest rates, which then may cause private sector spending — by households on consumption and by firms on investment — to decline, as the cost of borrowing has been increased. This process is known as the **crowding out** of private sector activity by the public sector. It limits the extent to which a government budget deficit can shift the aggregate demand curve, especially if the public sector activity is less productive than the private sector activity that it replaces. In principle, there could also be a **crowding in** effect if the government runs a surplus and thus puts downward pressure on interest rates.

When crowding out occurs, the public sector is effectively displacing private sector activity, so it affects the relative size of the public and private sectors.

Automatic and discretionary fiscal policies

It is important to distinguish between automatic and discretionary changes in government expenditure. Some items of government expenditure and receipts vary automatically with the business cycle. They are known as **automatic stabilisers**. For example, if the economy enters a period of recession, government expenditure will rise because of the increased payments of unemployment and other social security benefits, and revenues will fall because fewer people are paying income tax, and because receipts from VAT are falling. This helps to offset the recession without any active intervention from the government.

More important, however, is the question of whether the government can or should make use of discretionary fiscal policy in a deliberate attempt to influence the course of the economy. As already mentioned, the key issue is whether or not the economy has spare capacity, because attempts to stimulate an economy that is already at full employment will merely push up the price level.

There are many examples of how excessive government spending can create problems for the economy. Such problems arose in a number of Latin American economies during the 1980s. In Brazil, a range of policies were brought to bear in an attempt to reduce inflation — including direct controls on prices. However, with no serious attempt to control the fiscal deficit, inflation continually got out of control — reaching almost 3,000% in 1990. Only when the deficit was reduced did it become possible to bring inflation to a more reasonable level. More recently, the collapse of the economy of Zimbabwe was accompanied by inflation at such a high level that the printing presses could not keep up with the need for banknotes.

Extension material

The Barber boom

The UK has not been immune from this sort of effect. After the collapse of the Dollar Standard and at the time of the first oil price crisis of 1973–74, the then-chancellor of the exchequer, Tony Barber, launched a fiscal expansion, backed by a monetary expansion. This was to stem the rise in unemployment that was taking place. However, the result was that inflation soared to around 25%.

Balance between the public and private sectors

Both economic analysis and the UK experience support the view that fiscal policy should not be used as an active stabilisation device. However, this does not mean that there is no role for fiscal policy in a modern economy. Earlier, it was pointed out that decisions about the size of government expenditure and revenue influence the overall balance between the public and private sectors. The balance that is achieved can have an important influence on the overall level of economic activity, and upon economic growth, so the importance of designing an appropriate fiscal policy should not be underestimated. An important theme that runs through much economic analysis is that governments may be justified in intervening in the economy in order to correct market failure. Some of this intervention requires the use of fiscal policy: for example, taxes to correct for the effects of externalities, or expenditure to ensure the provision of public goods. In other words, fiscal policy can be an instrument that operates at the microeconomic level, as well as having macroeconomic implications.

Take infrastructure as an example. Infrastructure covers a range of goods that are crucial for the efficient operation of a market economy. Businesses need good transport links and good communication facilities. Households need good healthcare, education and sanitation facilities, not only in order to enjoy a good standard of life, but also to be productive members of the labour force. Both public goods and externality arguments come into play in the provision of infrastructure, so there needs to be appropriate government intervention to ensure that such goods are adequately provided. The consequence of failing to do this will be to lower the productive capacity of the economy below what would otherwise have been possible. In other words, the aggregate supply curve will be further to the left than it need be.

Synoptic link

Public goods were discussed in Book 1, Chapter 7.

On the other hand, too much government intervention may also be damaging. One of the most compelling arguments in favour of privatisation was that when the managers of public enterprises are insufficiently accountable for their actions, X-inefficiency becomes a major issue, so public sector activity tends to be less efficient than private sector enterprise. On this argument, too large a public sector may have the effect of lowering aggregate productive capacity below its potential level.

These arguments suggest that an important role for fiscal policy is in affecting the supply side of the economy, ensuring that markets operate effectively to make the best possible use of the economy's resources.

Synoptic link

X-inefficiency in public enterprises was discussed in Chapter 6.

Income distribution

The other key role for fiscal policy is in affecting the distribution of income within society. Taxes and transfers can have a large effect on income distribution. This in turn may have effects on the economy by affecting the incentives that people face in choosing their labour supply. This was discussed in Chapter 10.

Achieving a balance of taxation between direct and indirect taxes is an important aspect of the government's redistributive policy. A switch in the balance from direct to indirect taxes will tend to increase inequality in a society. The incentive effects must also be kept in mind. High marginal tax rates on income can have a disincentive effect: if people know that a large proportion of any income from additional work they undertake will be taxed away, they may be discouraged from providing more work. In other words, cutting income tax can encourage work effort by reducing marginal tax rates. This is yet another reminder of the need for a balanced policy — one that recognises that, while some income redistribution is needed to protect the vulnerable, disincentive effects may arise if the better-off are over-taxed.

The role of the government in different countries

In an international context, there are significant differences between countries in relation to the role of the government in the economy. Political ideology plays a part in this, countries with socialist governments tending to see a stronger role for the state in intervening in the economy. However, this is not the only important factor.

For many LDCs, tax collection is a challenge, with no effective administrative system in place. The situation is compounded when many people in the country are living on low incomes or in absolute poverty. Furthermore, where subsistence activity is significant, taxation cannot be effectively implemented. As a consequence, governments may have to play a relatively limited role in the economy, or try to raise finance for government expenditure by other means, perhaps by levying taxes on international trade. Another possibility is to fund expenditure by printing money, but this has been seen to have disastrous consequences for inflation, and was certainly a major factor in one of the most extreme episodes of hyperinflation, which took place in Zimbabwe in the late 2000s.

Figure 15.8 shows tax revenue as a percentage of GDP for selected countries around the world — notice that these are ranked in descending order of GDP per capita in PPP$. In interpreting these data, it is important to remember that tax revenue in a particular country may be low because the country does not have an effective tax collection system, or it may be that the government in power does not wish to take an active role in the economy — at least in the form of imposing high taxes in order to finance high expenditure. This is well illustrated by the difference between the

UK and the USA. Nonetheless, there is a tendency for the lower-income countries to display relatively low tax revenue relative to GDP. This is important because if the government has a limited capacity to raise tax revenue, this may limit the extent to which it is able to introduce policies to combat poverty, or to provide social infrastructure needed to encourage economic growth.

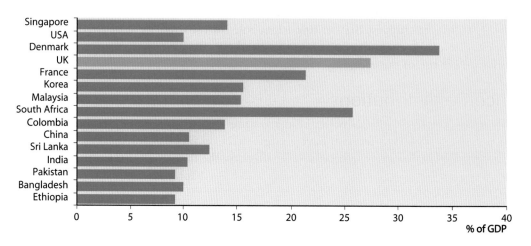

Figure 15.8 Tax revenue as a percentage of GDP, selected countries, 2011
Source: World Bank

Governments have also been aware that foreign firms may take account of relative tax rates in different countries when deciding where to locate their investment. Countries that are keen to attract foreign direct investment may thus feel pressured to keep corporate tax rates relatively low in the hope of attracting inflows of investment. Indeed, many multinational corporations have been able to negotiate tax holidays, leaving them free of taxation for a period after they bring their investment.

Sustainability of fiscal policy

Another important issue that came to the fore during the 1990s concerned the sustainability of fiscal policy. This is wrapped up with the notion that current taxpayers should only have to fund expenditure that benefits their own generation, and that the taxpayers of the future should make their own decisions, and not have to pay for past government expenditure that has been incurred for the benefit of earlier generations.

In this context, what is significant is the overall balance between receipts and outlays through time. If outlays were always larger than receipts, the spending programme could be sustained only through government borrowing, thereby shifting the burden of funding the deficit to future generations. This could also be a problem if it made it more difficult for the private sector to obtain funds for investment, or if it added to the national debt. The Labour governments of 1997–2010 introduced a so-called **'Golden Rule' of fiscal policy**, which stated that, on average over the economic cycle, the government should borrow only to invest and not to fund current expenditure. This was intended to help achieve equity between present and future generations. It should perhaps be noted that this was a self-imposed guideline, so there was no penalty for breaking the rule other than loss of political credibility. The Coalition government that followed was less committed to the concept of the Golden Rule, and the onset of the financial crisis — and the need to bail out commercial banks in order to safeguard the financial system — rendered the Golden Rule impossible to follow.

Key term

Golden Rule of fiscal policy a rule stating that over the economic cycle net government borrowing will be for investment only, and not for current spending

If receipts and outlays more or less balance over the economic cycle, the economy is not in a position whereby the current generation is forcing future generations to pay for its consumption. However, as the economy does go through the economic cycle, it is not practical to impose this rule at every part of the cycle, so the so-called Golden Rule was intended to apply over the economic cycle as a whole.

There was also a commitment to keep public sector net debt below 40% of GDP — again, on average over the economic cycle. Figure 14.3 in the previous chapter showed data for this on a quarterly basis since 1997. The financial support offered to Northern Rock and other banks in the bailout of 2008 had a noticeable effect on public sector net debt, as is clear in the figure. Even without the financial sector interventions, net debt rose over the 40% mark in the last quarter of 2008 and kept rising thereafter. This reflected other measures taken by the government to try to mitigate the effects of the recession. One example was the reduction in the rate of VAT from 17.5 to 15%. This is tantamount to a fiscal expansion, but when it was introduced, it was made clear that it was intended as a temporary boost for a specified period. This statement enabled the government to maintain that it was not breaching its long-term fiscal commitment. The rate of VAT returned to 17.5% in January 2010, and was increased to 20% in January 2011.

Summary

- Fiscal policy concerns the use of government expenditure and taxation to influence aggregate demand in the economy.
- If the economy is in a state in which the aggregate demand curve cuts the vertical segment of aggregate supply, demand-side policy affects only the overall price level, and not real output.
- If the government funds its expenditure by borrowing, higher interest rates may crowd out private sector activity.
- The stance of the government budget varies with the business cycle, as a result of the operation of automatic stabilisers.
- The overall balance between private and public sectors varies through time and across countries.
- Direct taxes help to redistribute income between groups in society, but if too progressive they may dampen incentives to provide effort.
- The Golden Rule for fiscal policy was that the government should aim to borrow only for investment, and not for current expenditure (averaged over the economic cycle).
- There was also a commitment to keep public sector net debt below 40% of GDP; this commitment did not survive the financial crisis and recession that began in the late 2000s.

Exercise 15.1

Discuss the extent to which the major British political parties adopt differing stances towards establishing a balance between the private and public sectors: that is, the extent to which each is 'high tax/high public spending' or 'low tax/low public spending'. Analyse the economic arguments favouring each of the approaches.

Macroeconomic policy design

Governments have a range of policies available to them, but also a range of possible objectives that they wish to achieve. Different countries face their own configurations of resources and challenges, and may set their own priorities. It is therefore no surprise to find that there is no unique approach that has been adopted to the design of macroeconomic policy.

Objectives of policy

First consider the range of policy objectives that a government may need to take into account when designing a policy mix.

Economic growth

It is through economic growth that the productive capacity of the economy is raised, and this in turn allows the living standards of the country's citizens to be progressively improved over time. In a sense, therefore, this is the most fundamental of the policy objectives, and has been pursued by governments all around the world. Although there are some policy measures that may be thought to affect growth directly, many other policy objectives may need to be met as a precondition for creating the environment in which growth may flourish.

Alleviating poverty and inequality

For less developed countries (LDCs), economic growth may be seen as a prerequisite for the alleviation of poverty and inequality. Without increasing the quantity of resources available, it may be impossible to improve living conditions for those living in poverty. A counter argument to this is that addressing basic needs may be a prerequisite for growth to be possible. However, LDCs are likely to give higher priority to this objective than the more developed countries.

Nonetheless, inequality in the distribution of income is a concern of governments that wish to influence the distribution of income within a society. This may entail transfers of income between groups — that is, from the rich to the poor — in order to protect the vulnerable. Such transfers may take place through progressive taxation (whereby those on higher incomes pay a greater proportion of their income in tax) or through a system of social security benefits such as the Jobseeker's Allowance or Income Support.

Macroeconomic stability

It is widely accepted that instability in the macroeconomy impedes the process of economic growth, so another key objective for governments is to provide a stable macroeconomic environment that will facilitate growth. This is important for countries at all stages of development.

Macroeconomic stability can be interpreted in different ways. For a long period from the 1970s onwards, the focus was primarily on monetary stability, seen in terms of achieving a low and stable rate of inflation. The underlying argument here was that a low and stable inflation rate would improve confidence in the future course of the economy, and thus encourage firms to invest. This would then increase the productive capacity of the economy, resulting in economic growth.

Poverty needs to be tackled to enable economic growth

The financial crisis that began in the late 2000s has drawn attention to the need to focus also on financial stability. In other words, there needs to be a sufficient and efficient flow of liquidity in the economy.

The need to safeguard the financial system by the bailout of failing banks further highlighted the need for fiscal stability. The sudden increase in public sector borrowing, and the consequent rise in debt, raised awareness of the need to prioritise measures to reduce fiscal deficits and national debt. For countries like Greece, this became the dominant priority in policy design.

Yet another element in reaching stability in the macroeconomic environment is the need to accommodate external shocks. These can come from many different sources, whether it be changes in the price of oil, or financial crisis spreading through globalised financial markets. Domestic policy may be needed to ensure macroeconomic stability is maintained in the face of such external shocks.

Full employment
Full employment is another objective for the macroeconomy. Unemployment imposes costs on society and on the individuals who are unemployed. From society's point of view, the existence of substantial unemployment represents a waste of resources and indicates that the economy is working below full capacity.

International competitiveness
As the world becomes increasingly interconnected through globalisation, it is increasingly important to maintain international competitiveness. This is partly about achieving productivity growth in line with international competitors. One way of viewing this is that it is about maintaining comparative advantage.

Balance of payments

Under a flexible exchange rate system, the overall balance of payments will always be zero because the exchange rate adjusts to ensure that this is so. Nevertheless, the balance of payments remains an objective, not so much to ensure overall balance as to maintain a reasonable balance between the current account and the financial account. If the current account is in persistent deficit, this could cause problems in the long run, as the implication is that the country is selling off its assets in order to obtain goods for present consumption. Under a fixed exchange rate system, the need to maintain the exchange rate acts as a constraint upon economic growth, which tends to lead to an increase in imports and creates a current account deficit.

Environmental considerations

It must be recognised that it is not only resources that contribute to living standards: conserving a good environment is also important. Sustainable growth and development means growth that does not prejudice the consumption possibilities of future generations, and this consideration may act as a constraint on the rate of economic growth. Another policy priority is therefore to look for sustainability in economic growth.

Correcting market failure

At the *microeconomic* level there are policy measures designed to deal with various forms of market failure. Competition policy is one example of this; it is designed to prevent firms from abusing monopoly power, and to improve the allocation of resources. Although such policies operate at the microeconomic level, they have consequences for macroeconomic objectives such as economic growth.

For LDCs, dealing with market failure is a high priority, if only because so many markets are underdeveloped or missing. For example, attention has been drawn to the need to improve the operation of financial markets in LDCs, in order to improve the flow of finance for investment. Measures may also be needed to ensure that inflows of external finance to LDCs can be effectively marshalled. This may entail improving the effectiveness with which flows of overseas assistance or international borrowing are utilised. It may also entail negotiating better deals with multinational corporations that bring foreign direct investment into LDCs, to ensure that the LDC can retain more of the benefits of such investment.

Policy options

Previous chapters have identified a range of policy options that governments can bring to bear in order to address these various objectives. Each has its own strengths and weaknesses, and is suited to the achievement of different sets of objectives. Governments will thus choose the range of policies most appropriate to the objectives that they are trying to achieve, which may in turn depend upon the particular challenges that are faced by economies in different circumstances.

Monetary and financial policy

Monetary policy entails the use of monetary variables such as money supply and interest rates to influence aggregate demand. The main objective of monetary policy in recent times has been to meet inflation targets, which is seen as a crucial part of macroeconomic stability. In the UK, the Bank of England used interest rates to keep inflation within its target range, whilst in Europe the European Central Bank (ECB) performed this role. In the USA, the Federal Reserve was also using interest rates to create a stable environment.

As explained in Chapter 14, this period of relative calm (the Great Moderation) was interrupted by rising commodity prices and financial crisis. The need to safeguard the financial system without plunging economies into deep recession switched the focus from monetary stability to financial stability. In the UK, inflation was allowed to rise above its target range whilst interest rates fell as far as they could fall. Quantitative easing (expansion of the money supply) was brought in to try to ensure an adequate flow of liquidity as some banks failed.

In the less developed countries, the priorities for monetary policy have been rather different. With financial institutions being relatively underdeveloped, and many rural communities lacking access to formal financial markets, monetary policy has partly been used to improve the coverage of financial markets and to boost confidence in the financial system. The provision of microfinance is one way in which attempts have been made to provide access to credit in rural areas, but this still has a long way to go.

This is not to say that monetary stability is not also important for LDCs. Countries in Latin America experienced hyperinflation in the 1980s, setting back progress with economic growth. Countries such as Zimbabwe have also seen bouts of extreme instability. This is a reminder that maintaining stability is an important precondition for achieving economy growth.

Fiscal policy

The term 'fiscal policy' covers a range of policy measures that affect government expenditures and revenues through the decisions made by the government on its expenditure, taxation and borrowing. Fiscal policy may be used to influence the level and structure of aggregate demand in an economy, but is also utilised to affect the distribution of income within a society. It also plays a role in addressing issues of market failure.

Using discretionary fiscal policy to combat unemployment by stimulating aggregate demand has been largely discredited, as it was seen to be ineffective, especially in the context of a floating exchange rate regime. Nonetheless, fiscal policy plays a key role in the economy through its impact on the balance between the public and private sectors.

For many developed countries, the privatisation of nationalised industries has reduced the size of the public sector. The presumption is that exposing such industries to competitive forces would improve accountability and efficiency, and thus result in improved allocation of resources. This rests on the assumption that the private sector tends to be more efficient than the public sector.

The development of fiscal rules was intended to ensure that current taxation would be used primarily for the present generation, and public borrowing for investment that would benefit future generations. The need to provide bailout funding for banks considered too big to fail led to the abandonment of such a rule-based system, given that public sector borrowing could not be maintained within the agreed limits. The bailouts also led to a sharp rise in public sector net debt. Fiscal policy thus had to be redirected towards reducing the debt, the danger being that this would deepen and prolong the recession.

Exchange rate policy

Since the collapse of the Dollar Standard in the early 1970s, floating exchange rates have become the norm. In other words, the policy towards the exchange rate has been to allow it to find its own equilibrium level in the foreign exchange market. This has implications for other policy approaches, making fiscal policy less effective but strengthening the impact of monetary policy on aggregate demand.

The implication of a floating exchange rate system is that a country is not able to use changes in the exchange rate in order to influence the competitiveness of its goods relative to the rest of the world. If a country does wish to improve its competitiveness, a more effective approach is to find ways of improving productivity.

China has been accused of intervening to improve the competitiveness of its exports by manipulating its exchange rate. During the early 2000s, this caused controversy. By undervaluing its currency, it was claimed that China was giving itself an unfair advantage, allowing exports to grow rapidly and thus fuelling its economic growth.

Such a policy has significant side-effects. Within China itself, this meant that resources were being diverted into the export sector, potentially at the expense of domestic consumption. Elsewhere, China's accumulation of US Treasury bills pushed up their prices. This implies lower interest rates than would otherwise have prevailed. It may have contributed to the housing bubble in the USA, which was one of the triggers for the financial crisis. This culminated in international pressure, to which China succumbed after 2005. The real value of China's currency (the yuan/renminbi) rose by some 30% between 2005 and 2014, suggesting that the exchange rate is now closer to its equilibrium value.

The establishment of the euro zone could be seen as an example of a drastic form of exchange rate policy, under which the euro zone members agreed to adopt the euro, thereby adopting a common exchange rate against the rest of the world, and a common monetary policy alongside it. With the ECB setting a common interest

China has been accused of manipulating its exchange rate

rate across all of the euro zone members, it became difficult for individual countries to adopt differential responses to the financial crisis, with some members suffering much more severe recessions than others as a result.

Supply-side measures

Supply-side policies are measures intended to have a direct impact on aggregate supply — specifically, on the potential capacity output of the economy. These measures are often microeconomic in character and are designed to increase output and hence economic growth.

For the UK, such policies have included measures intended to increase the provision of education and training, measures to improve the flexibility with which markets operate, the promotion of competition and attempts to improve the incentives faced by economic agents. All these are intended to affect the position of the long-run aggregate supply curve, and expand the productive capacity of the economy. These policies were discussed in Book 1, Chapter 16.

For LDCs, supply-side policies are crucial for growth and development. In particular, it is vitally important for LDCs to be able to invest in human capital. Improved provision of education and skills and enhanced healthcare delivery with better nutrition can have a dramatic impact on long-run growth by raising the productivity of the workforce. Markets can be made to work more effectively if transport and communication can be improved, or if such infrastructure as market facilities can be provided.

Notice that measures that lead to improvements in health, nutrition and education of the population also have direct effects on the alleviation of poverty and (potentially) inequality, so are doubly important for LDCs.

Regulation and control

This assembly of policy measures may not be enough. There may be situations in which the authorities may see the need to intervene directly through regulation or control. In particular, there may be a need to provide a legal and regulatory framework within which the behaviour of firms can be monitored in order to protect consumers.

A regulatory framework to promote competition may be needed, as was noted in Chapter 6 under Theme 3. The Competition and Markets Authority fulfils this role in the UK, and other countries have similar bodies.

For LDCs, it is important to establish an appropriate legal framework within which a system of secure property rights can be put in place. This is an essential underpinning for any economy to operate effectively. It was noted earlier that financial markets may fail to provide rural credit for investors, who may not be able to provide collateral against loans because of the lack of property rights. This is just one example of where a legal framework becomes important.

It is also important for LDCs to be in a position to negotiate with more experienced partners. For example, when a multinational corporation (MNC) decides to locate in an LDC, it must agree terms with the host government. Given the economic (and perhaps political) power of the MNC compared with the host government, the LDC can all too easily find itself making too many concessions in order to attract the investment of the MNC.

There are also circumstances in which an international body may be needed to regulate markets at a global level. For example, it has been noted that there may be externalities that cross national boundaries, and a worldwide agreement may be needed to combat global warming. The World Trade Organization (WTO) exists partly to arbitrate on disputes between trading partners, and to enforce agreements on tariffs and the conditions under which trade takes place.

One particular example is the need to regulate a process known as **transfer pricing**. There are MNCs that spread their supply chain around the world, with different stages of the production process being located in different countries. In such circumstances, the MNC undertakes a lot of internal transactions between its own branches in different countries, and can set the prices at which those transactions take place. It becomes possible for the company to minimise its tax liability by manipulating those internal prices in such a way as to take the profit in a country with a low tax rate.

There is widespread agreement that such practices should be prohibited, but the controversy surrounding the activities of companies such as Google, Starbucks and Amazon shows that it is no easy matter to intervene. Part of the problem is that the MNCs are operating globally, but governments only operate nationally.

Problems in designing and implementing policy

Policymakers face many problems when seeking to implement their chosen policies. For a start, they need information on which to base their policy design. A key problem here is that it takes time to collect data, so real-time data are not available. The policymaker only has data about how the economy was performing at some date in the past. And even this may be inaccurate, provisional or incomplete. Given the time that elapses in designing a policy and getting it approved, and then in it working its way through the system, a policy may only become effective after the need for it has passed. After all, the economic environment is always changing. Policymakers must take policy decisions based on their best forecasts (or guesses!) about the future, knowing that this is characterised by high levels of risk and uncertainty. In addition, the economy is open to the impact of sudden and unanticipated shocks.

Furthermore, a government needs to adopt a combination of policies that will enable it to achieve its objectives. One of the problems with this is that conflicts may arise, both between policies and between objectives. The policy adopted to deal with one objective may endanger achievement of another.

Indeed, the adoption of one policy measure may rule out the use of some other measure. For example, the authorities cannot adopt independent targets for money supply and the interest rate if they want the money market to remain in equilibrium. Targeting the exchange rate may mean that it is not possible to use monetary policy to influence aggregate demand. Introducing fiscal austerity in order to reduce public sector debt may prevent the achievement of economic growth. For an LDC, investing in healthcare or education may leave no funds available for spending on infrastructure such as roads and communications.

Exercise 15.2

Given the following list of policy objectives, discuss the possible conflicts that may arise between them, and discuss how these might be resolved:

- low inflation
- low unemployment
- high economic growth
- a low deficit on the current account of the balance of payments
- maintenance of a high environmental quality
- equity in the distribution of income

Summary

- Governments have several possible policy objectives — and a range of possible instruments to bring to bear.
- Economic growth is often seen as taking a high priority amongst objectives, but other targets of policy may be necessary for growth to take place.
- Less developed countries may have different priorities compared with more advanced economies.
- Approaches to policy include monetary and fiscal policy, together with supply-side measures.
- Other policies such as regulation may sometimes be required.
- Regulation may sometimes need to be coordinated to address concerns that cross national boundaries.
- Policymakers need to take decisions on the basis of inadequate information, and under conditions of risk and uncertainty.
- Conflicts may arise both between policy objectives and between policy measures.

Theme 4 key terms

absolute advantage the ability to produce a good more efficiently (e.g. with less labour)

absolute poverty the situation of a household whose income is insufficient to allow it to purchase the minimum bundle of goods and services regarded as necessary for survival

appreciation a rise in the exchange rate within a floating exchange rate system

automatic stabilisers a process by which government expenditure and revenue varies with the business cycle, thereby helping to stabilise the economy without any conscious intervention from government

Bank for International Settlements (BIS) an institution that acts as a bank for central banks and sets standards for regulation of banks that are accepted globally

bank rate the rate of interest charged by the Bank of England on short-term loans to other banks

BRIC countries a group of countries comprising Brazil, Russia, India and China that have made rapid progress in recent years (South Africa is also included in this group)

broad money (M4) M0 plus sterling wholesale and retail deposits with monetary financial institutions such as banks and building societies

buffer stock a scheme intended to stabilise the price of a commodity by buying excess supply in periods when supply is high, and selling when supply is low

capital account of the balance of payments an account identifying transactions in (physical) capital between the residents of a country and the rest of the world

capital adequacy ratio the ratio of a bank's capital to its current liabilities and risk-weighted assets

central bank the banker to the government, performing a range of functions, which may include issue of coins and banknotes, acting as banker to commercial banks and regulating the financial system

common market a set of trading arrangements in which a group of countries remove barriers to trade among them, adopt a common set of barriers against external trade, establish common tax rates and laws regulating economic activity, allow free movement of factors of production between members and have common public sector procurement policies

comparative advantage the ability to produce a good relatively more efficiently (i.e. at lower opportunity cost)

credit multiplier a process by which an increase in money supply can have a multiplied effect on the amount of credit in an economy

crowding in a process by which a decrease in government expenditure 'crowds in' private sector activity by lowering the cost of borrowing

crowding out a process by which an increase in government expenditure crowds out private sector activity by raising the cost of borrowing

current account of the balance of payments an account identifying transactions in goods and services between the residents of a country and the rest of the world, together with income payments and international transfers

customs union a group of countries that agree to trade without barriers between them, and with a common tariff barrier against the rest of the world

demographic transition a process through which many countries have been observed to pass whereby improved health lowers the death rate, and the birth rate subsequently also falls, leading to a low and stable population growth

depreciation a fall in the exchange rate within a floating exchange rate system

devaluation a process whereby a government reduces the price of its currency relative to an agreed rate in terms of foreign currency

development a process by which real per capita incomes are increased and the inhabitants of a country are able to benefit from improved living conditions, i.e. lower poverty and enhanced standards of education, health, nutrition and other essentials of life

direct tax a tax levied directly on income

economic and monetary union a set of trading arrangements the same as for a common market, but in addition having a common currency (or permanently fixed exchange rates between the member countries) and a common monetary policy

emerging economies economies that have experienced rapid economic growth with some industrialisation and characteristics of developed markets

Exchange Rate Mechanism (ERM) a system that was set up by a group of European countries in 1979 with the objective of keeping member countries' currencies relatively stable against each other

export-led growth a situation in which economic growth is achieved through the exploitation of economies of scale, made possible by focusing on exports and so reaching a wider market than would be available within the domestic economy

fair trade schemes schemes that set out to ensure that small producers in LDCs receive a fair price for their products

financial account of the balance of payments an account identifying transactions in financial assets between the residents of a country and the rest of the world

Financial Conduct Authority (FCA) a body separate from the Bank of England responsible for conduct regulation of financial services firms

financial intermediaries institutions such as banks and building societies that channel funds from lenders to borrowers

Financial Policy Committee (FPC) the decision-making body of the Bank of England responsible for macroprudential regulation

financial stability a situation in which there is a sufficient and efficient flow of liquidity in the economy

fiscal deficit occurs when government outlays exceed government receipts

fixed exchange rate a system in which the government of a country agrees to fix the value of its currency in terms of that of another country

floating exchange rate a system in which the exchange rate is permitted to find its own level in the market

foreign direct investment (FDI) investment undertaken in one country by companies based in other countries

foreign currency gap a situation in which an LDC is unable to import the goods that it needs for development because of a shortage of foreign exchange

foreign exchange reserves stocks of foreign currency and gold owned by the central bank of a country to enable it to meet any mismatch between the demand and supply of the country's currency

free trade area a group of countries that agree to trade without barriers between themselves, but having their own individual barriers with countries outside the area

futures market a market in which it is possible to buy a commodity at a fixed price for delivery at a specified future date; such a market exists for foreign exchange

General Agreement on Tariffs and Trade (GATT) the precursor of the WTO, which organised a series of 'rounds' of tariff reductions

Gini coefficient a measure of the degree of inequality in a society

globalisation a process by which the world's economies are becoming more closely integrated

Golden Rule of fiscal policy a rule stating that over the economic cycle net government borrowing will be for investment only, and not for current spending

government budget deficit (surplus) the difference between government expenditure and government revenue

government capital expenditure spending by government on capital projects

government consumption expenditure spending by the government on goods and services

Harrod–Domar model a model of economic growth that emphasises the importance of savings and investment

HIPC Initiative an initiative launched in 1995 to provide debt relief for heavily indebted poor countries

hot money stocks of funds that are moved around the world from country to country in search of the best return

Human Development Index a composite indicator of the level of a country's development, varying between 0 and 1

indirect tax a tax on expenditure, e.g. VAT

industrialisation a process of transforming an economy by expanding manufacturing and other industrial activity

infrastructure the complex of physical capital goods needed to support development in the form of roads, communication networks, market, education and healthcare facilities etc.

interbank lending borrowing and lending between banks to manage their liquidity and other requirements for short-term funds

International Monetary Fund (IMF) a multilateral institution that provides short-term financing for countries experiencing balance of payments problems

interventionist strategy a strategy for stimulating development that focuses on addressing market failure

invisible trade trade in services

Keynesian school a group of economists who believed that the macroeconomy could settle in an equilibrium that was below full employment

labour productivity a measure of output per worker, or output per hour worked

law of comparative advantage a theory arguing that there may be gains from trade arising when countries (or individuals) specialise in the production of goods or services in which they have a comparative advantage

lender of last resort the role of the central bank in guaranteeing sufficient liquidity is available in the monetary system

Lewis model a model developed by Sir Arthur Lewis which argued that less developed countries could be seen as being typified by two sectors, traditional and modern, and that labour could be transferred from the traditional to the modern sector in order to bring about growth and development

LIBOR the average rate of interest on interbank lending in the London interbank market

liquidity the extent to which an asset can be converted in the short term and without the holder incurring a cost

liquidity preference a theory that suggests that people will desire to hold money as an asset

liquidity ratio the ratio of liquid assets to total assets

Lorenz curve a graphical way of depicting the distribution of income within a country

macroprudential regulation financial regulation intended to mitigate the risk of the financial system as a whole

marginal tax rate tax on additional income, defined as the change in tax payments due divided by the change in taxable income

market for loanable funds the notion that households will be influenced by the rate of interest in making saving decisions, which will then determine the quantity of loanable funds available for firms to borrow for investment

market-friendly growth an approach to economic growth in which governments are recommended to intervene less where markets can operate effectively, but to intervene more strongly where markets are seen to fail

market-oriented strategy a strategy for encouraging development that relies on enabling markets to work effectively

microfinance schemes that provide finance for small-scale projects in LDCs

microprudential regulation financial regulation intended to set standards and supervise financial institutions at the level of the individual firm

Millennium Development Goals (MDGs) targets set for each less developed country, reflecting a range of development objectives to be monitored each year to evaluate progress

monetarist school a group of economists who believed that the macroeconomy always adjusts rapidly to the full-employment level of output, and that monetary policy should be the prime instrument for stabilising the economy

Monetary Policy Committee (MPC) the body within the Bank of England responsible for the conduct of monetary policy

monetary union a situation in which countries adopt a common currency

monetary stability a situation in which there is stability in prices relative to the government's inflation target

multinational corporation (MNC) a company whose production activities are carried out in a number of countries

narrow money (M0) notes and coins in circulation and as commercial banks' deposits at the Bank of England

national debt the total amount of government debt, based on accumulated previous deficits and surpluses

natural rate of output the long-run equilibrium level of output to which monetarists believe the macroeconomy will always tend

natural rate of unemployment the unemployment rate that exists when the economy is in long-run equilibrium

non-tariff barriers measures imposed by a government that have the effect of inhibiting international trade

official development assistance aid provided to LDCs by countries in the OECD

open market operations intervention by the central bank to influence short-run interest rates by buying or selling securities

progressive tax a tax in which the marginal tax rate rises with income, i.e. a tax bearing most heavily on the relatively well-off members of society

Prudential Regulation Authority (PRA) a decision-making body in the Bank of England responsible for microprudential regulation of deposit-takers, insurers and major investment firms

purchasing power parity theory of exchange rates a theory stating that in the long run exchange rates (in a floating rate system) are determined by relative inflation rates in different countries

quantitative easing a process by which liquidity in the economy is increased when the central bank purchases assets from the commercial banks

real exchange rate the nominal exchange rate adjusted for differences in relative inflation rates between countries

regressive tax a tax bearing more heavily on the relatively poorer members of society

relative poverty the situation obtaining if household income falls below 50% of median adjusted household disposable income

repo a sale and repurchase agreement, whereby one financial institution sells a financial asset to another with an agreement to buy it back at an agreed future date

retail banks banks that provide high-street services to depositors

revaluation a process whereby a government raises the price of domestic currency in terms of foreign currency

securitisation a process whereby future cash flows are converted into marketable securities

sharecropping a form of land tenure system in which the landlord and tenant share the crop

stages of economic growth a process described by economic historian Walt Rostow, which set out five stages through which he claimed that all developing countries would pass

sustainable development 'development which meets the needs of the present without compromising the ability of future generations to meet their own needs' (Brundtland Commission, 1987)

tariff a tax imposed on imported goods

terms of trade the ratio of export prices to import prices

tiger economies a group of economies in Southeast Asia (Hong Kong, South Korea, Singapore and Taiwan) that enjoyed rapid economic growth from the 1960s

total factor productivity the average productivity of all factors, measured as the total output divided by the total amount of inputs used

trade creation the replacement of more expensive domestic production or imports with cheaper output from a partner within the trading bloc

trade diversion the replacement of cheaper imported goods by goods from a less efficient trading partner within a bloc

trading possibilities curve shows the consumption possibilities under conditions of free trade

transfer payments occur when the government provides benefits (in cash or in kind) to poor households

transfer pricing a process by which a multinational corporation can minimise its global tax liability by manipulating the internal prices for transactions between its branches in different countries

universal banks banks that operate in both retail and wholesale markets

velocity of circulation (V) the rate at which money changes hands: the volume of transactions divided by money stock

visible trade trade in goods

voluntary export restraint (VER) an agreement by a country to limit its exports to another country to a given quantity or quota

wholesale banks banks that deal with companies and other banks on a large scale

World Bank a multilateral organisation that provides financing for long-term development projects

World Trade Organization (WTO) a multilateral body responsible for overseeing the conduct of international trade

7 Globalisation and trade

1 Figure 1 shows the production possibility curves for two countries, A and
B, which each produce two goods, X and Y. Suppose that there is no trade
between the countries, and that production takes place at point *R*. What is
the total (world) production of the two goods?

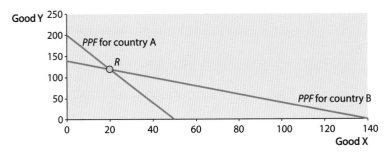

Figure 1 PPCs for countries
A and B

   A 20X and 120Y

   B 20X and 240Y

   C 40X and 240Y

   D 40X and 120Y

2 Referring to Figure 1, what would be the total (world) production of the two
goods if each country were to specialise in producing the good in which it has
a comparative advantage?

   A 140X and 200Y

   B 50X and 140Y

   C 140X and 140Y

   D 50X and 200Y

3 Which of the following defines the terms of trade?

   A The ratio of import prices to export prices

   B The ratio of export prices to import prices

   C Export prices multiplied by import prices

   D Export prices minus import prices

4 a Assess the view that transnational companies are the most important
cause of globalisation.

   b Evaluate the benefits of globalisation to a country of your choice.

8 Trading blocs and restrictions on trade

1 Figure 2 shows domestic demand and supply of a commodity before and after
the imposition of a tariff. The world price of the good is *OE*, and the country
can import as much as it wishes at that price. What would be the level of
imports in the absence of the tariff?

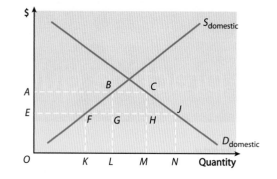

Figure 2 A tariff

A KL
B KM
C KN
D LM

2 Referring to Figure 2, if a tariff of the amount *AE* is imposed on the good, what would be the level of imports?
  A KL
  B KM
  C KN
  D LM

3 Referring to Figure 2, if a tariff of the amount *AE* is imposed on the good, which area would represent the tax revenue raised by the government?
  A ABGE
  B ABFE
  C BCML
  D BCHG

4 Figure 3 shows the effect of a voluntary export restraint (quota). *D* represents domestic demand for the good, and S_{dom} shows the quantity that domestic producers are prepared to supply at any price. The world price is *OE*, and in the absence of a quota, the country can import as much as it wishes at that price. What would be the level of imports in this situation?

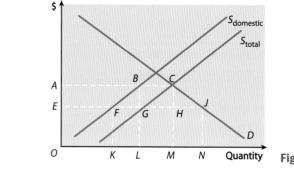

Figure 3 A quota

  A KL
  B KM
  C KN
  D LM

5 With reference to Figure 3, if a quota for imports is agreed such that the total supply of the good is given by S_{total}, what would be the level of imports?

  A KL

  B KM

  C KN

  D LM

6 Which of the following measures is **not** a non-tariff barrier to trade?

  A A regulation that specifies more rigorous safety standards than are applied to domestically produced goods

  B A requirement that imports of a particular good are processed by a small and remote customs office

  C A rule controlling the precise specifications of a product

  D A tax imposed on imported goods

7 a For over 40 years the value of world trade has been growing more quickly than the growth rate of world GDP. Examine the reasons that might explain this trend.

  b Assess the disadvantages of an increase in trade liberalisation to a country of your choice.

8 a Examine the economic effects of the growth of trading blocs on the global economy.

  b Evaluate the likely economic effects on the global economy of an increase in protectionism by developed countries.

9 a Examine the role of the World Trade Organization in world trade.

  b Evaluate the reasons why a country might wish to restrict free trade.

9 The balance of payments and exchange rates

1 Table 1 itemises components of a country's balance of payments in US$ million.

Direct investment (balance)	200
Exports of goods	25,000
Imports of goods	30,000
Income (balance)	–3,000
Portfolio investment (balance)	–150
Other investment (balance)	1,000
Services (credits)	6,500
Services (debits)	7,500
Transfers (balances)	12,000

What is the balance on current account?

  A +$1,050 million

  B +$3,000 million

  C +$60,000 million

  D –$10,000 million

2 Given the data in Table 1, what is the balance on the financial account?

  A −$50 million

  B −$850 million

  C +$2,950 million

  D +$1,050 million

3 Given the data in Table 1, what is the visible balance?

  A −$5,000 million

  B +$10,000 million

  C −$1,000 million

  D +$1,000 million

4 The UK's current account

Despite the 25% depreciation in the value of sterling in 2008, the UK's current account has remained in deficit. This deficit was estimated to be £56 billion in 2012, while the trade in goods deficit was over £100 billion. The continued problems in the euro zone combined with the UK's low productivity and its depleted manufacturing base have made it difficult for the UK to increase exports.

Some economists argue that a current account deficit is not significant for economic management if it can be financed by inflows into the financial account. However, others consider that such imbalances cannot be sustained in the long run and that measures should be taken to eliminate them.

  a Explain the difference between a trade in goods deficit and a current account deficit.

  b Analyse the likely impact of a depreciation in the external value of a currency on the balance of payments deficit on current account.

  c Apart from the impact on the current account of the balance of payments, examine **two** possible effects of a sharp fall in the external value of the pound.

  d Assess **two** factors which might explain the reasons for the continuation of the UK's current account deficit, despite the depreciation in the value of sterling.

  e Evaluate whether a deficit on the current account of the balance payments should be a primary concern to the UK government.

5 a Examine the reasons why the exchange rate of a country's currency might appreciate against another currency.

  b Evaluate the benefits of membership of the euro zone.

6 'The UK has experienced a persistent deficit on its trade balance.'

  a Assess the likely causes of the UK's trade balance deficit.

  b Evaluate measures by which the UK could reduce this deficit.

7 France's international competitiveness

According to the Global Competitiveness Index, France fell from eighteenth to twenty-first place between 2011/12 and 2012/13. One factor was that labour costs have risen more quickly in France than in other countries and, in particular, compared with those in Germany. Taxes on employers, the equivalent of national insurance contributions, are also high relative to those in other countries and twice those paid by German employers. Furthermore, France's public expenditure as a proportion of GDP is over 56%. Some economists have suggested that taxes on employers should be reduced while those on expenditure, such as VAT, should be increased.

a Distinguish between price competitiveness and non-price competitiveness.

b Analyse factors that could have caused a fall in France's international competitiveness.

c Examine the possible impact of France's membership of the euro zone on the competitiveness of its goods and services.

d Assess **two** measures that the French government might take to improve the competitiveness of the country's goods and services.

e Discuss the structural reforms that the French government might implement in order to improve the country's international competitiveness.

8 a Assess factors which might cause the exchange rate of a currency to fluctuate against other currencies.

b Evaluate the benefits of membership of the single European currency.

9 a Examine factors that could cause a deterioration in the international competitiveness of a country's goods and services.

b Evaluate measures by which the international competitiveness of a country's goods and services could be improved.

10 Poverty and inequality in developed and developing countries

1 Which of the following indicators is **not** used in calculating the human development index?

A GNI per capita in PPP$

B Percentage of people living on less than $1.25 per person per day

C Expected years of schooling

D Life expectancy at birth

2 a Examine factors that influence the level of income inequality in a country of your choice.

b Assess the impact of inequality on economic growth and on economic development.

3 Poverty in India

It has been estimated that, despite rapid economic growth in recent years, 450 million Indians are living in absolute poverty. Meanwhile, inequality is growing rapidly: the top 10% earned 12 times as much as the bottom 10% in 2012, compared to 6 times in 1992. Indeed, India is fourth in a world league table of the greatest number of billionaires: there were 61 at the last count, who have a combined wealth of $250 billion. The growth of capitalism has resulted in India's 100 richest people owning assets equivalent to 25% of the GDP.

Growth rates of 8–9% over an extended period have helped to create a large middle class who provide a large market for cars and white goods. However, problems have been created through significant urbanisation and the exploitation of the environment.

a Distinguish between absolute poverty and relative poverty.

b Explain how inequality may be measured. Illustrate your answer with an appropriate diagram.

c To what extent is inequality necessary for the operation of a market economy?

d Examine the view that poverty is a major constraint on economic development.

e Assess problems that might arise when a country such as India experiences a period of rapid economic growth.

11 Emerging and developing economies

1 Which of the following does **not** contribute towards investment in human capital?

    A Education

    B Provision of healthcare

    C Improved nutrition

    D Expenditure on new equipment

2 Dependence on primary production is said to be problematic for less developed countries for many reasons. Which of the following is **not** one such reason?

    A The prices of agricultural products can be volatile because of instability in supply.

    B The prices of mineral products tend to fluctuate with the economic cycle.

    C Specialising in primary products goes against the natural pattern of comparative advantage for many less developed countries.

    D The terms of trade have tended to deteriorate over time for primary products relative to manufactured goods.

3 **a** Referring to relevant examples, discuss the view that dependence on primary products is the most significant constraint on economic development.

    b Assess the impact of protectionist policies by developed countries on economic development in a country of your choice.

4 **a** To what extent is rapid population growth a constraint on economic growth and development? Refer to examples of specific countries in your answer.

    b Evaluate the significance of deficiencies in human capital as a limit to economic development in a country of your choice.

5 **a** Assess the factors that might prevent a country from undergoing a process of industrialisation.

    b To what extent might industrialisation contribute to an increase in economic development? Refer to examples of developing countries in your answer.

6 **a** Examine the ways in which deficiencies in human capital might limit economic growth.

    b Evaluate reasons why the patterns of development have differed between East Asia and Sub-Saharan Africa.

12 Promoting growth and development

1 **a** Assess the role of foreign direct investment in promoting growth and development in a country of your choice.

    b Apart from foreign direct investment, evaluate two other ways by which a developing country might be able to fill its savings gap.

2 **a** Examine reasons why a developing country of your choice has large international debts.

    b Discuss the case for cancelling the debts of the world's most heavily indebted poor countries.

3 **a** Discuss the role of the World Bank in promoting economic development.

    b To what extent is a policy of import substitution likely to promote economic growth and development? Refer to examples of developing countries in your answer.

4 a Contrast fair trade and microfinance as alternative means of promoting economic development.

b Evaluate the role of market-led approaches to the promotion of economic development.

13 The financial sector

1 Which of the following would be seen as the **most** liquid form of asset?

A Savings accounts in banks

B Wholesale deposits with banks

C Notes and coin

D Treasury bills

2 Money performs four key roles in the economy. Which of the following is **not** one of these?

A Medium of exchange

B Outlet for government borrowing

C Unit of account

D Standard of deferred payment

3 Suppose that the commercial banks in a country follow a rule such that they always aim to hold 5% of their assets in liquid form. What would be the total increase in bank lending if government action led to an extra $100 being lodged as bank deposits?

A $180

B $200

C $1,800

D $2,000

4 Suppose that the market for loanable funds is initially in equilibrium, but the government decides to enforce an interest rate ceiling in order to encourage firms to invest more. Which of the following is likely to happen?

A Firms will borrow more in order to invest more.

B Households will save more and firms will invest more.

C The supply of loanable funds will increase, enabling firms to invest more.

D Households will save less, there will be a shortage of loanable funds, and investment will fall.

5 a Many countries have experienced a rise in their national debt since 2008. Assess factors that could explain this trend, referring to examples of countries in your answer.

b Discuss the view that governments should take measures to engineer a reduction in their national debt as quickly as possible.

6 a Assess reasons why many countries have experienced a slow rate of economic growth since the financial crisis.

b Discuss the effectiveness of monetary policy as a means of increasing the rate of economic growth in a country of your choice.

14 The role of the central bank

1 Which of the following is **not** a role of the central bank?

A Banker to the government

B Issuing currency

C Setting the rate of value added tax

D Setting bank rate

2 a Outline the transmission mechanism by which a change in interest rates affects aggregate demand.

   b Evaluate the effectiveness of inflation targeting in the early 2000s.

3 a Discuss the importance of liquidity in the economy, and how this became an issue during the financial crisis of the late 2000s.

   b Explain how quantitative easing was utilised to overcome liquidity problems, and evaluate the extent to which it was necessary.

4 a Distinguish between monetary and financial stability.

   b Explain the measures used by the Bank of England to achieve monetary and financial stability.

15 The role of the state in the macroeconomy

1 Which of the following is **not** a fiscal policy measure?

   A An increase in indirect taxes

   B An increase in government expenditure on infrastructure

   C An increase in interest rates designed to influence aggregate demand

   D A reduction in income tax rates

2 Which of the following is **not** regarded as a supply-side policy?

   A Improving the flexibility of the labour market

   B Reducing income tax rates in order to provide incentives for people to work.

   C Reducing interest rates to encourage higher consumption

   D Encouraging firms to spend more on training their workers

3 The Spanish economy

The Spanish economy has had a double-dip recession, experiencing recession in 2009/10 and again in 2012. Forecasts suggest that the economy will contract further in 2013. The weakening of domestic demand during 2012 is explained by falls in all components, especially private consumption. This reduction in private consumption occurred as a result of cuts in government expenditure, a rise in VAT in September 2012 and a continuing rise in unemployment, which reached over 6 million or 27% in March 2013. The Spanish prime minister has promised to unveil fiscal policy measures in order to halt the recession in the euro zone's fourth-largest economy.

The only bright spot was an improvement in Spain's current account balance: although exports fell, there was an even sharper fall in imports.

   a Explain what is meant by a double-dip recession.

   b Using an appropriate diagram, analyse the impact of a fall in real incomes on the economy of Spain.

   c Examine the effect on inequality of the increase in unemployment in Spain.

   d To what extent might export-led growth be possible in Spain?

   e Evaluate the use of fiscal policies aimed at promoting economic growth in Spain.

Index

Page numbers in **bold** refer to **key term definitions**.

M

MO (narrow money) **268**

M4 (broad money) **268**

Maastricht Treaty 155

macroeconomic policy 181–182, 308–314

macroeconomic stability 223–224, 262, 308–309

macroeconomy 274–279

malaria 192

Malthus, Thomas 230

management, and economies of scale 14

marginal costs **10**

marginal physical product of labour (MPP_L) **79**–80

marginal productivity theory **80**

marginal revenue product of labour (MRP_L) **79**–80

marginal revenues **20**

marginal tax rate **206**

marine insurance sector 282

market concentration 53–55

market failure 25, 310

market for loanable funds **272**

market-friendly growth strategy **222**–225, 241–250

marketing, and economies of scale 14

market-oriented strategies **241**–250

market structure
  barriers to entry 29
  case study 47
  competitiveness 73–76
  definition **27**
  monopolistic competition 28, **48**–52
  monopoly 28, 37–46
  monopsony **62**–63
  oligopoly 29, **55**–62, 64
  perfect competition 28, **30**–37
  types 27

mark-up pricing 67

Marshall–Lerner condition 176

maternal health 192

maximum wages 95, 96

MDGs (Millennium Development Goals) **191**–194, 254

MERCOSUR 149

mergers 4–6, 138
  case study 23

Mexico 257

microeconomic markets 223

microfinance **248**

microprudential regulation **291**

Microsoft 28, 29, 41, 109, 116

migrant workers 89–90

migration 263

Millennium Development Goals (MDGs) **191**–194, 254

minimum efficient scale **16**

minimum wages **93**–95

MNCs (multinational corporations) **5**, 24, **135**, 138–139, 245–247, 313

monetarist schools 274, **301**

monetary base 268

monetary efficiency gain 157

monetary policy 155, 267, 289–290, 298, 310–311

Monetary Policy Committee (MPC) **287**

monetary stability **286**, 291–292, 308–309, 311

monetary union **151**, 153–158

money 267–272

monopolies 28, **37**–46, 102–104

Monopolies and Restrictive Practices Commission 105

monopolistic competition 28, **48**–52

monopsony **90**–91

moral hazard 279, 282, 283

Morgenstern, Oskar 56

mortgage market 276–277

Mozambique 243–244

MPC (Monetary Policy Committee) **287**

MPP_L (marginal physical product of labour) **79**–80

MRP_L (marginal revenue product of labour) **79**–80

Mugabe, Robert 225

multinational corporations (MNCs) **5**, 24, **135**, 138–139, 245–247, 313

N

NAFTA (North American Free Trade Agreement) 149, 166

NAPP Pharmaceutical Holdings 46

narrow money (MO) **268**

Nash equilibrium **58**

Nash, John 56, 57, 58

national debt **298**

National Minimum Wage (NMW) 93

natural monopolies **14**, **40**–41, 110

natural rate of output **301**

natural rate of unemployment **301**

Nestlé 15

Neumann, John von 56

New Deal 96

n-firm concentration ratio **53**

NMW (National Minimum Wage) 93

non-pecuniary benefits **85**

non-tariff barriers **163**–164